Social Media

Enduring Principles

Social Media

Enduring Principles

ASHLEE HUMPHREYS
Northwestern University
Medill School of Journalism, Media,
Integrated Marketing Communications

New York   Oxford
OXFORD UNIVERSITY PRESS

Oxford University Press is a department of the University of Oxford.
It furthers the University's objective of excellence in research,
scholarship, and education by publishing worldwide.

Oxford   New York
Auckland   Cape Town   Dar es Salaam   Hong Kong   Karachi
Kuala Lumpur   Madrid   Melbourne   Mexico City   Nairobi
New Delhi   Shanghai   Taipei   Toronto

With offices in
Argentina   Austria   Brazil   Chile   Czech Republic   France   Greece
Guatemala   Hungary   Italy   Japan Poland   Portugal   Singapore
South Korea   Switzerland   Thailand   Turkey   Ukraine   Vietnam

For titles covered by Section 112 of the US Higher Education
Opportunity Act, please visit www.oup.com/us/he for the
latest information about pricing and alternate formats.

Published by Oxford University Press
198 Madison Avenue, New York, New York 10016
http://www.oup.com

Oxford is a registered trademark of Oxford University Press

Library of Congress Cataloging-in-Publication Data
Humphreys, Ashlee.
    Social media : enduring principles / Ashlee Humphreys.
        pages cm
    Includes bibliographical references and index.
    ISBN 978-0-19-932843-7 (alk. paper)
1. Social media. 2. Online social networks. 3. Communication and technology. 4. Mass media—
Technological innovations. I. Title.
    HM742.H863 2016
    302.23'1—dc23

                                                                    2015012484

Printing number: 9 8 7 6 5 4 3 2 1

Printed in the United States of America
on acid-free paper

BRIEF CONTENTS

CONTENTS

—

PART II   PEOPLE

PREFACE

A lmost without our notice, social media has subtly crept into our lives. When we turn on the television, we see a scroll of Twitter comments. When we talk to our friends, they ask whether we saw the picture someone posted on Facebook or Instagram. When we want to know how to make pasta, or fix our phones, or do our hair, we find ourselves inevitably looking for how to do these things online and regularly being taught by others who live in far-flung places. Sometimes we even strike up friendships with these strangers or observe flame wars between them or see surprising acts of kindness and assistance as people link up to achieve a common goal.

So how do we come to understand this flurry of practices in social media? This is not a book that will tell you that everything is changing. It will not try to convince you that you should reshape your life around personal branding or "mastering" some social media platform. There are no tips for power users. This book takes a *social science* approach to understanding our online lives and provides a synthesis of what we *know* from previous research in communications, journalism, marketing, psychology, sociology, and anthropology. Drawing from these disciplines, we will focus on the core theories that are used to understand and explain human communication online.

Using the resources afforded by social science, this book examines the ways people use media socially, particularly on digital platforms. Even if the medium changes, our theories for explaining and predicting human communication change more slowly, if at all. Some of the foundational work on, say, self-presentation or community building is just as relevant today when we look at communicative practices online as it was when anthropologists were studying the Triobriand Islanders or sociologists were analyzing greeting rituals and face-saving at work. People's basic needs and goals tend to endure, even if the way they try to achieve those needs and goals changes. And yet, technological and social structures can also shape practices in surprising and unexpected ways. We may see people struggling to form community in a group that is geographically distanced or where anonymity creates a depersonalized or hostile environment. We may examine the ways that greeting rituals are extended or codified because of the textual nature of a medium. Part of the fun of this new territory is figuring out which principles change and which endure. Hope you enjoy the adventure.

Methodology

Any book, even a synthetic overview such as this one, has a methodology, and it is important to note how this text was composed. I began by reviewing syllabuses of social media and digital media courses from schools throughout the United States, Europe, and to a lesser extent East Asia. Based on these as a model, I created an outline of chapter topics or "buckets" that made sense within the way social media was taught and from my own experience teaching and researching the subject. I also noted the content of each syllabus and downloaded many of the texts that were assigned in these courses.

After developing a structure of topics, I searched for articles and sorted them into the appropriate bucket. This resulted in approximately seventy-five to one hundred articles per chapter that were saved and sorted into a folder system for each chapter. A detailed bibliography is available on request. After this collection stage, I read through each article, noting key themes, terms, and theories and taking notes on important contributions and findings from each author. These were cataloged into a database by my amazing research assistants.

Ethnography also played an unseen and unexpected role in the development of this book. While reading or revising in coffee shops, it was the norm rather than the exception for me to hear people talking about social media or digital technology, and, in addition to observing its use, I found myself taking examples and insights from these overheard conversations. During my two years teaching a course on the topic, students brought to light aspects of social media practices and new examples that would have never occurred to me and yet really brought to life many of the theories and concepts. Most of the vignettes in the book happened to me or someone I know, and several came through the voices of students. Finally, news stories about social media were so pervasive (and so overwhelming) during the time period of writing the book that I cataloged them as well and included them where I could.

After reading the academic articles for each chapter, I wrote a draft that included the basic core theories and examples for each topic, using my database of notes as a guide. I iteratively added content as new articles appeared and examples came up in popular culture and media. After all chapters were completed for each topic, the manuscript was reviewed by twelve reviewers, each of whom read three or four chapters each. During this time I also personally solicited feedback from other scholars who were experts in the field pertaining to a particular topic. These generous scholars offered trenchant and valuable insights that immeasurably improved each chapter. I am indebted to them and to the reviewers for making this a deeper and more relevant book.

Finally, after receiving comments and reviews, I incorporated these ideas into the text and further added timely examples and findings. Because the topic of social media is ever evolving, I would like to consider the manuscript an open text in the sense that I hope it provides a useful structure for classifying past, present, and future research and yet is also open to change. If you have new examples, theories, empirical findings, or anything else, please consider adding them to the wiki online or contacting me via email.

Acknowledgments

First, it is important to recognize that I simply could not have written this book without the teachers, scholars, and mentors who taught me how to evaluate, synthesize, and produce social science research. Thank you to Kent Grayson, Wendy Griswold, Cristina Lafont, Greg Carpenter, Angela Lee, Brian Sternthal, Alice Tybout, and many others at Northwestern who have guided me as a thinker and researcher. The intellectual community at Northwestern and Medill have quite literally produced me as a scholar, and I am grateful for the support I have received there over the past fifteen years.

I am also indebted to the scholars who generously agreed to read chapters of the book and provided excellent critiques, comments, and suggestions, which I hope I did justice in incorporating. Thanks to Jeremy Birnholtz, Bernard Cova, John Deighton, Jennifer Earl, Stephanie Edgerly, Eileen Fischer, Henry Jenkins, Alice Marwick, Matt Weber, and Jim Webster, in addition to twelve anonymous reviewers of the manuscript. This book is so much better because of all of your insights and suggested additions.

Three amazing research assistants, Kelly Hartzell, Lauren Kaufman, and Tania Arguello helped me put everything in this book together, and I am indebted to them for their calm demeanor, impeccable organization skills, and tireless hard work. They helped in a million ways too numerous to mention. Plus, they are brilliant in their own right and will no doubt have luminous careers.

Thanks also to Frank Mulhern, Ed Malthouse, Brad Hamm, and others at Medill for their support, which allowed me the flexibility and financial support to travel to conferences and teach the courses on which this book first got its trial runs.

I am grateful to the editorial team at Oxford University Press, including Mark Haynes, Paul Longo, Toni Magyar, Patrick Lynch, and that amazing Canadian permissions team. Thanks for all of your efforts to make this book the best possible. I am also indebted to Stan Wakefield, who first supported the book and found a publisher. Without him, the project would not have happened.

Thanks to my friends and family who offered their tireless support throughout the process of writing this book. Jonathan Berman, Markus Giesler, Lora Harding, Monica Kenny, Michelle Weinberger, and countless others were always willing to talk and ready to help. I have immeasurably benefited from their society.

Finally, thanks as always to my partner, Jeff Glover, for being a tireless supporter, advocate, friend, cheerleader, husband, editor, and a million other things. He has not only made this book better, but also made me better.

—Ashlee Humphreys

I would also like to acknowledge and thank the following reviewers for their helpful feedback:

Lance Strate	*Fordham University*
Nancy Jennings	*University of Cincinnati*
Scott L. Weiss	*Saint Francis College*
Leslie A. Rill	*Portland State University*
Fred Fejes	*Florida Atlantic University*
Todd Chambers	*Texas Tech University*
Kris M. Markman	*University of Memphis*
Herbert A. Terry	*Indiana University–Bloomington*
George L. Daniels	*University of Alabama*
Kenneth Hoffman	*Seton Hall University*
Richelle Rogers	*Loyola University, Chicago*
Ran Wei	*University of South Carolina*
Susan M. Simkowski	*University of Arkansas–Fort Smith*
Natalie Underberg-Goode	*University of Central Florida*
Mark Glantz	*St. Norbert College*
Po-Lin Pan	*Arkansas State University*
L. Ripley Smith	*Bethel University*
Elizabeth Lopez	*Georgia State University*
Katherine G. Fry	*Brooklyn College–City University of New York*
Todd O'Neill	*Middle Tennessee State University*
Donna L. Halper	*Lesley University*
Jonathan Crane	*University of North Carolina–Charlotte*
Bianca C. Reisdorf	*University of Cincinnati*
Kimberly Voss	*University of Central Florida*
Steven M. Schneider	*SUNY Polytechnic Institute*
Tessa Joseph-Nicholas	*University of North Carolina at Chapel Hill*

CHAPTER 1

—

Introduction

As I was driving through middle Tennessee on I-40, the clouds started darkening. Then the deluge started: hammering rain, gusting winds, drivers with flashing hazard lights. As I drove on, the downpour kept going, and going, and going. I decided I should turn the radio on to check for tornados in the area. On the FM dial, I tuned in to a man listing roadways: *I-24, Murfreesboro Pike, I-40 between I-65 and I-24, Briley Road west of the turnpike.* Standard fare; I assumed these roads were closed because of flooding. But then he took a call. The driver described her location—she was in a town called Antioch—and asked how she could get to the West End of Nashville. My first reaction was incredulity. *She* wanted the deejay to give *her* personal directions into town? What did she think this was, Google maps? But then the deejay responded without missing a beat. "We've had people calling in to report that I-24 is now closed between exit 52 and exit 54. A lady earlier coming from Antioch took Thompson Lane over to I-65 and then came north." The caller thanked the deejay and hung up. Then he took another call, this time from a man calling to report that crews were shutting down Murfreesboro Pike around Glenwood Springs. The deejay took down this information and thanked the caller, only to share it with the next caller who was trying to come from the airport. This continued for more than an hour. And as I entered Nashville, I found myself beginning to use the reports. A caller earlier had reported flooding around the fairgrounds, so when I arrived I was not surprised to find cars turning around and heading through the labyrinth of side roads to reach their destination. In fact, I was prepared to take an alternative route to the north and west.

This is social media.

Social media does not rely on any particular medium; rather, it is a practice, or set of practices, for using media socially. In the previous story, a community of people contributes knowledge to help other drivers find their way around flood waters. This practice is not much different from contributing to an article on Wikipedia or blogging tips on childcare. It is not the medium that matters, but the use of it. True, most of the examples of social media to be discussed in this book occur through digital communications, and social media undoubtedly has been greatly expanded by digital technologies such as the Internet, mobile phones, and tablets. But social media have existed within so-called "old media" as well.

Consider letters to the editor. Early newspapers were formatted with a blank back page to allow readers to write their own news reports, circulating the personally observed news to other readers who picked up the paper (Harris, 1690). Throughout their early history, newspapers were used as a compendium of first-hand reports by what we would now call "citizen-journalists." Although they provided a range of firsthand knowledge, these entries often lapsed into gossip, feuding, and contradictory reports. Consider whether and how this differs from the way many people use Twitter. Again, it is not the medium of paper printing that makes something "social media," but the way people use it to circulate information, form social worlds, and maintain social bonds. Where social media practices used to exist sparsely, there is now a dense forest emerging, with new saplings cropping up all the time. The aim of this book is to provide a structure for understanding social media practices, artifacts, and institutions without reducing them to a particular medium. It is crucial to understand developments in digital technology, but this is only one infrastructure that enables social media; it is not the whole of it.

The same can be said for the social groups highlighted by this shift to the digital. Fan communities existed long before online groups for discussing reality television or the latest HBO series. As Henry Jenkins and others have argued, the current groups we see online are better understood as continuations of cultures that predated the Internet (Jenkins, Ford, & Green, 2013). For instance, an early form of fantasy baseball cropped up in the 1980s as fans traded letters in "play-by-mail" leagues of "rotisserie baseball" (Friedman, 1984). Digital technology simply makes it easier and faster for fans of *Twilight* or *Harry Potter* to connect with each other and produce materials such as a fan fiction. It creates an infrastructure for producing YouTube celebrities overnight. But these social formations are structured by many of the same dynamics that have always structured fan cultures and communities.

And yet, it is also a new world. Material technology that allows public and semipublic broadcasting can also change social practices in important ways. In some cases—as in the opening vignette—the scale of practices has clearly changed, whereas in other cases, it might be worth considering how the structure of practices has changed as well. Figuring out how technology both enhances and constrains preexisting and emergent practices is the task of communication scholars and students. Welcome aboard!

PERSPECTIVE OF THIS BOOK

Any book on communication—any book period—is inevitably written from a particular perspective. This is a particular kind of book, and two distinctions are important for understanding what kind of book this is. First, this book aims to provide a *grounded academic* overview of social media. Unlike the myriad of business press books, this book is an academic text summarizing foundational and state-of-the-art research in the field of social media. It aims to cover existing research and to present a coherent framework for future research. The book draws from long-standing theories in communication, journalism, sociology, psychology, and marketing, but also includes a number of contemporary case examples that both illustrate enduring implications of the theories and point to new directions and modifications. Although the book includes case examples, it is primarily based on academic research in the social sciences rather than guru-like business mantras. Indeed, one of the challenges for the student of social media is distinguishing the two.

Second, this book takes a social science approach to studying social media. There are a number of ways to approach the emerging topic of social media. Computer scientists and engineers have methods for understanding the flows of data and content between networked computers. But this will not be a book that covers the technical aspects of creating and structuring digital worlds. Moreover, critical approaches from the humanities offer valuable and needed perspectives on the history of computing, the nature of our relationship with texts, and the way texts structure the way we think and communicate. Critical studies in the humanities can enlighten us to the importance of social media in political and cultural life and sensitize us to the continuing power imbalances that these discourses reproduce. However, this book will not take up the critical and historical issues prompted by social media at any great length.

In contrast to the approaches offered by the physical sciences or humanities, this book offers an overview and synthesis of social science research on social media. This means that the material will focus on the people using social media. Sociologists can enable us to see how dynamics emerge between groups of people as they communicate. Psychologists can tell us how people pursue goals online. Communication scholars can help us understand power relationships between audience and producer in historical context and enlighten us to the rhetoric and genres of social media as well as the interpersonal dynamics and human communication. Ethnography from anthropology can give us a grounded perspective on changing cultural practices.

There are obvious challenges for producing a book about a topic that is rapidly changing. Without a doubt, things you read here will be outdated. However, what tends to change much more slowly are the theories for understanding human communication and social structure. As the radio and print examples just discussed indicate, social media has been with us for longer than we realize. It is not dependent on a particular medium and so, if the medium changes, or even if genres within the medium change, the theory for understanding, explaining, and predicting human interaction will likely stand. And yet, although theories rarely change, we see new and fascinating examples of theories put to use in radically new circumstances. These new technological or institutional circumstances can completely change the way we thought we understood things.

It is an exciting time to dive into the study of social media. If you are going to understand social media from a social science perspective, there is a considerable amount of ground to cover.

ORGANIZATION OF THE BOOK

The book is divided into four sections: messages, people, networks, and culture. The first section, messages, covers the content and physical infrastructure that make up social media. We will examine the communication model, the various types and channels of social media communication, and the methods for measuring the effectiveness of social media platforms. The second section, people, focuses on the individual user experience of social media, including uses and benefits of social media, motivations for participating in new media, and processes of interaction and contribution to social media products. The third section on networks will discuss how the users of social media form groups and how this group structure can affect communication. In this section, we will examine the basics of network theory, discuss the relevance of networks for the distribution of content, and evaluate the research on virtual communities. The final section will cover the broader ways that social media has changed political, economic and cultural institutions. This includes examining the cultural production and distribution of content through online channels, the integration of social media into different cultures, and the consequences for economic practices and political action.

USES OF THIS BOOK

The study of social media is interdisciplinary by nature. Communication scholars, sociologists, anthropologists, and psychologists can all enlighten us to particular aspects of social communication, and that is to say nothing of the valuable contributions that have come from fields that are themselves multi- or inter-disciplinary, such as cultural studies, marketing, and informatics. This book has been written so that you can take or leave parts of it, depending on your interests. If you are coming from communications, you might find Sections I and IV of the book most familiar, those that cover messages and the macro-level impact of media technologies on social worlds. If you are coming from sociology, marketing, or psychology, Sections II and III might be most interesting to you because they cover the people and the groups of people using social media in great detail. However, if you are interested in social media as a topic, my hope is that you will explore all sides of it from each of these disciplinary angles. Feel free to explore what is most relevant to your curriculum, but in this volume you will, I hope, find some old familiar perspectives on human communication and some new exciting ones as well.

Each chapter is built around one or two core theories. These theories come from long-standing bodies of knowledge about how people interact and communicate. After an exposition of the theory, it will be time to dive in and cover its application to, and sometimes it's limitations in, the world of social media. After covering some examples, critical perspectives and tradeoffs will be offered.

Key terms, a chapter summary, discussion questions, and recommended readings will be provided to facilitate review of the important concepts. My hope is that each chapter will merely set you up for some careful and critical thinking about the topic in addition to some related reading.

REFERENCES

Friedman, J. (1984). The most peppery game since the Hot Stove League? It's rotisserie baseball. *People Weekly*, April 23, 2.

Harris, R. P. f. B. (1690). *Publick occurrences both forreign and domestick*. Boston: Richard Pierce.

Jenkins, H., Ford, S., & Green, J. (2013). *Spreadable media: Creating value and meaning in a networked culture*. New York: New York University Press.

CHAPTER 2

——

The Communication Model

When Anne was in middle school, she talked to her aunt on the phone every Sunday morning. They would catch up on the week's events, what was going on at school, and how her grandparents were doing. She could hear her aunt laugh at the funny things her grandfather did and hear the worry in her aunt's voice about her kids, Anne's cousins. Now, fifteen years later, Anne texts with her aunt several times a week, exchanging small observations and checking in whenever she sees something her aunt would like. She will text her aunt almost anywhere, at any time—the grocery store, the train, sometimes even in class. Her aunt posts pictures of her kids online, and Anne not only makes her own comments, but also reads what her aunt's friends have to say—people she does not even know! She talks to her aunt less frequently, but she communicates with her more often. Sometimes this causes her to wonder: are they more or less connected?

This chapter will lay out how social media fits into basic communication models and discuss the ways in which they have been modified to understand social media. It will also provide a brief history of theories for understanding how technology and media shape human communication and behavior.

WHAT *IS* SOCIAL MEDIA?

As the introductory chapter makes clear, social media is not dependent on digital communication. It describes a set of practices for communicating, usually collaboratively, and usually so that it is visible to more than one person. Social media generally goes beyond private, **dyadic** communication between two people, and it usually happens in a public or semipublic forum (for a related definition, see Miller, 2013).[1] Although many social media sites are owned by companies, social media as a form of communication cannot be limited to proprietary sites like Facebook or Twitter, and although social media is related to business concepts like Web 2.0 and user-generated content, it is not contained in these two ideas alone. As illustrated by radio call-in shows, letters to the editor, citizen journalism, and the like, social media does not inherently need a digitally based platform. However, Internet technology and infrastructure have changed collaborative communication, and further developments in technology will inevitably continue to structure how people communicate in unforeseeable ways. If we focus on theories for understanding social media as a set of practices for communicating, we will be able to understand these unforeseen changes and make sense of human behavior by linking old practices with new ones.

MODELS OF COMMUNICATION

Models for understanding social media fall directly between **interpersonal** and **mass communication** approaches. Because social media concerns not only the casual conversations people have with their friends, but also potentially sharing those conversations with a broader audience, both interpersonal and mass media approaches are valuable for understanding what happens when people communicate socially.

Interpersonal Approaches

Interpersonal communication is an approach to studying communication that is primarily based on the face-to-face dynamics of two people (or what we call dyadic communications). One of the founders of this approach, Erving Goffman, argues that in an interaction, people are always trying to gain information from others and test predictions about others from the information they receive (Goffman, 1959). For instance, if you meet someone at a party, one of the first questions you ask will likely be about that person's background. Just who *are* they and what are they doing here? Goffman calls this norm self-disclosure. You expect someone to casually answer some basic questions, and you feel compelled to reciprocate by answering them for yourself. Now, consider this same set of norms in the sphere of digital communication. How would you feel if this person now "friended" you on Facebook? Did he or she produce the right amount and type of disclosure before making the request? Did you exchange enough information to be "friends"?

Interpersonal communication stresses **relational norms**, or informal rules that govern communicative behavior between people. For instance, the norm of reciprocity suggests that there should be a give and take in a conversation; it is rude if one party monopolizes the discourse. This norm, called turn-taking, holds in almost all casual face-to-face communication. Many of the interpersonal norms in face-to-face communication structure online communication as well (Jeffrey & Mark, 2003; Martey & Stromer-Galley, 2007; Peña & Hancock, 2006; Sassenberg, 2002; Yee, Bailenson, Urbanek, Chang, & Merget, 2007). For instance, online multiplayer games like the Sims have many of the same entrance, welcoming, and leave-taking norms such as saying "hello" and "goodbye" (Martey & Stromer-Galley, 2007). In face-to-face interactions and online, these norms can vary slightly because of the frequency of communication and the familiarity with the partner. They are also influenced by gender, with women performing them more than men, a difference that is also found in offline communication (Martey & Stromer-Galley, 2007; Yee et al., 2007).

"On the Internet, nobody knows you're a dog."

Cartoon 2.1 Credit: Peter Steiner/The New Yorker Collections/The Cartoon Bank.

As the studies just cited indicate, interpersonal communication research of social media norms has begun to tell us a lot about similarities. However, they have also uncovered many differences between online and offline interpersonal communication. For instance, anonymity is more accepted online than in real life (Turkle, 1995/2011), and one of the first cartoons about online communication satirizes this fact (Cartoon 2.1). The development of different dialects and slang, in-group and out-group signaling, and trust are just a few areas of social media that can be informed by an interpersonal approach. There is much to uncover using the interpersonal approach, and these topics will be explored later when we consider uses and benefits in Chapter 6, as well as group behavior in Chapter 10.

Although interpersonal theories can tell us a lot about social media, there are also limitations. For example, dyadic communication is assumed to happen privately or semiprivately. In contrast, many dyadic conversations are visible online and can even spiral into full-scale community discussions. For instance, Twitter allows individuals to communicate with anyone, so when Oprah tweets a supporting message to her best friend, Gayle, about her new show, is it interpersonal communication or outright mass media promotion? To better understand this complex dynamic and many other phenomena in the social media universe, we must consult theories of audience and mass communication.

Mass Communication

In contrast to interpersonal communication, theories of mass communication tend to provide explanations of what people, either users or providers of media, do in the aggregate. This set of theories was developed for understanding how organizations communicate to a large, diffuse, and heterogeneous audience. Methods and institutions for transmitting information between producer and audience—newspapers, magazines, and television—are typically considered forms of mass communication, and mass communication is more often observed publically than in interpersonal settings.

Photo 2.1A and 2.1B Oprah Winfrey Tweets Gayle King.

In the traditional mass communication model, the source produces a message that is encoded in media, which is received by the receiver, who produces some feedback (Figure 2.1). This simple model has been enhanced to understand how mass media influence the general public. The concept of "two-step flow," for instance, says that mass media influence opinion leaders, who in turn influence a wider audience (Katz & Lazarsfeld, 1970). In a two-step flow model, media messages are not necessarily directly received by the audience, but filter down through opinion leaders. This implies that media organizations may not have direct influence on what information people receive, but instead have indirect influence through gatekeepers.

In social media models of communication, things are a little different. The communication model for social media has tended to be conceptualized as a network of platforms and users (Figure 2.2). Users communicate with each other both directly and through platforms, and the content of those platforms is itself produced by a number of other users. Information does not "flow" in one direction from sender to receiver. Rather, everyone is potentially a source, and everyone is potentially a receiver. Users are conceptualized as nodes in a network such

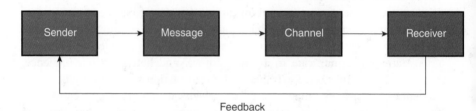

Figure 2.1 Traditional Communication Model.

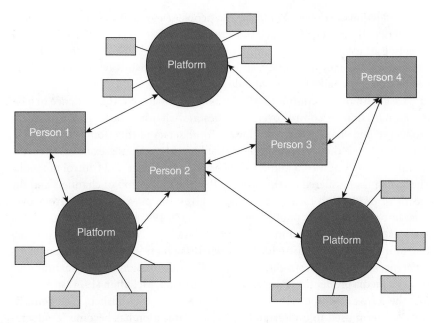

Figure 2.2 The Social Media Communication Model.

that an organization like CNN has the same status—at least technically—as a blogger or an eyewitness (although, as we'll discuss in Chapters 9 and 13, power differences can still impact the flow of communication).

There are three key differences between traditional and social media models. First, the audience is not necessarily passive, but often active (Jenkins, 2004), curating information, providing shared interpretations of texts, and rating the products of others. Media scholar Henry Jenkins, for example, says, "If old consumers were assumed to be passive, the new consumer is active" (Jenkins, 2004, p.37). **User-generated content** is the term that many now use to refer to the products made by users and user groups. We will cover more of this concept in Chapter 5. Some scholars have understood this difference in activity versus passivity as being tied with the type of media. As Marshall McLuhan argues, **hot media** require less involvement from the audience, whereas **cool media** requires more active engagement (McLuhan, 1968). For example, radio is a hot medium where you can sit back and listen, whereas the telephone is a cooler one where participation is usually required. No matter what we call it, it is clear that the audience is much more able to contribute to the conversation in the social media communicational model than in traditional mass media approaches.

Second, the audience is not only potentially more active, but also potentially much narrower. Consider, for example, making a status update on Facebook. One does not simply create and encode a message for the whole world to see. Rather, the message is crafted with a particular public (namely, your friends) in mind. Further, this activity can also take the form of collaborative engagement and production of content. You post, and people respond. In this sense, audience members both produce feedback more socially and are more socialized in their reception of information. Accordingly, audiences can sometimes be much narrower than in mass media. A Facebook conversation involving thousands of people would probably be hard to follow.

Last, with online communication it may be possible for the audience to have more ownership or control over messages and channels because the costs for producing and sharing them are lower. To understand this, some communication scholars use theory from political economy. These studies examine the ownership dynamics of media and form theories about power and control of media. The basic insight offered by this work is that the ownership of channels and the means of production for communication gives one power—and control—over what information enters public debate (Garnham, 1995). Some have argued that social media makes the communication landscape and even knowledge production more democratic (Sunstein, 2006), whereas others have pointed to enduring differences in power, oversight, and control of information despite institutional shifts in media production (Castells, 2007). Early on, McLuhan (1974) speculated that the Xerox machine would turn everyone into self-publishers. The **demotic turn** is a term used to understand how communication has become "democratized" (Jenkins, 2004). As a select few fashion bloggers demonstrate, even those who do not work for the fashion industry can use the Internet as a communication tool to gain cultural capital and become a recognized voice in the fashion world (McQuarrie, Miller, & Phillips, 2013).

However, despite this turn toward more democratic communication platforms, the channels through which people communicate are often still owned by companies (Hackett & Carroll, 2006). In the traditional communication model, companies both produce the content and control the message. In contrast, in the social media model, users—particularly groups of networked users who collaborate—may often control the message, but corporations often still own the physical and virtual infrastructure on which people communicate. Further, in recent years, this trend has been simultaneously accompanied by a consolidation of ownership in the mass media sphere (Jenkins, 2004). So although individuals or groups of media users have the ability to control messages, the institutions that produce news, movies, and music have consolidated, wielding more institutional power than in previous decades.

It is important to understand who owns the material infrastructure needed to create and disseminate information. Traditionally, a printing press was necessary to circulate information to a large number of people. But with the advent of digital communication, one can seemingly communicate with anyone and everyone. However, the competition for attention may be more intense, and just because someone *can* produce a message does not mean it will be received. Further, as many scholars have remarked, simply owning a computer is not enough to be included in the conversation. A critical component of participation is cultural capital—knowing how to participate and knowing what to say (a topic we will cover in Chapter 7).

In sum, the communication model for social media lies somewhere between the mass media and interpersonal approaches. The "audience" members can potentially be the source or the receiver. The audience not only is passive, but also can be active. The audience is not simply productive, but also produces with an eye toward *their own* audience. The means of production or the means of communication are often distributed more widely. Users are networked, and the network may produce content collaboratively. To be clear, it is not that mass media no longer exists. As a relatively powerful set of actors, mass media institutions are still relevant and important for understanding communication. However, our previous understanding of communication is now supplemented with, and embedded in, the world of social media, a world in which more people actively participate in producing and disseminating information.

Connecting Interpersonal with Mass Communication

How do our interpersonal approaches for understanding social media relate to mass media approaches? One way of understanding their relationship is through **structuration**. Structuration says that the larger normative patterns we see in mass communication are created and structured by the interactions of individuals. Conversely, the interactions of individuals are structured by constraints in communication technologies, legal structures, and social norms. For example, television viewers have routines for what channels they watch on television. Yet, those routines are constrained by the channels that are available. As people watch particular channels on television, those ratings are taken into account, thus changing the channels the cable company chooses to provide (Webster, 2011). People cannot watch what is not available, but they can also work around existing structure to get what they want (Hulu, anyone?).

The sociologist Anthony Giddens argues that these repeated, institutionalized patterns both *enable* and *constrain* behavior. Say you want to share news of a new job. Facebook will not determine what you say or what comments are left in response to the good news, but the structure of the platform will give people the option to "like" your update, an option many of them will take. Although there are many ways that your friends and family could congratulate you—they might call or email you—they may choose to do it through the like button on Facebook. Why? Because it is there. As some media coverage on the topic has pointed out, you cannot "dislike" an update (Rushkoff, 2013). This can lead to some awkward dynamics when the update is bad. Say you lost your job. People may want to offer support (as with like), but that is not an option.

Structuration can help us understand the relationship between interpersonal communication—what norms, rules, and routines structure the conversations you might have with your friends—and mass communication—the larger patterns of media consumption like whether a like button is available on Facebook. People act within a given structure to achieve their own ends. So, if a like button is not available, people will leave a comment. And the difference is not trivial. These comments are likely to be longer and require more engagement from the audience of friends who read your updates.

Understanding social media requires keeping both perspectives in mind as we move through the book. The ways that social media structure individual human interaction are manifold and complex. They potentially depend on technology, culture, law, and many other variables. Therefore, before we move further, it will help to briefly consider debates about the relationship among people, media, and technology.

HISTORICAL DISCOURSES
OF DIGITAL TECHNOLOGY

Do We Structure Technology or Does Technology Structure Us?

Consider the opening story about Anne and her aunt. They used to catch up on the telephone. Now they use text messaging and social networking sites to stay in touch. This difference in technology has changed how often they talk, what they say, and even who participates in the conversation. However, they could always still pick up the telephone. **Technological determinism** is the perspective that technology determines the nature of human communication. First extensively argued by the French thinker Jacques Ellul, technological determinism makes two claims: first, that technology develops autonomously from human control, and second, that technology determines the development and evolution of society (Bijker, 1987). From the determinist perspective, the communication between Anne and her aunt has been indelibly changed by the technology available to them.

In contrast to the deterministic approach, constructivist approaches explain that people use technology for a variety of personal and social ends and that they construct technology to achieve them (Bijker, 1987). In a study of the telephone, sociologist Claude Fischer found that the introduction of home telephones did not dictate how people communicated, but it did change some social practices. For instance, Fischer found that in contrast to fears that the telephone would make people lazy, interrupt domestic life, and decrease social interaction, people actually began socializing more because the telephone served to "widen and deepen existing social patterns rather than to alter them" (Fischer, 1992). People in rural areas, especially women, felt more connected to the broader world than ever before, and people used the home phone to achieve a variety of goals, from practical uses like ordering home goods to social uses like "visiting" with friends and neighbors more often. As we can see using the theory of structuration, technology *enabled* some social practices, but *constrained* others. First coined by Berger and Luckmannn (1966), **social construction** refers to the idea that reality is shaped by collective understandings. In contrast to the perspective of technological determinism, social constructionism holds that people play a critical role in shaping technology, adapting its uses and meanings to suit their own ends.

Media Ecology

We can see how technology might shape social relationships, but how might it affect "deeper" structures—how we perceive the world and ourselves? Neil Postman and Marshall McLuhan were among the first to theorize the role of media in shaping our perception of the world (see Postman, 1964, as well as McLuhan, 1968). **Media ecology** is the perspective that the mode of communication shapes human activity in both interactional and historical domains (Strate, 1999). The "fundamental principle" of media ecology is that "a medium is a technology within which a culture grows . . . it gives form to a culture's politics, social organization, and habitual ways of thinking" (Strate, 2004, p.3). Media ecologists argue that communicative technologies shape our institutions, our social practices, and even our cognitive structures. Implicit in this argument are shades of technological determinism, as discussed in the previous section.

There are three basic takeaways from the media ecology approach framework we will draw on throughout the book. The first is that the medium can shape the message. Media ecologists, at least at first, were focused on studying the ways in which media shaped the content, or the "message" contained within the medium. So the way something is communicated plays a critical role in shaping *what* is communicated. For example, the invention of cinema offered more than just new stories. By elongating narratives into roughly two hours and situating the viewer in a dark room with no distractions, it also changed the way people thought about space, time, and the connections between events (McLuhan, 1968). This perspective yields McLuhan's most famous insight that the "medium is the message," by which he means "it is the medium that shapes and controls the scale and form of human association and action" (p. 9). The way ideas are communicated has an influence beyond the ideas themselves, and in fact, looking at the content can obscure our understanding of the influence of the medium itself.

Photo 2.2 Marshall McLuhan.

The German philosopher and social thinker Walter Benjamin argues that technology provides an extension of the body and senses (Benjamin, 2008). For example, a telescope extends the ability of the eyes to see into outer space. A car extends the ability of the body to move through space quickly. Building on Benjamin's insight, McLuhan argues that traditional media are extensions of the body, whereas new media are extensions of the perceptual and nervous system (see also Hayles, 2008; McLuhan, 1968). We can "hear" a symphonic orchestra in another city through a vinyl record, and we can "see" into an apartment in New York City if someone has a webcam set up. Written text shapes human communicative practices and potentially extends cognitive abilities in the same ways that objects may extend physical capabilities (Ong, 1982). In cultures without written text, language is not archived through writing, and thus memorization, repetition, and mnemonics become more important. Elements of language such as rhyme and alliteration in Homer's *Odyssey*, for example, are shaped to facilitate recall and oral retelling (Ong, 1982). With written language, people take the permanence of the language for granted, and this shifts human practice and thought. Written text makes language more objectlike. Words are "out there" and can be "looked up." For primarily oral cultures, however, language comes through sound; it is an event that cannot be frozen, preserved, and analyzed (Ong, 1982). In this way, the form of our communication shapes the way we think. Computing capabilities may even take us one step further in the replacement of memory by text, and networked multimediated text shapes our ways and styles of thinking (Hayles, 2012; McLuhan, 1968). For example, we now outsource the task of remembering phone numbers, addresses, and a host of other information to computers. If we need to remember who was in that movie we saw last weekend, we look it up on Google.

The second important contribution of media ecology for studying social media is the consideration of how newly invented media cast light onto older forms of media. Levinson (2003) argues that the Internet is able to encompass and convey many previous forms of media. Radio, print, and video can all be found on the Internet, and the Internet is the conduit for these older forms, just as print used to be the conduit for handwriting or radio used to be the conduit for the spoken word. New media often help us see old media in a new light. Media also became the message in the sense that old media can take on characteristics of high art after their obsolescence. For instance, records, once a mere conduit for listening to music, are now appreciated for their material and aesthetic qualities as well (Farrugia & Swiss, 2005). In this way, certain media become naturalized, simply melting into the background as we focus on the content, while the forms of other, perhaps outmoded media are made explicit.

The third notable aspect of media ecology for understanding social media is its overarching goal of understanding different forms of media in relation to each other and within social context. Shaped by this perspective, Postman (1970) says, "Media ecology looks into the matter of how media of communication affect human perception, understanding, feeling, and value, as well as how our interaction with media facilitates or impedes their chances of survival. The word "ecology" implies the study of environments: their structure, content, and impact on people" (p. 161). We can understand social media as an environment, an ecology of different types, each with its own cultural and perceptual influence on how we communicate and how we perceive the world. Postman says, "We put the word 'media' in front of the word 'ecology' to suggest that we were not simply interested in media, but in the ways in which the interaction between media and human beings gives a culture its character, and, one might say, helps a culture to maintain symbolic balance" (p. 11).

There are, of course, many ways this ecology can be drawn, and indeed it is still changing as tools come into and out of existence. The idea that platforms exist relationally stems from taking an ecological perspective to studying media. As Harold Rheingold (1993), who conducted one of the first ethnographies of an online community, says, "in terms of the way the whole system is propagating and evolving, think of cyberspace as a social petri dish, the Net as the agar medium, and virtual communities, in all their diversity, as the colonies of micro-organisms that grow in petri dishes" (p. xx). That is, blogging is a "species" that may share many traits with microblogging, but also some differences. Which of these species survive depends on how they fit in with our existing and changing social practices and institutions. More will be said of these distinctions in Chapter 3.

NEW CONCEPTS IN SOCIAL MEDIA

In addition to basic theories of communication, there are several other, newer concepts that have been developed to understand how people communicate and collaborate online. In addition to media scholars, business writers, marketing scholars, and economists have all come up with new concepts for understanding social media. Some of them have stuck.

Web 2.0

Web 2.0 is a term used to indicate the historical turn toward creating communication and commercial platforms that are sustained by collective participation. Coined in 1999 by Darcy DiNucci, Web 2.0 was a play on scholars' understandings that the Internet was initially a system for producing a sharing content that easily fit into the mass communication model (DiNucci, 1999; O'Reilly, 2005). That is, a user created a webpage for others to simply read. Web 2.0 is meant to describe the process where the webpage itself is created by multiple users and updated by a collaborative group. The audience "talks back." Wikipedia is a commonly cited example of Web 2.0, but the term is usually used—and was first proposed—with commercial intent (Van Dijck & Nieborg, 2009). However, commercial examples of Web 2.0 include the shift from Amazon as a pure retailing site to a social shopping site that includes user reviews and ratings and platforms like Yelp! that take the idea of a business guidebook, like the yellow pages, and turn it into a site on which users can share and read reviews of restaurants and small businesses. Studies have shown that the information on Wikipedia is as reliable as that from the *Encyclopedia Britannica*, a traditional print publication of authorities' knowledge (Giles, 2005; Holman Rector, 2008). However, although Web 2.0 describes a range of sites that allow users to create and share content, many are the proprietary platforms of online retailers or other commercial companies.

Convergence

Convergence is the process through which certain institutional, functional, and user practices have merged into one platform and/or sphere. First proposed by Henry Jenkins, convergence occurs in at least two domains—the user domain and the producer domain. Specifically, in the user domain more and more functions are combined onto one device. One can now take a picture, make a call, watch a movie, or check email from a single smartphone. But convergence is also happening in the producer domain, as companies like Viacom combine ownership of multiple types of media such as films, video games, music, magazines, and newspapers. As Jenkins (2004 says, "Convergence is taking place within the same appliances . . . within the same franchise . . . within the same company . . . within the brain of the consumer . . . and within the same fandom" (p. 34). Convergence is primarily a concept for describing the production of media, but one issue to consider throughout the book will be how convergence impacts user practices. This can be seen, for example, in the appearance of microblogging platforms that allow users to broadcast text, image, video, and sound simultaneously. According to Jenkins (2004), "Media convergence is more than simply a technological shift. Convergence alters the relationship between existing technologies, industries, markets, genres and audiences" (p. 34). We will take up these issues in Chapters 11 and 12.

Platforms

A **platform** is a system that coordinates the exchange or interaction between two or more groups of people (Rochet & Tirole, 2003). For example, Facebook is a platform that hosts social communication between people, but it also facilitates advertising to people who visit the site. In economics, this is called a **two-sided market**, an economic platform where a company provides value to two different sets of customers. For example, a traditional magazine will sell its product to an audience of readers, but it will also sell advertising space to companies wishing to gain the attention of the magazine audience. As we will further discuss in Chapter 9 about social networks and in Chapter 14 on economic life, platforms can provide a place where value is created (Benkler, 2006; Piskorski, 2014).

    Managing a platform is a balancing act because the company must weigh the interests of one group against that of the other. For example, if advertising gets too annoying, consumers will leave. Yet if there is not enough advertising or there are too few readers, clients will go elsewhere to advertise. This prompts many organizations that are set up as platforms (like Facebook) to attempt to cultivate a particular kind of audience and develop metrics for measuring their characteristics, so they can be a "product" to be sold to an advertiser (Napoli, 2003). More on this will be covered in Chapter 4 as we consider how social media use is measured and aggregated.

SUMMARY AND CONCLUSION

This chapter has discussed what social media is and provided an overview of the perspectives for studying social media. In contrast to interpersonal and mass communication, social media practices are characterized by being public or semipublic, two-way, and relatively controlled by their creators. Although new technologies facilitate and indelibly shape the nature of communication in a social media ecology, people still work around and resist them, using or changing infrastructure to meet their needs. In the next chapter, we will dig deeper to understand the many different species in this rich ecosystem, the types and affordances of social media communication.

TOPICS

- Platform
- Media ecology
- Media convergence
- Technological determinism and social constructionism
- Structuration

DISCUSSION QUESTIONS

1. What is the demotic turn and how might it affect communication content?
2. What conditions might lead the audience to being more active versus more passive?
3. As a media ecology, how does social media shape the relationships between senders and receivers?
4. What is media convergence and what factors might enable or constrain it?
5. Is the media ecology perspective technologically deterministic? If so, how?

EXERCISE

Draw your own media ecology. What types of media do you think are important to include? How do the aspects of the media you include shape the way people communicate?

NOTE

1. Although what tends to be distinct about social media is that it concerns nondyadic or publically observable dyadic communication, we will also discuss some cases of dyadic communication, such as texting, direct messaging, or email.

FURTHER READINGS

Jenkins, H. (2004). The cultural logic of media convergence. *International Journal of Cultural Studies, 7*(1), 33–43.

McLuhan, M. (1977). http://www.youtube.com/watch?v=ImaH51F4HBw/.

REFERENCES

Benjamin, W. (2008). *The work of art in the age of mechanical reproduction.* London: Penguin UK.

Benkler, Y. (2006). *The wealth of networks: How social production transforms markets and freedom.* New Haven, CT: Yale University Press.

Berger, P., & Luckmann, T. (1966). *The social construction of knowledge: A treatise in the sociology of knowledge.* Soho, NY: Open Road Media.

Bijker, W. E. (1987). *Social construction of technology.* New York: Wiley.

Castells, M. (2007). Communication, power and counter-power in the network society. *International Journal of Communication, 1*(1), 29.

DiNucci, D. (1999). Fragmented future. *Print, 53*(4), 32.

Farrugia, R., & Swiss, T. (2005). Tracking the DJs: Vinyl records, work, and the debate over new technologies. *Journal of Popular Music Studies, 17*(1), 30–44.

Fischer, C. S. (1992). *America calling: A social history of the telephone to 1940.* Berkeley: University of California Press.

Garnham, N. (1995). The Media and the Public Sphere. In Craig Calhoun (ed.), *Habermas and the Public Sphere* (pp. 359–76). Cambridge, MA: MIT Press.

Giles, J. (2005). Internet encyclopaedias go head to head. *Nature, 438*(7070), 900–901.

Goffman, E. (1959). *The presentation of self in everyday life.* Garden City, NY: Doubleday.

Hackett, R., & Carroll, W. (2006). *Remaking media: The struggle to democratize public communication.* New York: Routledge.

Hayles, N. K. (2008). *How we became posthuman: Virtual bodies in cybernetics, literature, and informatics.* Chicago: University of Chicago Press.

Hayles, N. K. (2012). *How we think: Digital media and contemporary technogenesis.* Chicago: University of Chicago Press.

Holman Rector, L. (2008). Comparison of Wikipedia and other encyclopedias for accuracy, breadth, and depth in historical articles. *Reference Services Review, 36*(1), 7–22.

Jeffrey, P., & Mark, G. (2003). Navigating the virtual landscape: Coordinating the shared use of space. In *Designing information spaces: The social navigation approach* (pp. 105–124). New York: Springer.

Jenkins, H. (2004). The cultural logic of media convergence. *International Journal of Cultural Studies, 7*(1), 33–43.

Jenkins, H. (2006). *Convergence culture: Where old and new media collide.* New York: New York University Press.

Katz, E., & Lazarsfeld, P. F. (1970). *Personal influence, the part played by people in the flow of mass communications.* Piscataway, NJ: Transaction.

Levinson, P. (2003). *Digital McLuhan: A guide to the information millennium.* New York: Routledge.

Martey, R. M., & Stromer-Galley, J. (2007). The digital dollhouse context and social norms in the Sims online. *Games and Culture, 2*(4), 314–334.

McLuhan, M. (1968). *Understanding media: The extensions of man.* Cambridge, MA: MIT Press.

McLuhan, M. (1974). At the moment of Sputnik the planet became a global theater in which there are no spectators but only actors. *Journal of Communication, 24*(1), 48–58.

McQuarrie, E. F., Miller, J., & Phillips, B. J. (2013). The megaphone effect: Taste and audience in fashion blogging. *Journal of Consumer Research, 40*(1), 136–158.

Miller, D. (2013). "What is social media?"—A definition. Retrieved from http://blogs.ucl.ac.uk/social-networking/2013/05/01/what-is-social-media-a-definition/.

Napoli, P. M. (2003). *Audience economics: Media institutions and the audience marketplace.* New York: Columbia University Press.

O'Reilly, T. (2005). *What is Web 2.0?* Retrieved October 1, 2013.

Ong, W. J. (1982). *Orality and literacy: The technology of the word.* New York: Methuen.

Peña, J., & Hancock, J. T. (2006). An analysis of socioemotional and task communication in online multiplayer video games. *Communication Research, 33*(1), 92–109.

Piskorski, M. J. (2014). *A social strategy: How we profit from social media.* Princeton, NJ: Princeton University Press.

Postman, N. (1964). *The humanism of media ecology.* Paper presented at the Proceedings of the Media Ecology Association.

Postman, N. (2000). The humanism of media ecology. In *Proceedings of the Media Ecology Association* (Vol. 1, pp. 10–16). Available at http://www.media-ecology.org/media_ecology/#What%20is%20Media%20Ecology?%20(Neil%20Postman.

Rheingold, H. (1993). *The virtual community: Homesteading on the electronic frontier.* New York: Basic Books.

Rochet, J. C., & Tirole, J. (2003). Platform competition in two-sided markets. *Journal of the European Economic Association, 1*(4), 990–1029.

Rushkoff, D. (2013). *Present shock: When everything happens now.* New York: Penguin.

Sassenberg, K. (2002). Common bond and common identity groups on the Internet: Attachment and normative behavior in on-topic and off-topic chats. *Group Dynamics: Theory, Research, and Practice, 6*(1), 27.

Strate, L. (1999). Understanding MEA. *Medias Res, 1*(1).

Strate, L. (2004). A media ecology. *Communication Research Trends, 23*(2), 1–48.

Sunstein, C. R. (2006). *Infotopia: How many minds produce knowledge.* New York: Oxford University Press.

Turkle, S. (1995/2011). *Life on the screen.* New York: Simon & Schuster.

Van Dijck, J., & Nieborg, D. (2009). Wikinomics and its discontents: A critical analysis of Web 2.0 business manifestos. *New Media & Society, 11*(5), 855–874.

Webster, J. G. (2011). The duality of media: A structurational theory of public attention. *Communication Theory, 21*(1), 43–66.

Yee, N., Bailenson, J. N., Urbanek, M., Chang, F., & Merget, D. (2007). The unbearable likeness of being digital: The persistence of nonverbal social norms in online virtual environments. *CyberPsychology & Behavior, 10*(1), 115–121.

CHAPTER 3

—

Message Types

Imagine this: you are in the grocery store when suddenly you see Tom Cruise in the dairy aisle. Certainly, if ever you needed to share a piece of information, this is the moment! Who should you tell? How should you tell them? Should you tell them now or later, at length or in a short quip, in person, in a text, or online, and do you want people to respond or do you just "put it out there"? There are many different genres at your disposal in the world of social media. Understanding how these genres differ, change, and intersect is one of the main analytical challenges facing us if we want to understand how we use social media.

Say you want to tell your friends as a group, but you also want feedback. A social networking site like Facebook might be the answer. Or maybe you don't need approval and go to a feed like Twitter. Or perhaps you don't want people to think you're crazy and would prefer to text a few friends with a quick, but more personal "did I just see Maverick in aisle 6?" Whatever you decide to do, it will help to know the possibilities.

Social media comes in a variety of forms. This chapter will present a typology for categorizing messages and discuss properties of each type of social media message. It will draw from basic theories in linguistics and communication studies to present a model for understanding differences between messages in terms of audience, feedback, source, and genre. It will also provide a brief history of social media and discuss its evolution from niche message boards like Usenet to contemporary, widely adopted platforms like Facebook. Types of messages from blogs, message boards, networking sites, and chat rooms will be examined. But first, to understand why these different types matter, let's examine the relationship between the attributes of these tools and the way we use them.

AFFORDANCES

In the previous chapter we discussed the debate between technological determinism and social constructionism. Does technology shape us or do we shape technology? Rather than seeing technology as determining or constructed, it may help to resolve these two positions by understanding that the material and structural properties of technology enable some actions and uses while constraining others. Objects have **affordances** in the sense that their properties lend them toward some uses and away from others (Gibson, 1977). To take the basic example, think of the material properties of a chair. It has a horizontal surface that is placed about knee height. It has a vertical surface that supports one's back. It may have items placed at the side to rest one's arms. These traits, which we will call affordances, make it perfect for sitting; its material properties mean that humans naturally use it for that purpose and not for others, like transportation (Gibson, 1977). However, that does not mean that one couldn't use a chair for something else. For example, if you are at a party and need a place to put your food, a chair might be a natural table. If you are in a rush and need to put your clothes somewhere, it could double as a hamper. If you are tired and have two chairs, perhaps you will use one for a footrest, or if you need to change a light bulb, it can double as a stepping stool. These would all be positive affordances. However, there are certain things for which a chair would not have natural affordances or have negative affordances. You could not use a chair to call a friend or go to the store. An affordance is essentially a fit between the user's goals and the material environment.

Affordances are not abstract physical properties, but are relative to the user, and we tend to view objects mostly in terms of such uses, rather than their physical properties (Heidegger, 1954). For example, a hammer is a stick with a metal object on the end, but we tend to see that stick as a "handle" and the metal object as a "head." Affordances for humans are tied to norms and conventions for use that are learned (Hutchby, 2001), and we learn about the affordances of objects—how to use them—through socialization, just as we can also learn new uses by observing others.

In the same way as material objects, technologies have affordances (Hutchby, 2001). Social networking sites like Facebook might be great for keeping in touch with old friends, but not good for finding new friends—for that, see OKCupid (Piskorski, 2014). Mobile phones have the affordance of being connected and portable so we can take them almost anywhere (Wellman et al., 2003), but they are not so good for displaying detailed visual data or watching a movie. Twitter might have affordances for disseminating interesting news stories, but not for having long, personal conversations. Throughout this chapter, we will examine the attributes of social media with an eye toward how these attributes, as affordances, affect their use. As we will see, some attributes may make some types of social media more permanent, more mobile, or richer, and these properties will therefore structure common uses in systematic ways.

ATTRIBUTES OF SOCIAL MEDIA

Messages can be categorized based on a host of different variables. Six attributes are crucial for understanding how social communication differs: social presence, temporal structure, media richness, permanence, replicability, and mobility (Baym, 2010, pp. 7–11; see also Donath, 2004). Forms of media vary on these elements depending on affordances and social conventions for using the technology. Although media have certain objective characteristics, these characteristics are perceived in different ways depending on the user's experience and

Table 3.1 Attributes of Social Media Messages

ATTRIBUTE	DEFINITION	EXAMPLE
Social presence	The quality and amount of social information conveyed in a message	Skyping versus texting with a friend
Temporal structure	The level of co-presence with conversation partners in a communication context	Sitting in a chat room versus reading archives on reddit
Media richness	The amount of sensory information transferred between the sender and the receiver	Text-based email versus streaming video
Permanence	The degree to which previous messages are available to users	Texting a picture versus Snapchat
Replicability	The degree to which a message can be consistently reproduced	Downloading a file from Soulseek versus trying to share a song on iTunes
Mobility	The degree to which a medium's devices can be physically transported, enabling access from a variety of places	Checking scores on your iPhone versus watching the game on a television

knowledge of the medium (Fulk, Steinfield, Schmitz, & Power, 1987). Such differences in perception can lead to different usage routines and norms, an issue to which we will return in Chapter 6. First we will explore these different elements before we see how they are combined in different genres of social media.

Social Presence and Media Richness

One of the most important differences between types of social media is the degree of social presence they convey. **Social presence** (Short, Williams, & Christie, 1976) is the "degree to which the medium permits users to experience others as being psychologically present" (Fulk et al., 1987, p. 531). Factors such as sociability, warmth, personality, and sensitivity all determine whether social presence is conveyed in a particular medium. For instance, a webcam feed that offers facial expression, tone of voice, and background visuals would make the sender more socially present than sending a text message. **Conversational analysis** is the method used by linguists to study how these extralinguistic cues affect communication (Halliday & Hasan, 1976). One early study of office email use found that users try to convey social presence through cues like ellipses and parenthetical markers as well as smiley faces and winks (Fulk et al., 1987; see also Negretti, 1999). For example, Figure 3.1 shows an exchange between two teenagers. How many cues of social presence can you count?

The study of the extralinguistic aspects of communication is called *pragmatics*. Pragmatics involves everything from the intonation of a voice to norms about referring to close things as "this" and far things as "that." In short, context, not just content, matters (Berger & Calabrese, 1975).

Line 1 Buddy1: hey honey :-)
Line 2 Buddy1: you're home
Line 3 Guysome: tell your mom thanks for the pie
Line 4 Buddy1: i would, but i think she's asleep
Line 5 Guysome: brb
Line 6 Guysome: I just had a revelatory idea
Line 7 Buddy1: <gasp>
Line 8 Guysome: I am listening to a tape deep in my archives entitled simply 'john
Line 9 carroll'
Line 10 Guysome: and...
Line 11 Buddy1: and??
Line 12 Guysome: it contains 45 minutes of improvised music—he and I on electric
Line 13 guitar...kyle on drums
Line 14 Buddy1: and...
Line 15 Guysome: it is awesome
Line 16 Buddy1: so what's the idea?
Line 17 Guysome: however, the quality of it is bad because we recorded it on an old tape
Line 18 player
Line 19 Guysome: flash forward to the future---->
Line 20 Buddy1: <flashing>
Line 21 Guysome: I get a copy of the band's (abominable) tape and use their four
Line 22 track
Line 23 Buddy1: sounds good
Line 24 Buddy1: hey, i gtg, I think mom is getting up <tiptoes back to bed>
Line 25 Guysome: oh no :-(
Line 26 Buddy1: sorry! ttyl
Line 27 Guysome: night!

Figure 3.1 Extralinguistic Clues in an Instant Message Chat.

One important finding from pragmatics is the norm of turn-taking discussed in the previous chapter (Goffman, 1959; Schegloff, 1979). In face-to-face communication, one offers social cues such as pauses and intonation to signal completion or continuance. Who among us has not been in a conversation with someone who butts their way into the conversation with these cues? Some media, like iPhone's iMessaging and Google Chat, try to replicate at least one of these social cues by signaling when the other person is "typing."

Closely related to the idea of social presence, **media richness** describes the amount of sensory information transferred between the sender and the receiver (Daft & Lengel, 1986; Daft & Macintosh, 1981). Media richness is based on the speed of feedback, the types of channels, familiarity of the source, and richness of the language carried. From this perspective, face-to-face communication is the richest medium, whereas written formal media is the least rich. For example, a website that offers video, sound, and chat would be more rich—it can carry more information—than a text-only blog. It is important to note that richness is not the same thing as complexity or depth. A scientific paper or poem may exist only as text, but is more complex than a television advertisement having video and sound.

However, although a video with sound will be richer, it also requires a larger bandwidth, not only technologically (Lasswell, 1948), but also mentally

(Simon, 1971). Rich messages convey a lot of information, but they also require more attention and effort to cognitively process (Chaiken & Eagly, 1989; Petty & Cacioppo, 1986). A perspective called *signal detection theory* (Lasswell, 1948) is the study of how much "noise" to "signal" is required to convey the message with the minimum bandwidth. This is also a consideration when supporting the bandwidth for an entire network, not just between sender and receiver. For example, boyd and Ellison (2007) note that the early social network site Friendster failed in part because they were not prepared to offer the amount of bandwidth users, en masse, required. Thus bandwidth is a concept that can be used to understand the capacity required by both individual messages and the aggregate of messages sent by all users in the system.

People do not always value or always want to use rich media for everything they do. For example, the impersonality of email can actually be a good thing in the office because it allows workers to hide otherwise apparent social cues and therefore be better negotiators. As many college students can attest, it is much easier to text their parents than to have a long discussion on the phone about grades this semester. However, older users may have trouble interpreting social cues sent through less rich forms of media, particularly if they are not experienced in using them (Karimi & Neustaedter, 2011).

Early studies of media richness in computer-mediated communication viewed digital communications as less rich than a phone conversation or face-to-face communication. However, more recent work has shifted to considering many forms of digital communication as **situated**, which means that people use them according to personal needs and goals as well as practical and social conventions. Richer is not always better. For instance, receiving a text message in class or at work is far preferable to getting a call. Conversely, receiving a text while driving could mean a serious accident, but a call is relatively less problematic.

Temporal Structure

One of the most studied differences in social media is the distinction between synchronous and asynchronous communication. With **synchronous** communication, people are co-present in the same digital space. They can exchange messages almost immediately (although of course there are still technological limitations on this, such as connection speed). People must be available at the same time, if not physically co-present, to create a sense of synchronous communication (Donath, 2004). In contrast, other social media, like message boards, are intended to be relatively more **asynchronous**, with users posting a message and then returning hours or days later to view the responses. In studies of Internet communication, scholars find that turn-taking norms exist, but that unlike face-to-face communications, where both source and receiver have an evenly synchronous experience, in online communication the receiver only experiences silence as the sender types the message. This lag can lead to hitches in turn-taking norms (Garcia & Baker Jacobs, 1999). As we can see in the previous example, turn-taking can get out of sync in some forms of social media communication (see lines 14–17 of Figure 3.1).

Symmetry

Media can be symmetric, where the sender and the receiver exchange information, or it can be asymmetric, where one person or organization sends more information than is received. For example, in a study of elderly communities' use of social media, Xie (2008) finds that symmetrical communication like voice chat or instant messaging is better for emotional support, whereas an asymmetrical online forum is best for informational support (Xie, 2008). These elements can also make communication less formal and therefore more fun and flexible. The more asymmetric and formal a communication form is, the more it looks like mass media. For example, if you use email to send everyone in the office a notice about an upcoming holiday party, the communication is relatively asymmetrical and asynchronous. Communication that is symmetric and informal like messages exchanged while playing a video game, on the other hand, likely looks more like personal media than mass media. Social media clearly lies somewhere in between—with symmetric formal and informal communication occurring alongside asymmetric informal communication (Lüders, 2008).

Permanence

Social media also vary in their permanence. Permanence is how long the content of a message is accessible to its users. For instance, Snapchat allows users to take a snapshot that erases itself in ten seconds. Although workarounds are possible to capture the image, the normative social understanding is that the image should be fleeting. As many have noted, such an application can be useful for facilitating sexting, or the sending of sexually explicit images or messages, as well as other messages users may wish to keep private. With cloud-based computing, permanence is not always apparent. For example, in a 2014 hacking scandal, hundreds of celebrities were surprised to find that hackers could access their personal photos and share them with the world (Safronova, 2014). The permanence of social media has become related to reputation in an important way, and reputation management services have cropped up to help people expunge damaging information from their search results. According to a Pew survey, 81% of adults say they feel "not very" or "not at all secure" using social media sites to share private information (Madden, 2014). Although some commentators have claimed that teenagers have different ideas of privacy, 70% of teenagers reported being concerned with sharing private details on a site that stores information (Pew, 2013). Despite these concerns, 55% of people say they are willing to share some information about themselves with companies to use free online services (Madden, 2014). More on this will be covered in Chapter 6.

Although permanence can present reputational problems, whether we view permanence as a problem depends on the context. Permanence is not always a bad thing. In 2014 when Malaysian flight 17 was downed in Ukraine, the Way

Back Machine, an Internet archiving project, captured a separatist leader boasting, "We just downed a plane, an AN-26," with a picture of what looked like a Boeing 777. Although the post was later deleted, it was referenced by U.S. Ambassador Samantha Power and others as evidence that Russian separatists had been responsible for the attack (Lepore, 2015). Thus, in this case, permanence is not a threat to reputation, but rather a mode of accountability. Although we may assume that permanence is a natural feature of online communication, this is not necessarily the case, because organizations for preservation like libraries are not fully institutionalized. Many scholars have pointed to potential issues with disappearance and the ephemerality of content (Lepore, 2015), leading us to ask, Could everything we put online one day disappear?

Mobility and Replicability

Some media are more **mobile** than others. Harold Innis refers to this difference as "heavy" versus "light" media (Innis, 2007). Some media are heavy in the sense that they are durable, but hard to transport. Others are light in the sense that they are portable. Although media can help people communicate over space and time, they may themselves have physical properties (e.g., heavy or light) that impede or enable their ability to preserve or transmit knowledge (Strate, 2004). A desktop computer may allow the user the rich experience of playing *Call of Duty* with friends, but have few advantages when it comes to looking for a good place to get pizza (for that, a smartphone would be perfect).

Devices can be mobile, but so can content. For this, we use the concept of **media replicability**, the degree to which information is easy to reproduce (Lessig, 2004). Because of technological constraints for making copies, some media are easily copied, whereas others are harder to reproduce. For example, when the Recording Industry Association of America wanted to impede the copying of songs, they supported the Digital Millennium Copyright Act, a law Congress passed in 1998. This law made it possible for companies to protect copyrightable material by placing technological obstructions in the material as well as in users' computers and thus made the material less mobile.

Social media have countless differences in their material and functional properties. These "inherent" properties, although they do not determine use, both constrain and enable what humans do with them (Hutchby, 2001). And, of course, humans are themselves pretty crafty. There are many technologies (like the Internet itself) that begin with one use and end up being put to a completely different one. The next section will provide a brief overview for understanding the emergence of social media technology, forms, and genres.

A BRIEF HISTORY OF COMPUTER-MEDIATED COMMUNICATION

Before we discuss how different attributes combine to form different genres of social media, it will help to have a historical perspective on the emergence of the

Internet and mobile telephony. A full historical accounting of the Internet and its related forms is beyond the scope of this book, but a few references on the history of computer-mediated communication are listed at the end of this chapter. Here, we will adopt the perspective of historical progression based on layering of newer modes of communication on top of other forms, rather than on simple linear progress (Cartoon 3.1 illustrates a linear progression). As new genres emerge, they commingle and combine to create new forms that are similar but different (if anyone is interested in the philosophical underpinnings of this, see Hegel (1807/2004) and Polanyi (1944)). This idea of layering is important because it can help us trace the origins of current modes of communication while acknowledging their difference from previous modes. Although particular genres of communication change, human practice evolves much more slowly.

Internet

In the mid-1960s several parallel teams, one from MIT, one from RAND, and one from NPL, first drew up plans for exchanging messages or "packets" of information electronically over computer systems. These plans, with partial funding from the U.S. Department of Defense, converged in a project called ARPANET, and two computers, one at UCLA and another at the Stanford Research Institute, were connected in October 1969. Two other nodes, one at UC Santa Barbara and one at the University of Utah, were soon connected. ARPANET eventually grew into the Internet (Leiner et al., 2012). The basic idea was that there would be no global control of the system. Rather, each network would stand on its own and communicate to other networks through "blackboxes" or gateways, a system of routers. There were many further advances and structuring agreements required to provide common standards for communicating on the network, but the system expanded in the next thirty years to be adopted by communities of scholars and companies who used email systems and finally to home users in the mid-1980s. On January 1, 1983, the TCP/IP system was adopted by all users, providing a common standard to connect devices. Finally, a system for finding and linking webpages, called the World Wide Web, was implemented in 1991 and 1992 (Brügger, 2010).

Cartoon 3.1 Linear Progression. Credit: Mike Keefe, InToon.com.

From its inception, the Internet was a social medium—a system of exchanging information with communities of others, like the telephone. As it has evolved and changed, the ways of exchanging information have experienced periods of diffusion and convergence. In this brief history, we will catalog only a few historical genres that are related to social media as we now experience it.

Mobile Communication

Parallel to the development of personal computing, digital and mobile telephony emerged in the mid-1980s (most are familiar with these early images of phones the size of a shoe box; if not, Google "Zack Morris phone"). These systems for communicating were eventually enabled to send small bits of text as a subsidiary service because text took up little bandwidth. Growing out of previous models of personal digital assistants, in the early 2000s, mobile telephony began to merge with personal computing with the innovation and adoption of the Blackberry and iPhone and other "smartphones," devices that enabled Internet access, as well as audio and text communication in addition to pictures and music. According to Nielsen, in 2013, smartphone use reached a majority, with 60% of mobile users in the United States using a smartphone (Nielsen, 2013), and as of December 2014, 77% of people in the U.S. owned one (Nielsen 2014). Meanwhile, noting their ubiquity, social science researchers have begun to investigate the impact of cellphones and smartphones on the social norms of face-to-face communication (Humphreys, 2005; Mazmanian, Orlikowski, & Yates, 2005). A comparison of a picture taken at a Vatican funeral in 2005 to one of the announcement of the new Pope in 2013 (Photos 3.1A and 3.1B) illustrates the changes in the pervasiveness of smartphones and other small digital devices for recording experiences (and may also tell us something about the contextual norms of social media use).

FORMS AND GENRES OF SOCIAL MEDIA

In this section, we will cover only a few relevant genres in social media, keeping in mind that genres can often be mixed or blurred. For instance, YouTube is primarily a website that provides media content, some of which was produced before YouTube came into being. However, it also provides features of a social networking site, including profiles, private messages, and the ability to "follow" others. Genres of social media may converge or diverge over time, but we can still understand how their basic attributes may affect the ways that people use them.

Technology, Form, and Genre

Scholars like Marika Lüders (2008) helpfully make the distinction among a technology, a form, and a genre. A **technology** is a material configuration that allows for the production or reception of media. For instance, the printing press is a technology. A **form** is the type of media that results from a particular technology. For example, novels, newspapers, and pamphlets are all forms that came out of the technology of the printing press. A **genre** is a particular set of conventions

Photo 3.1A April 4, 2005, Mourners Gather for Viewing of Pope John Paul II.

Photo 3.1B March 13, 2013, The Announcement of Pope Francis.

within a form. For example, the Gothic novel was a particular type of novel that arose in the late 1700s. Features, op-eds, and sports stories are all genres within the form of the newspaper (online or not). To take another example, digital telephony was a technology developed in 1984 that allows a sender to encode a message and send it across a wireless signal to a receiver with a similar device, a phone. However, several forms can come out of this technology. SMS text messaging is a particular form of communication. Sets of conventions that emerge using SMS messaging (like sexting) could be called genres. As one moves from technology to form to genre, the social and agentic shaping of the communication becomes clear (Lüders, 2008). Conceivably, genres can vary widely from culture to culture and among social groups, but forms and technologies may vary less.

Remediation

It is important to understand how styles from older genres can affect the form of new genres. As we saw in the discussion of the media ecology perspective, new forms of media can shed light on certain aspects of old media that were previously unexamined. **Remediation** is the idea that stylistic elements from previous genres are carried forward into new styles and genres of communication (e.g., Fornäs, Klein, Ladendorf, Sundén, & Sveningsson, 2002; Bolter & Grusin, 2010). For example, email headers like "re:" and "cc:" (or carbon copy) were modeled on the form of physical memos that circulated in offices, where carbon copy referred to a physical process for copying and relaying a message to another party. Stemming from some of McLuhan's initial work, remediation comes from the idea that "the content of any 'medium' is always another medium" (McLuhan & Fiore, 1967). So, for example, speech is the content of writing. That is, writing was initially developed to represent speech. In the same way, writing is the content of print. Print was created to represent handwritten communication (McLuhan & Quentin, 1964, p. 8). McLuhan also points to the tendency of a medium to be naturalized until it displays some content. For example, an electric light does not seem like a medium, as something that communicates, until it displays a brand name. Suddenly, we note that light can be a medium for a particular message, for example, "Enjoy Coca-Cola."

Remediation takes this idea further to show how previous modes of communication show up in new modes. For example, the website Pinterest takes the form of a bulletin board, a physical space where one might pin photographs, aphorisms, and notes. Where did the idea of a bulletin board come from? From a preexisting medium, of course. Remediation can be found in many forms of social media, from Pinterest, to YouTube (where we see the image of a television in the logo), to blogs designed to look like notebooks (Photo 3.2). Remediation

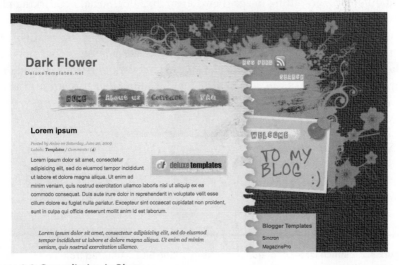

Photo 3.2 Remediation in Blogs.

even affects the way we label technology. For example, Internet "radio" bears only a passing resemblance to the FM or AM dial. In short, old genres can shape the look and feel of new genres, at least initially. Then those genres may themselves develop and be remediated by other future genres.

Social Network Sites

Social network sites are "web-based services that allow individuals to (1) construct a public or semi-public profile within a bounded system, (2) articulate a list of other users with whom they share a connection, and (3) view and traverse their list of connections and those made by others within the system" (boyd & Ellison, 2007, p. 211). Communication on these sites can occur synchronously or asynchronously, symmetrically or asymmetrically. Permanence is relatively high relative to other genres. These sites began as places where blogs were connected. For instance, one of the first social networking sites, "Open Diary," was a site that put together personal diary writers on the Internet (Kaplan & Haenlein, 2010). Although they began as simple ways to link profiles, personal pages that display information about the self, social networking sites have gradually changed to offer more features such as messaging and chatting (Figure 3.2).

The "backbone" of social network sites are profiles created by users where they present a public self, usually complete with a photograph and some personal information (boyd & Ellison, 2007). Some scholars have argued that the importance of the profile within these network sites has created a culture of narcissism and performance (Gabler, 2011). This debate will be taken up when we consider the self in Chapter 6.

Profiles are then linked according to associations or "friends" (Wilson, Gosling, & Graham, 2012). The average number of connections, or friends, one has on Facebook is 303 as of the writing of this book, although there are significant differences according to age (Pew Research, 2013). Social networking platforms tend to be structured by slightly different norms and offer different structures for either meeting new friends or deepening existing relationships (Piskorski, 2014). Some sites, like LinkedIn, create a professional network, whereas sites like Facebook create an informal network of friends, although as anyone who has ever been friended by their grandmother can attest, it is not always that simple.

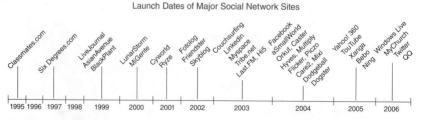

Figure 3.2 Launch Dates of Major Social Networking Sites. Adapted from boyd and Ellison (2007).

When communicating on social network sites, users likely imagine a particular public, one composed of their friends. A **public** is "a discursive space in which individuals and groups congregate to discuss matters of mutual interest and, where possible, to reach a common judgment" (Hauser, 1998, p. 86). When people get together to talk or write to each other, they form something larger than themselves, which can create a sense of unity (Anderson, 1991). A public can develop its own style, conventions, and cultural logic for communicating. The concept of a public, which we will talk more about in Chapter 10, helps us understand how communication within smaller publics can vary depending on the nature of particular subcultures (Warner, 2002), communities, or nations (Anderson, 1991). We will learn much more about these configurations when we discuss online communities.

Blogs

Blogs are asynchronous, relatively permanent forms of asymmetric communication. They are frequently updated and organized in reverse chronological order, with priority given to the most recent entry (Herring, 2004; Blood 2002). The term "blog" comes from "weblog," but was truncated to blog by a commentator (Kaplan & Haenlein, 2010). Blogs can be used for personal self-expression or for more formal, organizational communication, but they are usually written by a single author. More recently, however, multiauthor blogs have emerged, where several different authors share ideas around a common theme. The number of blogs has grown from less than 1 million in 2003 to more than 181 million (Nielsen, 2013). As blogs have grown in popularity, the genre has produced many subgenres, such as the political blog, the mommy blog, the tech blog, the gossip blog, the fashion blog, and the personal diary.

Message Boards or Forums

Early systems of asynchronous communication were developed based on the idea of a bulletin board; hence, they were called BBS, bulletin board systems. One of the first systems used to coordinate bulletin boards from all over the world was

Photo 3.3 Social Media Forms and Functions.

called Usenet, a system that is still in use today (Baym, 2010; Lueg & Fisher, 2003). These asynchronous communication tools evolved into what we now think of as a message board or forum. Reddit, soaps.com, 4chan, and Rivals.com are all examples of message boards, but it's also common for magazines like *Entertainment Weekly* and media organizations like ESPN to host message boards. Users on message boards write short entries under sections guided by a given topic, called a thread. Other users in the group then respond asynchronously to entries, generally under the guidance of conversational norms where information or opinions are exchanged. Sometimes, however, fights or "flame wars" can break out, where two or more members engage in a war of words. Although disputes can be settled, sometimes this results in the fission of the community. More about the etiquette and dynamics of message boards will be covered in Chapters 6 and 10.

Chatrooms

Chatrooms emerged in the early 1980s as a form of synchronous, impermanent group communication (Viegas & Donath, 1999). They are somewhat rich in that the immediacy of a response can be felt, but they lack many social cues that would come with a face-to-face group discussion, although participants will try to recreate social cues through emoticons and other text-based representations such as giving a rose: @---^--. Although they may lack some social cues, chatrooms adopt many of the same norms as face-to-face group communication like welcoming, self-disclosure, and turn-taking (Jenks, 2009).

First enabled by subscription-based services like CompuServe, the first chatroom, Compuserve "CB," was based on the idea of CB radio, with different "channels" on which people could talk about a particular topic. In contrast to message boards where people communicated asynchronously, chat rooms were virtual spaces where people began to gather, to casually chat about a common interest, or to exchange professional knowledge (Rheingold, 1993). One example of an early online community was *The WELL*. What emerged from *The WELL*, Harold Rheingold (1993) reports, was virtual communities: "social aggregations that emerge from the Net when enough people carry on those public discussions long enough, with sufficient human feeling, to form webs of personal relationships in cyberspace" (p. 5). We will further explore these and other community dynamics in Chapter 10.

Feeds

Feeds or microblogs like Twitter are relatively impermanent and low in richness. Although feeds can even offer video (like Vine) or images (like Instagram), their richness is still constrained in characters or seconds. Messages that are more recent generally take priority, but are searchable by user or by hashtag (Photo 3.4), a symbol used to code (and sometimes also comment on) the information. In fact, the word of the year for 2014 according to the American Dialect Society was

Photo 3.4 Birth of the Hashtag.

the hashtag "#blacklivesmatter" (American Dialect Society, 2015). Around 2010, breaking news began to be circulated via feeds (Kwak, Lee, Park, & Moon, 2010). For example, to find out the latest updates on the Boston bombing in 2013, an unprecedented number of people started following hashtags associated with locating the suspects, and followed along as the search unfolded (Jin, Dougherty, Saraf, Cao, & Ramakrishnan, 2013). Although some argue that feeds like Twitter helped drive political activism as in the Iranian Revolution in 2009, others argue that the role of social media in driving political outcomes is far from clear (Morozov, 2009). More about the role that social media plays in political life will be discussed in Chapter 13.

Content Sharing and Hybrid Forms

Content sharing sites can range from symmetric to asymmetric communication, but most often fall on the asymmetric side of the spectrum. Symmetric elements are incorporated through commenting features that are (sometimes) controlled by the platform. Apps used on smartphones may also often draw from one or more of these genres. An app like Yik Yak, for example, has most features identified with a feed, but is usually accessed as through a mobile device. Another important type of hybrid is the genre of the social shopping site (Stephen & Toubia, 2010). Social shopping sites like Amazon or Zappos offer traditional electronic retail, but importantly add social components like reviews and ratings. Features such as these can create a community in their own right that comes to exist outside the focal goal of the site. For example, Yelp! hosts events in many cities for its most loyal Yelpers, who themselves may come to yield considerable power over businesses (Piskorski, 2011). As these hybrid forms indicate, genres of social media will likely not stop changing any time soon, as they remediate older technologies and even begin to remediate recent forms of communication. However, these forms all tend to be structured by attributes such as social presence, temporality, media richness, mobility, and permanence that help us understand how they're likely to shape human communication.

SUMMARY AND CONCLUSION

This chapter has covered the attributes of social media and offered a brief account of the historical context for understanding the combination of these attributes to produce various genres. As affordances, these characteristics of social media can help us appreciate the diversity of types of communication in this complex ecosystem. From feeds to blogs, chat rooms, and social networking sites, there seems to be a mode for communicating about anything. If not, people then adapt and rework existing forms to new uses. Undoubtedly, there are and will be many more. Concepts like affordances, remediation, and genre help us understand how social media forms emerge, change, and structure human communication. In the next chapter, we will use this breakdown of attributes and genre to better understand how social media is studied and measured.

TOPICS

- Affordances
- Social presence, temporal structure, media richness, permanence, replicability, and mobility
- Technology, form, genre
- Media richness theory
- Remediation

DISCUSSION QUESTIONS

1. What differentiates one genre of social media from another genre?
2. What is the relationship between a particular technology like the mobile telephone and a particular genre like a feed?
3. When is social presence important?
4. Can you think of other contrasts between heavy and light media? Are there limitations to this theory?

EXERCISES

1. List ten instances of remediation in social media. What was the initial genre and how did that genre influence the new one? What impact did that have on user practices?
2. Make up a new genre of social media and write three samples of it. What are its conventions? What are its attributes? How do these attributes relate to user goals for communicating? Last, where does your new genre fit in the ecosystem?
3. Pick a relatively new genre of social media, perhaps one not even discussed here, and draw its family tree. Where did the genre come from and what older genres is it related to? What is the technology and form that supports it? Then, speculate on where the genre is going next. What attributes of social media could be added as features and what would be the purpose of these new functions?

FURTHER READINGS

Baym, Nancy K. (2010). *Personal connections in the digital age.* Cambridge, UK, and Malden, MA: Polity.

boyd, d., & Ellison, N. B. (2007). Social network sites: Definition, history, and scholarship. *Journal of Computer-Mediated Communication, 13*(1), 210–230.

Lüders, M. (2008). Conceptualizing personal media. *New Media & Society, 10*(5), 683–702.

Moschovitis, C. J. P. (1999), *History of the Internet: A chronology, 1843 to the present.* Santa Barbara, CA: ABC-CLIO.

To check out the first website, go to http://www.w3.org/History/19921103-hypertext/hypertext/WWW/.

REFERENCES

American Dialect Society. (2015). *2014 Word of the Year is "#blacklivesmatter"* [Press release]. Retrieved from http://www.americandialect.org/2014-word-of-the-year-is-blacklivesmatter/.

Anderson, B. (1991). *Imagined communities: Reflections on the origin and spread of nationalism.* New York: Verso.

Baym, N. K. (2010). *Personal connections in the digital age.* Cambridge, UK, and Malden, MA: Polity.

Berger, C. R., & Calabrese, R. J. (1975). Some explorations in initial interaction and beyond: Toward a developmental theory of interpersonal communication. *Human Communication Research, 1*(2), 99–112.

Blood, R. (2002). *The weblog handbook: Practical advice on creating and maintaining your blog.* New York: Basic Books.

Bolter, J. D., Grusin, R., & Grusin, R. A. (2000). *Remediation: Understanding new media.* Cambridge, MA: MIT Press.

boyd, d., & Ellison, N. B. (2007). Social network sites: Definition, history, and scholarship. *Journal of Computer-Mediated Communication, 13*(1), 210–230.

Brügger, N. (2010). *Web history* (Vol. 56). New York: Lang.

Chaiken, S., & Eagly, A. H. (1989). Heuristic and systematic information processing within and beyond the persuasion context. In Uleman, J. S., & Bargh, J. A. (eds.), *Unintended thought* (pp. 212–252). New York: Guilford Press.

Daft, R. L., & Lengel, R. H. (1986). Organizational information requirements, media richness and structural design. *Management Science, 32*(5), 554–571.

Daft, R. L., & Macintosh, N. B. (1981). A tentative exploration into the amount and equivocality of information processing in organizational work units. *Administrative Science Quarterly,* 207–224.

Donath, J. (2004). Sociable media. *Encyclopedia of Human–Computer Interaction, 2,* 629.

Fornäs, J., Klein, K., Ladendorf, M., Sundén, J., & Sveningsson, M. (2002). *Digital borderlands: Cultural studies of identity and interactivity on the Internet.* New York: Lang.

Fulk, J., Steinfield, C. W., Schmitz, J., & Power, J. G. (1987). A social information processing model of media use in organizations. *Communication Research, 14*(5), 529–552.

Gabler, N. (2011). *Life: The movie: How entertainment conquered reality.* New York: Random House.

Garcia, A. C., & Baker Jacobs, J. (1999). The eyes of the beholder: Understanding the turn-taking system in quasi-synchronous computer-mediated communication. *Research on Language and Social Interaction, 32*(4), 337–367.

Gibson, J. J. (1977). *The theory of affordances.* Hillsdale, NJ: Erlbaum.

Goffman, E. (1959). *The presentation of self in everyday life.* Garden City, NY: Doubleday.

Halliday, M. A., & Hasan, R. (1976). *Cohesion in spoken and written English.* London: Longman's.

Hauser, G. A. (1998). Vernacular dialogue and the rhetoricality of public opinion. *Communications Monographs, 65*(2), 83–107.

Hegel, G. W. F. (1807/2004). *The phenomenology of spirit.* Digireads.com.

Heidegger, M. (1954). The question concerning technology. In Hanks, C. (ed.), *Technology and Values: Essential Readings* (pp. 99–113). Chichester, UK: Wiley–Blackwell.

Herring, S. C. (2004). Slouching toward the ordinary: Current trends in computer-mediated communication. *New Media and Society, 6,* 26–36.

Humphreys, L. (2005). Cellphones in public: Social interactions in a wireless era. *New Media & Society, 7*(6), 810–833.

Hutchby, I. (2001). Technologies, texts and affordances. *Sociology, 35*(2), 441–456.

Innis, H. A. (2007). *Empire and communications.* Lanham, MD: Rowman & Littlefield.

Jenks, C. J. (2009). Getting acquainted in Skypecasts: Aspects of social organization in online chat rooms. *International Journal of Applied Linguistics, 19*(1), 26–46.

Jin, F., Dougherty, E., Saraf, P., Cao, Y., & Ramakrishnan, N. (2013). *Epidemiological modeling of news and rumors on Twitter.* Paper presented at the Proceedings of the 7th Workshop on Social Network Mining and Analysis. Chicago, IL, USA—August 11–14, 2013.

Kaplan, A. M., & Haenlein, M. (2010). Users of the world, unite! The challenges and opportunities of Social Media. *Business Horizons, 53*(1), 59–68.

Karimi, A., & Neustaedter, C. (2011). *My grandma uses facebook: Communication practices of older adults in an age of social media.* School of Interactive Arts & Technology, Simon Fraser University, Surrey, BC, Canada.

Kwak, H., Lee, C., Park, H., & Moon, S. (2010). *What is Twitter, a social network or a news media?* Paper presented at the Proceedings of the 19th International Conference on World Wide Web. Raleigh, NC, USA—April 26–30, 2010.

Lasswell, H. D. (1948). The structure and function of communication in society. In Bryson, L. (ed.), *The communication of ideas* (pp. 37–51). New York: Harper & Row.

Leiner, B. M., Cerf, V. G., Clark, D. D., Kahn, R. E., Kleinrock, L., Lynch, D. C., . . . Wolff, S. (2012). *A brief history of the Internet.* Retrieved from http://www.internetsociety.org/internet/what-internet/history-internet/brief-history-internet/.

Lepore, J. (2015, January 26). The cobweb: Can the Internet be archived? *The New Yorker.*

Lessig, L. (2004). *Free culture: How big media uses technology and the law to lock down culture and control creativity.* New York: Penguin Press.

Lüders, M. (2008). Conceptualizing personal media. *New Media & Society, 10*(5), 683–702.

Lueg, C., & Fisher, D. (2003). *From Usenet to CoWebs: Interacting with social information spaces.* New York: Springer.

Madden, M. (2014). *Public perceptions of privacy and security in the post-Snowden era.* Pew Research Internet Project. Retrieved from http://www.pewinternet.org website: http://www.pewinternet.org/2014/11/12/public-privacy-perceptions/.

Mazmanian, M. A., Orlikowski, W. J., & Yates, J. (2005). Crackberries: The social implications of ubiquitous wireless e-mail devices. In *Designing ubiquitous information environments: Socio-technical issues and challenges* (pp. 337–343). New York: Springer.

McLuhan, M., & Fiore, Q. (1967). The medium is the message. *New York, 123,* 126–128.

McLuhan, M., & Quentin, F. (1964). The medium is the message. *Hardwired, San Francisco,* 8–9.

Morozov, E. (2009). Iran: Downside to the "Twitter Revolution." *Dissent, 56*(4), 10–14.

Negretti, R. (1999). Web-based activities and SLA: A conversation analysis research approach. *Language Learning & Technology, 3*(1), 75–87.

Nielsen. (2013). *Mobile majority: U.S. smartphone ownership tops 60%.* Retrieved from http://www.nielsen.com/us/en/newswire/2013/mobile-majority--u-s--smartphone-ownership-tops-60-.html/.

Petty, R. E., & Cacioppo, J. T. (1986). The elaboration likelihood model of persuasion. In *Communication and persuasion* (pp. 1–24). New York: Springer.

Pew. (2013). *Where teens seek online privacy advice.* Pew Research, Amanda Lenhart, Mary Madden, Sandra Cortesi, Urs Gasser, Aaron Smith. Retrieved from http://www.pewinternet.org/2013/08/15/where-teens-seek-online-privacy-advice/

Piskorski, M. J. (2011). Social strategies that work. *Harvard Business Review, 89*(11), 116–122.

Piskorski, M. J. (2014). *A social strategy: How we profit from social media.* Princeton, NJ: Princeton University Press.

Polanyi, K. (1944). *The great transformation: The political and economic origins of our time.* Boston: Beacon Press.

Research, E. (2013). http://www.statista.com/statistics/232499/americans-who-use-social-networking-sites-several-times-per-day/.

Rheingold, H. (1993). *The virtual community: Homesteading on the electronic frontier.* New York: Basic Books.

Safronova, V. (2014, October 12). Jennifer Lawrence's strong stance on privacy. *The New York Times.* Retrieved from http://www.nytimes.com/2014/10/12/fashion/a-strong-voice-for-privacy.html/.

Schegloff, E. A. (1979). Identification and recognition in telephone conversation openings. In *Everyday language: Studies in ethnomethodology* (pp. 23–78). New York: Irvington.

Short, J., Williams, E., & Christie, B. (1976). *The social psychology of telecommunications.* New York: Wiley.

Simon, H. A. (1971). Designing organizations for an information-rich world. In Simon, H. A. (ed.), *Computers, communications, and the public interest* (pp. 37–72). Baltimore: Johns Hopkins University Press.

Stephen, A. T., & Toubia, O. (2010). Deriving value from social commerce networks. *Journal of Marketing Research, 47*(2), 215–228. doi:10.1509/jmkr.47.2.215

Strate, L. (2004). A media ecology. *Communication Research Trends, 23*(2), 1–48.

Viegas, F. B., & Donath, J. S. (1999). *Chat circles.* Paper presented at the Proceedings of the SIGCHI Conference on Human Factors in Computing Systems, Pittsburgh, Pennsylvania.

Warner, M. (2002). Publics and counterpublics. *Public Culture, 14*(1), 49–90.

Wellman, B., Quan-Haase, A., Boase, J., Chen, W., Hampton, K., Díaz, I., & Miyata, K. (2003). The social affordances of the Internet for networked individualism. *Journal of Computer-Mediated Communication, 8*(3).

Wilson, R. E., Gosling, S. D., & Graham, L. T. (2012). A review of Facebook research in the social sciences. *Perspectives on Psychological Science, 7*(3), 203–220.

Xie, B. (2008). Multimodal computer-mediated communication and social support among older Chinese Internet users. *Journal of Computer-Mediated Communication, 13*(3), 728–750.

CHAPTER 4

—

Measuring Social Media

Adam spends a lazy Saturday making a short video about his dogs, two Yorkies named Goldie and Sam. He and his wife draw up a brief "script," reuse some costumes left over from Halloween, and "direct" the, um, actors. Adam quickly edits the footage and posts it to YouTube, mostly so he can share it with his brother. The next morning, he logs on to find that his video has had more than 200,000 views, with 2,000 messages sitting in his inbox! There are 1,000 comments, a few response videos—and they are continuing to pour in. What in the world just happened?!

Chapter 4 will discuss the many ways social media can be measured. It will use the theory of attention economy to understand methods of measurement and the value of attention in social media. The chapter will also cover activity on social media documented for academic study. How do researchers learn about online behaviors and draw implications from data collected online? Last, we will consider the implications of both of these types of measurement for individual privacy.

Social media measurement is a topic that affects users and platform providers alike. It can tell us how many people have loved—or hated—what we said, but it also informs the revenue models of various social media platforms and is therefore a pivotal issue for advertisers, television networks, and journalists. Accordingly, in addition to user experiences, this chapter will also examine examples from marketing and journalism to evaluate the ways that messages are studied, measured, and incorporated into organizations.

ATTENTION ECONOMY

To understand what motivates and structures measurement online, it helps to think in terms of an **attention economy**. An attention economy is a system where people's attention comes to have economic value (Davenport & Beck, 2013; Simon, 1971). First coined by the scholar Herbert Simon, attention economy has come to represent a particular way of thinking about attention online. Simon argued that although information is plentiful, there are human constraints on processing and interpreting information, meaning that attention is scarce.

The more information overall, the scarcer attention becomes. For instance, on video-sharing sites like YouTube, metrics such as "views" tell us which videos have garnered more human attention, which can translate into ad revenue for both the site and the creators of content. Through revenue-sharing programs, many providers of content then have the opportunity to make money from advertising on their videos.

The fact that a site like YouTube is a platform—it provides a place for people to view videos, but also sells advertising to companies—means that having more viewers on the site makes the advertising space more valuable. If more people show up to watch Adam's Yorkie video, more eyeballs will also view a banner ad on the same page. In this way, the audience becomes a sellable asset (Napoli, 2013). Measuring the audience is therefore important to almost anyone running a platform because the audience's attention has monetary value.

MEASURING ATTENTION

There are seemingly infinite ways to measure attention online. In this chapter we will discuss how some traditional metrics have been adapted to new media and address the new metrics that have arisen as a result of both technological innovation and changes in social practice.

You may not realize it, but entire industries exist around measuring attention. Nielsen research, for example, publishes independent reports estimating how many people watch *American Idol*, visit a given Buzzfeed story, or saw the last episode of *The Real Housewives of Orange County*. Organizations like the Alliance for Audited Media measure how many people read *The New York Times* or the latest issue of *Vogue*. These companies, the companies they measure, and the companies to which they send reports all rely on a common standard for measuring "eyeballs" and develop collective agreements about what counts when it comes to measuring attention. These collective agreements, which are codified in payment schemes, contracts, standards, processes, and expectations, are called an **information regime** (Anand & Peterson, 2000; Andrews & Napoli, 2006; Napoli, 2011).

Information regimes are hard to change because they are entrenched in business processes and organizations. However, they may change slowly over time as technology for measuring viewership changes, companies develop different expectations, and powerful actors and organizations push for change. For example, Nielsen originally measured viewership by asking people to keep a diary of what they watched (and in some areas they still do). Then, in 1987, the company developed a set-top box to track television programing coming into a household (Lotz, 2007). Now, measurement can be even more advanced, such as the use of eye-tracking studies to measure ad viewership online. However, these new techniques are not always adopted because organizations will tend to go on what they know and new regimes may violate normative, cultural, technological, or regulatory structures. For example, measures of eye tracking currently lack technological structure that is universally adopted, and many feel that these forms of measurement violate norms of privacy and autonomy. For this reason, traditional metrics like reach, frequency, page views, and click-through rate can still have influence in addition to a few new metrics.

Information regimes are also important because deciding what to measure has important implications for what we know and what we value. As John Hayes, chief marketing officer of American Express, has remarked, "We tend to over-value the things we can measure and undervalue the things we cannot" (as quoted in Li, 2010, p. 76). Throughout this chapter we will see the power and influence of information regimes. Methods for measuring attention are not always the most efficient or technologically savvy, but they are the standards on which companies agree to track, buy, and sell attention.

Reach and Frequency

As noted in the previous section, two of the most traditional metrics of measuring attention are reach and frequency. **Reach** describes the total number of people who have seen an advertisement or other content online. For instance, events like the Super Bowl on television have a wide reach; millions of people's eyeballs are on the screen (that is, when they are not getting more buffalo wings). These people come from a number of different demographic segments. More than 100 million people watched the Super Bowl in recent years, so it provides one of the greatest reaches possible for an advertiser—hence, the big bucks they pay for advertising (*Sporting Charts*, 2014). Websites like *Huffington Post* and Wikipedia may not be the Super Bowl—okay, they are nowhere close—but they do represent a greater reach than other, smaller sites. In 2013, every click on an online ad cost its advertisers an average of 92 cents, although this figure can vary dramatically according to the demographics of the audience (Hochman, 2013).

Some social media advertising campaigns increasingly take advantage of the reach of mass media events by integrating or improvising related social media campaigns. For example, when the lights went out during the 2012 Super Bowl, Oreo quickly launched a Twitter message saying, "You can still dunk in the dark." This message generated 15,846 retweets—10,000 of which were within the first hour of its posting—and 6,524 favorites (Ives, 2013). Similarly, during the 2014 Academy Awards, Samsung took advantage of the large reach of the broadcast through product placement and integration of their phone to create, at the time, the most retweeted photograph, a selfie containing celebrities like Brad Pitt, Ellen DeGeneres, Jennifer Lawrence, and many others (Smith, 2014).

In contrast to reach, **frequency** is a measure of the number of times a person has seen the online content, be it an ad, a newspaper article, or simply a status update. Have you ever had the experience of seeing a banner ad over and over, even on different sites? To get a message across, we must be exposed to it multiple times. In fact, psychologists estimate that we must be exposed to a typical advertising message between three and five times to remember it (Keller, 1987; Napoli, 2013). The **mere exposure effect** says that the more people are exposed to a stimulus, the more they like it (Zajonc, 1968). However, once we have been exposed to a stimulus, it becomes uninteresting because people get bored and begin to come up with counterarguments (Cacioppo & Petty, 1979; Petty & Cacioppo, 1986). With complex messages, frequency can sometimes be more important than reach. For example, for a high-involvement product like a car or a computer, it will take many exposures for people to learn about and become familiar with the product, particularly to overcome the barriers to buying the product. As we will discuss in Chapter 11 on social media marketing, platforms usually sell advertising through a bidding system in which companies pay depending on exactly how valuable your attention may be to a particular company.

Platform Structures

All of these metrics play a role in platform structure. As noted previously, one key reason audiences are measured is because they provide value to the platform. More users mean more advertising revenue. Traditional newspapers and magazines, for example, have used this model to support cheap publications for decades. In Chapter 14, we will return to a more in-depth discussion of managing platform structures.

Based on these different measurements, social media platforms may adopt different revenue models, or ways of making money, usually based on some consideration of how they want to structure their platform. **Subscription** services, such as Netflix or HBO Go, offer membership for a fee, expecting the audience to directly pay for content. **Pay-per-use platforms**, in contrast, expect users to pay for each piece of content discretely. For example, some websites, like Byliner, sell

Photo 4.1 Douglas Coupland, installation view of Brilliant Information Overload Pop Head, Electric Laser Goo Pop Head, Liquid Video Game Pop Head, Supersonic Mustang Pizza Pop Head, 2010, in Douglas Coupland: everywhere is anywhere is anything is everything, Vancouver Art Gallery, 2014.

articles on demand, and Amazon "rents" movies for a twenty-four-hour time span. **Open-access or freemium models** offer content for free, hoping to build an audience that will support the production of content through advertising. For instance, blogs like the Awl provide open-access content, but then also sell other, curated collections of material.

Narrowcasting

A metric like views on YouTube is a measure that cannot disentangle reach and frequency. Sure, the fact that a video like "Gangnam Style" has been viewed more than 2 billion times means something (Photo 4.2). But we do not know whether 2 billion people have seen the video or if 2 million people have seen the video one hundred times. However, for a metric like "fans" or "followers," we can make the reasonable assumption that the reach of a message will be roughly equivalent to that number, or some systematic proportion of that number. For example, when Kim Kardashian, who has about 20.5 million followers, tweets out a product endorsement, advertisers count on about the same number of people being exposed to that message. Accordingly, they will pay celebrities and others with a large number of followers to promote products. Vine celebrity Jerome Jarre, for instance was offered $1 million by an advertising agency to promote a brand that he only identified as "an unhealthy food product" to his 8 million followers on the six-second video-sharing service (Bilton, 2015). Both reach and frequency are measures of exposure; they simply measure whether a person was co-present with a message.

Yet the social and technological structures that funnel attention can have consequences for what information we get and what information we do not. Since December 2009, Google has customized search results based on previous search history and location, regardless of whether you have logged in or agreed to be

PSY - GANGNAM STYLE (강남스타일) M/V

2,268,818,425

Photo 4.2 "Gangnam Style."

Photo 4.3   Can You Hear Me Now?

tracked. On the one hand, this means that you get "personalized" results. When you want to know where to order a pizza, you won't get a pizzeria in Hong Kong, but rather one right around the corner. However, on the other hand, this function also means that there are some results that others see that you may not (Pariser, 2011). This **filter bubble** means that people are exposed to different information, and this may have political and cultural consequences. For example, as Pariser (2011) finds, two different people with similar demographics (both educated, liberal women) received different search results following the BP oil spill. In response to the search query "BP," one woman received stock quotations and advertisements, whereas the other women received news of the catastrophic spill in 2010. Narrowcasting, the practice of disseminating a message to a specific audience, has implications for civic and commercial life. As the previous example suggests and as we will discuss in Chapter 13, narrowcasting means that we will tend to be exposed to information that confirms our beliefs. For commercial life, narrowcasting means that companies can use these narrowly defined audiences for targeting the practice of appealing to a specific group of consumers. Being sorted into different segments and types, as we will discuss, can have powerful effects.

Attention, Engagement, Conversion

So far, this chapter has discussed the ways in which people's attention and eventual exposure to a message are conceptualized and measured. Measures of attention include page views, number of followers, or site visits. But, as we discussed in Chapter 2, people do much more than passively consume content in social media. This section will discuss ways of measuring—and thus conceptualizing—the audience's active engagement in social media. The ultimate goal of much of social media content, both commercial and nonprofit, is to inspire the audience to do something (Figure 4.1). This end goal, which we will call conversion, is some desired action or behavior such as voting, downloading, or purchasing.

Measures of **engagement** attempt to represent how involved or responsive the audience is to a particular message. Recall our discussion of audience activity

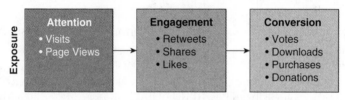

Figure 4.1 Attention, Engagement, and Conversion.

and passivity in Chapter 2; engagement is a metric of exactly that. Namely, because of differences in social practice and technological advancements for measuring these practices, viewers tend to be conceptualized as more active in social media than in traditional media, and thus activity can be measured as a sign of "engagement." Metrics based on the content or feedback of users in response to a message thus come to the fore in social media measurements. As Henry Jenkins puts it, "This next generation of audience research focuses attention on what consumers do with media content, seeing each subsequent interaction as valuable because it reinforces their relationship to the series and, potentially, its sponsors" (Jenkins, 2006, p. 38). How involved is the audience in either the consumption or the production of the message?

Measures of engagement are notoriously vague, but the idea is that the content we see online can—and sometimes does—translate to real-life behavior. For example, in 2012 a nonprofit called Invisible Children posted a YouTube video called "KONY 2012," depicting a plea to capture and stop the African military leader Joseph Kony. A compelling video, made with a clear and direct call to action, prompted millions of people to pass the video on to their friends, family members, and colleagues. Within a few weeks, the video had translated to more than 112 million views, and, more importantly, nearly 2 million visits to Invisible Children's donation webpage (Suddath, 2012). Clearly, viewer response went beyond simply viewing the video for many people, who not only donated, but also may have talked to their friends about it.

As this example illustrates, responses in social media can vary widely. We can repeat the message, comment on it, reinterpret it, or simply give it a thumbs up or thumbs down. For instance, one study found that the average Twitter user retweets only 1 in 318 links (Romero, Galuba, Asur, & Huberman, 2011). Yet recall the mere exposure effect discussed in the previous section. People can easily tire of a message and begin to counterargue after many exposures. In the case of Kony 2012, for example, people began to question the origin of the video and its viral spread (the fact that its narrator had a public meltdown did not help). Similarly, some people reported having the same response to the ALS ice bucket challenge (Hiltzik, 2014). In this way, media attention can turn from favorable to unfavorable seemingly overnight.

Because response itself can vary so widely, there are numerous ways to measure response to social media content. **Conversion** describes some action taken on the part of the user that the sender of that message desires (Ellis-Chadwick,

Johnston, & Chaffey, 2009). Purchasing, downloading, and voting are all measures of conversion. Between exposure and conversion there are a number of measures that are thought to lead to conversion—as reflections of increased involvement and investment.

One of these measures is pass-along, the rate at which a user passed the message to another person. Many social media marketing campaigns base some of their metrics for success on how much "buzz" or pass-along a particular campaign generated. Online advertisers use two other measures for advertising effectiveness online: **click-through rate**, which measures whether a user clicked on a link; or **pay-per-click**, which measures whether a user purchased something as a result of the online advertisement. These behavioral measures can be used to assess the success of the message and are often tracked through cookies, lines of computer code that track online activity, sometimes without the user's awareness or consent. We will return later in this chapter to the issues of privacy entailed by this kind of surveillance. However, imagine the following scenario: you place an ad on *Huffington Post*. How do you know whether your ad eventually leads to conversion and, more importantly, how do you measure it? **Conversion attribution** describes the process of linking, or attributing, exposure to conversion. Sometimes users could visit a site ten times before they make a purchase. Conversion attribution attempts to track exactly what message led to the conversion, even if it was several days and many clicks ago, and to track both direct and indirect effects of online advertisements (Qiu & Malthouse, 2009).

As we have seen, there are many ways of collecting and aggregating data online, and many more have likely been invented since this writing. However, a potentially more important investigation centers around how these data are interpreted and used to better understand social behavior online. In the next section, we will discuss methods for collecting and studying social media for both academic and commercial purposes.

METHODS FOR STUDYING SOCIAL MEDIA

Imagine you're assigned the task of figuring out why 200,000 people viewed Adam's Yorkie videos on YouTube. Where do you begin? There is so much data available and it is your job to turn it into information. One of the major challenges facing anyone interested in learning about social media practices is exactly how to study them. This section will discuss a few ways researchers gather, analyze, and interpret data from social media.

Digital Anthropology and Netnographic Analysis

One way to learn about social media practices is by using the traditional anthropological toolkit. Taking the view that human interaction, even face-to-face interaction, is always mediated (by social structure, norms, voice, etc.), **digital anthropology** studies the cultural and social structures that frame the human interaction that occurs through digital technology (Horst & Miller, 2013).

This perspective often includes the analysis of interactions between the digital and nondigital world and incorporates an understanding of the material elements of the digital. For example, studies in digital anthropology have found that people use text messaging on cellphones in Africa to leapfrog some stages of infrastructural development (Horst & Miller, 2006) and that immigrants use social networking sites to maintain social ties across a transnational diaspora (NurMuhammad, Dodson, Papoutsaki, & Horst, 2013; Panagakos & Horst, 2006).

Adapting the traditional practice of ethnography, which usually involves participant observation, interviewing, and immersion in a culture, **netnography**, or online ethnography, is the practice of conducting field research online (Kozinets, 2010). By becoming immersed in an online community, researchers can gain insight into the social and cultural dynamics of particular groups online. Netnographic analysis has been used to study everything from Apple devotees (Muniz & Schau, 2005), to open-source communities (Hemetsberger & Reinhardt, 2006), to soccer fans (Healy & McDonagh, 2013) and online fan communities of shows like *The X-Files* (Kozinets, 1999) and *The Sopranos* (Russell & Schau, 2014).

Methods for conducting netnography can include passive observation, where one simply observes or "lurks" around a message board or blog, or participant observation, where one engages with the community, disclosing ones identity and the purpose of research (Kozinets, 2010). Netnographic methods may also involve interviewing—through chat, video, phone, or Skype—as the researcher becomes more immersed in the community. And, of course, data collection online can be combined with methods for doing more traditional anthropological research about the offline worlds of informants. For instance, to learn about the status hierarchy in the tech culture of the San Francisco Bay area, Alice Marwick primarily adopts traditional ethnography, supplementing the method with observations of behavior and texts online such as Valleywag (Marwick, 2013). As she notes, the distinction itself can sometimes be problematic. She says, "the firm division between 'online' and 'offline' is immensely complicated in places like San Francisco with high rates of technology use" (Marwick, 2013, p. 10). Similarly, investigators of teenagers will often also ethnographically explore their offline worlds, as researchers simply follow the "native" wherever they go, attempting to understand how technology is deeply embedded in their social lives, both on and offline (boyd, 2014). Through this method, scholars have learned a great deal about group hierarchy, communication norms, and productive practices online (Kozinets, Hemetsberger, & Schau, 2008), all topics that will be covered in Chapter 10 on virtual communities.

Textual Analysis

In addition to studying social practices, there are many ways to study text itself online. **Content analysis** is a method of systematically collecting, analyzing, and interpreting textual or visual data online, usually with the intent of quantifying patterns for comparison or to draw inferences across time (Krippendorff, 2012).

Automated content analysis is a method for conducting content analysis using computers, and sentiment is one key metric often produced by this type of analysis. For example, researchers have used content analysis to study responses to political debates on Twitter, Facebook, and blogs (Fernandes, Giurcanu, Bowers, & Neely, 2010; Tumasjan, Sprenger, Sandner, & Welpe, 2010; Woodly, 2008). **Discourse analysis** is a method for studying text that focuses on interpreting the material with reference to broader patterns and structures in society, usually by taking into account the social role, position, and power of the person doing the typing. For example, a discourse analysis of #egypt tweets both before and after the resignation of Hosni Mubarak finds that tweets depicted the unfolding events as a drama created by the instantaneous nature of the medium and the language used within it (Papacharissi & de Fatima Oliveira, 2012). Discourse analysis will also not only tend to analyze the cultural dynamics of what is being said, but also look at the discourses used by particular actors. In the case of #egypt tweets, for example, media elites began to weigh in on the protests and lent their credibility to heighten awareness of particular leaders emerging in the protests.

Network Analysis

Content and discourse analysis study the content of online text, while network analysis studies who is behind it. **Network analysis**, which we'll also discuss in Chapter 7, is a way to map and analyze patterns of connection or information flow between people online (Backstrom, 2011; Burt, 2001; Wilson, Gosling, & Graham, 2012). On a site like Facebook, for example, scholars have traced how clusters of people form and assessed who has the most value in a network because of their role as a connector of other clusters (Backstrom, 2011). Mapping social structure in this way has important consequences for understanding how messages spread. For instance, Klout claims to measure social influence through network analysis. Your Klout score represents not only how many followers you have, but also how many followers your followers have. This kind of metric can be one way of measuring social influence using the data available online. In Chapter 9, we'll explore network analysis in more detail.

Machine Learning and Big Data

So far we have covered how academics might use the vast amounts of data available online to enrich our knowledge of social media. Generally, this involves choosing a **sample**, or smaller subset of the data available, in an attempt to understand a broader theoretical topic like social status, message flow, or norms of communication. Drawing from the social sciences, these approaches are based on well-established methods for studying social behavior. For instance, one might pick a particular community, say *Harry Potter* fans, to study the process through which fans create and circulate fan fiction. In a network analysis, you would pick a particular person or node and draw the network from there. These methods begin with the analyst identifying a priori the range of variables under study and proposing some initial expectations about the relationship between variables.

Within the universe of social behavior, these methods are good at telling us what things mean and why people behave as they do. Yet computer scientists, information systems scholars, and mathematicians have ways of aggregating and drawing inferences from vast amounts of data. Although the theoretical inferences one can draw may be more limited in scope, they are generally developed by studying the entire population, all of the data about a given topic that it's possible to collect, rather a sample of that population.

Although "big data" can mean a variety of things, it usually refers to an approach that uses a large amount of user data to generate predictive or descriptive insights (Podesta, Pritzker, Moniz, Holdren, & Zients, 2014). As a White House report notes, more than four zettabytes will be generated each year—but who's counting?[1] The National Science Foundation defines big data as "large, diverse, complex, longitudinal, and/or distributed datasets generated from instruments, sensors, Internet transactions, email, video, click streams, and/or other digital sources available today and in the future" (Podesta et al., 2014). It is characterized by volume, variety, and velocity (Podesta et al., 2014). That is, there is a great deal of information (volume) that covers a large scope of people and activities (variety), and the data are collected and reported in a fast-moving, real-time, and immediate way (velocity). Big data has become popular for a few reasons. First, increased audience fragmentation means that more data are required to understand and predict patterns of a particular audience, thus making big data desirable (Webster, 2014). It is also desirable to collect and keep all of these data because the data itself may be valuable if uniquely owned (O'Reilly & Battelle, 2009). Last, the feasibility and desirability of analyzing large data sets has emerged for a number of historical and economic reasons that will be discussed in Chapter 14. In brief, we can observe that because of the cost of storage space, automated data collection makes it feasible for these data to be generated by devices, online activities, or user input and stored on servers.

Yet it is important to realize that big data comes in a variety of forms. Transactional data, for example, are data generated through user behavior, usually purchase. Content, like messages posted on Facebook or Twitter, can constitute data related to personality or social interactions and perhaps tell us about user attitudes and response. Geolocation data are often automatically collected through one's phone or other device and can be used to communicate relevant information at a given place. Yet, despite the dramatic increase in available data, recall the dilemma of the attention economy. Just as we may feel overwhelmed by all of the information out there, companies too are constrained for attention and must be prepared to make sense of all of these data. It is not an easy task.

So there is a lot of data available, but what do we do with it? Big data usually refers to both a type of data collection and a set of tools for analysis (Webster, 2014). Analysis of large amounts of data is usually facilitated by **algorithms**, executable formulae or programs used to take particular inputs of data and provide an output that is either a prediction or aggregated result. They are a kind of "blackbox" through which data are input and retrieved, and for the most part they truly are blackboxes. Some of the most important algorithms, like Google's search algorithm or Amazon's recommendation algorithm, remain proprietary. Two of the primary strategies for analyzing big data are based on search and collaborative filtering (Webster, 2014).

Search

Search algorithms take the input of one or more keywords and outputs a set of webpages or links. Google's original search algorithm, called PageRank, is based on three factors: (1) incoming links, (2) outgoing links, and (3) the rank of incoming links according to existing PageRank rankings, or "relevance" to the search terms (Langville & Meyer, 2011). Because page rankings are dependent on the rankings of other linked pages, this can create a system where a few sites with a lot of traffic come to dominate the results.

Because the order and appearance of search listings is so important from an attention economy perspective, many companies will try to game the system through **search engine optimization**, a process through which companies design webpages and other online infrastructure to be as search-friendly as possible and to reach the highest position in the results. What is and is not allowable manipulation of the system is a topic of much debate. For example, in 2011 JC Penney was busted for creating fake webpages with incoming and outgoing links to manipulate their placement in Google's search results (Segal, 2011; Webster, 2014). In this way, companies are continually playing a cat-and-mouse game as Google tweaks its algorithm to prevent fraud and companies respond with workarounds.

Collaborative Filtering

Collaborative filtering is another type of algorithm that platforms use to analyze and synthesize data. Sites like Amazon, Netflix, and Facebook all produce recommendations through collaborative filtering tools. For example, sites like LinkedIn and Facebook have an algorithm to predict with whom you would like to connect. Netflix adds a social component to its service by having algorithms for predicting what "others like you" might like to watch, and Amazon develops recommendations based on what it learns from clusters of purchases by all users. Collaborative filtering is thus based on comparing people. The algorithm simply creates a profile generated through user data such as page visits, purchases, and location and compares that profile to others that are similar. Based on the similarity of some characteristics like location, age, and interests, the algorithm suggests items that are "missing" in two otherwise similar profiles. However, the functioning of these types of algorithms requires a great deal of data to be successful—both in scope of users and in depth of data—and they have important privacy implications that will be discussed in this chapter and Chapter 13.

One of the most important approaches for big data analysis is called machine learning. **Machine learning** is a process in which predictive information is produced using observed patterns in a large database that updates the process. Although, strictly speaking, e-commerce sites like Amazon are not "social" per se, many retailing and content services use machine learning to add social components to their offerings. When picking a movie, it helps to know what your friends watched last weekend.

Issues

Big data brings with it a number of epistemological, ethical, and practical issues. On the one hand, predictive algorithms can create self-fulfilling prophesies (Webster, 2014). If Amazon predicts you will like a particular book and you end up buying that book, the algorithm thinks it was right all along. In this way, collaborative filtering not only predicts what will happen, but also actually changes our behavior. From a filter bubble perspective, this could be politically problematic because we are sold only the things "Amazon thinks we might like." Another, much broader, issue is that large amounts of mostly quantitative data can limit our scope for what is knowledge and prompt us to overemphasize certain kinds of activities—namely those that can be measured and predicted—versus those that cannot (boyd & Crawford, 2012). In sum, bigger is not always better, and big data still requires thoughtful policies and theories for interpretation and analysis.

A final important issue for big data is that companies can use the data generated—usually unknowingly—by users to provide value to either themselves or others, such as advertisers. In the next chapter about co-creation, we will consider some of the ethical issues associated with user input. But first, we will look at some of the privacy concerns that emerge out of this information regime.

PRIVACY

Although privacy is connected with many other topics in social media, it helps to first consider it alongside the topic of measurement. Questions of what one can measure easily lead into what one *should* measure. Thus, the ability to measure brings with it questions about social norms and even laws for appropriate measurement. For instance, measurement issues came starkly to the fore in 2013 when Edward Snowden revealed practices of the U.S. government for storing and using phone records, email correspondence, and other online activity (Sullivan, 2013). Given the ability of technology to provide us with surveillance on just about anyone, what are the appropriate bounds of surveillance? A branch of sociology, called **surveillance studies**, tries to puzzle out just that (Lyon, 1994, 2001, 2007).

Although the issue of surveillance rightly comes with an ominous sense of limiting freedom, the issue is not always so simple. For example, consider the case of closed-circuit cameras, or CCTV. In the urban United Kingdom, cameras cover a broad swath of public space, meaning they record behaviors on public transportation, city blocks, and government buildings (Goold, 2004). But now imagine that a crime occurs and the culprit is easily caught because of this network. Does this success justify the system of surveillance?

In academic study, institutional research boards at each university govern the collection of data on human subjects. According to standards set within fields like anthropology, researchers must gain informed consent from the people with whom they interview and interact. Yet according to current standards, most textual data online are considered publicly observable behavior and therefore do not require consent. However, most scholars observe practices for making screen names and other identifying information anonymously, especially for sensitive topics such as therapy online groups, medical groups, or where potentially illegal activity has taken place. Recall that the variable of permanence discussed in Chapter 3 means archived online behavior can have important implications for people's lives long after they have made a post.

Despite these safeguards for handling data for research purposes, standards for the collection and storage of personal data in nonacademic settings are more varied. Associations like the Direct Marketing Association and the Association for Data-Driven Marketing and Advertising have informal guidelines, and there is some legal coverage provided by the Federal Communications Commission. However, companies are largely left to their own discretion in collecting, storing, and using information collected from people online. For example, the Federal Trade Commission requires that consumers be given an "opt-out" option to email solicitations ("Controlling the Assault of Non-Solicited Pornography and Marketing Act of 2003", 2003), and although roughly 70% of emails comply with this law, about 10% of companies provide broken or ineffective links (Alliance, 2014).[2] Congress passed the CAN SPAM Act in 2003, but it has had little deterrent effect, simply causing spammers to register outside of the United States (Kigerl, 2014). As Lanier (2014) notes, changes in regulation only prompt spammers to develop workarounds to pollute the Internet. We will return to some of these issues in Chapters 6, 13, and 14 on the self, political, and economic life.

SUMMARY AND CONCLUSION

This chapter has covered measurement in social media, both the methods for academic study of online practices and the more commercial side of measurement through which user information is collected, aggregated, and used by social media sites and services. Regardless of which side you're coming from, it helps to know how your own behavior can be, and often is, tracked online.

Based on the idea that media consumption is an attention economy, human attention, which is scarce, comes to have value both for advertisers and for other companies who want to offer their products or services. As we saw in the case of Adam's overnight success with his Yorkie videos, attention can be easy to measure and track on social media platforms but hard to transform into meaningful information.

In an attention economy, the activity of users in social media can come to have value. Unlike previous modes of media consumption, where the lines between the producer and consumer of value have been clear, social media provides the context in which users more actively participate in generating content. In the next chapter, User Interaction and Co-Creation, we will further explore how users produce value online.

TOPICS

- Attention economy
- Reach and frequency
- Information regimes
- Click-through versus pay-per-click
- Conversion and conversion attribution
- Netnography
- Content analysis
- Machine learning

DISCUSSION QUESTIONS

1. The idea of attention economy suggests that all attention is valuable. When, if ever, might attention not be valuable?
2. What is engagement? If you were a social scientist, how you would measure it?
3. Imagine that you make a video that goes viral. How would you respond to the attention and what metric would mean the most or the least to you?

EXERCISE

The chapter outlines several approaches to studying online behavior. Pick one method and use it to explore an online community with which you're unfamiliar. Why did you pick that particular method and what kind of understanding did it give you? How would another method have changed your interpretation and analysis?

NOTES

1. However, although vast amounts of data may be collected, that does not mean it will be permanently stored. As Lepore (2015), Boyd and Crawford (2012), and others have pointed out, archiving the data is not always practically feasible, and many have not made preservation a concern, particularly when the information does not relate to commercial or government interests.
2. http://www.fcc.gov/guides/spam-unwanted-text-messages-and-email/; see also things that could be lurking in unread terms-of-service agreements: http://business.time.com/2012/08/28/7-surprising-things-lurking-in-online-terms-of-service-agreements/.

FURTHER READINGS

boyd, d., & Crawford, K. (2012). Critical questions for big data: Provocations for a cultural, technological, and scholarly phenomenon. *Information, Communication & Society, 15*(5), 662–679.

Napoli, P. M. (2013). *Audience economics: Media institutions and the audience marketplace*. New York: Columbia University Press.

Webster, J. G. (2014). *The marketplace of attention: How audiences take shape in a digital age*. Cambridge, MA: MIT Press.

REFERENCES

Anand, N., & Peterson, R. A. (2000). When market information constitutes fields: Sensemaking of markets in the commercial music industry. *Organization Science, 11*(3), 270–284.

Andrews, K., & Napoli, P. M. (2006). Changing market information regimes: A case study of the transition to the BookScan audience measurement system in the US book publishing industry. *Journal of Media Economics, 19*(1), 33–54.

Backstrom, L. (2011). *Anatomy of Facebook*. Retrieved from http://www.facebook .com/note.php?note_id=10150388519243859/.

Bilton, N. (2015, January 28). Jerome Jarre: The making of a Vine celebrity, style. *The New York Times*. Retrieved from http://www.nytimes.com/2015/01/29/ style/jerome-jarre-the-making-of-a-vine-celebrity.html?_r=0/.

boyd, d. (2014). *It's complicated: The social lives of networked teens*. New Haven, CT: Yale University Press.

boyd, d., & Crawford, K. (2012). Critical questions for big data: Provocations for a cultural, technological, and scholarly phenomenon. *Information, Communication & Society, 15*(5), 662–679.

Burt, R. S. (2001). Structural holes versus network closure as social capital. *Social Capital: Theory and Research*, 31–56.

Cacioppo, J. T., & Petty, R. E. (1979). Effects of message repetition and position on cognitive response, recall, and persuasion. *Journal of Personality and Social Psychology, 37*(1), 97.

Controlling the Assault of Non-Solicited Pornography and Marketing Act of 2003, 108th Congress, Pub. L. No. Public Law 108-187, 117 Stat. 2699 Stat. (2003).

Davenport, T. H., & Beck, J. C. (2013). *The attention economy: Understanding the new currency of business*. Watertown, MA: Harvard Business Press.

NurMuhammad, R., Dodson, G., Papoutsaki, E., & Horst, H. (2013). Uyghur Facebook use and diasporic identity construction. In *IAMCR 2013: Crises,Creative Destruction'and the Global Power and Communication Orders* (pp. 1–23). International Association for Media and Communication Research.

Ellis-Chadwick, F., Johnston, K., & Chaffey, D. (2009). *Internet marketing: Strategy, implementation and practice*. Boston: Pearson Education.

Fernandes, J., Giurcanu, M., Bowers, K. W., & Neely, J. C. (2010). The writing on the wall: A content analysis of college students' Facebook groups for the 2008 presidential election. *Mass Communication and Society, 13*(5), 653–675.

Goold, B. J. (2004). *CCTV and policing: Public area surveillance and police practices in Britain*. Oxford: Oxford University Press.

Healy, J. C., & McDonagh, P. (2013). Consumer roles in brand culture and value co-creation in virtual communities. *Journal of Business Research, 66*(9), 1528–1540. doi:http://dx.doi.org/10.1016/j.jbusres.2012.09.014/.

Hemetsberger, A., & Reinhardt, C. (2006). Learning and knowledge-building in open-source communities: A social-experiential approach. *Management Learning, 37*(2), 187–214.

Hiltzik, M. (2014, August 18). A few (impolite) questions about the ice bucket challenge. *Los Angeles Times.* Retrieved from http://www.latimes.com/business/hiltzik/la-fi-mh-ice-bucket-challenge-20140818-column.html/.

Hochman, J. (2013). *The cost of pay-per-click (PPC) advertising—Trends and analysis.* Hochman Consultants. Retrieved from https://www.hochmanconsultants.com/articles/je-hochman-benchmark.shtml/.

Horst, H., & Miller, D. (2006). *The cell phone: An anthropology of communication.* Oxford: Berg.

Horst, H. A., & Miller, D. (2013). *Digital anthropology.* London: A&C Black.

Ives, N. P., Rupal. (2013, February 4). Marketers jump on Super Bowl blackout with real-time Twitter campaigns. *Advertising Age.*

Jenkins, H. (2006). *Convergence culture: Where old and new media collide.* New York: New York University Press.

Keller, K. L. (1987). Memory factors in advertising: The effect of advertising retrieval cues on brand evaluations. *Journal of Consumer Research, 14*(3), 316–333.

Kigerl, A. C. (2014). *Evaluation of the CAN SPAM Act: Testing deterrence and other influences of email spammer behavior over time.* Pullman: Washington State University Press.

Kozinets, R. V. (1999). E-tribalized marketing?: The strategic implications of virtual communities of consumption. *European Management Journal, 17*(3), 252–264.

Kozinets, R. V. (2010). *Netnography: Doing ethnographic research online.* Thousand Oaks, CA: Sage.

Kozinets, R. V., Hemetsberger, A., & Schau, H. J. (2008). The wisdom of consumer crowds collective innovation in the age of networked marketing. *Journal of Macromarketing, 28*(4), 339–354.

Krippendorff, K. (2012). *Content analysis: An introduction to its methodology.* Thousand Oaks, CA: Sage.

Langville, A. N., & Meyer, C. D. (2011). *Google's PageRank and beyond: The science of search engine rankings.* Princeton, NJ: Princeton University Press.

Lanier, J. (2014). *Who owns the future?* New York: Simon & Schuster.

Lepore, J. (2015). The Cobweb: Can the Internet be archived?, *New Yorker,* January 26, 2015.

Li, C. (2010). *Open leadership: How social technology can transform the way you lead.* New York: Wiley.

Lotz, A. D. (2007). *The television will be revolutionized.* New York: New York University Press.

Lyon, D. (1994). *The electronic eye: The rise of surveillance society—Computers and social control in context.* New York: Wiley.

Lyon, D. (2001). *Surveillance society: Monitoring everyday life*. New York: McGraw–Hill International.

Lyon, D. (2007). *Surveillance studies: An overview*. Cambridge, UK: Polity.

Marwick, A. E. (2013). *Status update: Celebrity, publicity, and branding in the social media age*. New Haven, CT: Yale University Press.

Muniz, A. M. Jr., & Schau, H. J. (2005). Religiosity in the abandoned Apple Newton brand community. *Journal of Consumer Research, 31*(4), 737–747.

Napoli, P. M. (2011). *Audience evolution: New technologies and the transformation of media audiences*. New York: Columbia University Press.

Napoli, P. M. (2013). *Audience economics: Media institutions and the audience marketplace*. New York: Columbia University Press.

Online Trust Alliance. (2014). *Email unsub best practices & audit*. Retrieved from https://otalliance.org/system/files/files/resource/documents/2014ota-unsubaudit.pdf/.

O'Reilly, T., & Battelle, J. (2009). *Web squared: Web 2.0 five years on*. Sebastopol, CA: O'Reilly Media.

Panagakos, A. N., & Horst, H. A. (2006). Return to Cyberia: Technology and the social worlds of transnational migrants. *Global Networks, 6*(2), 109–124.

Papacharissi, Z., & de Fatima Oliveira, M. (2012). Affective news and networked publics: The rhythms of news storytelling on #Egypt. *Journal of Communication, 62*(2), 266–282.

Pariser, E. (2011). *The filter bubble: How the new personalized Web is changing what we read and how we think*. New York: Penguin.

Petty, R. E., & Cacioppo, J. T. (1986). The elaboration likelihood model of persuasion. *Advances in Experimental Social Psychology, 19*, 123–205.

Podesta, J., Pritzker, P., Moniz, E. J., Holdren, J., & Zients, J. (2014). *Big data: Seizing opportunities, preserving values*. Retrieved from http://www.whitehouse.gov/sites/default/files/docs/big_data_privacy_report_may_1_2014.pdf/.

Qiu, D., & Malthouse, E. C. (2009). Quantifying the indirect effects of a marketing contact. *Expert Systems with Applications, 36*(3), 6446–6452.

Romero, D. M., Galuba, W., Asur, S., & Huberman, B. A. (2011). Influence and passivity in social media. In *Machine learning and knowledge discovery in databases* (pp. 18–33). New York: Springer.

Russell, C. A., & Schau, H. J. (2014). When narrative brands end: The impact of narrative closure and consumption sociality on loss accommodation. *Journal of Consumer Research, 40*(6), 1039–1062.

Segal, D. (2011, February 12). The dirty little secrets of search. *The New York Times*. Retrieved from http://www.nytimes.com/2011/02/13/business/13search.html?pagewanted=all&_r=0/.

Simon, H. A. (1971). Designing organizations for an information-rich world. *Computers, Communications, and the Public Interest, 72*, 37.

Smith, C. L. (2014, March 2). Ellen DeGeneres' Oscars selfie beats Obama retweet record on Twitter. *The Guardian*. Retrieved from http://www.theguardian.com/film/2014/mar/03/ellen-degeneres-selfie-retweet-obama/.

Sporting Charts. (2014). How many people watch the Super Bowl each year? *Sporting Charts.*

Suddath, C. (2012, August 30). "Kony 2012": Guerrilla marketing. *Bloomberg Businessweek.*

Sullivan, M. (2013, November 9). Lessons in a surveillance drama redux. *The New York Times.* Retrieved from http://www.nytimes.com/2013/11/10/public-editor/sullivan-lessons-in-a-surveillance-drama-redux.html?_r=0/.

Tumasjan, A., Sprenger, T. O., Sandner, P. G., & Welpe, I. M. (2010). Predicting elections with Twitter: What 140 characters reveal about political sentiment. *ICWSM, 10,* 178–185.

Webster, J. G. (2014). *The marketplace of attention: How audiences take shape in a digital age.* Cambridge, MA: MIT Press.

Wilson, R. E., Gosling, S. D., & Graham, L. T. (2012). A review of Facebook research in the social sciences. *Perspectives on Psychological Science, 7*(3), 203–220.

Woodly, D. (2008). New competencies in democratic communication? Blogs, agenda setting and political participation. *Public Choice, 134*(1–2), 109–123.

Zajonc, R. B. (1968). Attitudinal effects of mere exposure. *Journal of Personality and Social Psychology, 9*(2p2), 1.

CHAPTER 5

—

User Interaction and Co-Creation

Janie loves going to Threadless when she needs a basic, but cool t-shirt. After a few months on the site, she tries her hand at a few designs (she *is* a graphic designer after all!). She posts a few early ones to a discussion board on the site to get some early feedback. There are a few duds, but there is one she particularly likes. After making a couple tweaks suggested by the community, she submits it to the Threadless $20,000 grand prize competition alongside other t-shirt designs like those seen in Photo 5.1 for a community vote. Overnight, there are 105 votes! For *her*! Elated, she eagerly agrees to have Threadless produce her shirt. It seems unquestionably cool to have something she made put into production. After waiting a few weeks, Janie finally receives her shirt in the mail. It looks just as great as she imagined, so she takes a few pictures of herself in it to send to her friends. They publically comment on it, and apparently Threadless sells several hundred more t-shirts. Janie reflects on the many hours she put into this design. Shouldn't she be getting paid for this?

If you stop to think about it, a lot of the content we consume online is co-created. Tumblr, Facebook, Twitter, Instagram, Vine, and almost any other social

Photo 5.1 Threadless Designs.

media platform you can think of is composed of photographs, comments, and ratings produced by users of the site. These companies simply set up and maintain a platform on which users contribute content for the consumption of others.

Chapter 5 will discuss co-creation, the process through which consumers work with each other or with a company to produce something that has value for themselves or others. As the example just cited illustrates, co-created materials are a central input and output in social media. When users communicate in online forums, they produce things that others find useful, entertaining, or interesting. Users may produce content alone, with each other, or collaboratively with a company to produce social media. For example, what users experience as Facebook is not something produced by a company alone, but rather the cumulative creation of users. What is *valuable* about Facebook, the product itself, is made by the millions of people who log on every day. Wikipedia, YouTube, and many other sites work similarly (Van Dijck & Nieborg, 2009). Even Google uses previous searches, the product of a lot of user input, to produce their search results. Yet although users contribute a great deal of content to these sites, few people get paid for their efforts. Many scholars contend that co-creation is merely another way in which companies try to exploit users for their own gain (Humphreys & Grayson, 2008; Rey, 2012; Ritzer & Jurgenson, 2010; Van Dijck & Nieborg, 2009; Zwick, Bonsu, & Darmody, 2008). In this chapter we will unpack co-creation as a multifaceted concept and understand how it has changed the way people interact with companies, media organizations, and each other. We will then consider the ethical issues this shift poses for those who produce and profit from co-creative activities.

CO-CREATION AS A CONCEPT

As we saw in Chapter 2, social media involves a more active audience than in previous forms of traditional or mass media (Jenkins, Ford, & Green, 2013; Van Dijck, 2013). People become engaged in intellectual projects for their own sake and completely forget that they are "consuming" media at all. For instance, about 10% of Wikipedia's contributors produce 90% of the site's content by creating, writing, and correcting entries, with results that rival a traditional encyclopedia (Giles, 2005; Nov, 2007). The content of Instagram, for example—pictures, ratings, and comments—are all products made by the audience. So where does consumption end and production begin? This chapter will introduce some concepts we can use to begin to answer the question.

When the audience becomes especially active and begins to produce things of value (either to themselves or to others), we call this practice **co-creation**[1] (Bruns, 2008; Cova, Dalli, & Zwick, 2011; Humphreys & Grayson, 2008; Prahalad & Ramaswamy, 2004b; Ritzer & Jurgenson, 2010; Schau, Muniz Jr, & Arnould, 2009; Toffler, 1980). Surveys indicate that between 58 and 83% of people have engaged in some kind of co-creative activity (Arvidsson, 2008), yet in any particular context, a minority of users are especially active, only about 10% on average. The basic process of co-creation has been given many different names—prosumption, co-production, social production, produsage—and there are many varied shades of co-creation that we'll discuss in this chapter. Sometimes people create things by themselves and share them with others. Sometimes, they produce things in collaboration with a group. Other times, they will work with a traditional company or other organization to make objects or content that is valuable (and sometimes, but not always, reap the rewards). Each of these practices is slightly distinct in its motivation and outcomes, and this chapter will discuss some of these nuances. Further, it will introduce theoretical concepts like the value chain and use and exchange value that will be helpful for categorizing the different types of co-creation and for better understanding the role of these practices in the social media ecosystem.

History of Co-creation

The origins of co-creation are actually quite old. If you think about it, people have been modifying the goods and services they use ever since there were goods and services. For instance, if you buy something as simple as an orange, you still have to peel it. Arguably, this labor makes the product consumable. Similarly, if you buy coffee beans, you have to grind and brew them; if you buy an IKEA desk, you have to assemble it; if you buy meat, you have to cook it. You get the idea.

The first scholar to give a name to this idea was Alvin Toffler. Toffler, calling the process **prosumption**, argued that in the future consumers would become increasingly adept at fulfilling their own needs, primarily with technology (Toffler, 1980). For example, a bank uses the ATM to "outsource" the labor of making a deposit to the consumer, who works with the machine rather than a paid employee to complete the transaction (Dujarier, 2014). Sites like Expedia and TripAdvisor fulfill many of the functions once filled by travel agents. Although some modes of co-creation such as these can be utilitarian, more often they are the products of expressive and creative efforts of consumers. Prototypically, co-creation efforts tend to be "self-organized, emergent, bottom-up phenomenon, not primarily motivated by monetary concerns" (Arvidsson, 2008, p. 329). This kind of co-creation is seen as the result of a historic emergence of an "expressive age" (McLuhan, 1968) whereby people define themselves not by their family roles or jobs but by their own identity and self-expression (more on this in the next chapter). As many scholars have suggested, in the postwar era, people have become more invested in identity and are more productive of immaterial ideas and knowledge than ever before in human history (Calhoun, 1994; Deleuze & Guattari, 1988; Escobar, 1992; Hardt & Negri, 2009). This, together with unprecedented leisure time, readily available networked communication technology, eroding barriers between professional and private identities, and a historically educated population, creates the conditions under which people might want to voluntarily work together to produce products or content that interests them, perhaps for self-fulfillment, status, or sociality (Arvidsson, 2008).

Concomitant with this shift in user practices (or perhaps because of it), co-creation has become a popular marketing tactic and fundamental business model. Hailing the "wisdom of crowds," business journalist James Surowiecki argues that by **crowdsourcing** people can collectively produce knowledge that's greater than the sum of individual knowledge (Surowiecki, 2005). For example, Google reports that it can predict the spread of the flu from search data (Ginsberg et al., 2008). In contrast to previous models that could predict the spread of the flu within one to two weeks from doctors' hospital reports, using search data, scientists can predict the spread of the flu with a one day time lag, as long as there's sufficient web use in the population.[2] There has been much hype about the productive possibilities of user interaction and collaboration, but some scholars have pointed to issues such as misleading results because of a lack of expertise (Van Dijck & Nieborg, 2009), exploitation (Rey, 2012; Zwick et al., 2008) and the privileged status of those users who get to contribute over those who do not (Jönsson & Örnebring, 2011; Van Dijck, 2009). Plus, collaborative production— working with others—can be a long and arduous process (Humphreys, 2008; Weber, 2004). For some insight into this, look at the Talk page for your favorite Wikipedia topic.

Despite some of these drawbacks, social media platforms do seem to provide a way to coordinate user knowledge and efforts toward a larger project that can be cheaper and easier than previous face-to-face modes of collaborating. For example, the Linux operating system was first developed by a group of programmers coordinated by a Finish programmer, Linus Tourvald, beginning in 1991 (Weber, 2004).[3] Protected eventually under a General Free Public license (which means it is free to be used, copied, or modified), Linux has become an alternative operating system to commercial products like Windows and iOS, and it's promotion is supported by the Linux Foundation. Linux is used by the White House, the Department of Defense, and even in airplane flight entertainment systems for United, Delta, Qantas, and Virgin Airlines, to name a few (Varian & Shapiro, 2003; Wagner, 2008). And all this was started by a couple of hackers!

The co-creation of media content is called produsage (Bruns, 2008). For example, users of the website *Funny or Die* participate in a rating system for videos, voting them up or down based on their entertainment value using a toolbar (see Photo 5.2). On Quora, users "upvote" the best answers to questions posed by the website's users, which provides a mechanism for filtering content for other users, thereby providing value. Similarly, you can vote comments up or down on Yelp!, helping to promote reviews that are helpful and dismiss those that are not. For entertainment content, audiences will collaborate on extensions of a story or create costumes and artwork to compliment the original text that can be sold to others. **Participatory culture** means that audiences participate not only in consuming cultural products but also in producing them (Jenkins, 2006). However, audiences can also create more "serious" or informational content such as news and political commentary. We will return to these forms of participatory culture and participatory journalism at the end of this chapter and Chapters 12 and 13.

The more commercially focused products of co-creation—also called user-generated content—can provide a marketing boost for companies. For example,

Photo 5.2 Funny or Die Video Voting Bar System.

some early attempts at using user-submitted advertising included a Doritos Super Bowl ad and a Pepsi donation campaign (Elliot, 2010; Kuechenmeister, 2008). Consumers can co-create content-based objects like advertisements, encyclopedias, or software, but sometimes they also have a hand in adding value to material goods and services, which is often coordinated via an online platform. For example, Adidas offers a service where customers can build their own shoes to wear. Threadless (Photo 5.1), mentioned in the opening story, allows users to create t-shirt designs, and Jones soda uses its fans to develop flavors, packaging, and promotional materials (Brabham, 2010; Muñiz & Schau, 2011).

The Value Chain

So how do we make sense of all of these activities? There are many different types and levels of user involvement in the creation of online content. One way to understand how types of co-creation differ is by looking at the **value chain** (Porter, 1980; Prahalad & Ramaswamy, 2004b). The value chain describes the process that leads to the creation of a consumable good (Figure 5.1). Co-creation is any activity by a user or consumer that adds value at some part in the value chain. In this section, we will go through each step of the value chain, enumerating the ways in which users can potentially add value at each step.

The development of a good or service often begins with need recognition. People have a problem they want to solve. If coffee gets cold, you will need a thermos. If you wake up late, you will need an alarm clock. At their most basic, goods and services fulfill needs for tools, even if one might argue that those needs are stoked and channeled by marketers. Market research and need recognition are thus often cited as the first step in the value chain (Prahalad & Ramaswamy, 2004b; Schau et al., 2009). In co-creation, consumption communities such as

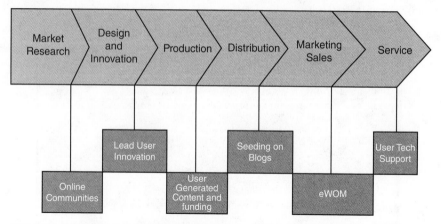

Figure 5.1 Co-Production in the Value Chain (adapted from Porter, 2001).

user groups or online fan communities are often studied to gather information about what people need or want. By studying user communities, Harley Davidson, for example, found a new market for families and women (Harley Davidson, 2013). Message boards and support groups are key venues in which people discuss problems they have and also sometimes even begin to suggest potential solutions (Bradford, Grier, & Henderson, 2012; Schau et al., 2009).

Design and innovation is the second step in the value chain. Consumers might produce ideas that serve as innovation in the design process (Figure 5.1). For example, some communities, like the mini-moto bike community, take existing marketplace objects and modify them to suit their needs (Martin & Schouten, 2014). Hiking communities will modify gear like tents and backpacks to make it better for hiking particular terrain (Füller, Schroll, & von Hippel, 2013). Surgeons will even modify their own surgical instruments (Von Hippel, 2005). Attempting to harness some of this user creativity, companies like OSRAM, a leading light manufacturer, sponsor contests for users to create the most innovative electronics or troubleshoot early versions of software (Hutter, Hautz, Füller, Mueller, & Matzler, 2011; Prahalad & Ramaswamy, 2004a).

The next step in the value chain is production. Consumers can add value to and even produce the content of a site by curating content through comments and "likes," promoting some entries that are high quality and downplaying others, or by writing entries themselves. On a site like YouTube, for example, users rate videos, which helps to curate videos for others and produce a final product. With sites like Kickstarter, audience members even literally facilitate production by contributing the money to make a product. For example, fans of the television show *Veronica Mars* contributed more than $5 million to help produce a Veronica Mars movie,[4] and fans who paid more than $2,500 were even allowed to be extras in the cast (Photo 5.3).[5] For event production, companies like Alfa Romeo will use brand loyalists as volunteer, quasi-employees that help the

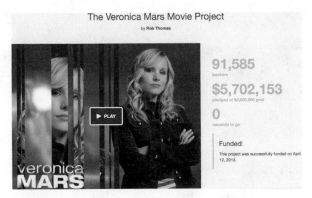

Photo 5.3 Kickstarter Campaign for Veronica Mars.

company execute events and curate message boards (Cova & Saucet, 2014). However, as we will discuss, norms often structure what is and is not okay in co-creation. For example, when Zach Braff attempted to fund a movie in a similar way, yet without a preexisting fan base, his efforts were met with controversy.

The next step in the value chain is distribution. Users co-create in this step by circulating content or acting as salespeople for a product they feel passionate about. For example, Jones soda is promoted heavily by those who participate in creating labels (Muñiz & Schau, 2011). In close relation, particularly in the case of media content, users may also help with promoting or marketing media content such as a movie, television show, or album. For example, they might create videos on YouTube to support the promotion of a new movie, helping to add value to the marketing efforts for that movie. Similarly, people create "haul" videos where they unpack bags after a big shopping trip or "unboxing" videos where people unpackage new technology. As user-generated content, these videos can promote the goods, services, and brands that are shown in the videos (Blythe & Cairns, 2009; Jeffries, 2011; Pace, 2008; Smith, Fischer, & Yongjian, 2012). Some companies have more formally incorporated user-generated content into marketing by sponsoring contests to produce advertisements. For example, during the 2012 Super Bowl, Doritos devoted a spot to airing the winning ad of its contest,[6] and in 2013, the winner received $1 million.[7]

The final step in the value chain is service. Consumers participate in servicing items by forming communities to help other customers with technical support or servicing existing items. For example, the JAVA Developer Forum is a group of computer users who answer queries by other users and solve problems in coding and other technical challenges. They do this not purely altruistically, but also for status in the community (Zhang, Ackerman, & Adamic, 2007).

Co-creation of Media Content

There is a value chain for physical products, but also one for media content (Figure 5.2). A news story does not just appear out of thin air; it is produced

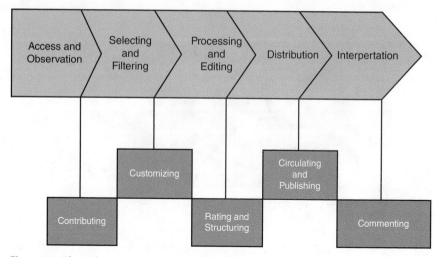

Figure 5.2 The Value Chain for News (adapted from Domingo et al., 2008).

through information gathering, filtering, fact-checking, writing, editing, distribution, and interpretation. Like the value chain for physical goods, users have the opportunity to play a role in contributing at any one of these steps (Domingo et al., 2008). For example, some modes of citizen journalism rely on Twitter for access to information about breaking news. When protests unfolded in Tehran, journalists like Andrew Sullivan used reports from Twitter as sources on the ground.[8]

Although quite old, **citizen journalism**, when nonprofessional journalists produce and disseminate journalistic knowledge, has been vastly enabled by social media platforms (Bruns, 2005; Deuze, 2005; Deuze, Bruns, & Neuberger, 2007; Domingo et al., 2008; Gillmor, 2003, 2004; Johnson, 2007; Monaghan & Tunney; Tsuruaki, 2005). For example, CNN iReport hosts a platform for coordinating the efforts of nonprofessional journalists. The site offers assignments and provides tips for producing a compelling story and taking good photographs. Another feature, called Open Stories, allows users to collectively build and comment on a news story with print and broadcast reporting.[9]

Information, particularly for breaking news stories, now readily comes from Twitter (Cassa, Chunara, Mandl, & Brownstein, 2013; Morozov, 2009; Murthy, 2011; Sutton et al., 2014; Thorson et al., 2013). Sites like reddit and Slashdot harness user input for filtering; Wikinews uses collaboration for processing and editing stories. Rather than circulating print newspapers with headlines, users on Twitter can act as hubs for circulating breaking news stories and other content (Weber & Monge, 2011). Even comments on sites like *Huffington Post* help to interpret news and, by providing perspectives or commentary, fulfill functions traditionally assigned to columnists. There are many ways in which people can become more involved in the production of news content, and we will further discuss them in Chapter 13.

Collaborative Production

So far we have primarily discussed the efforts of individual co-creators, but more often co-creation is done collectively by a group of people who share the rewards. We call this **collaborative production**, a type of co-creation that happens when fans or community members collaborate on a product. Collaborative production has some advantages over the traditional model of firm-produced goods and services. It usually attracts people who are intrinsically interested and motivated to contribute to a task, and these people will tend to self-select into tasks at which they are good and about which they are knowledgeable (Benkler, 2002). In contrast to a "normal" job at a company that would pay you money for your work, collaborative production generally attracts people who want to contribute and who get intrinsic rewards for doing so.

However, large collaborative projects have two potential downsides. First, from a purely economic perspective, participants' motivation may wane if there are no economic rewards. Because resulting products are often not ownable, no one can make money off of them. As we will discuss in the next section, people may get nonmonetary rewards like social capital and status, but often these come in the long rather than in the short term. Second, collaborative production is likely to fail without the coordination or organization to put the efforts of contributors together.[10] Novels and movies, for example, would probably make terrible collaborative projects (Benkler, 2002; although see http://www.storytimed.com/ for attempts at producing collaborative novels). Good potential collaborative projects generally have three traits. First, they are modular, which means they can be broken into parts. Second, these parts can be small and relatively manageable, requiring a reasonable amount of effort and attention, and third, these components should be easy to integrate (Benkler, 2002). For example, NASA ran a program called Clickworkers to coordinate the efforts of users to label photographs of Mars, identifying key topographical structures. A similar effort was organized after the Malaysian Airlines crash off the coast of Indonesia to look for the wreckage (Fishwick, 2014).

Last, collaborative production can suffer if the contributors lack expertise. Professionals are highly trained; they develop forms of deep knowledge and have access to pools of resources and thus may be better at many tasks than amateur co-creators (Kreiss, Finn, & Turner, 2011). In the sphere of journalism, for example, the credibility of the story can be in doubt if citizen journalists do not follow standard sourcing and fact-checking procedures (Johnson, 2007). Further, a great deal of resources go into producing mind-blowing technological and artistic innovations. Perhaps sometimes the best ideas come not from the "wisdom of crowds," but from a lone genius who can have total control over the product. We will return to the idea of collective production in Chapter 9 when we discuss online or virtual communities.

Motivations for Co-creation

So why would someone participate in creating value if they do not get paid? Some argue that contributors enjoy "not the product but the process" (Arvidsson, 2008).

Those who co-create either with a company or with a community of like-minded others may do it for its intrinsic value, for reasons of self-actualization, or to realize an artistic or creative goal. For example, in the opening vignette, Janie simply makes a t-shirt design because she thinks it would be cool. She is a graphic designer, and she enjoys the artistic process. Roughly 88% of people participate in co-creation for self-fulfillment (Hars & Ou, 2001). People are more likely to collaborate on software projects for self-enhancement, whereas they are more likely to participate in content-related projects like Wikipedia for altruistic motivations (Oreg & Nov, 2008).

However, people also get nonmaterial rewards from co-creation. First, there is a sense of esteem and respect from others for contributions to a project. People naturally get a little ego boost from making things that people recognize as worthwhile (we will return to this idea in the next chapter). For example, people reported contributing to Wikipedia because they enjoy giving something to the group, but secondarily because they enjoy the status and reputation building that can come with contributing to the community. Being the "expert" on something gives people a sense of accomplishment and worth (Kuznetsov, 2006; Nov, 2007). Another study of core participants in a peer-to-peer network finds that the core members of the group get informational resources, but unlike the peripheral members, hardcore members also benefit from the feelings of social support offered by the community (Mathwick, Wiertz, & De Ruyter, 2008). The motivations to co-create can often be community oriented, but people are simultaneously motivated by ego enhancement and self-interest (Arvidsson, 2008, p. 333).

One way to understand this tension is through the concept of **status**. Status describes the relative place of someone within a social grouping (Weber, 1978), and people gain or lose status according to the collective recognition of others. Contributions to co-creation in the aggregate can build community and reinforce social ties, giving community members social capital, a concept to which we will return in Chapter 9. The basic idea is that one wants to gain recognition in a social group, but there must be a social group around to recognize you. Yet despite these individual and group-oriented motivations, many scholars have pointed out that the value produced by consumers inevitably benefits the company, who pays nothing for the content (Cova et al., 2011; Hamilton & Heflin, 2011; Rey, 2012; Ritzer & Jurgenson, 2010). Other scholars point to what they perceive as a pernicious overlap between economic and communal discourses of sharing, friendship, and community building (Van Dijck & Nieborg, 2009). Further, people will often engage in co-creation in the hopes of becoming professionals at the task, but the inherent power dynamics of industries like music, art, or entertainment mean that these hopes are rarely realized. Thus, rather than acting as a liberating form of self-expression, co-creation can actually represent a form of consumer exploitation. The next section will explore this possibility.

ETHICAL ISSUES IN CO-CREATION

Co-creation does not come without its own set of ethical, legal, and political issues. On Google, for example, user input is used to refine the list of search results, thereby making Google a more valuable product. Should users get some of the $15.7 billion in revenue from Google last year? Millions of people produce tweets each day, but Twitter sells that data after it is produced. Co-creation is touted as a great tool for marketing and advertising, yet people rarely get a commission on the products they promote. In some cases, such as on YouTube, creators of video content can get proceeds from advertising before their videos. Although some scholars show that people co-create for self-improvement or non-monetary rewards like status, others contend that using consumer-produced products exploits freely given consumer labor (Cova et al., 2011; Humphreys & Grayson, 2008; Rey, 2012; Zwick et al., 2008). Even broader critiques make the point that business and technological systems for co-creation have constrained co-creative activities, channeling them into self-realization and commodity production (Comor, 2011). Co-creation, they claim, is completely suffused and shaped by capitalism and oriented toward satisfying and reinforcing its goals.

To unravel some of these debates, it helps to revisit their underlying economic principles. As we have discussed, consumers can play a part in creating value, but what kind of value? The political economist Karl Marx, along with other early economists (Smith, 1887) distinguished between two types of value, use value and exchange value. **Use value** is the value that one gets from using the object. This kind of value is usually idiosyncratic or specific to the user. When a consumer co-creates an object, he or she creates use value, or value to the end user but probably no one else. For example, when a consumer assembles a desk he or she bought at IKEA, this creates use value. When a reader enters her preferences to see news and sports on her MSNBC homepage, this creates value for her, but does not extend to other readers.

The other type of value is exchange value. **Exchange value** is the value that is produced whenever a person or company exchanges the good for another good or service or, more commonly, for money. In many cases, user innovations will be adopted by the company, incorporated to improve a product, service, or publication, and then resold to other consumers for an exchange value. Although people put time and effort into product development, they do not get part of this exchange value. Yet, those same consumers also seem fine with freely contributing their labor. This is where ethical issues arise, and scholars have argued that this represents a kind of exploitation without alienation (Rey, 2012; Zwick et al., 2008). At the personal level, people happily create content and feel connected to what they produce, but on the structural level, they seem to be exploited because a company, not the creator, profits from these activities. As Rey (2012) puts it, "If people are ignorant of, or unconcerned with, the value they create for companies, exploitation becomes only more insidious. And, whenever exploitation exists, social inequality follows in its wake" (p. 416).

To make matters more complex, consider the fact that many users produce content unintentionally in the form of search queries, messages to friends, or picture sharing (Zwick et al., 2008). What rights do platforms like Facebook have over this material? Many terms-of-service agreements give the platform the right to disseminate content posted on their platforms, which challenges both user privacy and economic fairness. For example, many users and celebrities, including the singer P!nk and the actress Tiffani Amber Thiessen, removed their content from Instagram in protest after the site released updated terms of service claiming that users' photos could be legally sold to advertisers (Timberg, 2012). In many cases, however, power disparities between users and companies mean platforms can dictate the terms of these user agreements. Alternative social networking sites like Ello have cropped up to address these issues, but switching to them is difficult because of the inherent switching costs and network effects of existing platforms (more on this in Chapter 14).

As you might imagine, ownership rights over co-created objects can get tricky. So far, this section has covered the economic issues, but what about legal protocols for co-created products? Generally speaking, political and regulatory structures are oriented toward protecting the rights of companies and intellectual property in traditional ways (Lessig, 2008). However, some legal changes are taking place in this area. For software, co-produced products can be protected by something called a **general public license** (GPL), an agreement that the work can be shared freely, used by anyone, and modified. The GPL includes a provision that keeps these rights in tact even if the object is transferred. For example, a couple years after the Linux operating system was created, it was protected by a GNU GPL. The **Creative Commons** license similarly protects images and artworks. Flickr, for example, distributes images that photographers mark as Creative Commons, which has both commercial and noncommercial options. Some of the images in this book, in fact, are the products of photographers who shared their images via Creative Commons. We will return to some of these copyright issues in Chapter 14 on economic life and legal structures.

SUMMARY AND CONCLUSION

This chapter has examined the ways in which the audience, and consumers more broadly, take part in the creation of value online. Because the tools for creating, sharing, and coordinating activities such as the production of encyclopedia articles, software development, and even automated tasks like search and tagging have become available to just about everyone, this kind of value creation has become more recognized and more institutionalized within corporate models. However, there is another piece to the puzzle as well. Why in the world would someone want to spend their time working on these projects? It turns out that people have many other and more varied incentives than pure economic motive. People will collaborate for self-development, community building, or just for the fun of it. As a model of economic production, the possibilities are interesting, if not always successful. In this chapter, we have further examined some of the ethical issues with the use and commoditization of audience labor. Is it wrong for a company to use someone's work for free, although they have freely given it? Will people continue to contribute to these projects if they feel their work will make someone else richer? Understanding, if not answering, these difficult questions requires a deeper evaluation of the uses and benefits of social media, a topic we will pursue in the next chapter.

TOPICS

- Value chain
- Co-creation
- Participatory culture
- Participatory journalism
- Collective production
- Use versus exchange value

DISCUSSION QUESTIONS

1. Where in the value chain can users contribute the most value? Is it different for different types of products?
2. What kinds of social media tools are the most helpful for facilitating co-creation? Can you give an example?
3. In the opening vignette, is it fair that Janie does not get paid for her work? Why or why not?
4. If you were to set up a platform for co-creation, how would you structure the ownership rights? If the product made money, how would it be distributed?

EXERCISE

Pick your favorite (media or nonmedia) product and draw its value chain. Where are the opportunities for providing value? Take one of these opportunities and develop it into a platform or business idea to facilitate co-production for this step.

NOTES

1. This chapter will refer to the process primarily as co-creation rather than co-production, prosumption, social production, or produsage. Scholars use these terms more or less interchangeably or according to common usage in their respective fields (marketing, sociology, communication, or media studies). Although researchers have discussed some theoretical differences between terms, by and large, these distinctions have not been empirically demonstrated. (See Humphreys & Grayson, 2008; Ritzer & Jurgenson, 2010.)
2. http://www.google.org/flutrends/us/#US/.

3. http://www.cs.cmu.edu/~awb/linux.history.html/.
4. http://deadline.com/2014/03/veronica-mars-kickstarter-donors-rob-thomas-699611/.
5. http://www.theguardian.com/film/2014/mar/13/veronica-mars-movie-fans-money-pressure-return-kickstarter-funded-marshmallows/.
6. http://www.adweek.com/adfreak/here-are-your-5-doritos-crash-super-bowl-finalists-137339/.
7. http://adage.com/article/special-report-super-bowl/doritos-crash-super-bowl-ad-contest-global/244121/.
8. http://www.theatlantic.com/daily-dish/archive/2009/06/the-revolution-will-be-twittered/200478/.
9. For an example on the open story for the shooting in Ferguson, Missouri, see http://ireport.cnn.com/open-story.jspa?openStoryID=1163258#DOC-1166220/.
10. In fact, one study, published in *Science*, shows that groups can outperform individuals on tasks involving collective intelligence, but only if there are members who play a role in coordination. Mixed-gender teams did best, and the groups with the smartest individual did not always perform the best (Woolley et al., 2010).

FURTHER READINGS

Benkler, Y. (2002). Coase's Penguin, or, Linux and "The Nature of the Firm." *Yale Law Journal*, 369–446.

Bruns, A. (2005). *Gatewatching: Collaborative online news production* (Vol. 26). New York: Lang.

Schau, H. J., Muniz, A. M. Jr., & Arnould, E. J. (2009). How brand community practices create value. *Journal of Marketing*, 73(5), 30–51.

von Hippel, E. (2005). *Democratizing innovation*. Cambridge, MA: MIT Press.

REFERENCES

Arvidsson, A. (2008). The ethical economy of customer coproduction. *Journal of Macromarketing, 28*(4), 326–338.

Benkler, Y. (2002). Coase's Penguin, or, Linux and "The Nature of the Firm." *Yale Law Journal*, 369–446.

Blythe, M., & Cairns, P. (2009). *Critical methods and user generated content: The iPhone on YouTube*. Paper presented at the Proceedings of the SIGCHI Conference on Human Factors in Computing Systems. New York, NY, USA: ACM Press, 2012.

Brabham, D. C. (2010). Moving the crowd at Threadless: Motivations for participation in a crowdsourcing application. *Information, Communication & Society, 13*(8), 1122–1145.

Bradford, T. W., Grier, S. A., & Henderson, G. R. (2012). Gifts and gifting in online communities. *Research in Consumer Behavior, 14,* 29–46.

Bruns, A. (2005). *Gatewatching: Collaborative online news production* (Vol. 26). New York: Lang.

Bruns, A. (2008). *Blogs, Wikipedia, Second Life, and beyond: From production to produsage* (Vol. 45). New York: Lang.

Calhoun, C. (1994). *Social theory and the politics of identity.* Malden, MA: Blackwell.

Cassa, C. A., Chunara, R., Mandl, K., & Brownstein, J. S. (2013). Twitter as a sentinel in emergency situations: Lessons from the Boston marathon explosions. *PLoS Currents, 5.*

Comor, E. (2011). Contextualizing and critiquing the fantastic prosumer: Power, alienation and hegemony. *Critical Sociology, 37*(3), 309–327.

Cova, B., Dalli, D., & Zwick, D. (2011). Critical perspectives on consumers' role as "producers": Broadening the debate on value co-creation in marketing processes. *Marketing Theory, 11*(3), 231–241.

Cova, B., & Saucet, M. (2014). Unconventional marketing. *The Routledge Companion to the Future of Marketing,* 217.

Deleuze, G., & Guattari, F. (1988). *A thousand plateaus: Capitalism and schizophrenia.* London: Bloomsbury.

Deuze, M. (2005). What is journalism? Professional identity and ideology of journalists reconsidered. *Journalism: Theory, Practice, and Criticism (Journalism), 6*(4), 442–464.

Deuze, M., Bruns, A., & Neuberger, C. (2007). Preparing for an age of participatory news *Journalism Practice, 1*(3), 322–338.

Domingo, D., Quandt, T., Heinonen, A., Paulssen, S., Singer, J. B., & Vujnovic, M. (2008). Paritcipatory journalism practices in the media and beyond: An international comparative study of initiatives in online newspapers. *Journalism Practice, 2*(3), 326–342.

Dujarier, M.-A. (2014). The three sociological types of consumer work. *Journal of Consumer Culture,* 1469540514528198.

Elliot, S. (2010, January 31). Pepsi invites the public to do good, media & advertising. *The New York Times.* Retrieved from http://www.nytimes.com/2010/02/01/business/media/01adco.html?_r=0/.

Escobar, A. (1992). Imagining a post-development era? Critical thought, development and social movements. *Social Text,* 20–56.

Fishwick, C. (2014, March 14). Tomnod—The online search party looking for Malaysian Airlines flight MH370. *The Guardian.* Retrieved from http://www.theguardian.com/world/2014/mar/14/tomnod-online-search-malaysian-airlines-flight-mh370/.

Füller, J., Schroll, R., & von Hippel, E. (2013). User generated brands and their contribution to the diffusion of user innovations. *Research Policy, 42*(6–7), 1197–1209. doi: http://dx.doi.org/10.1016/j.respol.2013.03.006.

Giles, J. (2005). Internet encyclopaedias go head to head. *Nature, 438*(7070), 900–901.

Gillmor, D. (2003). Moving toward participatory journalism. *Nieman Reports, 57*(3), 79–80.

Gillmor, D. (2004). *We the media: Grassroots journalism by the people, for the people.* Beijing and Sebastopol, CA: O'Reilly.

Ginsberg, J., Mohebbi, M. H., Patel, R. S., Brammer, L., Smolinski, M. S., & Brilliant, L. (2008). Detecting influenza epidemics using search engine query data. *Nature, 457*(7232), 1012–1014.

Hamilton, J. F., & Heflin, K. (2011). User production reconsidered: From convergence, to autonomia and cultural materialism. *New Media & Society, 13*(7), 1050–1066.

Hardt, M., & Negri, A. (2009). *Empire.* Cambridge, MA: Harvard University Press.

Harley Davidson. (2013). *Study: Women have a powerful option to find happiness in 2014.* Retrieved from http://www.harley-davidson.com/content/h-d/en_US/home/events/press-release/general/2013/news126.html/.

Hars, A., & Ou, S. (2001). *Working for free? Motivations of participating in open source projects.* Proceedings of the 34th Annual Hawaii International Conference on System Sciences. IEEE Computer Society Washington, DC, USA.

Humphreys, A. (2008). Understanding collaboration and collective production: New insights on consumer co-production. *Advances in Consumer Research, 35*, 63–66.

Humphreys, A., & Grayson, K. (2008). The intersecting roles of consumer and producer: A critical perspective on co-production, co-creation and prosumption. *Sociology Compass, 2*, 1–18.

Hutter, K., Hautz, J., Füller, J., Mueller, J., & Matzler, K. (2011). Communition: The tension between competition and collaboration in community-based design contests. *Creativity and Innovation Management, 20*(1), 3–21.

Jeffries, L. (2011). The revolution will be soooo cute: YouTube "hauls" and the voice of young female consumers. *Studies in Popular Culture*, 59–75.

Jenkins, H. (2006). *Convergence culture: Where old and new media collide.* New York: New York University Press.

Jenkins, H., Ford, S., & Green, J. (2013). *Spreadable media: Creating value and meaning in a networked culture.* New York: New York University Press.

Johnson, K. A. (2007). *The impact of hyperlinks and writer information on the perceived credibility of stories on a participatory journalism web site* (Ph.D. Diss.), Drexel University. Retrieved from http://libweb.cityu.edu.hk/cgi-bin/er/db/ddcdiss.pl?3286894/.

Jönsson, A. M., & Örnebring, H. (2011). User-generated content and the news: Empowerment of citizens or interactive illusion? *Journalism Practice, 5*(2), 127–144.

Kreiss, D., Finn, M., & Turner, F. (2011). The limits of peer production: Some reminders from Max Weber for the network society. *New Media & Society, 13*(2), 243–259.

Kuechenmeister, C. (2008). *Doritos puts up $1 million prize for consumer-created Doritos commercial that beats seasoned ad pros during Super Bowl XLIII* [Press release]. Retrieved from http://www.prweb.com/releases/Doritos/Contest/prweb1382474.htm/.

Kuznetsov, S. (2006). Motivations of contributors to Wikipedia. *SIGCAS Comput. Soc., 36*(2), 1. doi:10.1145/1215942.1215943.

Lessig, L. (2008). *Remix: Making art and culture thrive in the hybrid economy.* New York: Penguin. Also available under a Creative Commons license from Bloomsbury Academic at http://www.lessig.org/blog/2009/04/remix_now_ccfree.html/.

Martin, D. M., & Schouten, J. W. (2014). Consumption-driven market emergence. *Journal of Consumer Research, 40*(5), 855–870.

Mathwick, C., Wiertz, C., & De Ruyter, K. (2008). Social capital production in a virtual P3 community. *Journal of Consumer Research, 34*(6), 832–849.

McLuhan, M. (1968). *Understanding media: The extensions of man,* Cambridge, MA: MIT Press.

Monaghan, G., & Tunney, S. (2010). *Web journalism: A new form of citizenship?* Portland, OR: Sussex Academic Press.

Morozov, E. (2009). Iran: Downside to the "Twitter revolution." *Dissent, 56*(4), 10–14.

Muñiz, A. M., & Schau, H. J. (2011). How to inspire value-laden collaborative consumer-generated content. *Business Horizons, 54*(3), 209–217.

Murthy, D. (2011). Twitter: Microphone for the masses? *Media Culture and Society, 33*(5), 779.

Nov, O. (2007). What motivates Wikipedians? *Communications of the ACM, 50*(11), 60–64. doi:10.1145/1297797.1297798.

Oreg, S., & Nov, O. (2008). Exploring motivations for contributing to open source initiatives: The roles of contribution context and personal values. *Computers in Human Behavior, 24*(5), 2055–2073. doi:http://dx.doi.org/10.1016/j.chb.2007.09.007.

Pace, S. (2008). YouTube: An opportunity for consumer narrative analysis? *Qualitative Market Research: An International Journal, 11*(2), 213–226.

Porter, M. (2001). The value chain and competitive advantage. *Understanding Business Processes.* New York: Routledge (November 2000).

Porter, M. E. (1980). Industry structure and competitive strategy: Keys to profitability. *Financial Analysts Journal,* 30–41.

Prahalad, C. K., & Ramaswamy, V. (2004a). Co-creating unique value with customers. *Strategy & Leadership, 32*(3), 4–9.

Prahalad, C. K., & Ramaswamy, V. (2004b). Co-creation experiences: The next practice in value creation. *Journal of Interactive Marketing, 18*(3), 5–14.

Rey, P. (2012). Alienation, exploitation, and social media. *American Behavioral Scientist, 56*(4), 399–420.

Ritzer, G., & Jurgenson, N. (2010). Production, consumption, prosumption: The nature of capitalism in the age of the digital "prosumer." *Journal of Consumer Culture, 10*(1), 13–36.

Schau, H. J., Muniz, A.M. Jr., & Arnould, E. J. (2009). How brand community practices create value. *Journal of Marketing, 73*(5), 30–51.

Smith, A. (1887). *An inquiry into the nature and causes of the Wealth of Nations.* London: Nelson.

Smith, A. N., Fischer, E., & Yongjian, C. (2012). How does brand-related user-generated content differ across YouTube, Facebook, and Twitter? *Journal of Interactive Marketing, 26*(2), 102–113.

Surowiecki, J. (2005). *The wisdom of crowds.* New York: Random House.

Sutton, J., Spiro, E. S., Fitzhugh, S., Johnson, B., Gibson, B., & Butts, C. T. (2014). Terse message amplification in the Boston bombing response. *In Proceedings of the 11th International ISCRAM Conference* (pp. 612–621). Pennsylvania State University.

Thorson, K., Driscoll, K., Ekdale, B., Edgerly, S., Thompson, L. G., Schrock, A., ... Wells, C. (2013). YouTube, Twitter and the Occupy Movement: Connecting content and circulation practices. *Information, Communication & Society, 16*(3), 421–451.

Timberg, C. (2012, December 18). Instagram, Facebook stir online protests for privacy policy change. *The Washington Post.* Retrieved from http://www.washingtonpost.com/business/technology/instagram-facebook-stirs-online-protests-for-privacy-policy-change/2012/12/18/6c105d92-4948-11e2-b6f0-e851e741d196_story.html/.

Toffler, A. (1980). *The third wave.* New York: Morrow.

Tsuruaki, Y. (2005). Participatory journalism in Japan. *Economy, Culture & History Japan Spotlight, 24*(5), 17.

Van Dijck, J. (2009). Users like you? Theorizing agency in user-generated content. *Media, Culture, and Society, 31*(1), 41.

Van Dijck, J. (2013). *The culture of connectivity: A critical history of social media.* New York: Oxford University Press.

Van Dijck, J., & Nieborg, D. (2009). Wikinomics and its discontents: A critical analysis of Web 2.0 business manifestos. *New Media & Society, 11*(5), 855–874.

Varian, H. R., & Shapiro, C. (2003). *Linux adoption in the public sector: An economic analysis.* Manuscript. University of California, Berkeley.

Von Hippel, E. (2005). *Democratizing innovation.* Cambridge, MA: MIT press.

Wagner, V. (2008). *The Flying Penguin: Linux in-flight entertainment systems.* Retrieved from http://www.linuxinsider.com/story/65541.html/.

Weber, S. (2004). *The success of open source* (Vol. 897). Cambridge, UK: Cambridge University Press.

Weber, M. (1978). *Economy and society: An outline of interpretive sociology.* Berkeley: University of California Press.

Weber, M. S., & Monge, P. (2011). The flow of digital news in a network of sources, authorities, and hubs. *Journal of Communication, 61*(6), 1062–1081.

Woolley, A. W., Chabris, C. F., Pentland, A., Hashmi, N., & Malone, T. W. (2010). Evidence for a collective intelligence factor in the performance of human groups. *Science, 330*(6004), 686–688.

Zhang, J., Ackerman, M. S., & Adamic, L. (2007). *Expertise networks in online communities: structure and algorithms.* Paper presented at the Proceedings of the 16th International Conference on World Wide Web. Banff, AB, Canada—May 08–12, 2007.

Zwick, D., Bonsu, S. K., & Darmody, A. (2008). Putting consumers to work: Co-creationand new marketing govern-mentality. *Journal of Consumer Culture, 8*(2), 163–196.

CHAPTER 6

—

Uses and Benefits of Social Media

Annette signs on to Facebook one evening and receives something she has dreaded for a while: her mom's friend request. This has happened to all of her friends, but she never thought it would happen to her. She takes a deep breath. What is the worst that could happen? She gamely accepts the request and then sets about trying to figure out her privacy settings. About a month later, her best friend Marie posts pictures of a party. It was a great night, and Annette did not think much at the time about posing for pictures enthusiastically with a glass of wine in her hand. In fact, she had a great outfit on, and some of the pictures were pretty funny. Todd, her boyfriend who could not be there, might find these interesting, she thinks. The next morning she wakes up and signs on, only to discover a new comment: "Well, *that's* a nice face, Annette!" followed by twenty-five "likes" courtesy of her friends. This means trouble.

What do people get out of participating in social media? At an individual and interpersonal level, how do people use social media to help them achieve goals and express a sense of self? These fundamental questions will be addressed here. This chapter will use theories about the self from psychology and uses and gratifications of media from communication to understand the motivations for participation, including play, professionalization, and *communitas*. We will discuss self-presentation and relationship formation online and also use these concepts to understand social interaction and privacy in social media.

USES AND GRATIFICATIONS THEORY

Scholars have tended to view traditional media consumption such as that of books, magazines, newspapers, and movies using a perspective called uses and gratifications theory. **Uses and gratifications theory** argues that people consume media for some purpose and to receive some reward, or gratification (Blumler, 1979). Social media is no exception. For example, 96% of people use social networking sites to "keep in touch with old friends," and 91% of people use it to "keep in touch with current friends" (Bonds-Raacke & Raacke, 2010). This may seem obvious, but primary uses can have meaning in context withother, less common or salient uses. For example, only 34% of users reported using Facebook to learn about events, and merely 8% of users say they use it for dating (and most of these were men). Contrast this to the uses and gratifications that users seek from OkCupid (dating) or LinkedIn (professionalization), and uses and gratifications theory can have meaning in the social context of many different platforms and practices. The following sections will review just a few of the many uses and gratifications people get from various forms of social media, yet as we examine the role of self-perception and performance in online interactions, we will see just how deep uses and gratifications go.

Underlying most uses and gratifications is the idea of a **goal**. A goal is a desired end state, something people want to accomplish or something they want to avoid (Higgins, 1997). Goals can be conscious, such as when you sign in online to post pictures of a recent vacation, or they can be nonconscious (Bargh & Chartrand, 1999). For example, routines of checking Facebook or Instagram to see who has communicated with you might be the pursuit of a nonconscious goal to socialize or experience positive feelings of self-enhancement. At its most basic level, goal theory suggests that we seek positive rewards and shy away from negative punishments (Higgins, 1997). For example, when we post a picture and get positive feedback from others, this reinforces the behavior. If we were to receive negative feedback, it would likely weaken our behavior (although don't we all know people on whom negative feedback has no effect?).

SELF

Many of the goals we pursue online concern a desire to build, maintain, improve, or perform, a sense of self. The self is a complex philosophical construct, so complex that we could not possibly cover it all here. Philosophers in the Western tradition have taken many different perspectives on the self, from considering it a fixed "essence" of every person, to considering it always in flux, to considering it empty (Cushman, 1990; Taylor, 1989). In this context, however, what is important is that people tend to perceive a **self** that is a collection of relatively stable attributes and feelings about these attributes (James, 1890). This collection is continually being expressed and then modified through interaction and feedback from the social and physical world, a perspective called the **looking-glass self** (Cooley, 1902). Reactions that people have to us online can impact self-perceptions through this interactive and iterative process. For example, the positive comments that come from changing a profile picture can reinforce the behavior depicted, whereas online trolling can make us question or want to change aspects of ourselves. The way we see ourselves is—for better or worse—bound up with how others see us.

In fact, some modalities of online communication like Facetime and Skype can make the looking-glass self explicit in that we can see reflections of ourselves as we are talking (Miller & Sinanan, 2014). As Miller and Sinanan, two digital anthropologists, remark, these types of interactions mean that "for the very first time in human history, we routinely observe ourselves as we have appeared to others in the course of ordinary conversation" (Miller & Sinanan, 2014, p. 16).

The sociologist Erving Goffman has provided much of the foundation for how we think about the self, especially for theorizing about the way we interact with others. **Self-presentation** theory argues that we are always presenting our-selves for a perceived audience. In the opening story for this chapter, Annette performs for the camera at the party—and implicitly for Todd, the imagined audience—for whom she might emphasize her attractive qualities. For example, she may want to seem fun by holding up a drink or doing something silly. In the online dating world, 86% of users say that others have misrepresented their ap-pearance (Ellison, Heino, & Gibbs, 2006). By highlighting particular interests or activities on social media profiles, we may emphasize some (usually positive or culturally meaningful) aspects of the self and deemphasize other less desirable attributes, creating an **ideal self**. If, as Goffman suggests, the self is a perfor-mance, then there is a "front stage" where we do our formal impression manage-ment to others and a "backstage" where we are less self-conscious and may disclose our "real" selves. For example, celebrities will often use Twitter to pres-ent a backstage self, although to what degree this is in itself a performance can be debated (Marwick & boyd, 2011; Marwick, 2014).

Social Comparison Theory

We are continually engaged in presenting the self and receiving input from others. As we have discussed in the previous section, these interactions can change self-perception. We are affected not only by feedback on our own perfor-mances, but also by the performances of others. **Social comparison theory** says that we form evaluations of ourselves through comparison with others (Festinger, 1954). For instance, one study finds that passive Facebook use (looking at pic-tures versus posting them) prompts social comparison, which leads to reduced self-esteem after visiting the site (Zuo, 2014). Another study that tracked people over the course of the day found that feelings of anxiety and worry increased after visiting Facebook (Kross et al., 2013). When we compare ourselves to others, we

Photo 6.1 "Nobody Likes Me," Vancouver Canada.

may be more likely to notice attributes that we would not otherwise think about. For example, if you see several pictures of your friends having fun, you may think they are more social than you, forgetting that people strategically project themselves on social networking sites. Or if you see someone misspell a word in a status update, you might feel smarter, thinking "I would never do *that*!"

Performance Online

Western philosophical traditions have tended to consider the backstage self to be the real or "actual" self. However, others contend that all versions of self are ultimately a performance and that people essentially perform different roles depending on context. For instance, the term persona comes from the Latin persōna, which means a mask, character, or role, "that from which the voice comes" (Turkle, 1995/2011). This role-based, **dramaturgical theory of self** argues that we are always putting on a mask, performing different roles or selves on a "stage" with "props" for an intended audience. The opportunities for performing self on social media are vast and varied. One can produce a vlog of makeup reviews, debate policy issues on *The Huffington Post*, and create authoritative Wikipedia articles, relatively unchecked by the constraints of offline identity and contexts that might otherwise constrain performance. Yet performances can also be shaped by the norms of a particular platform or social world online. For example, we tend to perform a professional self on LinkedIn, but perhaps a friendly, casual self on Facebook and a flirtatious self on Tinder.

As we will see when we discuss age, race, gender and social class, these kinds of social categories are also performed in certain ways. For example, gender performances online can range from superfeminine performances in YouTube makeup tutorials (and video creators give notes on how to make such performances) to hypermasculine performances such as playing a massive multiplayer game like World of Warcraft, where one's avatar can be bigger and stronger relative to others than one might be in real life. We will return to the relationship of these performances to social identity in Chapter 8 on race and gender.

People not only present idealized self-representations online, but also may perform vulnerabilities that they do not express to others in the offline world (Turkle, 2011). This therapeutic self is not idealized; rather, its flaws are displayed and emphasized for an audience of sympathetic others. For example, one might post a status update to convey news about a sick friend or relative, a car accident, or a breakup, and the message may even be coded or vague so that it can only be understood by a particular audience (boyd, 2014). In this way, the therapeutic self can be different from the ideal self, but nonetheless a particular "slice" of our offline identities.

Both ideal and therapeutic selves represent a **virtual self**, the self that is presented in representations, particularly in representations online. Although early approaches to studying social media tended to represent the virtual self as being an escape from social and physical limitations such as gender, the rise of more mundane uses of social media have reminded us that there are many contexts in which our virtual selves remain tethered to our offline identities.

People create virtual selves all the time online, perhaps explicitly in role-playing games when one creates an avatar, but perhaps often implicitly as one creates pseudonyms for discussing politics or sports or simply by creating a more idealized self on a social networking site. Virtual selves can clearly range in their distance from one's self in "real life." Sometimes users embrace virtual selves with a sense of freedom or escape, whereas for others it can represent an unsettling departure from their physical selves. The July 5, 1993, issue of *The New Yorker* featured a cartoon by artist Peter Steiner that poked fun at Internet users' ability to manipulate their virtual selves by depicting a dog at a computer screen with the caption, "On the Internet, nobody knows you're a dog" (Steiner, 1993). Steiner's cartoon illustrates both the freedom and the perils of expressing the virtual self online. Of virtual selves, Turkle says, "When people adopt an online persona they cross a boundary into highly-charged territory. Some feel an uncomfortable sense of fragmentation, some a sense of relief. Some sense the possibilities for self-discovery, even self-transformation" (Turkle, 2011, p. 260). These digital selves represent the totality of self-representation online (Belk, 2010) and can persist even after death. Facebook, for example, even has procedures for shifting profiles to memorialize users after the termination of physical life.[1]

One often studied performance of self is the **selfie**, a shot one takes of oneself, usually close up and usually facing the camera (Nguyen, 2014; Murray 2015). As a genre, the selfie has garnered a lot of attention, becoming the international word of the year in 2013. Self-portraits, however, are not new. Artists from Van Gogh to Cindy Sherman and Vivian Maier have all used self-portraiture as a form of artistic expression (Photo 6.2). Yet, self-portraits turned selfies are often stigmatized as a narcissistic form of self-expression. Initially associated with teenage girls, selfies distributed online through platforms like Instagram, Twitter, and Snapchat can be used for personal branding (Marwick, 2013), play, and self-performance. In 2014, for example, Samsung paid for product placement on the Academy Awards, which resulted in the most retweeted selfie of all time (Photo 6.3).

Photo 6.2 Vivian Maier "Selfie."

Photo 6.3 Oscar Selfie.

Context Collapse

People may perform different selves for different audiences, but social media platforms can confront people with **context collapse**, situations in which two or more social worlds collide (Marwick & boyd, 2011). Because social media is available to virtually anyone, personal connections can sometimes mix in unexpected ways. Annette from our opening story experiences context collapse when her mother comments on her party pictures. The social world of her friends collides with the social world of her family. In the physical world, we often perform different aspects of ourselves in different contexts, but these are somewhat bounded by physical space. When we go to school, we are students, at home we are sons or daughters, at work, employees. However, in online space, these different contexts may converge because people from different parts of our lives mix in the same "virtual" space of a social networking site like Facebook. At a broader level, we see how technological tools like "circles" or friend groups are developed in an attempt to recreate the boundaries we have offline. However, in digital spaces, these boundaries always seem to be incomplete and porous, prompting concerns about etiquette and privacy.

Extended Self

Just as we can use technology to represent ourselves and to communicate those representations over great distances to many people, social media also provides astounding capabilities for extending ourselves, expanding them beyond physical and temporal limitations. For example, through the site Chatroulette or an app like Meerkat, we can see into the homes and lives of people across the world (http://www.chatroulette.com/). We call this idea the **extended self** (Belk, 1988). In the physical world, we extend our capabilities all the time, every time we drive a car, peer through binoculars, or pick up the telephone (Benjamin, 1968). For example, a Pew study reports that 74% of users use their cellphones to get directions or other information about their location. And we keep the objects close; 44% of people surveyed report sleeping in the bed with a cellphone (Pew Internet Project, 2014).

The phone extends our ability see traffic ahead, know the weather, and find the best restaurant in a strange neighborhood. As an extension of the brain, it likely contains contact information for everyone we know. It can embody memory by storing photos and videos of memorable events. Further, taking pictures can even change what we remember (Van Dijck, 2007). For example, one study conducted in an art museum found that people had more trouble remembering the art if they took pictures than if they had simply observed (Henkel, 2014). However, when participants were asked to take pictures by zooming in on particular aspects of the artwork, they were better able to remember both those details and others about the paintings.

There is much to be said for the way we use technology to extend our capabilities and the way that technology can become part of us over time. Philosophers like Donna Haraway argue that technology not only extends our physical capabilities, but also actually becomes embedded in who we are. Cyborg or **posthuman** theories see technology and human bodies as increasingly intertwined (Haraway, 1985; Hayles 2008). We may take many of these technological extensions for granted, but such shifts can challenge the boundary between human and machines in a way that challenges accepted cultural norms and complicates who we think we are.[2]

However, some have argued that the ubiquity of technologies can not only alter, but even diminish our existing capabilities. Because of the social pull of always-available technology, people are increasingly drawn toward multitasking (Carr, 2010). This can lead to **information overload**, which can be detrimental to **attention** (Klingberg, 2008)—the ability to focus on a given task—concentration (Ophir, Nass, & Wagner, 2009), and analytical thinking (Greenfield, 2009). Even talking to a friend using a hands-free device can divert attentional resources (Stayer et al. 2001; 2003; Patten et al 2004).

These neurological effects that come with continually communicating with friends on social media can have detrimental effects on our lives. For example, those who text and drive are twenty-three times as likely to crash as nondistracted drivers (Wilson & Stimpson, 2010). Researchers find that texting while

Photo 6.4 Smartphones as part of the extended self.

driving is as lethal as driving with a 0.10 blood alcohol level (Leung, Croft, Jackson, Howard, & Mckenzie, 2012). Less lethally, phone use can hinder other tasks in everyday life, such as learning in class or ordering coffee. For example, one popular restaurant in New York found that its Yelp! ratings took a nosedive. After studying changes in consumer behavior in the restaurant, they concluded that consumer cellphone use was actually the problem. Inattentive customers on their phones caused longer, more complicated interactions with wait-staff and gummed up the works for offering smooth service and quickly turning over tables.[3] Social media can help us do many new things, but it can also impact social relationships in unpredictable and unexpected ways. As a consequence, shifts in norms and cultural values are often required as new technologies are adopted and disrupt existing social practices and categories.

INTERPERSONAL RELATIONSHIPS

Self-Disclosure and Anonymity

So far we have discussed the different ways that people perform selves online. But what about how we perceive and interpret the self-presentation of others in social media? This section will discuss interpersonal interactions, how we both give and receive impressions in computer mediated contexts and form relationships in these mediated contexts.

Just as we are always performing self, we are also always interpreting the performances of others. One of the most basic insights coming from self-presentation theory is that there are a number of norms pertaining to interacting with others. **Self-disclosure**, for example, is the norm that one is expected to, at least gradually, disclose information about oneself to others (Chaikin & Derlega, 1974). Think of the situation of being at a social gathering among people you have never met. The expectation when greeting and talking to new people is that you answer some questions about yourself—why you are there, what you do, where you are from. Roughly the first fifteen minutes of any conversation among strangers consists of such information. This is also true in social media (Tidwell & Walther, 2002). We will examine how people get to know each other online, how they interact, and how they form trust through online interactions. Despite the similarities between online and offline greetings, there are many online contexts where the norms of self-disclosure vary from that of offline life. On the one hand, therapeutic contexts like mental health message boards or confessional blogs may be contexts in which people may disclose a lot of intimate information. On the other hand, there are information-sharing sites like Quora, where goals are to ask and answer questions that involve little self-disclosure. Curiously, self-disclosure, telling people about yourself, is not necessarily related to anonymity, or telling people who you are.

Anonymity is when someone's speech, writing, or actions do not contain personally identifiable information and thus cannot be linked to personal identity (Marx, 2004; Marx, 1999; Scott, 1998). Anonymity is different from

pseudonymity, in which a person's actions may be linked to a particular name, but not traced to an offline person. For example, some posters on reddit develop very rich identities in the community, but these identities remain untied to their offline lives (Bergstrom, 2011). Self-disclosure is also distinct from anonymity. For example, you might write a blog detailing you dating life, which contains a lot of self-disclosure in that you might talk about intimate details of dates. However, the blog could still be written anonymously—without information that would make it personally identifiable to you. In fact, scholars find that the more discursive anonymity a blog has, the more likely it is to contain self-disclosure (Qian & Scott, 2007).[4]

Anonymity online can lead to antisocial behavior. On 4chan, for example, where posts are anonymous by default, graphic, offensive, and obscene content abounds (Phillips, 2012). In contrast, on sites like Facebook where content is usually tied to one's offline identity, content can be bland and relatively conventional (Backstrom, 2011; Wilson, Gosling, & Graham, 2012). Philip Zimbardo (1969) was one of the first to study the effects of anonymity on human behavior by asking participants to perform hostile acts on others either when they were disguised or when they were identifiable and wearing their own clothes. He found that those who were anonymous behaved more aggressively than those in plain clothes.[5] Corroborating this classic finding, research on social media has found that those who are anonymous online are less willing to cooperate with each other (Cress & Kimmerle, 2008).

One reason that anonymity online causes aggression may be because of a certain kind of disinhibition. As we have all seen, people can get nasty when they are completely anonymous. Sites like YouTube, 4chan, and reddit, where posting can be done anonymously or pseudonymously, are notorious for the prevalence of flaming. **Flaming** is the use of hostile language online, including swearing, insults, and otherwise offensive language (Lapidot-Lefler & Barak, 2012, p. 434; Moor, Heuvelman, & Verleur, 2010; Steele, 1983). Flaming is more common in purely text-based versus visual communication (Castellá, Abad, Alonso, & Silla, 2000; Kiesler, Zubrow, Moses, & Geller, 1985) and occurs more often than in face-to-face communication (Kiesler et al., 1985; Siegel, Dubrovsky, Kiesler, & McGuire, 1986; Sproull & Kiesler, 1986). Although we usually consider flaming antisocial or counternormative behavior, some scholars have pointed out that in some online contexts like 4chan, flaming might actually be normative (Lea, O'Shea, Fung, & Spears, 1992). Many attribute flaming to anonymity, but the lack of personally identifiable information is merely one contributing attribute in a mix that includes deindividuation, textual mediation, lack of other social cues, and face-to-face accountability. For example, one study of YouTube found that flaming behavior was associated with a reduced awareness of people's feelings (Moor et al., 2010).

Disinhibition describes unrestrained or impulsive behavior without regard for social norms or consequences. The **online disinhibition effect** (Lapidot-Lefler & Barak, 2012; Suler, 2004) is the tendency to experience disinhibition because of the effects of computer-mediated communication. Anonymity online is one factor widely assumed to be associated with disinhibition (Lapidot-Lefler & Barak, 2012). For example, after a Korean law was passed requiring personal identification on Internet comments for major sites, a decrease in messages containing slanderous content and swear words quickly followed (Cho, Kim, & Acquisti, 2012). However, there can be multiple factors leading to disinhibition in addition to anonymity, including invisibility, asynchronicity, lack of eye contact, and textuality (Lapidot-Lefler & Barak, 2012; Suler, 2004). One study, for example, had people debate an issue under three conditions: purely textual communication, visual communication that included a webcam, or visual communication that include two webcams and instructions to make eye contact. Those who made eye contact were less likely to behave aggressively online than those with simply a webcam or textual communication (Lapidot-Lefler & Barak, 2012).

Yet anonymity online is not always a bad thing. The lack of personally identifying information can lead to pleasurable disinhibition associated with play and experimentation (Turkle, 2011). It can enhance self-disclosure and can thus allow people to talk about stigmatizing issues, to feel less marginal and receive emotional, and to receive therapeutic support. It can allow whistleblowers to reveal important information without the fear of reprisals. The deindividuating effects of anonymity online could make people feel more a part of the community (Postmes, Spears, & Lea, 1998). In sum, although anonymity can create aggression online, the norms and institutions of these online contexts as well as individual personality variables ultimately lead to either reinforcement or curtailment of aggression.

Trust

Imagine you receive a friend request from someone whose name you do not immediately recognize. How do you decide to accept or decline? If you are like me, you look to see how many shared connections you have and who these shared connections are. Publically displayed social connections present a warrant for trustworthiness; they help to assure people that one's actions and claims are truthful (Donath & boyd, 2004). **Signaling theory** argues that we are always "giving" and "giving off" social signals. Either we purposefully perform these cues or, often, we "give off" signals unintentionally.

There has been much debate about exactly *how* we get to know one another online. Initially, scholars argued that the lack of media richness, which we discussed in Chapter 3, would impact self-disclosure and thus hinder social interactions. One perspective, called the **social information processing (SIP) model**, says that we find a way to translate socially meaningful information into text-based formats (Walther, 1992). The social information processing model predicts that we still go through the same disclosure processes online, by interpreting cues from others and trying to reduce uncertainty about exactly who the person is and what they want (Tidwell & Walther, 2002). Interestingly, several studies have found that people disclose more personal information more quickly online and suggest that this is to compensate for the lack of richness. Another contributing factor may be the isolated one-to-one context where no one is "eavesdropping." Yet another explanation may be that we are slightly disinhibited by the lack of physical co-presence, being relieved of some of the demands of self-presentation like facial expression and eye contact.

Another perspective on interaction, called the **social identity deindividuation (SIDE) model**, suggests that we use social categories rather than interpersonal cues when we communicate online (Spears, Postmes, Lea, & Watt, 2001). Thus, in the absence of social cues, the social identity deindividuation model would predict that we consult **archetypes**, common categories of people formed by past experience, to extrapolate from limited information (Jung, 1981). For example, if someone disagrees with you in the comments section and seemingly supports gun control, you might imagine them as a stereotypical Rambo type from Texas, whereas they may actually be a peaceful hunter from Minnesota. Ultimately, in online communication we are likely using both interpersonal cues and archetypes—trying to puzzle out what someone is all about using the cues they give us and reconciling those with our prior social knowledge and experience (Walther, 1997).

There are many contexts like comments sections, message boards, and text messages where interaction remains text based. However, because there are now more modes of communication available such as video and sound, scholars have shifted to considering how people negotiate intimacy, build trust, and exchange information through "multiplex" ties that draw from a variety of media forms (Haythornthwaite, 2001; Haythornthwaite & Wellman, 1998).

One corollary of the fact that self-disclosure happens more quickly online is that we can develop intimacy faster when communicating through social media rather than offline. This hyperpersonal model of communication online says that in the absence of other cues, people will exaggerate features of their communication partners (Walther, 1996, 2006). In romantic relationships, intense feelings of intimacy can develop quickly, and this sometimes leads to gaps between online and offline perception and interaction—and some awkward situations when these merge (Turkle, 2011). In online interactions, people will engage in what psychologists would label projection; they impart their virtual partners with idealized qualities and infer rich intimacy in the absence of physical cues. Psychologist Sherry Turkle (2011) observes, "This situation leads to exaggerated likes and dislikes, to idealization and demonization. So it is natural for people to feel let down or confused when they meet their virtual lovers in person" (p. 207).

Are online relationships real? Sure, there is a difference between friends and Facebook "friends" (Donath & boyd, 2004), but are friendships formed online necessarily more superficial? Social media can expand our capabilities to form weak ties (a topic to which we will return in Chapter 9), but are these connections actually meaningful? When people attempt to answer this question, they are faced with different variables and dimensions of social contact. For instance, interaction can be frequent or scarce, but it can also be emotionally rich or shallow. We will return to some of these issues in Chapter 9 when we discuss social networks, tie strength, and forms of social capital.

Boundaries of Self and Privacy

We often experience a tradeoff between the benefits of social media and privacy. To enjoy some of the benefits, like connecting with old childhood friends, we must give up some privacy, such as making a profile "discoverable" to almost anyone. We may want to have a social presence and disclose aspects of ourselves to form bonds with others, but we also want to carefully select who those others are. How do people negotiate this fundamental tension? Because Western philosophy considers there to be a core, authentic self, people police the boundaries of the self. **Privacy** is "an *interpersonal boundary process* by which a person or group regulates interaction with others. By altering the degree of openness of the self to others, a hypothetical personal boundary is more or less receptive to social interaction with others. Privacy is, therefore, a dynamic process involving selective control over a self-boundary, either by an individual or by a group" (Altman, 1975, p. 6). In other words, people regulate the self-disclosure processes discussed in the previous section in their interactions with others. There are times and contexts in which they wish to disclose information about themselves and other times and contexts in which they want to regulate the boundaries of self-disclosure (Derlega & Chaikin, 1977; Nissenbaum, 2009). Yet in a networked public, we may not always have control over the information we share (Marwick & boyd, 2014). For this reason, people may negotiate these boundaries by encoding information through technology or strategically using the affordances of technology. As Marwick and boyd (2014) note, "if we understand privacy to be about the management of boundaries, networked privacy is the ongoing negotiation of context in a networked ecosystem in which contexts blur and collapse" (p. 1063). For this reason, some argue that privacy is now better regulated by maintaining **contextual integrity**, acknowledging and ensuring "adequate protection for privacy to norms of specific contexts, demanding that information gathering and dissemination be appropriate to that context and obey the governing norms of distribution within it" (Nissenbaum, 2004, p. 101). Thus, there is no simple answer to privacy protection. Rather, it depends on the context in which personal information is shared.

People's attitudes about privacy are generally mixed. A Pew study reveals that 50% of people surveyed are concerned about privacy online, but concern has increased from 33% in 2009.[6] Yet 86% of people have taken steps to remove traces of their online behavior such as deleting cookies, Internet histories, or previous posts. Scholars studying teens show that although they put a lot of themselves online (Madden et al., 2013; Marwick & boyd, 2014), they are nonetheless concerned about who is viewing and can view this information (Ito et al., 2008). Yet they are also confident in their abilities to understand and control privacy settings (Madden et al., 2013). In the face of shifting boundaries, informalization of roles, and changing social norms, teens police such boundaries of

The strategies people use to be less visible online
% of adult internet users who say they have done these thing online

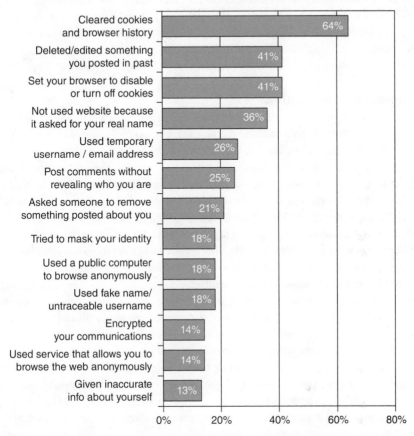

Figure 6.1 Pew Survey Results, "Anonymity, Privacy, and Security Online."

self-disclosure, for example, by considering someone "sketchy" if they transgress a socially or personally relevant boundary. Many feelings about privacy naturally relate to the receiver of the information and the use of that information. We will further examine the political dimensions of privacy and surveillance in Chapter 13 on political life.

Communitas

Self performance, comparison, and transformation are a critical set of goals people seek on and through social media. But many forms of social media help people pursue goals related to social needs; it *is* called social media, after all. **Communitas** is the feeling of being in a social group, part of a collective of like-minded individuals. Studies of social media use have found that socialization is one of the primary reasons people participate—they may want to talk about television shows online (Baym, 1995), participate in peer-to-peer software development (Mathwick, Wiertz, & De Ruyter, 2008), or figure out who will be the next winner of *Survivor* (Jenkins, Ford, & Green, 2013). Users cite the feeling of being part of the group as a key benefit and the primary reason they return to the group (Mathwick et al., 2008). However, the ways that people pursue sociality online can be diverse, reflecting the influence of cultures on connection. Chapter 10 on virtual communities will explore the many forms of building *communitas* online.

Information and Cultivation

Some uses and gratifications can be driven by the desire to learn new things, develop new talents, or gain cultural knowledge. For example, sites like Epicurious offer not only recipes online, but also social feedback on these recipes. Whether it is fixing a garbage disposal, learning to knit, or playing the guitar, people can learn a remarkable number of skills from others through social media in the form of YouTube videos, do-it-yourself blogs, or interest-based message boards.

When it comes to information seeking, people may seek out particular sources like a blog or news website and often attend to information that is congruent with what they already know. This is called **confirmation bias** (Nickerson, 1989), and scholars show that these kinds of behaviors are motivated by a desire to reduce **cognitive dissonance**. Cognitive dissonance theory (Festinger, 1962) says that people experience a sense of psychological discomfort when they encounter disconfirming information to their own beliefs or are blocked from pursuing a goal. From this sense of discomfort, they seek to reduce the dissonance as much as possible. For instance, people seek news groups of people with similar political points of view online rather than oppositional viewpoints, although some will look at oppositional sites just to see how "crazy" the other side is (Garrett, 2009). Cognitive dissonance can also drive behaviors like posting reviews online. We may seek to justify perceived wrongs or find others who like (or hate) the same things we do by posting or reading reviews on Yelp! or Amazon. We will return to the implications of these effects for word of mouth communication in Chapter 11 and political discourse in Chapter 13.

Therapeutic Uses

Social media such as discussion boards can also serve a therapeutic purpose, connecting those who suffer from physical or mental illness with others who share the same issues and who can provide both emotional support and information. For example, Figure 6.2 shows a real conversation on Yik Yak where students offer emotional and informational support to one another over financial aid.

Further, social media such as chat have been shown to help people overcome issues like extreme shyness (Stritzke, Nguyen, & Durkin, 2004) and loneliness (Ahn & Shin, 2013). However, the therapeutic function of social media can go in different ways for different people, sometimes improving their lives and sometimes negatively reinforcing existing issues. For example, Turkle (1995/2011) describes how some players of multiplayer games take out aggression on others that

Figure 6.2 Therapeutic Uses of Social Media.

they could not express in real life, what she describes as "acting out" versus "working through" issues that occur in the offline world (p. 200). And this type of aggression is tempting not only to produce but also to consume. One study conducted by researchers in China found that anger traveled more quickly over Sina Weibo, a Twitter-like platform than messages expressing other emotions like joy (Fan, Zhao, Chen, & Xu, 2013).

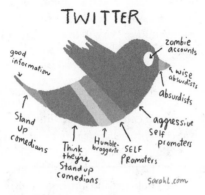

Cartoon 6.1: Credit: Courtesy Sarah Lazarovic.

Gossip, Bullying, and Drama

Social media can have these positive communal functions, but like many social phenomena, there's a dark side as well. Just as it can be a tool for social inclusion, it can also be a tool for social exclusion. For teens, platforms like Facebook and Twitter, but also apps like Yik Yak can provide a forum for "drama," the "performative set of actions distinct from bullying, gossip, and relational aggression, incorporating elements of them but also operating quite distinctly" (See also Ito et al., 2008; Marwick, 2011). Existing as a term that teens use about their own behavior, drama is distinct from bullying, gossip, or outright aggression, and the term is used to blur the lines between serious and trivial social behavior such as "bullying" as adults would define it. Drama, it is understood, can go back and forth, and there is not always a victim (either that, or everyone is a victim).

More severely, **cyberbullying** is the practice of socially or physically intimidating someone online, and this kind of activity can include spreading rumors, circulating illicitly taken pictures, taunting, or name-calling (Raskauskas & Stoltz, 2007). According to one survey, about 23% of children in primary or secondary school have experienced cyberbullying (DeHue, Bolman, & Völlink, 2008; Hinduja & Patchin, 2010), but this is still considerably less than the 37% of young adults who say they have been bullied offline (Whitney & Smith, 1993). Boys report participating in cyberbullying more than girls, whereas girls report being bullied online more often than boys (DeHue et al., 2008). Physical bullying peaks around eighth grade, but verbal and social bullying, and therefore cyberbullying, can exist well into high school (Williams & Guerra, 2007). Several high-profile examples of cyberbullying have led children and teens to commit suicide and resulted in legal prosecutions (Hinduja & Patchin, 2010).

Online vigilantes will also use social media tools to investigate and harass people who are themselves suspected of harassment or assault. For example, one online antibullying group, OpAntiBully, formed to expose the identities of cyberbullies or suspected sexual assailants who the group feels have not been brought to justice (Bazelon, 2014). Members of the group engage in "doxxing," or scouring the Internet for personal data in order to publicly link identity information to the perpetrator's transgression and shame them online (Bazelon, 2014).[7] Further, there is a range of antisocial behavior or trolling online that tends to wreak havoc in online communities. We will discuss trolling and other antisocial behavior further in Chapter 10.

Play

Self-development and interpersonal goals are two important motivations for participating in social media, but it can also just be fun. That is, sometimes there is no obvious goal—motivation is *intrinsic*, meaning that people enjoy social media for its own sake, not to accomplish something else. When one takes to Candy-Crush for hours, for example, it is likely not to build hand–eye coordination. First studied extensively by the psychologist and anthropologists, **play** is human activity that has no end goal, is pleasurable, and often spontaneous (Piaget, 2013).

For instance, play—rather than socialization or self-enhancement—is the primary reason that people play online games like EverQuest (Yee, 2006). These worlds can be complete, and this sense of play leads to several distinct psychological states, primarily because of a sense of **flow**, total absorption in a task that creates the feeling of escape and losing track of time. Flow theory describes the process by which people become so immersed in a task that they lose a sense of self and time (Csikszentmihalyi, 1975; Csikszentmihalyi & Csikszentmihalyi, 1992). Some argue that the experience of flow can lead to addiction (Song, Larose, Eastin, & Lin, 2004; Wan & Chiou, 2006), but others experience it for relaxation and to relieve stress.

Addiction

For the most part, scholars find that social media is yet another way people spend their leisure time—replacing time we might spend watching television, listening to the radio, or reading a book. However, for some, the feelings of transformation, escape, or flow can cause dependencies that impact offline lives (Turkle, 1995/2011). These feelings are triggered by the brain as it releases dopamine, the hormone responsible for giving us a "high" in response to stimuli (Kolker, 2014).

Although there is a lack of consensus about exactly how and when social media use constitutes addiction, many classify online addiction as "a dysfunctional preoccupation with some type of computer-mediated activity" (Suler, 2004, p. 354). "Within this broad category," argues Suler (2004), "there may be many distinct subtypes, each involving somewhat different underlying psychological processes. Some cyberspace addictions involve gaming and competition, some fulfill more social needs, some may be an extension of work compulsions" (p. 354). Researchers have found that checking our phones or social media profiles triggers a pleasurable response and gives us a rush similar to the feeling one experiences when under the influence of drugs, eating junk food, or playing video games (Photo 6.5). This kind of habit formation can

Photo 6.5 "Social Cigarettes."

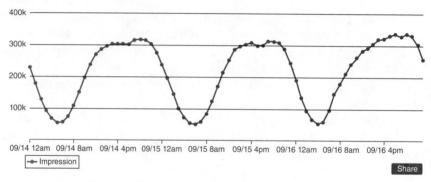

Figure 6.3: Daily Phone Use According to Locket.

occur when a positive stimulus is paired with a behavior (Skinner, 2014). For example, hearing the chime on your phone can produce the positive feelings of hearing from your friend or seeing a new "like" to something you have posted. According to data from an app called Locket, people check their phone an average of 110 times per day,[8,9] which amounts to checking, on average, once every six or seven minutes over a twelve-hour period (Figure 6.3). In effect, it is possible to be "addicted" to, or at least somewhat dependent on, social media (Kolker, 2014), although the line between normal and pathological behavior may not be clear and may also be the normative or political ground on which people marginalize others (Foucault, 1988).

To control such impulses, **self-regulation**—the process through which one controls short-term impulses—can play a role (Baumeister, Heatherton, & Tice, 1994). For example, to combat the urge to pick up the phone, people will play the game Phone Stack, where friends over dinner must put their phones in the middle of the table, and the first one to touch their phone loses the game (Photo 6.6). Phones have also been restricted at celebrity gatherings and parties, where the hosts want to control self-presentation[10] and privacy (Tell, 2013).

Photo 6.6 Phone Stack.

SUMMARY AND CONCLUSION

This chapter has covered the many wide and varied uses social media has for people as they go about their lives. Undoubtedly, social media will be put to more varied and surprising uses than this text could possibly cover. However, it is likely if not inevitable that issues of self-presentation, social relationship formation, and play will persist as people use social media to form images of themselves, communicate with others, and have fun. If we understand some of those basic issues, with any luck, we can understand more about how social media fits into the (selfie? Snapchat?) picture.

TOPICS

- Uses and gratifications of social media use (play, information, *communitas*, professionalization)
- Social comparison theory
- Self-presentation online
- Uses and gratifications theory
- Anonymity, pseudonymity
- Self-disclosure

DISCUSSION QUESTIONS

1. Scholar Sherry Turkle describes people being confused and disappointed when meeting their virtual partners offline. Has dating online changed in the past twenty years? Do you think people are still likely to experience disillusion when meeting their online paramours in real life? Why or why not?
2. Are relationships experience in social media contexts "real" and in what sense? What makes a relationship authentic? What criteria would suggest are important in answering this question?

EXERCISE

Pick a social networking platform and pull up three profiles. Analyze the performance of self as represented by these profiles. Are there forms of social feedback that shape the presentation of self? What aspects of the actual, ideal, and therapeutic selves are on display and what are the signifiers of each?

NOTES

1. http://www.huffingtonpost.com/2012/12/07/death-facebook-dead-profiles_n_2245397.html/.
2. It should also be noted that the idea of the cyborg also challenges essentialist concepts of gender. See Haraway (1985) and Hayles (2008).

3. http://www.nydailynews.com/life-style/eats/smartphones-blame-slow-service-restaurants-article-1.1879081/.

4. However, this was not the case with visual anonymity, or pictures that are personally identifiable.

5. Stanley Milgram found similar results, although his experiments were focused on the effects of authority and power.

6. http://www.pewinternet.org/2013/09/05/anonymity-privacy-and-security-online/.

7. http://www.nytimes.com/2015/02/15/magazine/how-one-stupid-tweet-ruined-justine-saccos-life.html?_r=0/.

8. http://www.buzzfeed.com/charliewarzel/heres-the-cold-hard-proof-that-we-cant-stop-checking-our-pho#3ymoa1x/.

9. http://abcnews.go.com/blogs/technology/2013/05/cellphone-users-check-phones-150xday-and-other-internet-fun-facts/.

10. http://www.nytimes.com/2013/09/22/fashion/step-away-from-the-phone.html?pagewanted=all&_r=0/.

FURTHER READINGS

Miller, D., & Sinanan, J. (2014). *Webcam.* New York: Wiley.

Richtel, M. (2014). *A deadly wandering: A tale of tragedy and redemption in the age of attention.* New York: HarperCollins.

Turkle, S. (2011). *Life on the screen.* New York: Simon & Schuster.

REFERENCES

Ahn, D., & Shin, D.-H. (2013). Is the social use of media for seeking connectedness or for avoiding social isolation? Mechanisms underlying media use and subjective well-being. *Computers in Human Behavior, 29*(6), 2453–2462.

Altman, I. (1975). The environment and social behavior: Privacy, personal space, territory, and crowding. Monterey, CA: Brooks/Cole.

Backstrom, L. (2011). *Anatomy of Facebook.* Retrieved from https://www.facebook.com/notes/facebook-data-team/anatomy-of-facebook/10150388519243859/.

Bargh, J. A., & Chartrand, T. L. (1999). The unbearable automaticity of being. *American Psychologist, 54*(7), 462.

Baumeister, R. F., Heatherton, T. F., & Tice, D. M. (1994). *Losing control: How and why people fail at self-regulation.* San Diego, CA: Academic Press.

Baym, N. K. (1995). The performance of humor in computer-mediated communication. *Journal of Computer-Mediated Communication, 1*(2).

Bazelon, E. (2014, January 15). The online avengers: Are antibullying activists the saviors of the Internet—Or just a different kind of curse? *The New York Times.* Retrieved from http://www.nytimes.com/2014/01/19/magazine/the-online-avengers.html?module=Search&mabReward=relbias%3Ar%2C%7B%222%22%3A%22RI%3A18%22%7D/.

Belk, R. (2010). Sharing. *Journal of Consumer Research, 36*(5), 715–734.

Belk, R. W. (1988). Property, persons, and extended sense of self. *Proceedings of the Division of Consumer Psychology, American Psychological Association 1987Annual Convention,* 28–33.

Benjamin, W. (1968). *Illuminations* (Vol. 241). New York: Random House.

Bergstrom, K. (2011). "Don't feed the troll": Shutting down debate about community expectations on Reddit. com. *First Monday, 16*(8).

Blumler, J. G. (1979). The role of theory in uses and gratifications studies. *Communication Research, 6*(1), 9–36.

Bonds-Raacke, J., & Raacke, J. (2010). MySpace and Facebook: Identifying dimensions of uses and gratifications for friend networking sites. *Individual Differences Research, 8*(1), 27–33.

Carr, N. (2010. June 4). Does the Internet make you dumber? *The Wall Street Journal.*

Castellá, V. O., Abad, A. Z., Alonso, F. P., & Silla, J. P. (2000). The influence of familiarity among group members, group atmosphere and assertiveness on uninhibited behavior through three different communication media. *Computers in Human Behavior, 16*(2), 141–159.

Chaikin, A. L., & Derlega, V. J. (1974). Variables affecting the appropriateness of self-disclosure. *Journal of Consulting and Clinical Psychology, 42*(4), 588.

Cho, D., Kim, S., & Acquisti, A. (2012). Empirical analysis of online anonymity and user behaviors: The impact of real name policy. Paper presented at *(HICSS), 2012 45th Hawaii International Conference on System Science* (pp. 3041–3050). IEEE. 2012 47th Hawaii International Conference on System Sciences (2012), Maui, Hawaii USA, Jan. 4, 2012 to Jan. 7, 2012.

Cooley, C. H. (1902). The looking glass self. *O'Brien,* 126–128.

Cress, U., & Kimmerle, J. (2008). Endowment heterogeneity and identifiability in the information-exchange dilemma. *Computers in Human Behavior, 24*(3), 862–874.

Csikszentmihalyi, M. (1975). *Beyond boredom and anxiety.* San Francisco: Jossey–Bass.

Csikszentmihalyi, M., & Csikszentmihalyi, I. S. (1992). *Optimal experience: Psychological studies of flow in consciousness.* Cambridge, UK: Cambridge University Press.

Cushman, P. (1990). Why the self is empty: Toward a historically situated psychology. *American Psychologist, 45*(5), 599.

DeHue, F., Bolman, C., & Völlink, T. (2008). Cyberbullying: Youngsters' experiences and parental perception. *CyberPsychology & Behavior, 11*(2), 217–223.

Derlega, V. J., & Chaikin, A. L. (1977). Privacy and self-disclosure in social relationships. *Journal of Social Issues, 33*(3), 102–115.

Donath, J., & boyd, d. (2004). Public displays of connection. *BT Technology Journal, 22*(4), 71–82.

Ellison, N., Heino, R., & Gibbs, J. (2006). Managing impressions online: Self-presentation processes in the online dating environment. *Journal of Computer-Mediated Communication, 11*(2), 415–441.

Fan, R., Zhao, J., Chen, Y., & Xu, K. (2013). Anger is more influential than joy: Sentiment correlation in Weibo. *arXiv Preprint arXiv*:1309.2402.

Festinger, L. (1954). A theory of social comparison processes. *Human Relations, 7*(2), 117–140.

Festinger, L. (1962). *A theory of cognitive dissonance* (Vol. 2). Stanford, CA: Stanford University Press.

Foucault, M. (1988). *Madness and civilization: A history of insanity in the age of reason*. New York: Vintage.

Garrett, R. K. (2009). Echo chambers online?: Politically motivated selective exposure among Internet news users. *Journal of Computer-Mediated Communication, 14*(2), 265–285.

Greenfield, P. M. (2009). Technology and informal education: What is taught, what is learned. *Science, 323*(5910), 69–71.

Haraway, D. J. (1985). *A manifesto for cyborgs: Science, technology, and socialist feminism in the 1980s*. San Francisco: Center for Social Research and Education.

Hayles, N. K. (2008). *How we became posthuman: Virtual bodies in cybernetics, literature, and informatics*. Chicago: University of Chicago Press.

Haythornthwaite, C. (2001). Exploring multiplexity: Social network structures in a computer-supported distance learning class. *The Information Society, 17*(3), 211–226.

Haythornthwaite, C., & Wellman, B. (1998). Work, friendship, and media use for information exchange in a networked organization. *Journal of the American Society for Information Science, 49*(12), 1101–1114.

Henkel, L. A. (2014). Point-and-shoot memories: The influence of taking photos on memory for a museum tour. *Psychological Science, 25*(2), 396–402. doi:10.1177/0956797613504438.

Higgins, E. T. (1997). Beyond pleasure and pain. *American Psychologist, 52*(12), 1280.

Hinduja, S., & Patchin, J. W. (2010). Bullying, cyberbullying, and suicide. *Archives of Suicide Research, 14*(3), 206–221.

Ito, M., Horst, H., Bittanti, M., boyd, d., Herr-Stephenson, B., Lange, P. G., . . . Robinson, L. (2008). *Living and learning with new media: Summary of findings from the digital youth project*. Chicago: John D. and Catherine T. MacArthur Foundation.

James, W. (1890). The consciousness of self. *The Principles of Psychology, 8*.

Jenkins, H., Ford, S., & Green, J. (2013). *Spreadable media: Creating value and meaning in a networked culture*. New York: New York University Press.

Jung, C. G. (1981). *The archetypes and the collective unconscious*. Princeton, NJ: Princeton University Press.

Kiesler, S., Zubrow, D., Moses, A. M., & Geller, V. (1985). Affect in computer-mediated communication: An experiment in synchronous terminal-to-terminal discussion. *Human–Computer Interaction, 1*(1), 77–104.

Klingberg, T. (2008). *The overflowing brain: Information overload and the limits of working memory.* Oxford: Oxford University Press.

Kolker, R. (2014, September 25). Attention must be paid: "A deadly wandering" by Matt Richtel. *The New York Times.* Retrieved from http://www.nytimes.com/2014/09/28/books/review/a-deadly-wandering-by-matt-richtel.html/.

Kross, E., Verduyn, P., Demiralp, E., Park, J., Lee, D. S., Lin, N., . . . Ybarra, O. (2013). Facebook use predicts declines in subjective well-being in young adults. *PloS One, 8*(8), e69841.

Lapidot-Lefler, N., & Barak, A. (2012). Effects of anonymity, invisibility, and lack of eye-contact on toxic online disinhibition. *Computers in Human Behavior, 28*(2), 434–443.

Lea, M., O'Shea, T., Fung, P., & Spears, R. (1992). *"Flaming" in computer-mediated communication: Observations, explanations, implications.* London: Harvester Wheatsheaf.

Leung, S., Croft, R. J., Jackson, M. L., Howard, M. E., & Mckenzie, R. J. (2012). A comparison of the effect of mobile phone use and alcohol consumption on driving simulation performance. *Traffic Injury Prevention, 13*(6), 566–574.

Madden, M., Lenhart, A., Cortesi, S., Gasser, U., Duggan, M., Smith, A., & Beaton, M. (2013). *Teens, social media, and privacy.* Washington, D.C.: Pew Research Center.

Marwick, A. E. (2011, September). The drama! Teen conflict, gossip, and bullying in networked publics. In *Teen Conflict, Gossip, and Bullying in Networked Publics (September 12, 2011).* A Decade in Internet Time: Symposium on the Dynamics of the Internet and Society: Oxford, UK.

Marwick, A. E. (2013). *Status update: Celebrity, publicity, and branding in the social media age.* New Haven, CT: Yale University Press.

Marwick, A. E., & boyd, d. (2011). I tweet honestly, I tweet passionately: Twitter users, context collapse, and the imagined audience. *New Media & Society, 13*(1), 114–133.

Marwick, A. E., & boyd, d. (2014). Networked privacy: How teenagers negotiate context in social media. *New Media & Society,* 1461444814543995.

Marx, G. (2004). Internet anonymity as a reflection of broader issues involving technology and society. *Asia-Pacific Review, 11*(1), 142–166.

Marx, G. T. (1999). What's in a name? Some reflections on the sociology of anonymity. *The Information Society, 15*(2), 99–112.

Mathwick, C., Wiertz, C., & De Ruyter, K. (2008). Social capital production in a virtual P3 community. *Journal of Consumer Research, 34*(6), 832–849.

Miller, D., & Sinanan, J. (2014). *Webcam.* New York: Wiley.

Moor, P. J., Heuvelman, A., & Verleur, R. (2010). Flaming on YouTube. *Computers in Human Behavior, 26*(6), 1536–1546.

Murray, D.C. "Notes to self: the visual culture of selfies in the age of social media," *Consumption Markets & Culture*, Vol. 18, No. 6, 1–27.

Nickerson, R. S. (1998). Confirmation bias: A ubiquitous phenomenon in many guises. *Review of general psychology*, 2(2), 175.

Nguyen, A. J. (2014). *Exploring the selfie phenomenon: The idea of self-preservation and its implications among young women* (Doctoral dissertation). Smith College School for Social Work: Northampton, MA.

Nissenbaum, H. (2004). Privacy as contextual integrity. *Washington Law Review*, 79(1).

Nissenbaum, H. (2009). *Privacy in context: Technology, policy, and the integrity of social life*. Stanford, CA: Stanford University Press.

Ophir, E., Nass, C., & Wagner, A. D. (2009). Cognitive control in media multi-taskers. *Proceedings of the National Academy of Sciences, 106*(37), 15583–15587.

Patten, C. J., Kircher, A., Östlund, J., & Nilsson, L. (2004). Using mobile telephones: cognitive workload and attention resource allocation. *Accident analysis & prevention*, 36(3), 341–350.

Pew Internet Project. (2014). *Mobile technology fact sheet*. Retrieved from http://www.pewinternet.org/fact-sheets/mobile-technology-fact-sheet/.

Phillips, W. (2012). *This is why we can't have nice things: The origins, evolution and cultural embeddedness of online trolling*. Doctoral Dissertation. University of Oregon.

Piaget, J. (2013). *Play, dreams and imitation in childhood* (Vol. 25). New York: Routledge.

Postmes, T., Spears, R., & Lea, M. (1998). Breaching or building social boundaries?: SIDE-effects of computer-mediated communication. *Communication Research, 25*(6), 689–715. doi:10.1177/009365098025006006.

Qian, H., & Scott, C. R. (2007). Anonymity and self-disclosure on weblogs. *Journal of Computer-Mediated Communication, 12*(4), 1428–1451.

Raskauskas, J., & Stoltz, A. D. (2007). Involvement in traditional and electronic bullying among adolescents. *Developmental Psychology, 43*(3), 564.

Scott, C. R. (1998). To reveal or not to reveal: A theoretical model of anonymous communication. *Communication Theory, 8*(4), 381–407.

Siegel, J., Dubrovsky, V., Kiesler, S., & McGuire, T. W. (1986). Group processes in computer-mediated communication. *Organizational Behavior and Human Decision Processes, 37*(2), 157–187.

Skinner, B. F. (2014). *Contingencies of reinforcement: A theoretical analysis* (Vol. 3). Cambridge, MA: BF Skinner Foundation.

Song, I., Larose, R., Eastin, M. S., & Lin, C. A. (2004). Internet gratifications and Internet addiction: On the uses and abuses of new media. *CyberPsychology & Behavior, 7*(4), 384–394.

Spears, R., Postmes, T., Lea, M., & Watt, S. E. (2001). A SIDE view of social influence. *Social Influence: Direct and Indirect Processes*, 331–350.

Sproull, L., & Kiesler, S. (1986). Reducing social context cues: Electronic mail in organizational communication. *Management Science, 32*(11), 1492–1512.

Strayer, D. L., & Johnston, W. A. (2001). Driven to distraction: Dual-task studies of simulated driving and conversing on a cellular telephone. *Psychological science, 12*(6), 462–466.

Strayer, D. L., Drews, F. A., & Johnston, W. A. (2003). Cell phone-induced failures of visual attention during simulated driving. *Journal of experimental psychology: Applied, 9*(1), 23.

Steele, G. L. (1983). *The hacker's dictionary: A guide to the world of computer wizards*. New York: Harper & Row.

Steiner, P. (1993). On the Internet, nobody knows you're a dog. *The New Yorker.*

Stritzke, W. G., Nguyen, A., & Durkin, K. (2004). Shyness and computer-mediated communication: A self-presentational theory perspective. *Media Psychology, 6*(1), 1–22.

Suler, J. (2004). The online disinhibition effect. *CyberPsychology & Behavior, 7*(3), 321–326.

Taylor, C. (1989). *Sources of the self: The making of the modern identity*. Cambridge, MA: Harvard University Press.

Tell, C. (2013). Step away from the phone! *The New York Times.* Retrieved from http://www.nytimes.com/2013/09/22/fashion/step-away-from-the-phone.html?pagewanted=all&_r=1&/.

Tidwell, L. C., & Walther, J. B. (2002). Computer-mediated communication effects on disclosure, impressions, and interpersonal evaluations: Getting to know one another a bit at a time. *Human Communication Research, 28*(3), 317–348.

Turkle, S. (1995/2011). *Life on the screen*. New York: Simon & Schuster.

Van Dijck, J. (2007). *Mediated memories in the digital age*. Stanford, CA: Stanford University Press.

Walther, J. B. (1992). Interpersonal effects in computer-mediated interaction: A relational perspective. *Communication Research, 19*(1), 52–90.

Walther, J. B. (1996). Computer-mediated communication: Impersonal, interpersonal, and hyperpersonal interaction. *Communication Research, 23*(1), 3–43.

Walther, J. B. (1997). Group and interpersonal effects in international computer-mediated collaboration. *Human Communication Research, 23*(3), 342–369.

Walther, J. B. (2006). Nonverbal dynamics in computer-mediated communication, or:(and the net:('s with you:) and you:) alone. *The Sage Handbook of Nonverbal Communication,* 461–480.

Wan, C.-S., & Chiou, W.-B. (2006). Psychological motives and online games addiction: Atest of flow theory and humanistic needs theory for taiwanese adolescents. *CyberPsychology & Behavior, 9*(3), 317–324.

Whitney, I., & Smith, P. K. (1993). A survey of the nature and extent of bullying in junior/middle and secondary schools. *Educational Research (NFER), 35*(1), 3–25.

Williams, K. R., & Guerra, N. G. (2007). Prevalence and predictors of internet bullying. *Journal of Adolescent Health, 41*(6), S14–S21.

Wilson, F. A., & Stimpson, J. P. (2010). Trends in fatalities from distracted driving in the United States, 1999 to 2008. *American Journal of Public Health, 100*(11), 2213–2219.

Wilson, R. E., Gosling, S. D., & Graham, L. T. (2012). A review of Facebook research in the social sciences. *Perspectives on Psychological Science, 7*(3), 203–220.

Yee, N. (2006). Motivations for play in online games. *CyberPsychology & Behavior, 9*(6), 772–775.

Zimbardo, P. G. (1969). *The human choice: Individuation, reason, and order versus deindividuation, impulse, and chaos.* In Levine, D., & Arnold, W. J. (Eds.), *Nebraska symposium on motivation* (Vol. 17). University of Nebraska Press.

Zuo, A. (2014). *Measuring up: Social comparisons on Facebook and contributions to self-esteem and mental health.* Masters Thesis, University of Michigan. http://hdl.handle.net/2027.42/107346.

CHAPTER 7

—

Digital Inequality, Age, and Social Class

On the advice of his daughter, Bill decides to move into a senior community. He is nowhere near being an "old fogey," but his daughter thinks it would be a good opportunity for him to meet other people and make more friends. Since his wife died two years ago, Bill has stopped doing a lot of the things they used to enjoy, like going to movies and plays. Plus, given that he would no longer have to cut the grass outside his home, he is inclined to agree with his daughter. He moves in and within months he is the life of the party. On Wednesday night they have card games, and on Fridays Bill leads a lecture series. One day he discovers a computer room full of shiny new Macs that no one has bothered to mention. He asks one of his neighbors, who tells him that a grant a few years back paid for a new computer lab so the adults could have "access," but no one ever uses it. Determined to start recording and sharing his life experiences with others online, Bill takes to the computer lab immediately. He does not have much experience with technology, but, being a former college professor, he easily learns how to set up his own YouTube channel and record some videos. He quickly gains a following online and starts spending more time in the lab. Soon people are asking him to teach them how to set up email, check the news, join Facebook, and look up health information. One neighbor, Adele, seems particularly interested in learning more and has asked Bill for private lessons. "Wait a second," Bill thinks to himself, "is this a date?"

As we saw in the previous chapter, social media plays a role in people's everyday lives—it helps them fulfill goals and solve problems both practical and social. However, not everyone uses social media the in same way. Social media practices—from what platforms you use to how you attempt a Google search to how you talk to friends online—are indelibly shaped by factors about us and our social worlds. Chapter 7 will use fundamental concepts from sociology to understand differences in social media use by age, and social class. The chapter will first present the concepts of literacy, economic, social, and cultural capital and use these concepts to understand digital inequality as well as differences in use according to social class and age. Then, drawing from a decade or more of research, Chapter 8 will elaborate on how social identities such as race and gender shape social media use.

LITERACY AND CAPITAL

Literacy

The digital divide was a term first popularized by the U.S. Department of Commerce's National Telecommunications and Information Administration (McConnaughey, Everette, Reynolds, & Lader, 1999) to denote the separation between those who had access to computers and the Internet and those who did not. Computer literacy, some claimed, was the key to erasing social inequality. However, as scholars have argued and demonstrably shown, the digital divide is a profound simplification. It implies that there is a binary distinction between the haves and the have-nots, when actually computer literacy exists on a spectrum (Selwyn, 2004; Warschauer, 2004). It also overly emphasizes the importance of physical infrastructure over social and cultural factors in achieving electronic literacy. Based on studying Internet use, scholars argue that digital literacy should be thought of as a "hierarchy of access to various forms of technology in various contexts, resulting in differing levels of engagement and consequences" (Selwyn, 2004, p. 351). Understanding these subtleties requires that we know more about literacy as a concept.

So exactly what is literacy? Most basically, it is "having mastery over the processes by means of which culturally significant information is encoded" (De Castell & Luke, 1983, p. 374; see also Warschauer, 2004). Literacy describes not only one's individual ability to read and write a language, but also one's ability to effectively use information and tools for access to information (Gee, 1996). Reading is a social practice, and one must have not only the ability to parse the words, but also an understanding of the context for what is being read and the motivation that comes from seeing it as useful and meaningful. Bill in our opening story sees the computer lab as meaningful because he wants to record his life experiences and share them with friends. Thus, literacy includes practical as well as social and cultural knowledge. For example, consider the knowledge one would need to make sense of a post to Yahoo! Answers. This would require not only the practical skills of using the keyboard and mouse, but also the skills of

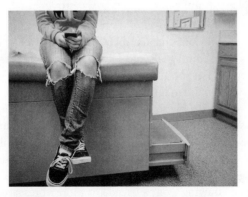

Photo 7.1 Digital Literacy in the Search for Health Information.

interpreting information and its sources, understanding the mode in which it was conveyed, and decoding the "netiquette" of others who wrote the answers.

Digital literacy requires multiple types of skills, not just the ability to read and write, but also knowledge of how to access trustworthy information, produce digital artifacts, and communicate effectively with others through digital devices.[1] Computer literacy, information literacy, multimedia literacy, and computer-mediated communication literacy all contribute to the ability to work with technological objects to access information (Warschauer, 2004; Figure 7.1). Figure 7.1 outlines these different types of legitimacies.

Computer-mediated communication literacy, for example, includes the knowledge of norms for social media communication (or netiquette), the understanding of genre, as well as strategies of rhetoric and persuasion that are effective in that particular social media genre. For example, if you are posting on a message board about college basketball, it might be effective to undercut someone's point with a satirical animated gif or the strategically deployed use of an acronym (e.g., SMH). These skills are unique to the communication context and are learned through socialization and use (Mossberger, Mary, Tolbert, & Stansbury, 2003; Van Dijk, 2005; Zillien & Hargittai, 2009).

Digital literacy, which describes these literacies taken together, is potentially important if one considers how many everyday tasks have now moved online. Managing finances, finding a job, participating in civic discussion, and finding health information are all basic tasks for which new media literacy is helpful if not essential. Those who do not have the same proficiency as others are

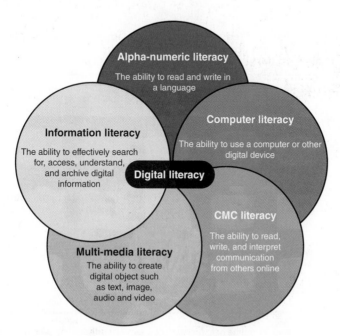

Figure 7.1 Digital Literacy. Adapted from Warschauer, 2004.

thus lacking a key resource for social advancement and personal betterment (let's leave aside, for now, the downsides of dealing with technology). In fact, it might make more sense to think about **digital inequality** rather than a "digital divide" (Zillien & Hargittai, 2009). Digital inequality describes the difference in access to social, cultural and material resources necessary to access, use, and interpret digital information and technologies.

Economic, Social, and Cultural Capital

Contrary to initial hopes, new media literacy varies according to offline inequalities (Robinson, 2009). But what creates social inequality? What marks one social class as distinct from another? How do you know who is rich and who is not? Even better: how do you become rich? And once you are rich, how do you stay rich? The seemingly simple answer is that to become rich you must have capital. Capital is any resource that is used to produce more wealth. Capital, and in particular economic capital, describes the materials such as factories, equipment, or money that can be used to reproduce wealth, which are called the **means of production** (Marx, 1867/1976; see also Smith, 1776/1937). Think of it this way: if you own a factory, you can use that wealth to produce and sell things to make a profit, thus producing more wealth. This is important because it means that the rich become richer while the poor remain poor. Economic capital is clearly needed to first acquire technology—hardware, software, and access (Selwyn, 2004)—but as our discussion of literacy suggests, it takes other kinds of capital to know how to use it (Table 7.1).

Table 7.1 Different Forms of Technological Capital, adapted from (Selwyn, 2004)

CAPITAL TYPE	EXAMPLES
Economic capital	Material resources, such as money to purchase hardware or software, such as the newest tablets or computers
Cultural capital	*Embodied*
	Spending time developing computer skills
	A "natural" interest in computers and social media
	Participation in informal learning
	Objectified
	Signification of tastes through display of preferences and activities online. For example, retweeting a post by the *New York Times*
	Institutionalized
	Formalized or credentialized training in computing or formal recognition of status (e.g., Twitter designation as being The Real celebrity)
Social capital	Networks of social contacts that provide support either face to face or remotely
	Face to face: family, friends, neighbors, tutors, other "significant others", membership of groups/organizations
	Remote: online help facilities, connections on social networking sites

Capital, as a reproductive resource, is not only limited to economic wealth. As the sociologist Pierre Bourdieu (Bourdieu, 1984) points out, you can get ahead by having **social capital**, connections with other people that serve as a resource. For example, if you are friends with someone whose brother works at JP Morgan and you would like to get an internship in investment banking, connecting either in real life or on LinkedIn will give you a better chance of securing that position. If you are having problems installing Windows, an expert friend may serve as a resource for help and advice. As a form of social capital, these kinds of connections may give you advantages in terms of literacy that you would not otherwise have.

Another type of capital is **cultural capital**, the set of knowledge, tastes, and practices that signal your social class to others and create a sense of affiliation between you and others who are of the same class. Cultural capital can be the explicit articulation of tastes, embodied in practices, or institutionalized through formal education (Bourdieu, 1986/2006; Table 7.1). Cultural capital can thus create a sense of distinction from some and an affiliation with others. For example, if you retweet something from the *New York Times*, this signals to others that you might have cultural capital in the most straightforward sense. Although some might wonder how you could possibly wade through all of that information and find it interesting, others will marvel, "Ah, I love A. O. Scott," remarking on your excellent taste in critics. In contrast, if you retweet a post from *US Weekly* or the *The Smoking Gun*, people will likely make different inferences about the amount of cultural capital you possess.

However, despite this trivial example, cultural capital can be much more complicated and much more pervasive than simply listing interests or tastes (after all, one can retweet the *New York Times* and then skip the hundreds of pages published each week). As illustrated in the example above, cultural capital can be *objectified* in artifacts like books, movies, and music. However, it can also be *embodied*; it subtly shapes our social worlds through taste and, more particularly, through **habitus**. Habitus is the life world, the context into which one is socialized (Bourdieu, 1984). By being exposed to particular tastes and habits at a young age, you might learn to prize simplicity over "bling" or appreciate artichoke over pork rinds. Studies find that those with low cultural capital have a "taste of necessity" that emphasizes practical efficiency or comfort, whereas those with high cultural capital have a "taste of liberty or luxury" that emphasizes self-expression or manner that may overlook functionality (Bourdieu, 1984; Holt, 1998).

These patterns not only structure particular interests, but also represent different ways of looking at the world and at technology more specifically. Applying this concept to Internet use, Robinson (2009) shows that people's "information habitus" structures their online activities. Those with low cultural capital have a taste for necessity and thus view social media activity instrumentally—as a tool to find a job or look for information, whereas those with higher cultural capital see it as a space for creative expression and self-building (Robinson, 2009).

Another study shows how different approaches to technology use can reproduce social class. Those with high socioeconomic status use the Internet for "capital-enhancing" activities like checking stock prices, reading political news, and looking up travel information, whereas those with low socioeconomic status are more likely to chat online (Hargittai & Hinnant, 2008; Zillien & Hargittai, 2009). What this means is that the digital divide will not be bridged merely through access to hardware and bandwidth. In many ways, existing patterns of inequality in knowledge and social advantage are only reflected in and reproduced by online activities (Merton, 1973; Zillien & Hargittai, 2009). For example, in the opening vignette, Bill takes naturally to the computer lab because of the embodied cultural capital he developed as a college professor.

Last, cultural capital can be *institutionalized*, usually through formal education (Bourdieu, 1986/2006). Those who have a college or postcollege education have higher cultural capital than those who do not, primarily because there is collective agreement that educational institutions grant status and skills to those who have matriculated (Bourdieu, 1986/2006). For example, one can be credentialed on Twitter as "real" to distinguish fake accounts from real ones. On Threadless, you can earn a "badge" for creating high-quality content (Threadless, 2014). In this way, a particular platform can bestow a formal sign of capital onto users.

There are a number of paradoxes inherent in studying cultural capital (Lamont & Lareau, 1988). For one thing, cultural capital has two perspectives. On the one hand, it can be hierarchical, meaning that there is collective agreement about what tastes are most advantageous. For example, most people will agree that a college degree gives you more cultural capital than a high school diploma. On the other hand, since cultural capital can be more localized, it means that tastes signify something to a small group of people (Arsel and Bean 2013). We will use the term **subcultural capital** to describe the knowledge, tastes, and practices that are valued within a particular subculture or group (Thornton, 2013). For example, if you participate in a fan group online like Survivor Maps, knowledge about the show serves to distinguish you from others (Jenkins, 2006). If you follow indie rock on Pitchfork, knowing the new unreleased EP of a band may garner you more credibility than riding the coattails of an already beloved band. In social groups, people build status, social esteem relative to others (Sauder et al 2012; Weber 1922/1978). Like capital, status is a social fact—most people agree that being a doctor is a high-status profession—but it can also be localized—apparently being a heart surgeon is higher status than being a psychologist (Abbott, 1981). However, unlike capital, status is determined by positive or negative social honor rather than by the combination of personal wealth and ability (Weber, 1922/1978).

A second paradox about cultural capital is that it has at least two dimensions: one's specific tastes versus one's range of tastes and flexibility moving between taste cultures. In the United States, those with high cultural capital tend actually to have a wide range of musical preferences rather than a particular set of them

(Johnston & Baumann, 2007; Peterson & Kern, 1996). A broad set of omnivorous tastes helps one fit in with many different types of people and contexts. Yet, there is often a code to selecting objects of affection on any tier of cultural production. One must like not simply any wrestler, but also the *right* wrestler. Just imagine what the breadth of tastes as a class marker implies for mashup culture, where cultural products both high and low can be combined and reworked for entertainment or commentary (Jenkins, Ford, & Green, 2013). Perhaps those with more cultural capital will be better mashup artists.

SOCIAL CLASS

Social Class and Literacy

As we've seen, capital—economic, social, and cultural—serves as a resource for people. Taken together, they predict one's social class. **Social class** is the combination of education, income, and prestige of occupation that places one in a hierarchy relative to others (Weber 1992). It is further reflected in and reinforced by consumption and media habits such as what one wears, buys, uses, reads, and watches (Holt, 1998; Levy, 1981). We will use capital, and in particular cultural capital, as an organizing framework for understanding patterns of use in social media according to social class. Understanding how cultural capital creates similarity and difference within social groups can help us understand and explain the patterning of consumption, tastes, and practices that are routinely observed in social life.

Understanding the digital divide ultimately depends on capital. This means that explaining (and solving) digital inequality has material, social, and cultural components. Materially, scholars have found that differences in hardware ownership (Livingstone, 2004; Zillien & Hargittai, 2009), connection speed (Schradie, 2011), and up-to-date software (DiMaggio, Hargittai, Celeste, & Shafer, 2004; Selwin 2004; Van Dijk, 2005) are important determinants of new media literacy. For example, people who do not own, but have access to a public computer are less likely to use one regularly, whereas having a computer in the home increases use for tasks like searching for medical advice. There are things like medical or relationship advice one simply does not want to look up in a library. Having greater access to the Internet, say from both home and work, makes people more likely to participate in creating content online (Schradie, 2011).

However, physical devices are not enough to compensate for digital inequality. For example, consider the case of Ennis, a small town in Ireland that won a contest where private technology company, Eircom, gave it $22 million to build technological infrastructure throughout the town—computers for every citizen, webpages for local business, and electronic payments for shoppers. Although the town had no shortage of material resources, they lacked the education and social programs to effectively implement the changes. Further, they did not quite appreciate some of the social benefits that had previously come along with supposed technological "inefficiency." For example, before the technological shift, the unemployed population of the town visited an office a couple times a week to pick up payments and fill out paperwork. Although the program outfitted each one of them with a computer so they could process their payments electronically and skip a visit to the office, people found that they missed the visits as a key outlet for social and emotional support (Warschauer, 2004). In contrast, towns that received less money were able to slowly integrate technology with existing social institutions. As this example illustrates, access to hardware is one thing, but there is also considerable inequality in knowledge and literacy (Deursen & van Dijk, 2010; Hargittai, 2008; Mossberger et al., 2003). As Bourdieu says, "To possess the machines, [one] only needs economic capital; to appropriate them and use them in accordance with their specific purpose . . . [one] must have access to embodied cultural capital; either in person or in proxy" (Bourdieu, 1986/2006, p. 50). As illustrated in the opening story, although seniors have access to a new computer lab, they may not necessarily have the skills, knowledge, or ability to use it.

Access and knowledge vary according to economic and cultural capital, but what about actual use? Cultural capital clearly shapes the way people use technology in general and social media more specifically. For example, in one study of one hundred computer users in New Jersey, Hargittai demonstrates that the low socio-economic status participants were less likely to use the "back" button, which made browsing more difficult, more time consuming, and more frustrating (Hargittai, 2005). Those with higher socioeconomic status see the Internet as a space for learning new skills and making new social connections versus activities like chatting with existing friends (Hargittai & Hinnant, 2006). These differences also carry over to the production, not just the consumption, of content. People with higher income and education are more likely to produce content online, which is important because the production of content can have an impact on who and what is represented and legitimated in social media (Schradie, 2011).

Taste and Social Reproduction
Social reproduction is when inequalities in the past or present reinforce structures of inequality in the future. **Homophily** is the tendency for people to affiliate with others who are like them. As they say, birds of a feather flock together. Homophily is one important, yet often subtle, way in which social reproduction occurs (see McPherson, Smith-Lovin, & Cook, 2001), usually through self-segregation rather than outright discrimination (Lawrence & Tatum, 1997). For example, many high schoolers report that people of the same race tend to self-segregate into groups during lunchtime (Eckert, 1989; Photo 7.2). Sociologists observe that the patterns created by homophily commonly arise on social media (Wimmer & Lewis, 2010). For example, in a study of this pattern among fifteen San Francisco high schools, kids from the wealthy high schools used Facebook, whereas those at the poorer high schools used Myspace. Similar patterns have been found by boyd (2008) and commented upon in news media (Hare 2009). Parental education, race, and ethnicity determine which social network platform people used. Whites, Asians, and those whose parents had college or postcollege degree tended to use Facebook,

Photo 7.2 Homophily.

whereas Hispanics and those with only high school education tended to use Myspace (boyd, 2006, 2008; Hargittai, 2007). Although patterns may have now shifted, disparities persist. For example, those with more education and income are more likely to use sites like LinkedIn and Facebook (Smith, 2014).

Some scholars look at social network choice as a kind of taste performance (boyd, 2008; Liu, 2007). For example, Myspace permitted various customized, colorful backgrounds that appeal to teens (Boyle & Johnson, 2010), whereas Facebook presented an aesthetic typical of middle- and upper-middle-class taste (Holt, 1998). Although this may seem like ancient history, it is a cautionary tale about how tastes—and thus platforms—can swiftly shift. One day you are in, and the next day you are out. Because taste can be embodied in aesthetic preferences, many of us may not even be aware of the reasons we may find one site "gaudy" and another "clean" or one site "sparse" or "boring" and another "exciting" and "cool." Social network sites can be an expression of a particular *taste culture*, a system of styles and practices that are related in a particular social class or subculture (Liu, 2007).

Use—accessing, reading, and consuming social media content—varies according to social class, largely because of cultural capital. But what about the creation of social media content? Here, scholars observe what Jenkins calls the "participation gap" (Jenkins, 2006, p. 208). Although anyone *could* produce online content, the people who create content tend to have more cultural capital than those who read and circulate content (Jenkins, 2006). For example, blogs, like the mainstream media before them, lack diversity (Hindman, 2008). Bloggers are 1.5 times more likely to have a college degree. Those who post photos and videos are two times as likely to have gone to college, whereas posters to a newsgroup were three times more likely to have a college degree.

AGE

Digital Natives or Digital Naives?
A wave of popular press books have proclaimed that the generation born after 1980, so-called Millennials, are "digital natives," people who have been socialized

Photo 7.3 Digital Natives or Digital Naïves?

with digital technology throughout their lives (Prensky, 2012; Rushkoff, 1999; Photo 7.3). Some argue that because these kids were socialized to use technology at an early age, this generation would be more computer literate than their parents or grandparents. To some extent this is true; young people use social media overall more than adults (Lenhart, Purcell, Smith, & Zickuhr, 2010). Although this might be true for some segments of the population and some technological practices (and—let's be honest, anyone who has sat with parents trying to post a photo can believe it), profound differences still exist among people in the same age group although similarities across age groups are also taking shape (anyone "friended" their mom lately?). Scholars have demonstrated that many young people, particularly those with low socioeconomic status, are not as digitally literate as we would like to think (Correa, 2010; Hargittai & Litt, 2011), prompting some to wonder whether young people are not digital natives, but rather digital naives (Hargittai, 2010).

When studying social media use and age, it is important to distinguish between cohort effects of age and generational effects. An **age cohort** describes a group of people who are about the same age. In contrast, a generation is a historically specific group of people who have experienced seminal historical events at a similar age. A generation may have stable traits that define the group over decades, traits that do not change although they collectively age. For example, the Baby Boom generation has been characterized by historians as optimistic regarding their personal lives, youthful, and self-confident (Goldsmith, 2008), whereas Millennials when surveyed were more open-minded, tolerant, and, of course, technology focused than previous generations (Pew, 2010). In contrast, a particular age cohort may use social media to overshare personal information now, when they are eighteen, but this does not mean that the cohort will continue to overshare like that as they age.

Starting from infancy, humans face different needs and encounter unique tensions at various stages in life. For example, when first entering school, children face the issue of establishing autonomy from the family unit (Eccles, 1999).

In early adolescence, they face issues of identity. Midlife adults confront issues of raising children while taking care of older parents, yet experience a sense of financial and emotional stability. Older adults face issues maintaining social connections, dealing with reduced physical abilities, and losing autonomy. Although these patterns vary according to the other factors discussed in this and the next chapter—social class, race, ethnicity, and gender—some patterns remain relatively consistent. Because of known inequalities with research focusing on the Western world, this section will largely cover social media and life stage transitions in the West, particularly in the United States.

Childhood

In early childhood, media consumption is limited primarily to television, DVD watching, and books (Gutnick, Robb, Takeuchi, & Kotler, 2011). However, between ages seven and nine, media habits begin to shift as children begin going online regularly. At age six, only 30% of children own their own media device, yet by age eight, 59% of them have their own device. "Once children get to 7 and 8 years, they are able to focus on activities for longer stretches of time, and their memory, logical reasoning, and problem solving skills sharpen. Children at this age can also apply their literacy skills to operate or communicate with digital media (e.g. via Internet searching or texting)" (Gutnick et al., 2011, p. 32). At this age, children have something social to do on social media—they form peer relationships and begin interacting more extensively with children their age. For example, Club Penguin offers a virtual world for socializing, playing games, and personalizing avatars (Gutnick et al., 2011; Marsh, 2008). However, virtual worlds like these require high bandwidth, which may not be available to those with less economic capital.

Preteens and Teens

Culturally, one thing is for sure: teen culture has shaped a number of social media practices from styles of video production to language for communicating quickly in text (e.g., LMAO, OMG, TTYL, etc.). As one study aptly puts it, new media literacy involves "certain literacy practices that youth have been central participants in defining: deliberately casual forms of online speech, nuanced social norms for how to engage in social network activities, and new genres of media representation such as machinima, mashups, remix, video blogs, web comics, and fanclubs. Often these cultural forms are tied to certain linguistic styles identified with particular youth culture and subcultures" (Ito et al., 2008, p. 12).

Teens engage primarily in two genres of participation—friendship-driven genres that are built primarily on existing relationships and interest-driven genres, which can exist more independently online as teens discover and pursue interests and fandom (Ito et al., 2010). Teens, particularly those with high cultural capital, engage largely in self-directed learning, informally picking up skills and knowledge from social media use, but also from peers online (Ito et al., 2008).

Overall, scholars observe that social media use, particularly social networking, blogging, and website creation, is relatively intense from ages thirteen to fifteen, but then drops off between sixteen and nineteen, as offline social lives replace some online activities. However, mobile phone use throughout these periods does not change, indicating that perhaps teenagers simply switch devices. There are expectations that one be "always on," continually available to close intimates, and yet teens will often maintain personal boundaries with others outside one's inner circle (Ito et al., 2008). Social bonding can also occur through offline sharing of online content through collective mobile watching, the ability to call up any media product for collective consumption (Ito et al., 2010; Photo 7.4).

Self-presentation online varies considerably, from elaborate performances, to ironic depictions, to minimal customization. In general, preteens and teens undergo a transition from identity building online, setting up and conveying markers of interests, to building social connections (Livingstone, 2008). For example, as they become teenagers, girls may switch from platforms that have affordances for self-expression and customization to platforms that have affordances for social connections (Livingstone, 2008). Both technical and social knowledge for social media use trickles down from older age cohorts and in some cases will trickle up, as young children teach their parents. For example, Weber and Mitchell (2008) interview a girl, Isabella, who learns how to make her social media profile from her older sister. Her sister not only teaches her how to set up her page and create related pages, but also conveys norms of what to create—she should have a home page, best friends page, profile page with interests (Weber & Mitchell, 2008).

What constitutes the "self" also shifts slightly through the adolescent life cycle. Livingstone finds that although girls will start out building a profile, based on content they themselves created, as they grow older, self is constructed not only by these materials but also, more importantly, by interaction with and connection to others. The self is not simply what one posts on the page, but rather an entity composed of the comments of others. Phatic comments and relatively "bland" entries on each other's walls may seem trite to removed observers, but they actually perform a key social function of "reaffirming one's place within the

Photo 7.4 Co-listening.

peer network" (Livingstone, 2008, p. 10). Through this kind of social linking and display, teens develop social identities in addition to personal identities (Weber & Mitchell, 2008).

Tools like status updates not only perform a dyadic (or one-on-one) relationship maintenance function, but also, because they are "broadcast" rather than sent dyadically, communicate identity to a broader audience. Teens "post status updates—how they are faring in their relationships, their social lives, and other everyday activities—that can be viewed by the broader networked public of their peers. In turn, they can browse other people's updates to get a senses of the status of others without having to engage in direct communication" (Ito et al., 2008, p. 15). They also sometimes encode these entries using vague pronouns or other subtleties to mask the true message from parents or other friends (Marwick & boyd, 2014).

In terms of relationships, teens maintain roughly two spheres: a semipublic sphere of weak connections maintained on social networking sites and a private sphere of close intimates, for whom they are always available. For example, a couple may start "talking" via casual, but flirtatious posts on each other's walls and a few phone calls, but then move quickly to a relationship, where eventually they become "Facebook official" and keep in contact continuously throughout the day, texting each other when they wake up and updating each other through mobile phones throughout the day (Ito et al., 2008, p. 17). After high school, social media can provide a valuable repository of social capital (Ellison, Steinfield, & Lampe, 2007) from which students draw through college. For example, college students will form social ties with peers, sometimes even before physically arriving on campus.

Middle Adulthood

Scholars know a good deal about how social media fits with childhood, preteen, teen, and college life stages, but we know considerably less about how social media fits into other life stages, such as early adulthood after college, mother and fatherhood, and middle and old age. Undoubtedly, the role that technology plays in one's life changes throughout young adulthood and parenthood, yet scholars have yet to extensively study these transitions. With identity issues and social networks largely settled, midlife adults will use social media for social support through life transitions such as having a child, losing a parent, having an illness, or getting a divorce.

In middle adulthood, people experience the highest self-esteem, feelings of security, and control of any age group (Orth, Robins, & Widaman 2012; Dörner et al., 2005). Most people in the current generation of middle-aged adults experience a control over their online identity not afforded to those who grew up with the Internet (Quinn, 2013). Adults in midlife will use social media to reactivate dormant social ties such as college friends, old neighbors, or former colleagues through social networking sites, email, or contextual search (Quinn, 2013), and affordances of social media provide ways to manage these interactions

(Quinn, 2014). For example, the asynchronicity of some tools can serve as a buffer for rejection or allow time for thoughtful communication. Asymmetry can also allow people to look up information but stop short of reconnecting (Quinn, 2013). Adults may also use social media as a vehicle for nostalgia, posting and sharing old photos with others.

Seniors

During late adulthood, social media use shifts further, as people use it for gaining information and learning (Google, 2013; Photo 7.5). Social media can be a place for computer-mediated social support (Xie, 2008). For example, some older Chinese users (fifty to seventy years of age) meet on a platform called *lao xiaohai*, the Old Kids. Users of the site gain social capital to help them with computer issues through online message boards. However, they also gain emotional support through instant messages and companionship over voice chat. In this way, they enjoy the affordances of each medium, such as the relative privacy of instant messaging versus the publicity of message boards for discussing personal and health issues (Xie, 2008). Participants would never discuss a mental health issue, for example, in a public forum, but would conduct an intimate conversation about depression via instant message. As a consequence of using these different modes of communication, relationships among older users can be multidimensional and multi-modal.

Despite these uses, the elderly (people older than sixty-five) experience their own digital divide because computer use can be reduced based on a lack of access or because of other factors such as expectations of performance, expectations of the effort it will take to use social media, and the social influence of peers (Niehaves & Plattfaut, 2014). One study of elderly computer use in Spain also finds a gender gap in use, whereby more elderly men than women use social media because of their perceptions of ease of use (Ramón-Jerónimo, Peral-Peral, & Arenas-Gaitán, 2013).

Photo 7.5 Elderly Uses of Social Media.

REGION

Rural versus Urban

The rural population, those who live in towns of less than 2,500 people (U.S. Census Bureau, 2010), make up one-fourth of the U.S. population. Because of the differences in space, these types of users tend to form social capital in different ways—often with a higher proportion of strong to weak connections than those who live in urban areas. The rural tend to be older, less educated, poorer, and less mobile (Bell, Reddy, & Rainie, 2004) and have been shown to suffer more often from social isolation, which can increase depression and other health issues (Gilbert, Karahalios, & Sandvig, 2010).

In terms of technology, those who live in rural communities start from an inherent disadvantage because both hardware and Internet access were slow to reach rural communities (Horrigan & Murray, 2006). In 2005, 24% of rural households had broadband Internet access. Dialup connections, of course, are associated with lower participation (Horrigan & Murray, 2006), presumably because of the hassle of signing online.

Comparing rural to urban use of social networks, one study finds many of these patterns of social isolation were reproduced (Gilbert et al., 2010); those who live in rural areas have fewer friends in their network, and those friends live closer together (eighty-eight miles away on average) than the friends of urban residents. Interestingly, women tend to be the technological gatekeepers in these communities (Gilbert et al., 2010; Larkin, 2008). Women in rural areas are more likely to be on social networking sites (versus the opposite pattern in urban areas), and yet rural women have higher privacy settings than others (Gilbert et al., 2010).

As we'll further discuss in Chapter 8, social media can also provide cultural scripts that may be unavailable in one's offline world. For example, rural gay youth use sites like PlanetOut and Gay.com as resources for coming out and for learning from a community of others (Gray, 2009). As opposed to mass media representations that tend to represent the lives and interests of urban gay culture, these "real" gay men and women offer resources for working out identity and relating to others. Because social media allows us to connect with people far away, it offers opportunities to find people like us for support, comfort, and advice about being different.

SUMMARY AND CONCLUSION

In sum, this chapter has demonstrated the many ways that social media use can vary not only individually but also according to differences in cultural capital, literacy, and age. Differences in subcultural capital as well as life stage mean that people's social media practices will change throughout their lifetime. Today you are interested in subverting the parental filter, but tomorrow you may be trying to set one of your own. Last, subcultural capital can also help us understand regional differences in social media use, as people in different regions develop different cultures of use and technological knowledge. Although many depict the internet as a great equalizer (Hancock, 2001), in this and the next chapter we see just how varied and interesting things can get.

TOPICS

- Capital (social, cultural, and economic)
- Digital literacy
- Habitus
- Homophily
- Age cohorts

DISCUSSION QUESTIONS

1. This chapter has presented the concepts of economic, social, and cultural capital. How might one signify these different types online, say in a SNS profile?
2. Imagine that you need to find out whether your headaches are part of a chronic condition or something more minor. How would you go about figuring this out? What kinds of literacies would be required?

EXERCISE

Make a map or a timeline of the human life cycle. What particular tensions occur at each stage? List these above the timeline. Then, below the timeline, list the technologies, practices, and platforms that people may use to address them.

NOTES

1. As we discussed in Chapter 2, we may outsource some of our abilities such as memory or calculation to digital systems, and so it is important that we be able to have control over these new "bodies" (Hayles, 2012).

FURTHER READINGS

boyd, d. (2014). *It's complicated: the social lives of networked teens.* New Haven, CT: Yale University Press.
Warschauer, M. (2004). *Technology and social inclusion: Rethinking the digital divide.* Cambridge, MA: MIT Press.

REFERENCES

Abbott, A. (1981). Status and status strain in the professions. *American Journal of Sociology,* 819–835.

Arsel, Z., & Bean, J. (2013). Taste regimes and market-mediated practice.*Journal of Consumer Research, 39*(5), 899–917.

Bell, P., Reddy, P., & Rainie, L. (2004). Rural areas and the Internet. *Washington, DC: Pew Internet & American Life Project, 7–37.*

Bourdieu, P. (1984). *Distinction: A social critique of the judgment of taste.* Cambridge, MA: Harvard University Press.

Bourdieu, P. (1986/2006). The forms of capital. In Richardson, J. (ed.), *Handbook of Theory and Research for the Sociology of Education.* New York: Greenwood.

boyd, d. (2006). White flight in networked publics? How race and class shaped American teen engagement with MySpace and Facebook. In Nakamura, L., & Chow-White, P. (eds.), *Race after the Internet* (pp. 203–222). New York: Routledge.

boyd, d. (2008). Can social network sites enable political action? *International Journal of Media & Cultural Politics, 4*(2), 241–244.

Boyle, K., & Johnson, T. J. (2010). MySpace is your space? Examining self-presentation of MySpace users. *Computers in Human Behavior, 26*(6), 1392–1399.

Correa, T. (2010). The participation divide among "online experts": Experience, skills and psychological factors as predictors of college students' web content creation. *Journal of Computer-Mediated Communication, 16*(1), 71–92.

De Castell, S., & Luke, A. (1983). Defining "literacy" in North American schools: Social and historical conditions and consequences. *Journal of Curriculum Studies, 15*(4), 373–389.

Deursen, A. v., & van Dijk, J. A. (2010). Measuring Internet skills. *International Journal of Human–Computer Interaction, 26*(10), 891–916.

DiMaggio, P., Hargittai, E., Celeste, C., & Shafer, S. (2004). Digital inequality. *Social Inequality: From Unequal Access to Differentiated Use, 355–400.*

Dörner, J., Mickler, C., & Staudinger, U. M. (2005). Self-development at midlife. In S. L. Willis & M. Martin (Eds.), *Middle adulthood: A lifespan perspective* (pp. 27–17). Thousand Oaks, CA: Sage.

Eccles, J. S. (1999). The development of children ages 6 to 14. *The Future of Children, 30–44.*

Eckert, P. (1989). *Jocks and burnouts: Social categories and identity in the high school.* New York: Teachers College Press.

Ellison, N. B., Steinfield, C., & Lampe, C. (2007). The benefits of Facebook "friends": Social capital and college students' use of online social network sites. *Journal of Computer-Mediated Communication, 12*(4), 1143–1168.

Gee, J. P. (1996). On mobots and classrooms: The converging languages of the new capitalism and schooling. *Organization, 3*(3), 385–407.

Gilbert, E., Karahalios, K., & Sandvig, C. (2010). The network in the garden: Designing social media for rural life. *American Behavioral Scientist, 53*(9), 1367–1388.

Goldsmith, J. (2008). *The long baby boom: An optimistic vision for a graying generation.* Baltimore: Johns Hopkins University Press.

Google. (2013). *Reaching today's boomers & seniors online*. Retrieved from https://www.thinkwithgoogle.com/research-studies/reaching-todays-boomers-and-seniors-online.html/.

Gray, M. L. (2009). Negotiating identities/queering desires: Coming out online and the remediation of the coming-out story. *Journal of Computer-Mediated Communication, 14*(4), 1162–1189.

Gutnick, A. L., Robb, M., Takeuchi, L., & Kotler, J. (2011). *Always connected: The new digital media habits of young children*. New York: Joan Ganz Cooney Center at Sesame Workshop.

Hancock, A. (2001). Technology: The great equalizer. *Community College Journal, 72*(2), 16–21.

Hare, B. (2009). Does your social class determine your online social network. *CNN.com, October, 14*.

Hargittai, E. (2005). Survey measures of web-oriented digital literacy. *Social Science Computer Review, 23*(3), 371–379.

Hargittai, E. (2007). Whose space? Differences among users and non-users of social network sites. *Journal of Computer-Mediated Communication, 13*(1), 276–297.

Hargittai, E. (2008). The digital reproduction on inequality. In Grusky, D. (ed.), *Social Stratification* (pp. 936–944). Boulder, CO: Westview Press.

Hargittai, E. (2010). Digital na (t) ives? Variation in Internet skills and uses among members of the "net generation." *Sociological Inquiry, 80*(1), 92–113.

Hargittai, E., & Hinnant, A. (2006). Toward a social framework for information seeking. In *New directions in human information behavior* (pp. 55–70). New York: Springer.

Hargittai, E., & Hinnant, A. (2008). Digital inequality: Differences in young adults' use of the Internet. *Communication Research, 35*(5), 602–621. doi:10.1177/0093650208321782.

Hargittai, E., & Litt, E. (2011). The tweet smell of celebrity success: Explaining variation in Twitter adoption among a diverse group of young adults. *New Media & Society, 13*(5), 824–842.

Hayles, N. K. (2012). *How we think: Digital media and contemporary technogenesis*. Chicago: University of Chicago Press.

Hindman, M. (2008). *The myth of digital democracy*. Princeton, NJ: Princeton University Press.

Holt, D. B. (1998). Does cultural capital structure American consumption? *Journal of Consumer Research, 25*(1), 1–25.

Horrigan, J., & Murray, K. (2006). *Rural broadband Internet use*. Washington, D.C.: Pew Internet & American Life Project.

Ito, M.., Baumer, S., Bittanti, M., boyd, d., Cody, R., Herr-Stephenson, B., . . . Tripp, L. (2010). *Hanging out, messing around, and geeking out: Kids living and learning with new media*. MIT press.

Ito, M., Horst, H., Bittanti, M., boyd, d., Herr-Stephenson, B., Lange, P. G., . . . Robinson, L. (2008). *Living and learning with new media: Summary of findings from the Digital Youth Project.* Chicago: John D. and Catherine T. MacArthur Foundation.

Jenkins, H. (2006). *Convergence culture: Where old and new media collide.* New York: New York University Press.

Jenkins, H., Ford, S., & Green, J. (2013). *Spreadable media: Creating value and meaning in a networked culture.* New York: New York University Press.

Johnston, J., & Baumann, S. (2007). Democracy versus distinction: A study of omnivorousness in gourmet food writing. *American Journal of Sociology, 113*(1), 165–204.

Lamont, M., & Lareau, A. (1988). Cultural capital: Allusions, gaps and glissandos in recent theoretical developments. *Sociological Theory, 6*(2), 153–168.

Larkin, B. (2008). *Signal and noise: Media, infrastructure, and urban culture in Nigeria.* Durham, NC: Duke University Press.

Lenhart, A., Purcell, K., Smith, A., & Zickuhr, K. (2010). *Social media & mobile Internet use among teens and young adults.* Washington, D.C.: Pew Internet & American Life Project.

Levy, S. J. (1981). Intepreting consumer mythology: A structural approach to consumer behavior. *The Journal of Marketing*, 49–61.

Liu, H. (2007). Social network profiles as taste performances. *Journal of Computer-Mediated Communication, 13*(1), 252–275.

Livingstone, S. (2004). Media literacy and the challenge of new information and communication technologies. *The Communication Review, 7*(1), 3–14.

Livingstone, S. (2008). Taking risky opportunities in youthful content creation: Teenagers' use of social networking sites for intimacy, privacy and self-expression. *New Media & Society, 10*(3), 393–411.

Marsh, J. (2008). *Out-of-school play in online virtual worlds and the implications for literacy learning.* Magill, South Australia: Centre for Studies in Literacy, Policy and Learning Cultures, University of South Australia.

Marwick, A. E., & boyd, d. (2014). Networked privacy: How teenagers negotiate context in social media. *New Media & Society*, 1461444814543995.

Marx, K. (1867/1976). *Capital: A critique of political economy.* Harmondsworth, Middlesex, England, and New York: Penguin Books in association with New Left Review.

McConnaughey, J., Everette, D., Reynolds, T., & Lader, W. (1999). *Falling through the net: Defining the digital divide.* Report by the U.S. Department of Commerce, National Telecommunications and Information Administration (NTIA). [Available online at http://www.ntia.doc.gov/ntia home/fttn99/contents.Html/].

McPherson, M., Smith-Lovin, L., & Cook, J. M. (2001). Birds of a feather: Homophily in social networks. *Annual review of sociology*, 415–444.

Merton, R. K. (1973). *The sociology of science: Theoretical and empirical investigations.* Chicago: University of Chicago Press.

Mossberger, K., Mary, K. M. C. J. T., Tolbert, C. J., & Stansbury, M. (2003). *Virtual inequality: Beyond the digital divide.* Washington, D.C.: Georgetown University Press.

Niehaves, B., & Plattfaut, R. (2014). Internet adoption by the elderly: Employing IS technology acceptance theories for understanding the age-related digital divide. *European Journal of Information Systems, 23*(6), 708–726.

Peterson, R. A., & Kern, R. M. (1996). Changing highbrow taste: From snob to omnivore. *American Sociological Review, 61*(5), 900–908.

Pew. (2010). *Millennials confident. Connected.* Retrieved from http://www .pewsocialtrends.org/2010/02/24/millennials-confident-connected-open-to-change/.

Prensky, M. R. (2012). *From digital natives to digital wisdom: Hopeful essays for 21st century learning.* Thousand Oaks, CA: Corwin Press.

Quinn, K. (2013). WE HAVEN'T TALKED IN 30 YEARS! Relationship reconnection and internet use at midlife. *Information, Communication & Society, 16*(3), 397–420.

Quinn, K. (2014). An ecological approach to privacy: "Doing" online privacy at midlife. *Journal of Broadcasting & Electronic Media, 58*(4), 562–580. doi:10.1 080/08838151.2014.966357

Ramón-Jerónimo, M. A., Peral-Peral, B., & Arenas-Gaitán, J. (2013). Elderly persons and Internet use. *Social Science Computer Review, 31*(4), 389–403.

Orth, U., Robins, R. W., & Widaman, K. F. (2012). Life-span development of self-esteem and its effects on important life outcomes. *Journal of personality and social psychology, 102*(6), 1271.

Robinson, L. (2009). A taste for the necessary: A Bourdieuian approach to digital inequality. *Information, Communication & Society, 12*(4), 488–507.

Rushkoff, D. (1999). *Playing the future: What we can learn from digital kids.* New York: Riverhead Trade.

Sauder, M., Lynn, F., & Podolny, J. M. (2012). Status: Insights from organizational sociology. *Annual Review of Sociology, 38*, 267–283.

Schradie, J. (2011). The digital production gap: The digital divide and Web 2.0 collide. *Poetics, 39*(2), 145–168.

Selwyn, N. (2004). Reconsidering political and popular understandings of the digital divide. *New Media & Society, 6*(3), 341–362.

Smith, A. (1776/1937). *An inquiry into the nature and causes of the wealth of nations.* New York: Modern Library.

Smith, C. (2014). *Business insider.* Retrieved from http://www.businessinsider .com/demographics-on-pinterest-that-make-the-social-network-attractive-to-marketers-2014-4/.

Lawrence, S., & Tatum, B. (1997). Teachers in transition: The impact of anti-racist professional development on classroom practice. *The Teachers College Record, 99*(1), 162–178.

Thornton, S. (2013). *Club cultures: Music, media and subcultural capital.* New York: Wiley.

Threadless. (2014). Retrieved September 28, 2014, from https://www.threadless .com/make/submit/.

U.S. Census Bureau. (2010). *2010 Census urban and rural classification and urban area criteria.* Retrieved from https://www.census.gov/geo/reference/ua/ urban-rural-2010.html/.

Van Dijk, J. A. (2005). *The deepening divide: Inequality in the information society.* Thousand Oaks, CA: Sage.

Warschauer, M. (2004). *Technology and social inclusion: Rethinking the digital divide.* Cambridge, MA: MIT Press.

Weber, M. (1922/1978). *Economy and society: An outline of interpretive sociology.* Berkeley: University of California Press.

Weber, S., & Mitchell, C. (2008). Imaging, keyboarding, and posting identities: Young people and new media technologies. *Youth, Identity, and Digital Media,* 25–47.

Wimmer, A., & Lewis, K. (2010). Beyond and below racial homophily: ERG models of a friendship network documented on Facebook. *American Journal of Sociology, 116*(2), 583–642.

Xie, B. (2008). Multimodal computer-mediated communication and social support among older Chinese Internet users. *Journal of Computer-Mediated Communication, 13*(3), 728–750.

Zillien, N., & Hargittai, E. (2009). Digital distinction: Status-specific types of Internet usage. *Social Science Quarterly, 90*(2), 274–291.

CHAPTER 8

—

Race and Gender

Trisha has gotten into programing lately and taught herself through books and online, often seeking advice from other programmers on a community site. Mostly she wants to create a game, but lately she has enjoyed just staying up late, listening to music, and figuring out some code. After about six months, she feels like she is finally getting the hang of it. She really values the help of two friends she has made on the site, but lately she has started to suspect they do not know who she really is. One of them said something kind of racist the other day, and they are generally not too kind to women either. One day she decides to "out" herself by talking about some of her other, more "girly" interests. They seemed OK with it, if a little surprised. Relieved, she sets about honing her skills in C^{++}. Everything is fine until about two weeks later, when she posts an answer to a new problem posed by an admin. The responses are relentless. Some newbies get trolled like this, but usually not someone who has been around as long as she has. Then, as she skims the comments, she finds the one that explains it all: "Hey Trish, you code like a girl." Yes, she is a girl. But what does it mean to code like one?

Although early research hailed the Internet as a place where people could freely adopt different gender, age, or racial personas, the more visual turn in social media has meant that representations are increasingly racialized and gendered (Nakamura, 2002/2013), both in that race and gender are conveyed through social media discourse and in that the race and gender of users are interpreted by others. As noted by Lisa Nakamura (2002/2013), "Though it's true that users' physical bodies are hidden from other users, race has a way of asserting its presence in the language users employ, in the kind of identities they construct, and in the ways they depict themselves online, both through language and through graphic images" (p. 31). The same can be said of gender. In one study of gender and language (Herring & Martinson, 2004), researchers found that participants in a text-only chat inferred gender cues from ways of speaking. For example, women use more hedging language ("I might," "I think," "it seems"), apologies, and emoticons, whereas men use more assertions and asked fewer questions (Herring, 2003; Herring & Martinson, 2004; see also Herring & Stoerger, 2013; Thomson & Murachver, 2001; Wolf, 2000).

In this chapter we will use the concepts of identity and performance to understand how race and gender shape social media use. As we will see, identity can shape the way we use social media, both because we internalize different norms and because different things are expected of us by others. Further, we will see how identity translates to political and civic discourse online as people confront the racist and misogynistic discourse created in an atmosphere of anonymity and depersonalization.

IDENTITY AND PERFORMANCE

As we discussed in Chapter 6, people perform one or more selves online through performance. Yet these projected selves are enacted in a world with existing social categories such as male, female, black, white, and Latino, to name only a few. Performances are received and interpreted in particular ways based on our collective understanding of what it means to be white, black, Latino, male, or female. We call this intersection of who we see ourselves to be and how others see us a **social identity**. Although we may have some latitude over how we identify, we are born into such categories and socialized accordingly. For example, if born female, our parents might receive pink clothes and blankets to meet our arrival and call us "beautiful" or "sweet" rather than "bold" or "daring." Although we can change or combine identities along a spectrum, cultural categories tend to be structured by strong culturally-constructed assumptions oriented along opposing dimensions such as weak or strong, emotional or rational, and soft or hard (Lévi-Strauss, 1966).

We usually begin identification with a recognition of similarities with some people and differences with others (Lacan, 2002). As Stuart Hall (1996) says, "Identification is constructed on the back of a recognition of some common origin or shared characteristics with another person or group with an ideal" (p. 6). Although race and gender online can be articulated or performed in particular ways, its signification is a two-sided process where the act of identification puts the user into a particular train of discourse and association that is largely determined by others collectively. Identification also puts us into a particular symbolic nexus of meanings that we do not control, but are socially constructed by others.

We may not even be aware of these social meanings until they become glaringly obvious through social interaction. For example, in the opening story Trisha does not think much of her identity as a woman until she receives a torrent of negative responses to her answer. The fact that someone calls her a "girl" suddenly casts her into a social role that has all sorts of meanings—that she may be weak or indirect or emotional—that she does not necessarily embody. The ability of names to do this, to "hail" us as a particular kind of person, is a process called **interpellation**. Interpellation is the process by which the dominant meanings of a social role come to constitute subjective identity, the ways we might feel, think, or act (Althusser, 1976; see also Fanon, 1967).[1] As we'll see for the categories of race and gender, although social identity usually begins with the recognition of some common characteristic or origin with others, the identity itself can have meanings that we do not determine and that may even shape our performance of self. Although social identities are socially constructed, they can also seem very real when we read a magazine, watch a television show, go online, or interact with others. As we will see, social media can both reflect and reproduce the social identities of race and gender, partly by shaping the performances of ourselves and others.

RACE

With its origins at the Department of Defense and then later in Palo Alto, California, the structure of the Internet was created by an industry will little racial diversity (Pitti, 2003). Although to the majority the Internet may seem unmarked by racial codings, to racial and other minorities it can be subtly and pervasively framed as white (De la Peña, 2010; Feagin, 2013), a space that is taken for granted as a white space and that centers on the interests of the white majority.[2] Structurally, racial divisions are coded into technology in ways both large and small. For example, most "hand" pointers are white (White, 2006), and until recently emojis lacked representation of races other than white (although Apple released a more "diverse" set of emojis in 2015 in conjunction with the Unicode Consortium[3]). Further, lagged gaps in access along racial lines mean that, as Nakamura (2002/2013) argues, "people of color were functionally absent from the Internet at precisely that time when its discourse was forming its distinct contours" (p. xii). The structure and culture of the Internet—and to some degree social media—was largely in place before access spread more broadly, and some gaps in access, of course, still remain (Pew Research, 2014).[4] In 2014, 80% of African Americans had Internet access compared to 87% of whites (Pew Research, 2014).

Considering the nuanced definition of literacy presented in the first section, we can certainly see how technological structures can work against those with different interests, abilities, and values. Yet, as we have discussed in Chapters 2 and 6, people often use infrastructure for their own goals, which can, in turn, change the technology. So just what is race and how might it shape the way people use social media?

As we discussed in the previous section, identification is a two-way street. The labels of social identity hail us into different subject positions, meaning that people expect certain types of performances from us if we identify as, for example, black or white. For example, on Twitter the hashtag #blacktwitter is used to denote the network of connections and content known as Black Twitter,[5] a community of African Americans who tweet about issues of common concern, primarily in the United States. However, after the emergence of this informal network, debate quickly turned to whether Black Twitter is or should be concerned solely with activism or whether it should extend to discussion of popular culture.[6] That is, some assume that because people on Black Twitter identify as black, this places them in a nexus of linked fate (Dawson, 1995; Tate, 1991), a sense of common political struggle, with other African Americans. So, although race is socially constructed through identification, it comes to shape how people perceive and interact in real, objective ways. It can create obligations and meanings over which we have no control, but can also open certain lines of action or possibility.

Representation Online

As we discussed in Chapter 2, although the initial utopian hopes about the Internet were that it would level social distinctions and bridge social identities, the reality is different. As a form of representation, social media is in many ways a mirror of culture and society, a media that reflects the prejudice and social boundaries of the offline world. We can see this in part by looking at representation online. For example, studies find that white men are overrepresented in video games, whereas African American men are slightly, and Latinos largely, underrepresented compared to the population (Williams, Martins, Consalvo, & Ivory, 2009). Further, when represented, African American men and Latinos tend to be depicted as thugs, as in *Grand Theft Auto* franchise (Leonard, 2009). So although social media makes room for technologically crossing color lines and reinventing racial representations, it more often reflects existing imbalances and stereotypes observed in other media and in the offline world.

Race and Social Media Use

As Daniels (2013) aptly states, "people use the Internet to both form and reaffirm individual racial identity and seek out communities based on race and racial understandings of the world" (p. 5). Racially based communities abound online as people share their interests and experiences. For example, some Asian American bloggers write online diaries to provide a way to maintain connections with friends and loved ones far from home (Karlsson, 2006). In a study of the Facebook walls of eighty-three students, Grasmuck et al. (2009) found that African American, Latino, and Indian students express a sense of collective identity with their respective racial or ethnic groups, whereas the pages of white and Vietnamese students did not.

Race and social class are inextricably linked (Cox, 1948; McCall, 2005). Researching one without the other simply gives one a partial picture of the world. However, some differences in social media use according to race are notable and supplement what we know about differences as a result of socioeconomic status. People exist in subcultures that pattern social media use just like any other cultural, media, or consumption practice. Further, patterns of historical and contemporary discrimination have resulted in forms of spatial segregation, meaning that in the offline world, people often live in racially homogeneous groups, and this spatial segregation is reflected in online spaces as well (boyd, 2006/2013).

In most studies, education makes the most difference in how people use social media. Yet because of homophily—the tendency to affiliate with others like you—social ties along racial lines can also exist on social media platforms. For example, early in the use of social networking sites, scholars observed that Facebook was used more by whites and Asian Americans than African Americans and Hispanics (boyd, 2006/2013; Watkins, 2009). In a study of friendship that looked at the social ties represented by pictures posted on Facebook, all racial groups were likely to form homophilous ties, with African Americans being the most homophilous and white being the least (Wimmer & Lewis, 2010). Despite these tendencies toward homophily, the study also found that friend selection on Facebook is based not solely on race, but also on ethnicity, region, and education and driven by mechanisms such as balancing (i.e., having friends of friends in common) and **propinquity**, or physical nearness, such as living in the same neighborhood or dorm (Wimmer & Lewis, 2010).

Further, although people's everyday use of the Internet tends to involve affiliating with people who are like you (Wimmer & Lewis, 2010), some people use it to engage in "identity tourism" (Nakamura, 2008), where racial features can be disguised and users can role-play, much like we discussed in Chapter 6.

As a result of both taste performance (Liu, 2007) and network effects, a divergence in social media platforms can begin early and continue in a kind of path dependence (Subrahmanyam, Reich, Waechter, & Espinoza, 2008). As we saw in the case of Black Twitter, segregation need not be built into the system for people to form homophilous ties within the platform. That said, there can also be more explicit and purposeful segregation according to race and ethnicity. For example, Blackplanet, AsianAvenue, and MiGente are all platforms for people of similar racial and ethnic backgrounds to socialize (Photo 8.1). These patterns, again a product of homophily, are not uncommon in groups that are not based around race such as ChristianMingle or SeniorPeopleMeet.

Although there are many similarities in social media use across race when controlling for social class, use still varies in some ways according to racial differences. For example, African Americans[7] were among the first to adopt Twitter (Smith & Rainie, 2010; Webster, 2010) and differences in use persist. In 2014, 22%

Photo 8.1 Asian Avenue Homepage.

of these African Americans use Twitter compared to 16% of whites (Pew Research, 2014). As Hargittai and Litt demonstrate using survey data, this was largely because of an interest in entertainment and celebrity culture (Hargittai & Litt, 2011). Others explain these differences by pointing out that mobile devices, which had high early adoption among African Americans and for which Twitter has a natural affordance, are useful to those who may not have a desktop computer (Lenhart, Purcell, Smith, & Zickuhr, 2010).

Controlling for education, African Americans are more creative with online content. They are more likely to post to chat rooms and social network sites and to create blogs and websites than any other group (Schradie, 2011). After accounting for differences in social class, African Americans are more likely to blog and are more politically active online (Harp, Bachmann, Rosas-Moreno, & Loke 2010; Jones, 1997), whereas Hispanics are more likely than others to share files.

As we will see, these patterns of use matter when it comes debate in the public sphere. For example, during the riots in Ferguson, Missouri, in 2014, outrage circulated continually on Twitter, whereas the feel-good ice bucket challenge to raise awareness for ALS predominated on Facebook (http://digiday.com/platforms/facbeook-twitter-ferguson/).

Discussion, Debate, and Hate Speech

In the public sphere, groups with different interests fight for dominance in framing public debate, disseminating information, and legitimizing certain points of view (McCombs & Shaw, 1972), and social media can serve as the battleground on which many of these struggles play out before being translated to mainstream media (Humphreys & Thompson, 2014). Online commenting on news stories, blog posts, and videos is one way public debate occurs. Although there are forums where open racial dialog can occur (Morris, 2011), many have noted the prevalence of racist discourse on Twitter, Facebook, and YouTube.[8] Scholars explain this prevalence—which is typically higher than in offline communication—as "two-faced racism" (Picca & Feagin, 2007), the idea that people can use online spaces to vent their private feelings about race without public accountability (Hughey & Daniels, 2013). As we saw in Chapter 6, features of anonymity can create a depersonalized atmosphere where aggression is acted out seemingly without consequence. In this way, social media can provide a space for what some have called "nonconsensual racial fantasies," acting out racial power online in ways they would not in real life (Steinfeldt et al., 2010).

Just as offline communities form groups online, so too do hate groups (Lee & Leets, 2002). **Hate speech** is defined as speech that attacks, threatens, or insults a person or group based on race, religion, national origin, gender, sexual orientation, disability, or other traits (Walker, 1994). Yet Daniels (2013) distinguishes between old models of hate speech, where speech is directly insulting, and new hate speech, in which hate groups will participate in more covert forms of speech such as trolling or the creation of cloaked sites, webpages that are ostensibly about a public figure or issue but that are actually owned and created by a group with an agenda counter to the apparent purpose of the page. For example, the site MartinLutherKing.org is owned by white supremacists (Daniels, 2009). The use of hate speech is treated as legally distinct, although punishment of offline hate speech is more common than online hate speech. Further, national differences in legal structures can impact the prosecution of hate speech online. Europe tends to take a restrictive approach to hate speech—limiting it and punishing those who create it—whereas courts in the United States have interpreted the first amendment as granting wide protection to racist speech (e.g., *Snyder v. Phelps*, 2011).

Social media can also be used for coordinated racist action. For example, in one incident mobile technology facilitated the targeting of "foreign"-looking men on a beach in Australia, which eventually caused a riot (Goggin, 2008). As we have seen in this section, social media can be both a conduit for attitudinal racism and a vehicle for structural racism, whereby racial minorities are structurally or symbolically excluded from conversations online (Bonilla-Silva, 1997). Ultimately, however, both forms play a part in structuring racial dynamics in social media.

Collective Action and Antiracism Online

Social media can also host a space for coordinating many other forms of civic and political action. Blogs provide forums for civic engagement for African Americans and Latinos that center around collective identity (Pole, 2010). Sites like HollabackNYC.org fight sexual harassment by allowing victims to upload pictures of their harassers (Rapp, Button, Fleury-Steiner, & Fleury-Steiner, 2010). In the larger media ecosystem, activism online can change political and racial conversations in the mainstream media. For example, in response to a rape case in Florida, feminist African American bloggers rallied online against actions taken by the NAACP and NAN including Al Sharpton to protect the assailants. In response to the group's protests, Sharpton publically apologized and hosted one of the activists on his show (Rapp et al., 2010). There are many ways in which social media provides a forum for ongoing dialog about race and racial issues.

Perhaps the most striking instance of the influence of social media on public discourse about race occurred in 2014 and 2015 when social media conversations and coordinated political action arose in response to black men being killed by police officers in Ferguson, Missouri, New York City and North Charleston, South Carolina. Among other functions, social media provided a way for people to disseminate information about the deaths, rally with others, and link these and other events like them into a larger narrative about police brutality. Eventually congealing around the hashtag #blacklivesmatter, the movement sparked protests and marches throughout the country, broad public debate, and extensive mainstream media coverage (Photo 8.2).[9] As we can see in this and other cases, social media can provide a space for communication and coordination across racial lines, as civic leaders enroll others outside of the community into political action and movements for social justice. We will explore this more extensively in Chapter 13 on political life.

Photo 8.2 #blacklivesmatter Protest in Atlanta.

GENDER

Race and social class clearly structure social media use because of differences in both access to economic resources and in cultural tastes and practices. These become even more complex when we consider gender. As Alice Marwick (2013) notes, "social media both reflects and produces gender" (p. 60). That is, social media platforms represent existing offline differences in gendered meanings, interests, and interaction, but these technologies can also further reinforce norms, ideas, and stereotypes of gender (Marwick, 2013).

In studying gendered performance in social media, it is important to distinguish between sex and gender. Sex is the set of biological traits that one is born with, whereas gender is the socially constructed expression of attitudes, behaviors, gestures, or appearance (Connell, 1987). Gender exists on a continuum and can be fluid or contextual (Fausto-Sterling, 2000). Yet part of the rhetorical power of gendered meanings and performances comes from the fact that they are essentialized into biological differences. That is, many people take masculine and feminine traits to be "the way things are," and this gives the distinction a particular kind of power over people and their behaviors. Further, as we saw with the concept of interpellation, being labeled with a particular gender identity has implications for the internalization of norms and expectations applied to us (e.g., "you play Halo like a girl").

Gender and Performance

As we discussed in Chapter 6 on uses and benefits, people are continually performing selves online (Hogan, 2010). They project idealized versions of themselves, strategically exposing the "backstage" of their authentic self or playing with these boundaries. Recall that **role theory** suggests that people inhabit different roles that consist of social and cultural norms for how to behave (Biddle, 2013). Through texting, online discussion, Instagram posting, and many other online activities, we perform roles and examine how our performances have been received by others. As Rose et al. (2012) notes, "Gender display, as a continuous communication loop, is defined by society and expressed by individuals as they interact while shaping evolving societal expectations regarding gender" (p. 589).

Gender is one aspect of self that many scholars argue is shaped by or even constituted by performance (Butler, 1990; Herring & Martinson, 2004). For example, when posting selfies online, young women will often perform traditional ideals of heterosexual femininity by appearing submissive or dependent (Kapidzic & Herring, 2011; Rose et al., 2012). By performing what Dobson (2008) calls "heterosexiness," they deploy and combine signs of traditional femininity by conveying coyness, shyness, or passivity through dress, pose, and voice (Kalof, 1993; La France & Ickes, 1981). One study of Facebook profile pictures finds that men tended to post pictures that emphasize active, dominant, and independent traits, whereas women tended to post pictures that emphasize being attractive and dependent (Rose et al., 2012).

Gender theorists study how gendered behavior is rewarded or sanctioned, depending on how that performance aligns with existing norms of masculinity and femininity. For example, makeup tutorials online instruct women on how to accentuate feminine traits (Photo 8.3A), and sites like Pinterest, a platform heavily used by women, are used to collect recipes and decorating ideas, activities that represent feminine investments in domestic spaces. Although female performances tend to be the focus of much gender research, male performances online are also prevalent. For example, men may perform gender through bathroom selfies, flexing in the mirror to show strength. Or on gaming platforms, men can perform masculinity by choosing characters based on bigness and being aggressive (Photo 8.3B).

To understand gender performances, it helps to relate them to previous modes of visual communication in traditional media such as film. For instance, film theorists distinguish between two idealized modes of watching—fetishistic versus voyeuristic modes (Dobson 2008; Mulvey, 1975). In fetishistic performances, the object on screen is idealized. It looks perfect, unapproachable. In contrast, voyeuristic modes of watching seek to find some truer reality of the object portrayed, hoping to devalue or humiliate the target. For example, fetishistic watching may occur when we see a slick, idealized representation in a show like Sex in the City, but voyeuristic watching occurs on TMZ or reality television when we revel in seeing Lindsay Lohan get in a fight or Orlando Bloom punch Justin Bieber. By accessing a candid, behind-the-scenes view, we become voyeurs rather than viewers of idealized representation.

Different linguistic styles are yet another way gender is performed online. Males use more assertive language, sarcasm, and challenges, whereas women use more personal pronouns, polite language (e.g., thanks and sorry), and hedging (e.g., "maybe" and "perhaps") (Hall, 1996; Herring, 2003; Thomson & Muvacher, 2001; see also Lakoff, 1975/2004). For example, in one experimental study, participants were asked to identify the gender of the author of an email using a constellation of linguistic cues such as apology, self-derogatory language, and adjectives (Thomson & Muvacher, 2001; Hills, 2000). Most people were able to

USE A FLESH TONE EYELINER TO "ERASE" ANY STRAY HAIRS

Michelle Phan brows tutorials || Beauty basic brows

Michelle Phan Makeup tutorials

▶ Subscribe   242

1,218

👍 12   👎 0

Let's Play Halo 4 - Castle Map Pack

Rooster Teeth

▶ Subscribe   8,129,222

1,034,697

👍 13K   👎 233

Photo 8.3A and 8.3B Michelle Phan Makeup Tutorial and Halo Play on YouTube.

infer gender from language online. Further, when men and women tried to impersonate the opposite gender, they could not hide these linguistic markers, despite performing stereotypical traits (Herring & Martinson, 2004). Differences in language use, primarily the products of socialization into traditional gender roles, are apparently subtle and hard to fake (Donath, 1998; Herring & Martinson, 2004).

Although gender swapping online is made possible by mediated communication, the increasing visuality of online life makes such swapping less common. Although early Internet research found some instances of gender "switching" through textually mediated social media (Bruckman, 1993; Hall, 1996; McRae, 1996), it has remained low according to most studies (Herring, 1992; Collins-Jarvis, 1997). Males gender swap more than females (Samp, Wittenberg, & Gillett, 2003), and some have suggested that people will engage in gender swapping for strategic goals such as enticing cooperation in online gaming (Martey, Stromer-Galley, Banks, Wu, & Consalvo, 2014) or fitting in on a platform where gender might make you "different" (Herring, 2003).

Representation Online

As we saw in the case of race, technologies may have been built by and quite literally around those who have historically been in power (Satchell, 2010; Weber, 1997). For instance, some have argued that cellphones are built around the size of male hands (Sanghani, 2014). As we discussed in the previous section, the Internet was built by a group with little racial or gender diversity with particular interests in sharing scientific information, and these historical gender imbalances continue today. Three percent of tech startups are founded by women (Coleman and Robb, 2009), and approximately 20% of women make up the workforce in technology (U.S. Department of Labor, 2013).

The structure and affordances of technological platforms may in some cases reproduce existing stereotypes. For instance, sites like Polyvore and ShopBop have functionality for curating and displaying images, with little room to discuss other issues, a structure that reproduces the stereotype of women as shoppers and cultivators of personal appearance (Marwick, 2013). Similarly, platforms like reddit, Digg, and Quora are male-dominated spaces where "important" issues are discussed, in contrast to other platforms like Instagram and social networking sites like Facebook, where women dominate.[10] In online games the default subject position is usually a white male, and women tend to be cast into marginal roles in ways that represent them as dependent on men and/or hypersexualized (Burgess, Stermer, & Burgess, 2007; Downs & Smith, 2010).

GENDER AND USES OF SOCIAL MEDIA

The amount of engagement online has been another topic of gender research. Women and men are largely similar in their amount of social media use (Muscanell & Guadagno, 2012), but of course vary in types of use according to (socially shaped) interests. Women consult health information online more often than men (Percheski & Hargittai, 2011). Further, there are some imbalances in the type and amount of co-creation online. Eighty percent of Wikipedia contributors are male (Antin, Yee, Cheshire, & Nov, 2011), which reflects existing imbalances in the production of offline OpEd content (Harp, Bachmann, & Loke, 2014).

Drawing from self-determination theory, Correa (2010) finds that although women and men have equal abilities online, women perceive themselves as less skilled and will thus participate less (Correa, 2010; also see Hargittai & Shafer, 2006; also see Livingstone, 2004). Indeed, women post fewer messages in discussion groups and women are less persistent in online discussions (Broadhurst, 1993; Herring, 1992). When women do engage in debate, fewer people—both men and women—respond (Herring, 1992) are less successful at directing the terms of discussion, even in groups where women predominate. However, context does matter. Men will be less aggressive in online groups dominated by women, and women will be more aggressive in male-dominated groups (Baym, 1996; Herring, 1996). In synchronous communication like chat, turn-taking is more balanced (Herring, 1999). Further, the content produced is itself structured by gender dynamics.

Gender, Harassment, and Misogyny Online

Perhaps the clearest place to see the role of gender online is to examine online responses to the activities of men versus women. For example, responses to female-produced content such as online videos tend to be more aggressive than those to male-produced videos (Herring, 1999). In one experiment, researchers played massive multiplayer games with a prerecorded voice that was either male or female, and they found that harassment was three times more likely when using the female voice (Kuznekoff & Rose, 2012). Female journalists and bloggers like Laurie Penny and Helen Lewis-Hasteley have spoken out against the hostile and violent tweets and comments they regularly receive, illustrating the misogyny and harassment aimed at women online (Thorpe and Rogers 2011; see also Taylor 2014 and Faludi 2014).

Although these forms of misogyny are obvious, there are differential effects of overt "hostile" sexism versus more subtle "benevolent" sexism (Lemonaki, Manstead, & Maio, 2015). That is, women can be demeaned as lacking competence and efficacy or they can be "damned with faint praise," encouraged for their socioemotional abilities versus other traits that are not gender normative, such as being rational, assertive, or independent. These distinct types of sexism have different effects on women's behavior. Although hostile sexism can make women less likely to be socially competitive with men (Lemonaki et al., 2015), it is more often called out than benevolent sexism, which is less likely to be challenged (Becker & Wright, 2011).

Despite harassment online, women have become key opinion leaders and market mavens, offering advice on makeup, fashion, and etiquette (O'Leary, 2013).

Through blogs and self-branding, women have built both cultural and social capital by developing online followings that cross over into traditional media. Yet, notably, women most easily build this kind of social capital when their activities are confined to particular socially sanctioned spheres of activity that are congruent with dominant norms. For example, Michelle Pham turned posting makeup tutorials on YouTube into a sponsorship for which she received $1 million to create twenty hours of content (Campbell, 2013). Women have been more limited in their ability to build cultural and social capital in male-dominated spheres such as gaming (Kuznekoff & Rose, 2012) and computer science and face harassment if they do not conform to particular gendered performances online.

Although social media can be a hostile place to be a woman across many domains, it can also provide a space for building supportive community (Herring, 2004) and rallying around issues like equal pay for women or sexual assault on campus. However, as we will address in Chapter 13 on political action, the efficacy of social media activism on offline political structures and institutions is not always clear and definitely not inevitable.

Sexuality

Sexuality, one's capacity for and orientation toward the desire for others, is similarly essentialized into binary opposition of heterosexual versus homosexual, when it is actually experienced as continual, fluid, and gradated (Sedgwick, 1990). In many spheres of public life, **heteronormativity** is assumed such that others assume that women desire men and men desire women. As we saw with taken-for-granted whiteness online, heterosexuality is assumed in many spaces, whereas homosexuality is coded as different or odd, and although many spaces for homosexual men and women exist in social media, these spaces may still be coded according to dominant norms of type. For example, although Grindr was developed to coordinate casual dating or sex among urban gay men, men in rural areas may equally use it to identify partners for emotional support and long-lasting relationships (Mowlabocus, 2010).

Further, social media platforms tend to be spaces for people of distinctly different sexual orientations rather than spaces for those in the middle (e.g., Tinder vs. Grindr). Here again, binary classifications on social networking and dating sites can further reinforce binary identification for both gender and sexuality. Yet the ability to communicate with and receive emotional support from others who feel different is arguably one of social media's greatest achievements. For example, It Gets Better (Photos 8.4A and 8.4B), a campaign in which gay and lesbian celebrities offered videos of support, ultimately generated more than 650 videos, which garnered more than 50 million views on YouTube and received mainstream media coverage (Savage & Miller, 2011).[11] Although the campaign was aimed at supporting gay youth throughout the United States, it had a particularly strong effect on conveying support to those who live in areas where it might be harder to find institutional support (It Gets Better Project, 2010).

Photo 8.4A and 8.4B Tim Gunn and Dan and Terry Videos on Behalf of the It Gets Better Project.

SUMMARY AND CONCLUSION

This chapter has examined how social identity and performance of race and gender are reflected in social media practices and reproduced by representations online. In contrast to early hopes that the Internet would be a more egalitarian and harmonious place, more current scholarship has turned to considering the ways in which existing power differences have migrated online. Yet social media does hold out the possibility of positive social change. Platforms allow people to coordinate political action and find social support in ways not previously possible or easy.

DISCUSSION QUESTIONS

1. Can someone change their identity through performance? Why or why not? Give an example to illustrate your point.
2. Is homophily always a good or a bad thing? Discuss an instance where it may be helpful to group members and one case where it may be harmful.
3. What is hate speech? Do you think it should treated the same as or different from regular speech? If so, why or why not?

EXERCISES

1. Pick a controversy about race that has occurred within the past year. What was the timeline of the controversy and what role did social media play in the controversy? What publics around the issue formed and how did they use social media?
2. Choose five female and five male celebrities with a social media presence. Collect and analyze data from their social media performances and evaluate the comments from others to celebrities online. What are the differences, if any, between the female and male celebrities? Why do you think there are differences?

NOTES

1. Drawing from Althusser (Althusser, 1976), Hall (1996) says identity is a "point of suture, between, on the one hand, the discourses and practices which attempt to 'interpellate,' speak to us or hail us into place as the social subjects of particular discourses, and on the other hand, the processes which product subjectivities, which construct us as subjects which can be 'spoken'" (p. 19).
2. However, it is important to note that according to census projections, the white population in the United States will lose racial majority by the year 2043. Also, one should note that although this dynamic of a white majority shapes internet content in the US, it can have different manifestations throughout the world, as the Internet can come represent language of the first-world or "core" versus the periphery (see Wallerstein 1974; Guillén, M. F., & Suárez 2005).

3. http://abcnews.go.com/Technology/wireStory/apples-latest-update-emoji-diverse-29186204/.
4. Namely, a Pew Report finds that 87% of whites have regular access to the Internet, whereas 80% of African Americans and 78% of Latinos use the Internet. http://www.pewhispanic.org/2013/03/07/ii-internet-use-3/, http://www.pewinternet.org/2014/01/06/african-americans-and-technology-use/.
5. http://www.salon.com/2013/09/03/black_twitters_not_just_a_group_its_a_movement/.
6. http://www.salon.com/2013/09/03/black_twitters_not_just_a_group_its_a_movement/.
7. Scholars have noted that measurement of race can misrepresent the inherent variability and subtlety in racial identification. Further, measures of race also tend to exclude non-English speakers in racial categories, particularly in Asian American and Latino groups. (See Zuberi, 2001).
8. http://www.businessinsider.com/internet-racism-2012-5/, http://www.theguardian.com/commentisfree/2012/jul/12/consequences-of-online-racism/.
9. http://www.motherjones.com/politics/2015/01/black-lives-matter-martin-luther-king-day-civil-rights-protests/; http://www.npr.org/2014/12/04/368408247/black-lives-matter-slogan-becomes-a-bigger-movement/.
10. http://www.pewresearch.org/fact-tank/2013/09/12/its-a-womans-social-media-world/.
11. http://www.itgetsbetter.org/.

FURTHER READINGS

Herring, S. C., & Stoerger, S. (2013). Gender and (a)nonymity in computer-mediated communication. In *Handbook of language, gender, and sexuality* (2nd ed., pp. 567–586). Hoboken, NJ: Wiley–Blackwell.
Nakamura, L. (2013). *Cybertypes: Race, ethnicity, and identity on the Internet.* New York: Routledge.

REFERENCES

Althusser, L. (1976). Ideology and ideological state apparatuses (notes towards an investigation). In *The anthropology of the state: A reader* (pp. 86–111). Hoboken, NJ: Wiley.
Antin, J., Yee, R., Cheshire, C., & Nov, O. (2011). *Gender differences in Wikipedia editing.* Paper presented at the Proceedings of the 7th International Symposium on Wikis and Open Collaboration, Mountain View, California.
Becker, J. C., & Wright, S. C. (2011). Yet another dark side of chivalry: Benevolent sexism undermines and hostile sexism motivates collective action for social change. *Journal of Personality and Social Psychology, 101*(1), 62.
Baym, N. K. (1996). Agreements and disagreements in a computer-mediated discussion. *Research on language and social interaction, 29*(4), 315–345.

Biddle, B. J. (2013). *Role theory: Expectations, identities, and behaviors.* San Diego, CA: Academic Press.

Bonilla-Silva, E. (1997). Rethinking racism: Toward a structural interpretation. *American Sociological Review,* 465–480.

boyd, d. (2006/2013). *White flight in networked publics? How race and class shaped American teen engagement with MySpace and Facebook.* In Nakamura, L., & Chow-White, P. (Eds.), *Race after the Internet* (p. 203–221). Routledge.

Broadhurst, J. (1993). Lurkers and flamers. *Online Access, 8*(3), 48–51.

Bruckman, A. S. (1993). Gender swapping in cyberspace. *Proceedings of INET 1993.*

Burgess, M. C., Stermer, S. P., & Burgess, S. R. (2007). Sex, lies, and video games: The portrayal of male and female characters on video game covers. *Sex Roles, 57*(5–6), 419–433.

Butler, J. (1990). Feminism and the subversion of identity. *Gender Trouble,* 1–25.

Campbell, G. (2013). YouTube makeup guru Michelle Phan on becoming a beauty superstar: "My only goal was to help my family." *Glamour.*

Coleman, S., & Robb, A. (2009). Characteristics of New Firms: A Comparison by Gender. *Kauffman Firm Survey Report.* Available at SSRN: http://ssrn.com/abstract=1352601 or http://dx.doi.org/10.2139/ssrn.1352601

Collins-Jarvis, L. (1997, November). Discriminatory messages and gendered power relations in on-line discussion groups. In *Annual Meeting of the National Communication Association, Chicago, IL.*

Connell, R. W. (1987). *Gender and power: Society, the person and sexual politics.* Stanford, CA: Stanford University Press.

Correa, T. (2010). The participation divide among "online experts": Experience, skills and psychological factors as predictors of college students' web content creation. *Journal of Computer-Mediated Communication, 16*(1), 71–92.

Cox, O. C. (1948). *Caste, class and race: A study in social dynamics.* New York: Knopf.

Daniels, J. (2009). Cloaked websites: Propaganda, cyber-racism and epistemology in the digital era. *New Media & Society, 11*(5), 659–683.

Daniels, J. (2013). Race and racism in Internet studies: A review and critique. *New Media & Society, 15*(5), 695–719.

Dawson, M. C. (1995). *Behind the mule: Race and class in African-American politics.* Princeton, NJ: Princeton University Press.

De la Peña, C. (2010). The history of technology, the resistance of archives, and the whiteness of race. *Technology and Culture, 51*(4), 919–937.

Dobson, A. S. (2008). *The "grotesque body" in young women's self presentation on MySpace.* Paper presented at the Australian Sociological Association Conference. Re-Imagining Society, Melbourne.

Donath, J. (1998). Identity and deception in the virtual community. *Communities in Cyberspace,* 30.

Downs, E., & Smith, S. L. (2010). Keeping abreast of hypersexuality: A video game character content analysis. *Sex Roles, 62*(11–12), 721–733.

Faludi, S. (2014), **"New Media/Old Misogyny,"** Open Society Foundations, http://static.opensocietyfoundations.org/misc/future-of-work/women-new-media-and-old-misogyny.pdf

Fanon, F. (1967). *Black Skin, White Masks [1952]*. C. L. Markmann (Ed.). New York.

Fausto-Sterling, A. (2000). *Sexing the body: Gender politics and the construction of sexuality*. New York: Basic Books.

Feagin, J. R. (2013). *The white racial frame centuries of racial framing and counter-framing: Centuries of racial framing and counter-framing*. New York: Routledge.

Goggin, G. (2008). Reorienting the mobile: Australasian imaginaries. *The Information Society, 24*(3), 171–181.

Grasmuck, S., Martin, J., & Zhao, S. (2009). Ethno-racial identity displays on Facebook. *Journal of Computer-Mediated Communication, 15*(1), 158–188.

Guillén, M. F., & Suárez, S. L. (2005). Explaining the global digital divide: Economic, political and sociological drivers of cross-national Internet use. *Social Forces, 84*(2), 681–708.

Hall, K. (1996). Cyberfeminism. *Pragmatics & Beyond. New Series, 39*, 147–170.

Hargittai, E., & Litt, E. (2011). The tweet smell of celebrity success: Explaining variation in Twitter adoption among a diverse group of young adults. *New Media & Society, 13*(5), 824–842.

Hargittai, E., & Shafer, S. (2006). Differences in actual and perceived online skills: The role of gender. *Social Science Quarterly, 87*(2), 432–448.

Harp, D., Bachmann, I., & Loke, J. (2014). Where are the women? The presence of female columnists in US opinion pages. *Journalism & Mass Communication Quarterly, 91*(2), 289–307.

Harp, D., Bachmann, I., Rosas-Moreno, T. C., & Loke, J. (2010). Wave of hope: African American youth use media and engage more civically, politically than whites. *The Howard Journal of Communications, 21*(3), 224–246.

Herring, S. C. (1992). *Gender and participation in computer-mediated linguistic discourse*. Paper presented at the Annual Meeting of the Linguistic Society of America, Philadelphia, PA, January 9–12.

Herring, S. C. (1996b). Two Variants of an Electronic Message Schema. In S. C. Herring (Ed.), *Computer-Mediated Communication: Linguistic, Social, and Cross-cultural Perspectives* (81–106). Amsterdam: John Benjamins.

Herring, S. C. (1999). The rhetorical dynamics of gender harassment on-line. *The Information Society, 15*(3), 151–167.

Herring, S. C. (2003). Gender and power in online communication. In *The handbook of language and gender* (pp. 202–228). Malden, MA: Blackwell.

Herring, S. C. (2004). Slouching toward the ordinary: Current trends in computer-mediated communication. *New media & society, 6*(1), 26–36.

Herring, S. C., & Martinson, A. (2004). Assessing gender authenticity in computer-mediated language use evidence from an identity game. *Journal of Language and Social Psychology, 23*(4), 424–446.

Herring, S. C., & Stoerger, S. (2013). Gender and (a)nonymity in computer-mediated communication. In *Handbook of language, gender, and sexuality* (2nd ed., pp. 567–586). Hoboken, NJ: Wiley–Blackwell.

Hills, M. (2000). You are what you type: Language and gender deception on the Internet. *Unpublished bachelor's honors thesis, University of Otago, Dunedin, New Zealand. Retrieved April, 17,* 2008.

Hogan, B. (2010). The presentation of self in the age of social media: Distinguishing performances and exhibitions online. *Bulletin of Science, Technology & Society,* 0270467610385893.

Hughey, M. W., & Daniels, J. (2013). Racist comments at online news sites: A methodological dilemma for discourse analysis. *Media, Culture & Society, 35*(3), 332–347.

Humphreys, A., & Thompson, C. J. (2014). Branding Disaster: Reestablishing Trust through the Ideological Containment of Systemic Risk Anxieties. *Journal of Consumer Research, 41*(4), 877–910.

It Gets Better Project (Producer). (2010). *It Gets Better: Dan and Terry.* Retrieved from https://www.youtube.com/watch?v=7IcVyvg2Qlo/.

Jones, Q. (1997). Virtual-communities, virtual settlements & cyber-archaeology: A theoretical outline. *Journal of Computer-Mediated Communication, 3*(3).

Kalof, L. (1993). Dilemmas of femininity: Gender and the social construction of sexual imagery. *The Sociological Quarterly, 34*(4), 639–651.

Kapidzic, S., & Herring, S. C. (2011). Gender, communication, and self-presentation in teen chatrooms revisited: Have patterns changed? *Journal of Computer-Mediated Communication, 17*(1), 39–59.

Karlsson, L. (2006). The diary weblog and the travelling tales of diasporic tourists. *Journal of Intercultural Studies, 27*(3), 299–312.

Kuznekoff, J. H., & Rose, L. M. (2012). Communication in multiplayer gaming: Examining player responses to gender cues. *New Media & Society,* 1461444812458271.

La France, M., & Ickes, W. (1981). Posture mirroring and interactional involvement: Sex and sex typing effects. *Journal of Nonverbal Behavior, 5*(3), 139–154.

Lacan, J. (2002). *Ecrits: A selection.* New York: Norton.

Lakoff, R. T. (1975). *Language and woman's place: text and commentaries* (Vol. 3). Oxford University Press.

Lee, E., & Leets, L. (2002). Persuasive storytelling by hate groups online examining its effects on adolescents. *American Behavioral Scientist, 45*(6), 927–957.

Lemonaki, E., Manstead, A. S. R. and Maio, G. R. (2015), Hostile sexism (de) motivates women's social competition intentions: The contradictory role of emotions. *British Journal of Social Psychology.* doi:10.1111/bjso.12100

Lenhart, A., Purcell, K., Smith, A., & Zickuhr, K. (2010). *Social media & mobile Internet use among teens and young adults.* Washington, D.C.: Pew Internet & American Life Project.

Leonard, D. J. (2009). Young, Black (& Brown) and don't give a fuck: virtual gangstas in the era of state violence. *Cultural Studies –Critical Methodologies* 9(2): 248–272.

Lévi-Strauss, C. (1966). *The savage mind.* Chicago: University of Chicago Press.

Liu, H. (2007). Social network profiles as taste performances. *Journal of Computer-Mediated Communication, 13*(1), 252–275.

Livingstone, S. (2004). Media literacy and the challenge of new information and communication technologies. *The Communication Review, 7*(1), 3–14.

Martey, R. M., Stromer-Galley, J., Banks, J., Wu, J., & Consalvo, M. (2014). The strategic female: Gender-switching and player behavior in online games. *Information, Communication & Society, 17*(3), 286–300.

Marwick, A. (2013). Gender, sexuality, and social media. in Hunsinger, J., & Senft, T. M. (eds.), *The Social Media Handbook.* New York: Routledge.

McCall, L. (2005). The complexity of intersectionality. *Signs, 30*(3), 1771–1800.

McCombs, M. E., & Shaw, D. L. (1972). The agenda-setting function of mass media. *Public Opinion Quarterly, 36*(2), 176–187.

McRae, S. (1996). Coming apart at the seams: Sex. *Text and the Virtual Body.* Retrieved from http://dhalgren.english.washington.edu/~shannon/vseams.html.

Morris, J. (2011). *Gender and race, online communities, and composition classrooms.* PhD Diss., Wayne State University.

Mowlabocus, S. (2010). *Gaydar culture.* Farnham, UK: Ashgate.

Mulvey, L. (1975). Visual pleasure and narrative cinema. *Screen, 16*(3), 6–18.

Muscanell, N. L., & Guadagno, R. E. (2012). Make new friends or keep the old: Gender and personality differences in social networking use. *Computers in Human Behavior, 28*(1), 107–112.

Nakamura, L. (2002/2013). *Cybertypes: Race, ethnicity, and identity on the Internet.* New York: Routledge.

Nakamura, L. (2008). *Digitizing race: Visual cultures of the Internet* (Vol. 23). Minneapolis: University of Minnesota Press.

O'Leary, A. (2013, April 12). The woman with 1 billion clicks, Jenna Marbles. *The New York Times.* Retrieved from http://www.nytimes.com/2013/04/14/fashion/jenna-marbles.html?_r=0&adxnnl=1&pagewanted=all&adxnnlx=1412273136-NIaZQaNCb9SIcrkUJ3UCUA/.

Percheski, C., & Hargittai, E. (2011). Health information-seeking in the digital age. *Journal of American College Health, 59*(5), 379–386.

Picca, L. H., & Feagin, J. R. (2007). *Two-faced racism: Whites in the backstage and frontstage.* New York: Routledge/Taylor & Francis.

Pitti, S. J. (2003). *The devil in Silicon Valley: Northern California, race, and Mexican Americans.* Princeton, NJ: Princeton University Press.

Pole, A. (2010). *Blogging the political: Politics and participation in a networked society.* New York: Routledge.

Pew Research. (2014). *African-Americans and Internet use.* Pew Research Center, Internet Science, and Technology. Retrieved from http://www.pewinternet.org/2014/2001/2006/african-americans-and-technology-use/.

Rapp, L., Button, D. M., Fleury-Steiner, B., & Fleury-Steiner, R. (2010). The Internet as a tool for Black feminist activism: Lessons from an online antirape protest. *Feminist Criminology, 5*(3), 244–262.

Rose, J., Mackey-Kallis, S., Shyles, L., Barry, K., Biagini, D., Hart, C., & Jack, L. (2012). Face it: The impact of gender on social media images. *Communication Quarterly, 60*(5), 588–607.

Samp, J. A., Wittenberg, E. M., & Gillett, D. L. (2003). Presenting and monitoring a gender-defined self on the Internet. *Communication Research Reports, 20*(1), 1–12.

Sanghani, R. (2014). *"My iPhone 6 is tearing out my hair": How tech isn't designed for women.* Retrieved from http://www.telegraph.co.uk/women/womens-life/11143856/Apple-iPhone-6-is-tearing-out-my-hair-How-tech-isnt-designed-for-women.html/.

Satchell, C. 2010. *Women are people too: The problem of designing for gender.* Atlanta: CHI.

Savage, D., & Miller, T. (2011). *It gets better: Coming out, overcoming bullying, and creating a life worth living.* New York: Penguin.

Schradie, J. (2011). The digital production gap: The digital divide and Web 2.0 collide. *Poetics, 39*(2), 145–168.

Sedgwick, E. (1990). *Epistemology of the closet.* London: Penguin.

Smith, A., & Rainie, L. (2010). *8% of online Americans use Twitter.* Washington, D.C.: Pew Internet & American Life Project.

Snyder v. Phelps, No. 09-751, 131 1207 (Supreme Court 2011).

Steinfeldt, J. A., Foltz, B. D., Kaladow, J. K., Carlson, T. N., Pagano, L. A. Jr., Benton, E., & Steinfeldt, M. C. (2010). Racism in the electronic age: Role of online forums in expressing racial attitudes about American Indians. *Cultural Diversity and Ethnic Minority Psychology, 16*(3), 362.

Subrahmanyam, K., Reich, S. M., Waechter, N., & Espinoza, G. (2008). Online and offline social networks: Use of social networking sites by emerging adults. *Journal of Applied Developmental Psychology, 29*(6), 420–433.

Tate, K. (1991). Black political participation in the 1984 and 1988 presidential elections. *American Political Science Review, 85*(04), 1159–1176.

Taylor, Ashra (2014), "How the Cult of Internet Openness Enables Misogyny," *Mother Jones,* Apr. 10, 2014. http://www.motherjones.com/media/2014/04/open-internet-closed-to-women

Thomson, R., & Murachver, T. (2001). Predicting gender from electronic discourse. *British Journal of Social Psychology, 40*(2), 193–208.

U.S. Department of Labor. (2013). *Labor force statistics from the current population survey.* Retrieved from http://www.bls.gov/cps/cpsaat11.htm/.

Wallerstein, I. (1974) *The Modern World-System,* New York,: Academic Press.

Walker, S. (1994). *Hate speech: The history of an American controversy.* Lincoln: University of Nebraska Press.

Watkins, S. C. (2009). *The young and the digital: What the migration to social-network sites, games, and anytime, anywhere media means for our future.* New York: Beacon Press.

Weber, R. N. (1997). Manufacturing gender in commercial and military cockpit design. *Science, Technology & Human Values, 22*(2), 235–253.

Webster, T. (2010). *Twitter usage in America: 2010*. Somerville, NJ: Edison Research.

White, M. (2006). *The body and the screen: Theories of internet spectatorship*. Cambridge, MA: MIT Press.

Williams, D., Martins, N., Consalvo, M., & Ivory, J. D. (2009). The virtual census: Representations of gender, race and age in video games. *New Media & Society, 11*(5), 815–834.

Wimmer, A., & Lewis, K. (2010). Beyond and below racial homophily: ERG models of a friendship network documented on Facebook. *American Journal of Sociology, 116*(2), 583–642.

Wolf, A. (2000). Emotional expression online: Gender differences in emoticon use. *CyberPsychology & Behavior, 3*(5), 827–833.

Zuberi, T. (2001). *Thicker than blood: How racial statistics lie*. Minneapolis: University of Minnesota Press.

CHAPTER 9

——

Social Networks

Christine has had a long day at class when she comes home to find her room-mate, Jenn, with a new haircut. After the requisite—and true!—compliments, she asks where Jenn got the fabulous cut. Jenn says she decided to try this different place downtown, about thirty minutes away in a remote location. "Why in the world would you go there?" Christine demands. Jenn explains that she heard about it from her friend, Megan. Christine does not know Megan—no surprise, Jenn has a million friends—but something sounds familiar about this place. Just two weeks ago her friend Mark had gone to the same out-of-the-way place because he read about it on Yelp!. "Wait a second," Christine ponders. "Something is going on here." Christine and Jenn puzzle out the connections. "Aha!" they both exclaim simultaneously. It turns out Mark knows Megan and Megan knows Jenn. Satis-fied, Christine goes to make dinner, thinking, "Maybe I should get my hair cut . . ."

This one lucky hair salon has been the beneficiary of the strength of weak ties. Suddenly an entirely new group is going there, just because of one key person, Mark, who ventured to gather information outside of his group of friends. By understanding the dynamics of networks, we can see how word-of-mouth communication can travel in surprising ways. There is a lot of information in this one flimsy connection.

In this chapter, we will cover the basic concepts of network theory and dis-cuss its importance for understanding social media. The chapter will begin by providing definitions of networks and their properties and then apply this re-search to understand phenomena in social media, the diffusion of innovations, and word-of-mouth communication.

NETWORK ANALYSIS

Understanding networks is all about understanding our social world as a spider-web of connections. Sometimes the spiderweb can be dense; other times, it is loose. Sometimes it falls apart altogether. Network analysis looks at social con-nections as if they were a map. This basic perspective is based on **graph theory**, an area of research from mathematics that studies the properties of nodes, their connections, and their relationships. Graph theory, and the theories of net-works have arisen from it, has been applied to just about everything—from understanding how the brain works, to studying interstate traffic patterns, to mapping how we find out about a new coffee shop or get a job (Barabási, 2014).

The graphs produced by the study of networks are based around nodes, which can represent a person, organization, object, or idea (Monge & Contractor, 2003). In social science, these nodes usually represent a person. Sociologists have taken this basic perspective and applied social network analysis to a wide range of problems, from studying how businesses thrive to understanding how kids make friends at school (Wasserman, Faust, & Faust, 1994). From the perspective of **networked individualism**, individuals are a node in many different networks (Rainie & Wellman, 2012). Through these networks, we operate as individuals, but draw from latent connections in the network when we need help or want to share information.

As we can see in Figure 9.1, each person in the opening vignette is represented as a node. When they have a relationship, this is represented by a line, which we will call a link, tie, or **edge**. An edge represents some connection of interest. Here, it represents the transmission of information from one person to the next. Dan C. from Yelp! tells Mark about the hair salon, Mark tells Megan, and Megan tells Jenn. Christine and Jenn are able to put all of this together because Mark had mentioned the salon to Christine, as did Jenn. In graph theory, edges are sometimes represented as having **directionality**, an arrow to represent the flow of the relationships. In this example, we marked the edge between Dan C. and Mark with an arrow to indicate that information went *from* Dan C. to Mark. In this way, ties can represent the flow of information through directionality. Communication can flow one way, as when you access a product review website to learn about the newest digital cameras. Or information could flow from you to the website if you post a review of your latest digital camera purchase. Or it can be reciprocal, as you exchange information equally with the website, reading and posting content. Whether a platform offers reciprocal or nonreciprocal links can be an important factor in structuring the flow of information and influence. For instance, social network sites are often structured through the creation of reciprocal ties (i.e., if you are friends on Facebook, the link is reciprocal), whereas Twitter is based on one-direction links (i.e., if you "follow" Kim Kardashian, this does not mean that she will follow you) (boyd, Golder, & Lotan, 2010). In a system with nonreciprocal links, a social structure where a small set of users have enormous followings without themselves following many others is possible and even

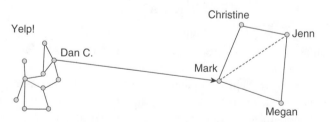

Figure 9.1 Networks in Word-of-Mouth Communication.

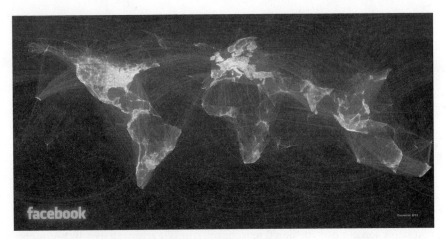

Photo 9.1 Facebook Connections Worldwide, 2010.

likely. Unlike a system with reciprocal links such as Facebook, status hierarchy can be much more clearly symbolized in a system with nonreciprocal links (to see what the network looks like globally, see Photo 9.1).

Network analysis can tell us about social distance—how close together or far apart we are via connections with other people. A **degree** describes how far removed one person or node is from another person or node. For instance, Christine has a second-degree relationship with Megan (they are connected by Jenn), but a first-degree relationship with Mark. Degrees are often displayed on social networking sites like LinkedIn and can even determine access to other users and privacy settings (Papacharissi, 2009). On Facebook, 92% of users are connected by four degrees or less (Backstrom, 2011). It turns out we are surprisingly close to people who may feel very far away.

It's a Small World, After All!

Say you are looking for a job in California and you live in Wisconsin. How many connections will you need to get in touch with someone who lives in Los Angeles and works in the movie industry? The psychologist Stanley Milgram asked just such a question in an early experiment about social networks. From his office in Cambridge, Massachusetts, Milgram mailed letters to 160 people he picked randomly from the phone book in Omaha, Nebraska. In this letter, Milgram instructed the recipient to forward the letter to someone they knew who might know the "target" of the experiment, a person Milgram knew personally in Cambridge, Massachusetts. The recipients were instructed to only forward the letter to someone they knew personally on a first-name basis. Letters went out, and within two weeks Milgram received a response that took only two degrees. Responses continued to pour in, and after averaging out the number of degrees needed for the letters to reach their targets, Milgram came up with the now famous, magic number: 5.5. The average number of links required for a letter to reach its target was, more casually, 6 degrees. Many people are probably familiar with this idea through the game *Six Degrees of Kevin Bacon*, which involves linking Kevin Bacon to other celebrities through a network of co-stars. It's come to be called the "small-world phenomenon" and has been replicated in everything from movies, to job connections, to Internet links. The small-world phenomenon has many different implications, but to understand some of these, we first must know a little more about networks.

Properties of Ties

Think of all the ways you might know someone. Your acquaintance could be a friend, a co-worker, or a family member of somebody you met at a party. Network analysis is based on boiling these many different types of relationships down to a few critical properties. Relationships can be represented as either binary (either you know someone or you don't) or a continuum. **Tie strength** usually represents the closeness between nodes. If two people communicate often and communicate through more than one medium, they are said to have strong, or close ties (Granovetter, 1973). Further, it turns out that people are more likely to form social ties with those who are like them on some dimension (gender, race, educational background), which is called homophily. The tendency to form homophilous ties means that we have close ties with people who think and act a lot like we do. This is why when you sign online you may see five people who have chosen to share the same point of view on the latest news scandal. Homophily means that we often end up "preaching to the choir" on social media.

Strong ties are important. Close relationships provide us help and support as we face hardships, raise kids, and do homework (Putnam, 1995). However, in one of the most cited studies about networks, sociologist Mark Granovetter shows that *weak ties* can also be important (Granovetter, 1973). Say you are looking for a new place to eat. All of your friends likely have the same information you do. They know the best Mexican, Italian, and sushi places where you live. There is nothing new there. However, consulting someone outside your close circle of friends might yield some new and helpful information. There may be a great place that your friends have simply never tried. This is the basic insight behind the opening vignette. Through the weak tie of a review on Yelp!, this lucky salon has garnered a new set of clients. For savvy users of word-of-mouth communication, this is crucial.

In some cases, ties can also have a positive or negative value. In a study of Epinions, Slashdot, and Wikipedia, where users could form positive or negative ties by reviewing or voting for each other, 80% of ties were positive. However, certain patterns emerged based on **balance theory**, the idea that we seek a balance in our attitudes and opinions about others (Leskovec, Huttenlocher, & Kleinberg, 2010; see also Wimmer & Lewis, 2010). Think of it this way: if you are friends with someone and they like someone else, it is likely that you like that person as well (it can get pretty awkward if you don't!). You are also likely to have common enemies (Figure 9.2). By this logic, certain patterns of ties occur more

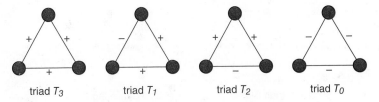

triad T_3 triad T_1 triad T_2 triad T_0

Figure 9.2 Balanced and Unbalanced Triads. Adapted from Leskovec, Huttenlocher, & Kleinberg, 2010.

than others in social networks. For instance, it is extremely rare in these types of networks for your friend to like someone and for you to dislike them (Leskovec et al., 2010; Wasserman et al., 1994).[1]

Network analysis helps us understand one-to-one or **dyadic** relationships as well as **triadic** relationships, but stepping back and looking at the network as a whole can also grant us a lot of insight (Wasserman et al., 1994). In the next section, we will consider properties of the network itself.

Properties of Networks

Remember high school? If so—or if you've seen a few John Hughes' movies—you might remember that there were separate friend groups, or cliques. They ate lunch together, they walked down the hall together, and they may have had classes together. In fact, a study shows classes are the primary way high school relationships are formed (Muller & Mueller, 2013). These groups of close friends can be described as highly clustered. For instance, the network of Facebook friendships in Figure 9.3. shows clusters from different periods in life: one cluster of colleagues, one cluster of family members, one cluster of college friends, and one dense cluster from high school that itself has clusters within it. **Clustering** is when nodes

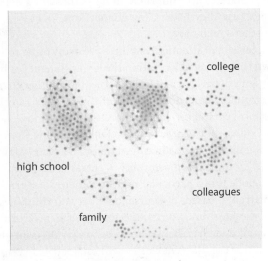

Figure 9.3 Clusters in the Author's Facebook Network.

High Clustering Low Clustering

Figure 9.4 High versus Low Clustering.

tend to be closely related by one-degree connections (Watts, 1999). A measure called the clustering coefficient describes the number of links that a given set of nodes has. So, for example, if seven nodes have twelve different connections, that would be a lot of clustering; everyone knows everyone else. However, if seven nodes have only seven connections, that would represent less clustering; there may be some people in the network who only know one other person in the group (Figure 9.4. When two different clusters have different sets of information, but no way to share it, this is called a **structural hole**. In many cases, someone in a position to bridge this structural hole has a lot of value to the network (Burt, 2001). Understanding where clusters exist means that some people, or "nodes," can have more influence depending on where they are located in the network.

Properties of Nodes

Some people simply have more acquaintances, and we call these people **connectors** or **hubs**. Connectors are important because they bring together people who would otherwise be unrelated. Think back to our opening example of the hair salon. Because Jenn knows a lot of people, she is the crucial link between these different friend groups. Typically hubs have many diverse connections, and they are critically important to how information flows through a network (Weber & Monge, 2011). Because they have many connections, hubs connect clusters of people who are otherwise far apart.

Connectors get a lot of attention, but there are many other roles in a network, each with its own strategic position within the larger system. For instance, a gatekeeper is a node with privileged and unique access to another cluster. A bridge is someone who is actually embedded as part of two clusters and therefore unites them. Unlike gatekeepers, there can be more than one bridge. And finally, the poor isolate is a node with few or no connections (Monge & Contractor, 2003).

So how do you know if you are a connector or an isolate? Many of these roles can be measured by calculating centrality. **Centrality** is a term for describing how important a node is in a particular network. There are several different ways of describing centrality, based, of course, on what you think is important. For instance, one of the most basic types of centrality is **degree centrality**, or how many connections a node has. Betweenness centrality describes how important the node is in connecting different clusters. To calculate betweenness centrality, you would need to first calculate clustering in the network and then see who lies between these clusters. Finally, closeness centrality measures whether a node tends to be directly or indirectly connected to other nodes in the network.

Networks themselves can have different properties that can be important when we compare them. A network is **centralized** if there are only one or two people with a lot of connections and hence a lot of power in the network. A network is **decentralized** if most of the people are connected to most of the other people. Therefore, no one person has a lot of power, at least when it comes to relaying information.

Emergence: How Networks Form

Studying networks requires a slightly different way of thinking than we may be used to. In psychology, the basic idea tends to be that if we can understand how one person responds, we can build that into an understanding of how a group of people will respond. This idea is called **methodological individualism** or reductionism. From this perspective, the whole is simply the sum of its parts. However, with networks, or any complex system that has lots of moving parts, something funny happens called emergence. **Emergence** is "any order, structure, or pattern appearing in complex random events that cannot be attributed to some specific pre-pensive purposeful activity or decision by some identifiable official or unofficial component or entity" (McKelvey 1997, p. 359, quoted in Monge & Contractor, 2003, p. 11). Imagine a beehive. In a beehive, bees have different roles—some bring food, others build the hive, others make more bees—and this system of roles and their relations make the hive what it is. Without one of these components, the hive would break down; it would cease to be a hive. In this sense, the whole is greater than the sum of its parts.

Closely related to this idea is the concept of **network effects**. Network effects describe the gains in a system when more and more people use the network. For example, consider text messaging. If just one other person in the world had the capability to receive a text message, it would be a useless technology. If your parents but not your friends had the ability to receive a text message, it would be a little more useful, but still not great. However, by 2011 more than 73% of people in the United States had the ability to send and receive a text (Pew Research, 2011; see also Pew Research 2015). The fact that the network of users is so large means that texting is a lot more valuable and useful. Economists study network effects in many systems— from interstate networks to phone, Internet, and movie distribution networks—and we will discuss the economic side of these effects in Chapter 14. The system of stable relationships between people or nodes has some serious value (Benkler, 2006).

NETWORK THEORY IN SOCIAL MEDIA

Social Capital

Connections have value. But what kind of value? The previous section covered the value that comes from a network of information and conduits for that information (Burt, 2001), but there is a more robust way to think about the value of networks. These nodes in our networks give us what sociologists call social capital. The measurement of **social capital** is relatively straightforward—it is simply the number and strength of social connectivity. But the consequences of social capital can go far beyond mere connections (Appel et al., 2014).

The sociologist Pierre Bourdieu first coined the term social capital to mean "the aggregate of the actual or potential resources which are linked to possession of a durable network of more or less institutionalized relationships of mutual acquaintance and recognition." This social network "provides each of its members with the backing of the collectivity-owned capital, a 'credential' which entitles them to credit, in the various senses of the word" (1985, p. 248). Social relationships are like a stock; they can store value until you need to activate it—to get a job (Lin, 1988), to meet potential dates, or to pick up your sister from school. The network of social relationships that surrounds us has value and can sometimes even be converted to financial capital (Cartoon 9.1), as when a business deal goes through because of mutual friendships. But social capital is a resource in many other ways. Our friends can comfort us when we lose our job or befriend us on a Saturday night. Surveys show that Internet users have more social connections, more social capital than non-Internet users (Ellison, Steinfield, & Lampe, 2007; Horrigan, Boase, Rainie, & Wellman, 2006; Rainie & Wellman, 2012).[2]

This new world of networked individualism is situated around looser, more fragmented networks that provide social capital (Rainie & Wellman, 2012). The hallmark of networked individualism is that people function more as connected individuals and less as embedded group members. Many fulfill their social, emotional, and economic needs by tapping flexibility into sparsely knit networks of diverse associates rather than relying on tight connections with a relatively small number of close friends (Rainie & Wellman, 2012; Wellman et al., 2003). For example, Rainie and Wellman (2012) describe a woman who was hospitalized after a fall and, through the efforts of her husband, received overwhelming support—both emotion and financial—from a diverse set of acquaintances and their acquaintances, both local and far away, some people whom the couple had never met.

"Jessica tells me you have a Twitter following in the six figures."

Cartoon 9.1 **"Jessica tells me you have a Twitter following in the six figures."** Twitter Followers as a Form of Social Capital.

Many Kickstarter campaigns operate on the same principle, where people seek to fund their projects through friends and friends of friends.

Social capital is a resource, but its activation can have distinct consequences in social life (Coleman, 1988). Social capital can entail obligations and expectations. For example, if you post on your friend's Facebook wall for her birthday, she will likely feel obligated to do the same on your birthday. Although we feel little, but some, reciprocal obligation with people we do not know (Cialdini, 1993), it is much stronger for those we know. Trust is another consequence of the norms and expectations that follow from social bonds. If you need to know whether a new dress looks good on you, texting a picture to your friend and soliciting her feedback might be more helpful than sending it out to the world for judgment. Your network of friends can, in itself, give people a reason to trust you because it provides evidence that others already trust you (Donath & boyd, 2004).

Social capital can also serve as an information channel. For example, if you happen on a new coffee shop that is a good study spot, you may convey that information to your friends with a status update (just don't tell too many people). By virtue of their social relationship with you, your friends now have more information about where to study than they did previously (Katz & Lazarsfeld, 1970). This function of social capital will be important when we return to considering word-of-mouth communication.

Last, social capital can be instrumental in enforcing social **norms**, or informal rules of collective agreement. When we have ties with people, we are affected by their judgments and feel pressure to act in accordance with their expectations. In many cases, this can be a good thing, but consider what happens when norms of our social network are not in our own best interest.

Social capital can be an individual resource, but it can also be a group resource, providing the basis for trust in a society. Since the foundational work on social capital, sociologists have used the number and depth of social connections as a measure of social cohesion. For example, in his book *Bowling Alone*, Robert Putnam (1995) argues that social capital has eroded in the United States, which he attributes in part to the "individualizing" effects of technology and Internet use. Networks of close offline friends are typically rather small, between five and six people (Wang & Wellman, 2010), but numbers change throughout one's life stage as well as historically over time. According to one study, the closeness of these relationships has diminished, with people reporting an average of about three close friendships in 1985, but only two close relationships in 2004. More troubling, the most common response to a 2004 question about strong ties was that respondents had no one with whom they could discuss important matters (McPherson, Smith-Lovin, & Brashears, 2006). Yet as Rainie and Wellman (2012) argue, dormant networks of acquaintances can actually be quite large. Because of shifts in communication technology and social life, rather than living in tight, geographically bound networks, people now exist as networked individuals, able to call on a large and diverse set of connections when they really need them.

The claims about the decline of social capital in the United States have been hotly debated (Norris, 2002; Paxton, 1999). Scholars using measures of social trust rather than membership in social organizations find that it is just as high in the United States as it has ever been (Norris, 2002). Further, social trust is correlated with newspaper readership and television ownership, tools that connect citizens with a broader imagined community (an idea to which we will return in Chapter 11). These debates about whether social capital is declining bring us to important refinements of different types of social capital and their effects on people's lives.

Types of Social Capital

There are at least two kinds of social capital: bridging and bonding. **Bridging social capital** is the value that friendship has to unite two different groups of people. The weak ties discussed earlier in the chapter have bridging capital. On the other hand, **bonding social capital** is the value a relationship might have to provide lasting and meaningful social support. Strong ties provide this kind of resource. Ellison et al. (2007) found that Facebook gives college students both bridging and bonding social capital, providing a sense of community and social trust among newfound peers at college as well as bridging ties with former high school networks. In a follow-up study, they found that using Facebook resulted in having more friends a year later and improvements in measures of psychological well-being, such as life satisfaction and self-esteem. Further, those who benefited the most were those who initially had low self-esteem (Steinfield, Ellison, & Lampe, 2008).

As we have seen in this chapter, although there are many good things about social networks, there can also be bad things. Through the enforcement of norms, social networks can inhibit or enable actions that may not be in one's self-interest or that of others. For example, in cases of cyberbullying, the fact that dense social connections exist—everyone knows everyone—can mean that rumors spread quickly and can make harassment seem inescapable (Alvarez, 2013).

Online versus Offline Social Networks

Throughout this chapter we have examined the role social networks play in organizing online worlds. But how do they relate to offline worlds? Although scholars used to think people would use online communication to primarily make new connections online (Rheingold, 1993), it turns out that online communication is more often used to strengthen and maintain existing offline social ties (Ellison et al., 2007). It is becoming more apparent that online and offline social worlds are deeply embedded in one another. Online interactions supplement existing social ties, and yet people still communicate more frequently with people who are physically nearby (Wellman, Haase, Witte, & Hampton, 2001). Offline ties are readily apparent by observing online data, and researchers were able to predict tie strength in offline social networks using data available only through Facebook based on the number and type of messages exchanged as well as indicators of homophily such as level of education (Gilbert & Karahalios, 2009). So, although scholars initially considered online social worlds to be different from offline social worlds, more recent research has started to view them as embedded. Sometimes we expand our offline social networks through online communication. For example, people may make new connections for the purpose of exploration, shared interests, emotional support regarding a stigmatized issue, or simply for fantasy and fun (Turkle, 1995/2011). However, we also strengthen and maintain offline social ties online. Some social networking sites like Match.com are developed specifically for meeting new friends, whereas others like Facebook are developed around strengthening existing social ties (Piskorski, 2014). Online communication, in fact, enables us to manage a large and diverse set of social ties, which can serve as a potential resource when we need social, emotional, or financial support (Rainie & Wellman, 2012).

SOCIAL NETWORKS IN PRACTICE

Diffusion of Innovations

Roles in the network play a critical role in the diffusion of a product or idea. For example, **market mavens** are actors who gather and disseminate marketplace information about prices, products, and consumption practices (Feick and Price, 1987). Some bloggers as well as YouTube reviewers who post "haul" videos showing off their new purchases are two examples of market mavens online. As journalists like Malcolm Gladwell have popularized, connectors, people who serve as hubs of human relationships, can be key conduits for the spread of trends (Gladwell, 2006; Granovetter, 1973). Because of their relationships with many different types of people, connectors make it possible for new information to flow through the network. However, although connectors clearly play an informational role, the *adoption* of a trend also depends on the participation of a critical number of people in your network (Granovetter, 1978).

Social networks play a critical part in the dissemination of information and influencing behavior. However, some scholars have countered this view of diffusion, arguing there are obvious and influential barriers to the viral spread of ideas such as laws, norms, and cultural understandings (Humphreys, 2010). For instance, in one of the foundational works of diffusion, Rogers (2010) shows how cultural ideas of hot and coldness impeded the adoption of boiling water in Peru. Although people were exposed to the idea of boiling water to prevent infection— an idea that could drastically decrease the risk of waterborne illness—this was not enough to ensure adoption. People could not just "catch" the idea like a cold. Rather, it needed to be made congruent with prior cultural norms and beliefs. So the process can be complex, and thus more about word-of-mouth communication will be covered in Chapter 12 on social media and culture.

Social Influence

Because people can occupy different places in the network, they have different amounts and types of **power**, or social influence (Castells, 2007). Market mavens, for example, collect a lot of marketplace information and thus have the ability to influence purchase decisions (Feick & Price, 1987). YouTube endorsers of makeup, for example, can influence what products viewers purchase, and those who become popular, many of them still in high school, receive products from luxury makeup brands like MAC and Bobby Brown. Similarly, fashion bloggers can develop devoted followings and thus also social influence when it comes to designers and brands. In some cases, popular fashion bloggers even "cross over" to the offline fashion industry, having developed the cultural capital to influence trends and styles (McQuarrie, Miller, & Phillips, 2013). We will return to some of these roles in the next chapter on virtual communities when we consider how people gain status in communities online.

SUMMARY AND CONCLUSION

As this chapter has illustrated, the way people are connected has important implications for social communication and influence online. Social networking sites like Facebook or LinkedIn can offer us maps of social relationships, but to put these to use, it helps to understand properties of nodes, ties, and networks as a whole. As it turns out, it may be a smaller world than we think. In the next chapter, we will go further to consider how persistent and repeated interaction between a group of people over time can create more permanent and meaningful social groups—communities—that can develop their own distinct set of norms, values, rituals, and traditions. As we will see, there is no richer world of variegated and intense interests than the world of online communities.

TOPICS

- Network properties (centrality, tie strength, directionality)
- Roles in networks (connector, gate keeper, bridge, hub, isolate)
- Strong versus weak ties
- Bridging versus bonding

DISCUSSION QUESTIONS

1. What kinds of power exist in a network? Are there different kinds of social influence according to different roles? What role does network structure play in who has power?
2. Do you think that social media increases or decreases social capital at a societal level? If so, what types of social capital are created?

EXERCISE

Create a network for your friend group. Then describe which nodes are connectors, bridges, liaisons, and isolates. What are the clusters and how dense are they? How centralized or decentralized is your network?

NOTES

1. There are exceptions. Leskovec et al. (2010) show that the exceptions are explained by status. For instance, if you like someone and your friend does not, it is likely that your friend has higher status than both you and the person in question.
2. Note, however, that there is some disagreement on exactly how social capital should be measured. The main disagreement centers around distinguishing social capital—one's social connections—from its consequences, such as social support and trust. See Appel et al. (2014).

FURTHER READINGS

Monge, Peter R., and Contractor, N. S. (2003), *Theories of communication networks*. New York: Oxford University Press.

Rainie, H., & Wellman, B. (2012). *Networked: The new social operating system*. Cambridge, MA: MIT Press.

REFERENCES

Alvarez, L. (2013, September 13). Girl's Suicide points to rise in apps used by cyberbullies. *New York Times.*

Appel, L., Dadlani, P., Dwyer, M., Hampton, K., Kitzie, V., Matni, Z. A., . . . Teodoro, R. (2014). Testing the validity of social capital measures in the study of information and communication technologies. *Information, Communication & Society, 17*(4), 398–416.

Backstrom, L. (2011). *Anatomy of Facebook*. Retrieved from http://www.facebook.com/note.php?note_id=10150388519243859/.

Barabási, A.-L. (2014). *Linked: How everything is connected to everything else and what it means for business, science, and everyday life*. New York: Basic Books.

Benkler, Y. (2006). *The wealth of networks: How social production transforms markets and freedom*. New Haven, CT: Yale University Press.

Bourdieu, Pierre (1985), "Forms of Capital," In Biggart, N. W. (Ed.). (2008). *Readings in economic sociology* (Vol. 4). John Wiley & Sons. 280–291.

boyd, d., Golder, S., & Lotan, G. (2010). *Tweet, tweet, retweet: Conversational aspects of retweeting on twitter*. Paper presented at the 2010 43rd Hawaii International Conference on System Sciences (HICSS).

Burt, R. S. (2001). Structural holes versus network closure as social capital. *Social Capital: Theory and Research*, 31–56.

Castells, M. (2007). Communication, power and counter-power in the network society. *International Journal of Communication, 1*(1), 29.

Cialdini, R. B. (1993). *Influence (rev): The psychology of persuasion*. New York: HarperCollins.

Coleman, J. S. (1988). Social capital in the creation of human capital. *American Journal of Sociology*, S95–S120.

Donath, J., & boyd, d. (2004). Public displays of connection. *BT Technology Journal, 22*(4), 71–82.

Ellison, N. B., Steinfield, C., & Lampe, C. (2007). The benefits of Facebook "friends:" Social capital and college students' use of online social network sites. *Journal of Computer-Mediated Communication, 12*(4), 1143–1168.

Feick, L. F., & Price, L. L. (1987). The market maven: A diffuser of marketplace information. *The Journal of Marketing*, 83–97.

Gilbert, E., & Karahalios, K. (2009). *Predicting tie strength with social media.* Paper presented at the Proceedings of the SIGCHI Conference on Human Factors in Computing Systems.

Gladwell, M. (2006). *The tipping point: How little things can make a big difference.* New York: Hachette Digital.

Granovetter, M. (1973). The strength of weak ties. *American Journal of Sociology*, 1360–1380.

Granovetter, M. (1978). Threshold models of collective behavior. *American Journal of Sociology, 83*(6), 1420–1443. doi:10.2307/2778111

Humphreys, A. (2010). Megamarketing: The creation of markets as a social process. *Journal of Marketing, 74*(2), 1–19.

Katz, E., & Lazarsfeld, P. F. (1970). *Personal influence, the part played by people in the flow of mass communications.* New Brunswick, NJ: Transaction.

Leskovec, J., Huttenlocher, D., & Kleinberg, J. (2010, April). *Predicting positive and negative links in online social networks.* Paper presented at the Proceedings of the 19th International Conference on World Wide Web.

Lin, N. (1988). "Social Resources and Social Mobility: A Structural Theory of Status Attainment." In Social Mobility and Social Structure, edited by Ronald Breiger. Cambridge: Cambridge University Press.

McKelvey, B. (1997). Perspective-quasi-natural organization science. *Organization Science, 8*(4), 351–380.

McPherson, M., Smith-Lovin, L., & Brashears, M. E. (2006). Social isolation in America: Changes in core discussion networks over two decades. *American Sociological Review, 71*(3), 353–375.

McQuarrie, E. F., Miller, J., & Phillips, B. J. (2013). The megaphone effect: Taste and audience in fashion blogging. *Journal of Consumer Research, 40*(1), 136–158.

Monge, P. R., & Contractor, N. S. (2003). *Theories of communication networks.* New York: Oxford University Press.

Muller, C., & Mueller, A. S. (2013). The embeddedness of adolescent friendship nominations: The formation of social capital in emergent network structures. *American Journal of Sociology, 119*(1), 216–253.

Norris, P. (2002). Social capital and the news media. *The Harvard International Journal of Press/Politics, 7*(1), 3–8.

Papacharissi, Z. (2009). The virtual geographies of social networks: A comparative analysis of Facebook, LinkedIn and ASmallWorld. *New Media & Society*, *11*(1–2), 199–220.

Paxton, P. (1999). Is social capital declining in the United States? A multiple indicator assessment. *American Journal of Sociology*, *105*(1), 88–127.

Pew Research (2006). The strength of Internet ties. *Pew Internet & American Life Project report*. Horrigan, J., Boase, J., Rainie, L., & Wellman, B. http://www.pewinternet.org/2006/01/25/the-strength-of-internet-ties/

Pew Research (2011). Pew internet & american life project. *Americans and Text Messaging*. http://www.pewinternet.org/2011/09/19/americans-and-text-messaging/

Pew Research (2015). Pew internet & american life project . U.S. Smartphone Use in 2015 http://www.pewinternet.org/2015/04/01/us-smartphone-use-in-2015/

Piskorski, M. J. (2014). *A social strategy: How we profit from social media*. Princeton, NJ: Princeton University Press.

Putnam, R. D. (1995). Bowling alone: America's declining social capital. *Journal of Democracy*, *6*(1), 65–78.

Rainie, H., & Wellman, B. (2012). *Networked: The new social operating system*. Cambridge, MA: MIT Press.

Rheingold, H. (1993). *The virtual community: Homesteading on the electronic frontier*. New York: Basic Books.

Rogers, E. M. (2010). *Diffusion of innovations*. New York: Simon & Schuster.

Steinfield, C., Ellison, N. B., & Lampe, C. (2008). Social capital, self-esteem, and use of online social network sites: A longitudinal analysis. *Journal of Applied Developmental Psychology*, *29*(6), 434–445.

Turkle, S. (1995/2011). *Life on the screen*. New York: Simon & Schuster.

Wang, H., & Wellman, B. (2010). Social connectivity in America: Changes in adult friendship network size from 2002 to 2007. *American Behavioral Scientist*, *53*(8), 1148–1169.

Wasserman, S., Faust, & Faust, K. (1994). *Social network analysis: Methods and applications*. New York: Cambridge University Press.

Watts, D. J. (1999). Networks, dynamics, and the small-world phenomenon 1. *American Journal of Sociology*, *105*(2), 493–527.

Weber, M. S., & Monge, P. (2011). The flow of digital news in a network of sources, authorities, and hubs. *Journal of Communication*, *61*(6), 1062–1081.

Wellman, B., Haase, A. Q., Witte, J., & Hampton, K. (2001). Does the Internet increase, decrease, or supplement social capital? Social networks, participation, and community commitment. *American Behavioral Scientist*, *45*(3), 436–455.

Wellman, B., Quan-Haase, A., Boase, J., Chen, W., Hampton, K., Díaz, I., & Miyata, K. (2003). The social affordances of the Internet for networked individualism. *Journal of Computer-Mediated Communication*, *8*(3).

Wimmer, A., & Lewis, K. (2010). Beyond and below racial homophily: ERG models of a friendship network documented on Facebook. *American Journal of Sociology*, *116*(2), 583–642.

CHAPTER 10

—

Virtual Communities

Jeff loves basketball. But not just any team—one team in particular: Duke University. When he went to college there, Jeff might have gone to a game or two, but did not spend much time thinking about the team. Now that he has graduated and has a job, he wants to keep up with Duke basketball. To do this, he logs on to Rivals.com. He joined about a year ago and was amazed to find people sharing lots of information about the team—who the new recruits were, rumors about the coaches' salaries, and words to the fan chants for the upcoming Carolina game. It was a gold mine! These were his people! About six months—and several thousand posts—into his immersion, Jeff decides to pay the site to get privileged information, or "premium" access. All of his virtual friends on the site have access, and Jeff does not want to be left out. This "inner circle" has norms and rituals like parodying the coach from Duke's rival team and posting animated GIFs of Duke's greatest triumphs. Although Jeff lives far away, he decides he wants to go to a real live game against Duke's rival, University of North Carolina. But he checks StubHub only to find the tickets to be outrageously expensive. Dismayed, he goes on the message board to figure out what to do. Minutes later, a fellow member of the community, a season ticket holder with whom Jeff often jokes, offers him tickets at face value for being "one of us."

Chapter 10 discusses online or virtual communities,[1] the creation and maintenance of social groups online. Online communities have been one of the most

Photo 10.1 The Cameron Crazies at Duke University.

prolific areas of research in social media. In this chapter we will cover traits of online communities and come to understand the role that online communities play in people's lives. From foundational theories of community, we can understand practices of online communities today. We will then move to considering the different kinds of online communities and the different roles that exist within these sometimes tight-knit groups.

TRAITS OF COMMUNITY

What is the difference between a network and a community? Communities are not just groups of people. They share particular, identifiable social traits, indicators of bonds that go deeper than mere acquaintance or co-presence. The sociologist Emile Durkheim was one of the first thinkers to enumerate these traits and explain how they created a social grouping that was larger than the sum of its parts. For Durkheim, a feeling of collective identity was the hallmark of community. As Howard Rheingold (1993), one of the first to study virtual communities says, "Virtual communities are social aggregations that emerge from the Net when enough people carry on those public discussions long enough, with sufficient human feeling, to form webs of personal relationships in cyberspace" (p. 5). A sense of common identification and affiliation simply emerges from repeated communication with others over a span of time (Collins, 2004).

Think of the last time you went to a sporting event or a concert. Likely as the crowd clapped or cheered together, a sense of cohesion was created. Whereas previously there were a lot of people just sitting or standing in an arena, after a cheer they become a cohesive group who are perceived to act as one. In fact, our language for talking about these events mirrors this feeling: we say, "The crowd did this," or "The crowd did that." This sense of a mass of people acting as one entity is a concept called **deindividuation**. On message boards, massive multiplayer games, and blogging communities, the belief that "everyone loved that" or "everyone hated that" can form through the patter of interactions, producing the feeling that subsumes individual identity in that of the group (Blanchard, 2004). Online media that allow synchronous, or near synchronous, communication can create this sense of unity as people experience events collectively. For example, through instantaneous sharing of news information, Twitter may create a collective sense of experiencing historical events (Thorson et al., 2013). Then again, bonds can also form over long periods of asynchronous communication through message boards, listservs, or blog commenting.

However, deindividuation can also have a downside. Just as this feeling of unity can create risky behaviors in offline crowds, it can also cause people to say and do things they otherwise would not. This phenomenon occurs because of **diffusion of responsibility**; when people do things in groups, each individual feels less responsible for the outcome. For example, an email request for help sent to one person garners more responses than when it is sent to multiple people (Barron & Yechiam, 2002). Scholars thus find evidence for the bystander effect online. In one study, the more people who were in a chat group, the longer it took someone to receive help from the group (Markey, 2000). Further, as we discussed in Chapter 6, anonymity online can also lead to a lack of accountability, with some nasty results.

Online communities have coalesced around just about any interest you can imagine. From soap operas (Baym, 1995), to car tuning (Frey & Lüthje, 2011), to sports fandom, to politics, people come together and form social bonds around the things they love. Unlike offline communities, people tend to join virtual communities voluntarily because of their interest or a common goal (Blanchard, 2008). As Henry Jenkins says, "[T]hese new communities are defined through voluntary, temporary and tactical affiliations, are reaffirmed through common intellectual enterprises and emotional investments and are held together through the mutual production and reciprocal exchange of knowledge" (Jenkins, 2004, p. 35). Further, although you might belong to only one or two geographical communities (i.e., your neighborhood or city), you can belong to many online communities. The entry and exit costs of online community membership are usually somewhat lower than those of membership offline (Norris, 2004). It would probably be costly to up and leave your neighborhood, but it is relatively easy to switch message boards or listservs. Despite these differences, strong social bonds can develop among those who communicate online. Although virtual communities can revolve around different interests and intellectual projects, as social groups, we generally understand them as having three traits (Muniz & O'Guinn, 2001).

The first trait of community is *consciousness of kind* (Gusfield, 1975). Consciousness of kind is a sense of belonging, of mutual recognition between group members that they are part of a collectivity. Language is one critical way that people signify belonging online. Online groups will develop specialized vernaculars, intentional misspellings, and abbreviations for commonly used words (Androutsopoulos, 2006; Crystal, 2001). For example, members of the 4chan community often use coded terms like lulz or kkthnxby to show in-group membership (Bernstein et al., 2011; Coleman, 2014). Building a recognizable identity is another key part of building the affective ties necessary for a social bond (Blanchard, 2008; Obst, Zinkiewicz, & Smith, 2002). However, in some cases individual identity can compete with group identity (Postmes, Spears, & Lea, 1998). For example, when message board posters begin to think of themselves as distinct from others on the board, they will correspondingly begin to view themselves as less a part of the group, which mitigates the effects of deindividuation (Postmes et al 1998).

The second trait of community is *shared rituals and traditions*. A **ritual** is an action or series of actions, usually performed collectively, that has meaning for the actor or the group. Doing things together, especially when people are copresent at the same time, can create a sense of what Durkheim calls "collective effervescence" (Collins, 2004). Online community life is suffused with rituals and traditions. For instance, watching television while using Twitter, or "livetweeting" an event, can create a sense of collective effervescence with other fans of a show. During the 2008 presidential debates, a sense of collectivity formed as people commented on and selected portions of the debate for extended comments (Vraga et al., 2014). On sites like Yik Yak, people can get this sense of collective effervescence by posting about the events or realities occurring in their offline communities. For example, on many college campuses, students will post about campus events like football games, parties, or weather, providing running commentary on offline events (Rozsa, 2015).

The third trait of community is a sense of *moral responsibility*, or duty to other members of the community. The social bonds created by a community instill not just a sense of collectiveness, but also a sense of responsibility to other members. If a community member is wronged, other members of the community may rush to that person's defense. In online games like *World of Warcraft*, for example, users defend one another's honor, and clan members will seek revenge for an attack on another clan member (Nardi & Harris, 2006). This phenomenon can be seen in many online communities when trolling occurs (Shachaf & Hara, 2010). Outsiders will seek to wreak havoc on the discussion thread of a community, but participants often bond together in coordinated action against outsiders. Participants' sense of norms will thus cause them to identify more strongly with the community (Blanchard, 2008).

Certain norms may guide these feelings of obligation in online communities. For example, the norm of **reciprocity** is a common obligation felt in online communities. If a member takes something from the community, he or she will feel obligated to give back in some way. **Generalized reciprocity** is when people contribute to the group without any particular expectation of immediate payback (Giesler, 2006; Mathwick, Wiertz, & De Ruyter, 2008). Rather, they contribute something to the community with the expectation that they will use the group's resources in the future or the consciousness that they have used them in the past. For instance, in a study of online file sharing, group members were exiled from the community, or "banned," if they did not reciprocate by sharing (uploading) files (Geisler, 2006). Usually, however, reciprocation is internally motivated, rather than coerced (Mathwick et al., 2008; see also Ostrom, 1990). In fact, the act of reciprocating itself reinforces a sense of membership. **Social exchange theory** explains that the exchange of goods or services over time will lead to the development of social ties (Emerson, 1976).

As we have discussed in this section, communities tend to have three properties: consciousness of kind, rituals and traditions, and moral responsibility. Consider how Rivals.com, the community of fans obsessed with college sports recruiting, exhibits these three properties. Members meet regularly online to discuss top prospects, trade rumors about ongoing recruiting efforts, and evaluate rivals. As we saw in the opening vignette, the obligation to other community members resulted in Jeff getting face value tickets for being "one of us," a true fan. Although all communities share these three properties, they also vary in kind. The next section will investigate the many species of online community and introduce some concepts for understanding these varied groups.

THEORETICAL APPROACHES TO COMMUNITY
AND TYPES OF ONLINE COMMUNITY

The concept of community was created to understand the social bonds between people who live or work together, but mass and social media have changed the way we think about how people form connections over long distances (Rainie & Wellman, 2012). Many different theories and concepts can be useful for thinking about online communities, and some may be more appropriate than others for particular *types* of communities.

Because online communities tend to group around lifestyles and interests, there are as many different communities as there are hobbies, television shows, subcultures, interests, and orientations. Previous research has tended to group online communities into two broad types—those that relate to an interest, hobby, or professional activity and those that relate to health or emotional support (Ridings & Gefen, 2004). Generally, this is because these two types of communities cater to distinctly different needs and motivations. People who participate in communities related to a particular interest or hobby tend to be driven by the motivation to share information and are therefore task oriented (Blanchard & Markus, 2004), whereas those who participate in communities such as health groups like dieting, smoking, mental illness, or cancer seek social and emotional support, not just information (Ridings & Gefen, 2004). Of course, these behaviors can also overlap—with interest-based groups crossing over to provide some support and support groups offering information—but the primary drivers of these groups tend to be distinct.

There are many different kinds of communities, and scholars have had different ways of describing these different types of groups. In this section we will cover different types of online communities, but guided by previous theoretical conceptualizations of community.

Imagined Community

Benedict Anderson coined the term **imagined community** to describe the way in which media such as newspapers create a sense of belonging to one nation or one community (Anderson, 1991). By reading the same headlines, discussing the same issues, and feeling affected by the same occurrences, all conveyed through media, a group of people can come to identify as part of the same group although they may be hundreds or thousands of miles apart and live in different circumstances. For example, although Twitter is designed for one-to-many communication and asymmetric linking (i.e., I can follow you, but you do not need to follow me), imagined communities nevertheless form through the use of shared linguistic conventions, consciousness of having simultaneous experience, and a collective recognition of those with "high" status (Gruzd, Wellman, & Takhteyev., 2011). Yet although the concept of imagined community was initially developed to understand the effect of one-to-many communication in a community through newspapers, social media provides its own twist by enabling community formation through many-to-many or networked inter-actions as well (Jenkins, 2014).

Subcultures

In some cases, online communities may be an expression of—and further impe-tus to—existing offline subcultures. Originally used to understand countercul-tural groups like punks (Hebdige, 1995), a **subculture** is a smaller grouping within a culture that shares particular norms, values, and practices that may run counter to the dominant culture. For example, the straight-edge punk subcul-ture, which initially existed through close face-to-face interactions at concerts as well as through DIY (or "do it yourself") publications like zines grew to have rich virtual communities as well. Whereas members who were more involved in the face-to-face community used virtual channels for information, those without the access or desire to participate face-to-face considered the virtual community a "space" in which they could socialize with others in the subculture (Williams, 2006). Many subcultures form a vibrant and mutually supportive community online, one that unites them with like-minded others and can reinforce offline interactions. For example, Comic-con and other offline events unite offline and online communities of so-called fan or geek culture (Jenkins, 1992/2012).

Audience Communities

Fan subcultures can be understood as a distinct type of online community, and many originated from previously existing audience communities. An **audience community** is a social group that forms around a particular media product such as a movie (e.g. *Star Wars*), television show (e.g. *Mad Men*), or book (e.g. *Harry Potter*). As an interpretive community, the group may discuss the text, developing its own unique interpretations that are informed by their particular backgrounds and identities (Fish, 1980). Such activities can range from puzzling out plot twists to disagreeing about characters' motivations to more metadiscursive conversa-tions about what the writers should do next. For instance, in the mid-1990s many Usenet message boards developed around television shows such as soap operas. In these groups, community members not only exchanged show updates and in-terpretations of plotlines, but also talked about wide-ranging issues in their lives, exchanging social support as well as information (Baym, 1999). More recently, the audience community for *America's Next Top Model* played a pivotal role in the life of the show. As an audience community, members of the group began to de-velop interpretations that questioned certain contestants, rules, season arcs, and even the show's host, Tyra Banks. Such discussions took on a life of their own, ulti-mately leading to a decline in viewership and fandom (Parmentier & Fischer, 2015). In this way, fans, together with technological platforms and show elements, formed an assemblage, or network of connected actors (DeLanda, 2006), that eventually dissolved over time because of narrative and group dynamics.

Some fan groups focus more squarely around sharing information and col-laborating on projects. For instance, the *Survivor* spoiler community takes information gathering to extremes through distributed work groups developed to investigate and reveal the winner of the show *Survivor* before the show airs. By developing connections with sources such as travel agents and using Google Earth, these groups take extreme measures to collectively investigate the final winner (Jenkins, 2006).

Fan fiction is often a product of many audience communities. Although fan communities predate the Internet, virtual communities provide a way for fans to create and share texts featuring characters from mass media products. In this way, audience communities can actually begin to produce, not just consume, cultural artifacts, a process to which we will return in Chapter 12.

Gaming communities are another kind of audience community, albeit one where fans actively play out the text while forming community. Gaming communities like *League of Legends* and *Little Big Planet* develop rich subcultures whose players form friendships, alliances, enemies, and factions (Kou & Nardi, 2014; Westecott, 2011). The cooperative and competitive elements of these groups often heighten or make explicit community ties that might be more obscure in other types of communities. Gaming communities thus combine elements of audience communities and our next type, communities of practice, in that they interpret texts, but also work together to accomplish a task.

Communities of Practice

Another type of online community used to understand group behavior, is a community of practice. A **community of practice** is a group that is "informally bound together by shared expertise and passion for a joint enterprise" (Wenger, 2000). For instance, after Apple discontinued production of an early personal digital assistant, the Newton, a community of users gathered together to produce software and bug fixes and provide technical support for a product disowned by the company that produced it (Muniz & Schau, 2005).

Communities of practice can form around leisure or professional endeavors. For instance, one of the largest lighting companies in the world, OSRAM, regularly runs design competitions to see who can design the best, most innovative

Photo 10.2 The Tribe has Spoken.

light. Through a voting process, other members vote on the designs until one is chosen and put into production (Hutter, Hautz, Füller, Mueller, & Matzler, 2011). Dell Computers created a platform for a group of software experts who trouble-shoot new products and offer fixes. Wikipedia, of course, is one of the largest communities of practice, with 31,000 people who are actively engaged in produc-ing and editing content on the English version (Simonite, 2013). As these exam-ples illustrate, online communities are often a site for co-creation or collaborative production. Members will come together to share knowledge and may perhaps self-organize to create objects of value such as computer software (Hemetsberger & Reinhardt, 2009), outdoor equipment (Füller, Bartl, Ernst, & Mühlbacher, 2006), or any other number of innovations. In Chapter 14 about economic life, we will return to the legal and property structures that these activities can challenge.

STATUS AND ROLES IN ONLINE COMMUNITIES

Theories of community will often stress the positive aspects of social belonging—help during hardship and emotional well-being from sociability—but there are also dynamics in a community that create a sense of difference even within the collective. Status, the relative and socially constructed position of someone within a social grouping (Weber, 1946/2009), is one such issue. Generally, mem-bers in a virtual community build status through length of time spent being active in the community (Mathwick et al., 2008), and even those who come in with a good deal of knowledge are suspect until proven trustworthy. For instance, in the *Survivor* spoiler community—the group dedicated to learning the winner of the show *Survivor* before the show aired—a newcomer to the group with a great deal of information was vetted extensively, a process that took almost the entire season (when, after all, his knowledge was proven roughly accurate by the airing of show itself) (Jenkins, 2006). On reddit, users gain status through "karma" points awarded through up or down votes by other users in response to a post or submission (Backstrom, 2011). A user's karma then comes to reflect his or her status or reputation within the community.

Sometimes status can have systems of formal recognition. For example, an online community of graphic design software enthusiasts has an annual contest to "name that font," and the winner receives the title of Johann (for Johann Guttenberg) for the year (Mathwick et al., 2008). On Wikipedia, status is for-mally recognized by being an admin, which grants the user a good deal of control over the content of pages and other users' abilities.

Communities such as Rivals.com go through a life cycle. Early on, they ac-quire new, involved members who contribute comments, but as time progresses some members "tune out," whereas others move up the hierarchy. Communities can also fission, as when an Internet message board for soap opera fans separated from the general television Usenet group and then further subdivided according to network (ABC, CBS, NBC) (Baym, 1999). It is also possible for one community to develop several subgroups that are encompassed within one broader community (Baym, 1999). Further, communities can die out altogether. For example, the assemblage we discussed for *America's Next Top Model* was disrupted and ultimately disbanded because of a move of the message board site, problematic interpretations of certain show elements, and the emergence of factions of fans who sabotaged the community (Parmentier & Fischer, 2015). For this reason, scholars have proposed methods for measuring the health of an online community (Preece, 2000). Measures of success might include obvious variables like the number of messages posted, the number of participants, and member satisfaction as well as less obvious measures like the degree of reciprocity, the percentage of on-topic messages, and trust among community members (Preece, 2000).

Status is one reason people participate in online communities, but there are many other, stronger motivations as well. For instance, a study of Wikipedia contributors finds that ideological motivators and a sense of intrinsic satisfaction are the primary motivations for contributing (Nov, 2007). However, motivations for being in an online community vary depending on the length of membership. Whereas information is more important motivator for newbies—or recent joiners—experienced members of online communities are more motivated by the social support the site offers (Mathwick et al., 2008).

Roles in Online Communities

Members in online communities develop **social roles**. A social role is a systemic pattern of behavior in interaction with others (Merton, 1968). For example, the social role of mothering might include caring for a child and purchasing things like food, clothing, and personal care items. In online communities, people will take different roles. As we have discussed, social hierarchies often develop in online communities according to length of affiliation and levels expertise, and "hardcore" members may emerge at the top of the hierarchy. However, there are many other roles. For instance, previous work has indicated that around 85% of all community members are relatively passive **lurkers**, who rarely contribute content in an online community (Bagozzi & Dholakia, 2002; Mathwick et al., 2008). The percentage of lurkers in a community varies greatly by community type. For example, in a support community, they make up 55% of users, whereas in software support communities, 82% are lurkers (Nonnecke & Preece, 2000). Lurkers can also come to feel like they are part of the community, although they do not actively participate (Baym, 1999).

Newbies are new members to the community. Sometimes ignored or flamed (Jacobson, 1999), newbies generally have the lowest status in an online community. Reputation through a history of previous posts is one critical way that people assess trust online (Ridings, Gefen, & Arinze, 2002). In the absence of other cues that might be present in offline communities such as the references of others, reputation comes to have outsized importance, such that anyone without a history in the community may be suspect. However, lack of cultural knowledge can also leave newbies at a disadvantage. Many online communities have norms for communicating and particular ways of signifying (Androutsopoulos, 2006).

The lack of this particular, contextual knowledge can leave newbies at a disadvantage until they become socialized into the culture of the group.

Roughly 15% of members regularly contribute content, and of those, about 3% are hardcore members who contribute a lot (Mathwick et al., 2008). Others in the community may be **information gatherers**, who bring new specialized knowledge to the group. For example, answer people are "individuals whose dominant behavior is to respond to questions posed by others" (Welser, Gleave, Fisher, & Smith, 2007). Welser et al. (2007) use network analysis to identify the place of answer people within the community. They tend to be tied to isolates and do not have many intense, reciprocal ties with other community members. Other than roles like newbies or hardcore members, which are based on status, there can be a number of other, more specific roles based on function. Those with high status or admin status might play a **gatekeeper** role, people charged with regulating spam and curating the content of a community. Others synthesize information, provoke discussion, or quell dissent as the peacemaker.

As we discussed in Chapter 6, anonymity online can lead to antisocial behavior. On 4chan, for example, anonymity enables users to engage in racist, sexist, and otherwise virulent behavior without fear of personally targeted backlash (Coleman, 2014; Phillips, 2012). In contrast, on platforms like Facebook or Twitter, users largely participate using their real names or pseudonyms that build a reputation through a history of posts and community membership. In Chapter 6, we discussed many of the effects that anonymity can have on individual behavior, but in the setting of online communities, anonymity can take on a new life that affects roles and role taking.

Usually reviled, **trolls** are users who attempt to disrupt the community in some way. These users are usually anonymous or have masked identities that cannot be tied to offline identities. Trolling entails "luring others into pointless and time-consuming discussions," (Herring, 2004), often involves identity deception (Donath, 1999), and is constituted by repetitive, argumentative behavior (Backstrom, 2011; Phillips, 2012; Shachaf & Hara, 2010). On Wikipedia, for instance, one study finds that trolling behavior acts as a kind of vandalism, as trolls create user names to delete or maliciously edit Wikipedia pages that constitute collective property (Shachaf & Hara, 2010). Further, trolls can work to undermine communication norms of the community itself and flame debate between high-status members (Dahlberg, 2001), and trolls view these reactions as validation. This type of deviant behavior online can disrupt community structure, leading to aggressive harassment of newbies, fission of the community, or attrition, as members go elsewhere. In response, many communities adopt the mantra "don't feed the trolls," meaning that if trolling behavior is ignored, the troll will grow bored and leave (Donath, 1999; Herring, 2004; Phillips, 2012). Yet scholars offer different theories for trolling behavior. Some view it as akin to tricksterism (Coleman, 2010) or role-play (Backstrom, 2011), whereas others frame it as antisocial behavior (Buckels, Trapnell, & Paulhus, 2014) or vandalism (Shachaf & Hara, 2010).

Photo 10.3 Trolls.

Studies have further documented the creation of multiple aliases in virtual communities. Often called **sock puppets**, alias identities may be created for a number of reasons. In one high-profile case, the chief executive officer of Whole Foods was discovered to have created a sock puppet to bash a rival grocery chain and defend himself against people who criticized his hair (Kesmodel & Wilke, 2007). Sock puppets have also been created to disseminate false information, such as their use in terrorist networks online (Fielding & Cobain, 2011). In more mundane community behavior, sock puppets can be created to voice points of view that one wants disconnected from an existing, reputable account. Since reputation, as we have discussed, is so important, high-status members have an incentive to create aliases to express provocative or problematic points of view within the community.

Group Boundaries

Generally, group boundaries are more porous in online communities than they are in physical communities (Blanchard, 2008). However, because belonging is not only indicated through longevity, but also signaled through language and knowledge, boundaries are often not completely open. This kind of knowledge

Photo 10.4 Sockpuppets.

forms a kind of cultural capital or literacy as discussed in Chapter 7. Group boundaries may be maintained by social consensus about what constitutes "legitimate" membership or by setting expectations for knowledge, norms of behavior, or linguistic codes. Potential group members must overcome these boundaries if they want to be included. Spam is another way to see how an online community reacts to outsiders or interlopers and maintains its boundaries. That is, to gain the rights to promote something, one must earn them through longevity and participation in the community.

SUMMARY AND CONCLUSION

In conclusion, we see that the formation of meaningful social connections online is not the exception; it is more generally the rule. This chapter has discussed the traits of online communities and introduced some theoretical tools for looking at the how online communities become embedded in people's lives and interests. Through an examination of status, we have learned about the formation of roles within online communities. In the next chapter we will further explore the ways in which these groups, and the high-status member types within them, can be the targets of marketing efforts by both companies and nonprofit organizations.

TOPICS

- Community traits, definition
- Community hierarchy
- Deindividuation
- Diffusion of responsibility
- Ritual
- Reciprocity and generalized reciprocity
- Social exchange theory
- Subculture
- Imagined community
- Audience community
- Community of practice
- Status
- Lurkers, hardcore users, newbies
- Trolls, sock puppets

DISCUSSION QUESTIONS

1. What is the difference, if any, between a network and a community?
2. How is status conveyed in an online community? Can this differ by genre, and if so, how?

3. What are some potential differences between audience communities and communities of practice? Give an example and describe the differences in social practices and goals.

EXERCISE

Pick an online community and conduct a netnographic study (see Chapter 4 for details on the method). Collect detailed data on its three traits of community and conduct an analysis of status, if it exists. What roles are there in the community, and if you participate, which role do you play?

NOTES

1. Here I will refer to virtual communities and online communities interchangeably. Some scholars prefer the term online community to virtual community because the word virtual implies that the social grouping is not "real," when in fact much of the research has shown that indeed people do form meaningful group affiliations online and that online and offline communities can overlap.

FURTHER READINGS

Jenkins, H. (2006). *Convergence culture: Where old and new media collide*. New York: New York University Press.

Rheingold, H. (1993). *The virtual community: Homesteading on the electronic frontier*. Cambridge, MA: MIT Press.

REFERENCES

Anderson, B. (1991). *Imagined communities: Reflections on the origin and spread of nationalism* (new ed.). New York: Verso.

Androutsopoulos, J. (2006). Introduction: Sociolinguistics and computer-mediated communication. *Journal of Sociolinguistics, 10*(4), 419–438.

Backstrom, L. (2011). *Anatomy of Facebook*. Retrieved from http://www.facebook.com/note.php?note_id=10150388519243859/.

Bagozzi, R. P., & Dholakia, U. M. (2002). Intentional social action in virtual communities. *Journal of Interactive Marketing, 16*(2), 2–21.

Barron, G., & Yechiam, E. (2002). Private e-mail requests and the diffusion of responsibility. *Computers in Human Behavior, 18*(5), 507–520.

Baym, N. K. (1995). The performance of humor in computer-mediated communication. *Journal of Computer-Mediated Communication, 1*(2).

Baym, N. K. (1999). *Tune in, log on: Soaps, fandom, and online community* (Vol. 3). Thousand Oaks, CA: Sage.

Bernstein, M. S., Monroy-Hernández, A., Harry, D., André, P., Panovich, K., & Vargas, G. G. (2011). *4chan and/b/: An Analysis of anonymity and ephemerality in a large online community.* Paper presented at the International Conference on Weblogs and Social Media. Barcelona, Spain.

Blanchard, A. (2004). Virtual behavior settings: An application of behavior setting theories to virtual communities. *Journal of Computer-Mediated Communication, 9*(2).

Blanchard, A. L. (2008). Testing a model of sense of virtual community. *Computers in Human Behavior, 24*(5), 2107–2123.

Blanchard, A. L., & Markus, M. L. (2004). The experienced sense of a virtual community: Characteristics and processes. *ACM Sigmis Database, 35*(1), 64–79.

Buckels, E. E., Trapnell, P. D., & Paulhus, D. L. (2014). Trolls just want to have fun. *Personality and Individual Differences, 67,* 97–102.

Coleman, G. (2010). Hacker and troller as trickster. *Social Text.*

Coleman, G. (2014). *Hacker, hoaxer, whistleblower, spy: The many faces of anonymous.* New York: Verso.

Collins, R. (2004). *Interaction ritual chains.* Princeton, NJ: Princeton University Press.

Crystal, D. (2001). *Language and the Internet.* Cambridge, UK: Cambridge University Press.

Dahlberg, L. (2001). Computer-mediated communication and the public sphere: A critical analysis. *Journal of Computer-Mediated Communication, 7*(1).

DeLanda, M. (2006). *A new philosophy of society: Assemblage theory and social complexity.* London: A&C Black.

Donath, J. S. (1999). Identity and deception in the virtual community. *Communities in Cyberspace, 1996,* 29–59.

Emerson, R. M. (1976). Social exchange theory. *Annual Review of Sociology, 2,* 335–362.

Fielding, N., & Cobain, I. (2011). Revealed: US spy operation that manipulates social media. *The Guardian, 17.*

Fish, S. (1980). *Is there a text in this class?: The authority of interpretive communitites.* Cambridge, MA: Harvard University Press.

Frey, K., & Lüthje, C. (2011). Antecedents and consequences of interaction quality in virtual end-user communities. *Creativity and Innovation Management, 20*(1), 22–35.

Füller, J., Bartl, M., Ernst, H., & Mühlbacher, H. (2006). Community based innovation: How to integrate members of virtual communities into new product development. *Electronic Commerce Research, 6*(1), 57–73.

Giesler, M. (2006). Consumer gift systems. *Journal of Consumer Research, 33*(2), 283–290.

Gruzd, A., Wellman, B., & Takhteyev, Y. (2011). Imagining Twitter as an imagined community. *American Behavioral Scientist, 55*(10), 1294–1318.

Gusfield, J. R. (1975). *Community: A critical response.* New York: Harper & Row.

Hebdige, D. (1995). Subculture: The meaning of style. *Critical Quarterly, 37*(2), 120–124.

Hemetsberger, A., & Reinhardt, C. (2009). Collective development in open-source communities: An activity theoretical perspective on successful online collaboration. *Organization Studies, 30*(9), 987–1008.

Herring, S. C. (2004). Slouching toward the ordinary: Current trends in computer-mediated communication. *New Media and Society, 6*, 26–36.

Hutter, K., Hautz, J., Füller, J., Mueller, J., & Matzler, K. (2011). Communitition: The tension between competition and collaboration in community-based design contests. *Creativity and Innovation Management, 20*(1), 3–21.

Jacobson, D. (1999). Impression formation in cyberspace: Online expectations and offline experiences in text-based virtual communities. *Journal of Computer-Mediated Communication, 5*(1).

Jenkins, H. (1992/2012). *Textual poachers: Television fans and participatory culture.* New York: Routledge.

Jenkins, H. (2004). The cultural logic of media convergence. *International Journal of Cultural Studies, 7*(1), 33–43.

Jenkins, H. (2006). *Convergence culture: Where old and new media collide.* New York: New York University Press.

Jenkins, H. (2014). Rethinking 'rethinking convergence/culture'. *Cultural Studies, 28*(2), 267–297.

Kesmodel, D., & Wilke, J. R. (2007). Whole Foods is hot, Wild Oats a dud—So said "Rahodeb." Then again, Yahoo poster was a Whole Foods staffer. The CEO to be precise. *Wall Street Journal,* (July 12), A1.

Kou, Y., & Nardi, B. (2014). Governance in *League of Legends*: A hybrid system. In Proceedings of the 9th International Conference on the Foundations of Digital Games, Fort Lauderdale, FL.

Markey, P. M. (2000). Bystander intervention in computer-mediated communication. *Computers in Human Behavior, 16*(2), 183–188.

Mathwick, C., Wiertz, C., & De Ruyter, K. (2008). Social capital production in a virtual P3 community. *Journal of Consumer Research, 34*(6), 832–849.

Merton, R. K. (1968). *Social theory and social structure.* New York: Simon & Schuster.

Muniz, A. M. Jr., & O'Guinn, T. C. (2001). Brand community. *Journal of Consumer Research, 27*(4), 412–432.

Muniz, A. M. Jr., & Schau, H. J. (2005). Religiosity in the abandoned Apple Newton brand community. *Journal of Consumer Research, 31*(4), 737–747.

Nardi, B., & Harris, J. (2006). *Strangers and friends: Collaborative play in World of Warcraft.* Paper presented at the Proceedings of the 2006 20th Anniversary Conference on Computer Supported Cooperative Work. Banff, Alberta, Canada.

Nonnecke, B., & Preece, J. (2000). *Lurker demographics: Counting the silent.* Paper presented at the Proceedings of the SIGCHI Conference on Human Factors in Computing Systems. The Hague, Netherlands.

Norris, P. (2004). *The bridging and bonding role of online communities*: Thousand Oaks, CA: Sage.

Nov, O. (2007). What motivates Wikipedians? *Communications of the ACM, 50*(11), 60–64. doi:10.1145/1297797.1297798.

Obst, P., Zinkiewicz, L., & Smith, S. G. (2002). Sense of community in science fiction fandom, Part 1: Understanding sense of community in an international community of interest. *Journal of Community Psychology, 30*(1), 87–103.

Ostrom, E. (1990). *Governing the commons: The evolution of institutions for collective action*. New York: Cambridge University Press.

Parmentier, M.-A., & Fischer, E. (2015). Things fall apart: The dynamics of brand audience dissipation. *Journal of Consumer Research, 41*(5), 1228–1251.

Phillips, W. (2012). *This is why we can't have nice things: The origins, evolution and cultural embeddedness of online trolling*. Doctoral Dissertation. University of Oregon.

Postmes, T., Spears, R., & Lea, M. (1998). Breaching or building social boundaries? SIDE-effects of computer-mediated communication. *Communication Research, 25*(6), 689–715.

Preece, J. (2000). *Online communities: Designing usability and supporting socialbilty*. New York: Wiley.

Rainie, H., & Wellman, B. (2012). *Networked: The new social operating system*. Cambridge, MA: MIT Press.

Rheingold, H. (1993). *The virtual community: Homesteading on the electronic frontier*. New York: Basic Books.

Ridings, C. M., & Gefen, D. (2004). Virtual community attraction: Why people hang out online. *Journal of Computer-Mediated Communication, 10*(1).

Ridings, C. M., Gefen, D., & Arinze, B. (2002). Some antecedents and effects of trust in virtual communities. *The Journal of Strategic Information Systems, 11*(3), 271–295.

Rozsa, L. (2015, January 11). Spying on college life, via Yik Yak, Motherlode. *The New York Times.* Retrieved from http://parenting.blogs.nytimes.com/2015/01/11/spying-on-college-life-via-yik-yak/?_r=0/.

Shachaf, P., & Hara, N. (2010). Beyond vandalism: Wikipedia trolls. *Journal of Information Science, 36*(3), 357–370.

Simonite, T. (2013, October 22). The decline of Wikipedia. *MIT Technology Review.*

Thorson, K., Driscoll, K., Ekdale, B., Edgerly, S., Thompson, L. G., Schrock, A., . . . Wells, C. (2013). YouTube, Twitter and the Occupy movement: Connecting content and circulation practices. *Information, Communication & Society, 16*(3), 421–451.

Vraga, E. K., Bode, L., Yang, J., Edgerly, S., Thorson, K., Wells, C., & Shah, D. V. (2014). Political influence across generations: Partisanship and candidate evaluations in the 2008 election. *Information, Communication & Society, 17*(2), 184–202.

Weber, M. (1946/2009). Class, status, party. In Mills, H. H. G. a. C. W. (ed.), *From Max Weber: Essays in sociology* (pp. 180–181). Milton Park, Abingdon, Oxon, and New York: Routledge.

Welser, H. T., Gleave, E., Fisher, D., & Smith, M. (2007). Visualizing the signatures of social roles in online discussion groups. *Journal of Social Structure, 8*(2), 1–32.

Wenger, E. (2000). Communities of practice and social learning systems. *Organization, 7*(2), 225–246.

Westecott, E. (2011). Crafting play: Little Big Planet. *Loading . . . 5*(8).

Williams, J. P. (2006). Authentic identities: Straightedge subculture, music, and the Internet. *Journal of Contemporary Ethnography, 35*(2), 173–200. doi:10.1177/0891241605285100.

CHAPTER 11

Social Media Marketing

"I'd like to teach the world to sing, in perfect harmony,"[1]—a nice, albeit somewhat sappy, sentiment. This line is the popular refrain from a song in Coke's iconic 1971 campaign (Photo 11.1), "I'd Like to Buy the World a Coke," or the Hilltop campaign. In the face of Cold War tensions, Coke's commercial depicting a multicultural group singing in unison from a hilltop resonated with a young Baby Boomer target audience. The campaign was launched by the advertising agency McCann–Erikson across multiple media and largely hailed as a success. Although it was reprised during the 1990 Super Bowl and again by NASCAR drivers in 2010, the song was all but forgotten. Then, in 2012, Google partnered with several brands to reimagine classic advertising campaigns using mobile and digital technology. Working with one of the initial creators, they created a campaign where you could buy the world a Coke—literally. Vending machines were set up in major world cities like Cape Town, London, Buenos Aires, and Tokyo. Using a mobile app or browser interface, people could pick a vending machine location, purchase a Coke for someone passing by, and send along a message that would be translated into the appropriate language by Google translate. When the recipient walking by picked up their Coke, they had the option to record a video or text message to the giver, which was delivered by email. The campaign was blogged about by prominent sites like AdAge and Gizmoto and eventually won the prestigious Cannes Lions Grand Prix award for mobile. As a piece of social media marketing, the "I'd like to buy the world a Coke" campaign reminded consumers of Coke's global presence and integrated the brand with positive values like world peace.[2]

As this marketing campaign illustrates, companies can integrate social media tools and practices into a marketing strategy to create some interesting and innovative ways of garnering consumer attention and creating emotional attachment. No matter what position you take on the role of advertising in society, we can probably all agree that companies like Coca-Cola have excelled at becoming integral parts of culture. Studies have shown, for instance, that regions of the brain associated with emotion light up when consumers see the Coca-Cola Santa Claus, a figure popularized by the company in 1931.[3] The "Buy the World a Coke" campaign yet again illustrates the enduring rhetorical and cultural power of marketing communications to provide a way for a company or organization to

Photo 11.1 "I'd Like to Buy the World a Coke," Original Television Commercial, 1971.

communicate with its customers, constituents, or donors. But social media can play a marketing role beyond simply offering a new communication channel. As we will see, it has changed other business processes such as product development, branding, and customer service.

Understanding the way that marketing is pursued within social media is important for anyone who wants to understand social media institutions and practices. As members of a culture that is saturated with marketing messages, it is critical to understand and be able to evaluate these tactics as a citizen and consumer. Further, as social media develops historically, it is important to understand how fields like marketing vie for power and attention, shaping platforms and metrics to suit particular commercial goals. Bringing together what we learned in Chapters 9 and 10, this chapter will examine how both social networks and virtual communities are used as tools for product development, word-of-mouth communication, and customer service. Unlike previous chapters, this chapter will focus on how organizations use social media to communicate with a designated audience for a strategic purpose.

Companies are not the only ones who can potentially benefit from marketing. All kinds of organizations—from universities, to churches, to charities and museums—engage in marketing (Twitchell, 2004), and nonprofit groups have similarly used social media as a communication tool to reach new and different audiences including potential donors and advocates, a concept called **social marketing** (Kotler & Zaltman, 1971). For example, a campaign called the "Ice Bucket Challenge," went viral in 2014, raising awareness and money for ALS, amyotrophic lateral sclerosis (Photo 11.2).[4] Social media marketing has also helped political candidates cultivate audiences who spend less time watching television and reading traditional print publications (Cogburn & Espinoza-Vasquez, 2011). For example, the Obama campaign in 2008 mobilized interest in young and

Photo 11.2 ALS Ice Bucket Challenge.

minority voters by maintaining a presence on platforms such as Twitter and Facebook as well as sites like AsianAvenue and BlackPlanet (Baumgartner et al., 2010). Tellingly, on election day, John McCain had 4,942 Twitter followers to Obama's 118,107 followers (which eventually grew to 60 million) (Solop, 2010). By inspiring viral videos like Obama Girl and a celebrity-studded video by producer and performer will.i.am, the campaign was able to steer social media content to create a sense of grassroots activism (Powell, Hendricks, & Denton, 2010). Both commercial and noncommercial organizations have developed specialized ways of using social media to communicate with customers.

As we can see in these two examples, social media marketing is neither straightforward nor predictable. In this chapter we will examine how some of the core marketing principles undergird social media marketing and look at how social media has engendered shifts in the dynamics of communicating to a constituency—be they consumers, voters, or donors.

INFORMATION OR PERSUASION?

Is advertising information or persuasion? This debate is one of the most basic questions in marketing, and social media seems to cut across the divide. Consumers need information to understand goods and services, but they are also clearly persuaded by what information they are given. Further, in a competitive landscape, companies are eager to provide information as well as emotional and symbolic appeals to self-image and social belonging. Although some argue that marketers simply help people meet their needs and align companies with these needs, others argue that they manipulate vulnerabilities or act in short-term versus long-term interests of consumers and citizens. Many scholars have adopted the definition of **advertising** as persuasive communication (for commentary see Kotler & Levy, 1969; Schudson, 2013). In a traditional communication model like the one we learned about in Chapter 2, this is quite straightforward: the advertiser (source) encodes a message (medium) to be decoded by the customer (receiver), who provides some feedback. However, in a networked communication model like the one we find in social media, the process is less clear.

One difference is that both the company and the consumer play the role of sender and receiver. For example, Delta set up social media monitoring on Twitter to detect any time a customer mentioned Delta, usually in reference to customer service issues like flight delays, mishandled baggage, and poor treatment. Customers produce communications, and Delta receives and responds to those communications. In this model, although power differences between companies and consumers still exist, who is influencing whom becomes less clear.

A second difference is the nature of the medium. When companies and consumers communicate, it is across multiple channels, and companies make an attempt to coordinate their marketing efforts. For example, in 2013 Dove created a campaign around an event where artists drew pictures based on women's descriptions of themselves and compared those to how others saw them. Out of this event, Dove created a traditional television ad, a gallery event, and social media messages on YouTube, Twitter, and Facebook, which themselves were picked up and circulated among people online. In this way, companies usually want to coordinate their efforts across channels to create additional attention and engagement with the message.

A final difference is the nature of influence. Recall that in a social media communication model, consumers communicate not only with the company but also with other consumers. This means that although the company may exert some control over the brand message, there is substantial brand, production, and company-related content co-created by consumers, either individually or collectively (Diamond et al., 2009). For example, a viral video wherein people create geysers from Diet Coke and Mentos eventually garnered more than 17 million views, inspired countless response videos,[5] and crossed over into mainstream media mentions on shows like the *Late Show with David Letterman*. Coke did not commission someone to make this video, and yet, following this phenomenon, sales of Diet Coke increased (Deighton & Kornfeld, 2011). Although there was some initial consternation about the harm this might do to brand value—after all people were buying Coke to play with it, not to consume it—Coke eventually decided to approach co-created brand content through a "brand ambassador" model (Deighton & Kornfeld, 2011), co-sponsoring a video with Mentos and revamping their website. Shifting their approach to social media content, the company started looking for ways to work with, not against, social media content.[6]

One way to resolve the debate is to understand that advertising does a combination of both informing and persuading—but it does different things at different times, in different contexts, for different products. When the company conveys a message to the consumer, we call this **push marketing** whereas when consumers seek out information about a company, we call this **pull marketing**. For example, push marketing is when Coke spends a million dollars on a television ad to tell you about a new product. Pull marketing is when you look up the lowest calorie soft drink on Google. It is no surprise, then, that companies are thinking of ways to encourage consumer pull by placing themselves in channels like search and trying to create push that will garner consumer word of mouth.

Paid, Earned, and Owned Media

Scholars divide media coverage into paid, owned, and earned media (Table 11.1). **Paid media** is when the company buys time or space on an existing channel. For example, a banner ad on IMDB (internet movie database) or a Google Adwords ad would be paid media. **Owned media** is when the company advertises on a channel that it owns. For example, a company website, direct mail or email, and promotional flyers are all types of owned media. **Earned media** is media coverage created by someone else. Earned media can either be traditional, such as coverage in a newspaper like the Style section of *The New York Times*, or it can be social media, such as coverage by a fashion blogger or a mention on Twitter (although, as we will discuss in Chapter 13, the line between these two forms of media is sometimes blurry).

Most of what we consider social media would be classified as earned media. In most contexts, earned media is the most persuasive and usually the cheapest form of communication, but also the hardest to control. It seems more authentic than paid or owned media because it comes from a source other than the company, which has an obvious bias in conveying information. Testimonials from other consumers such as those posted on social network sites also lend credibility to the message because the source is probably more like you (Brown & Reingen, 1987). So which is more important? One study finds that traditional earned media had a much larger immediate effect on sales than social media, but social media mentions ultimately had a larger long-term impact because they occurred more frequently (Stephen & Galak, 2012). Think of it this way: a traditional print outlet is probably produced every day (at best!), yet millions of people are tweeting multiple times per hour. Chances are that social media will contain word of mouth (more than 3.3 billion impressions every day) (Keller & Libai, 2009), and even if this effect is relatively small, the results can accumulate quickly.

Social media can also reach audiences that traditional media would not otherwise reach, and these audiences are defined by more specialized interests. For example, advertising on Vine, usually through spokespeople, reaches a

Table 11.1 Media Types in Marketing

MEDIA TYPE	DEFINITION	EXAMPLE
Paid	When a company buys time or space on an existing platform	Ads shown before a YouTube video; Twitter feed ad
Owned	When a company builds and owns a platform	A company website or sponsored virtual community
Earned	When a company benefits from consumer word-of-mouth or press attention	Retweets of an ad campaign; testimonial on a blog; product suggestion on a social networking site

particular audience of eighteen to twenty year olds. LinkedIn and Twitter have relatively more men, aged twenty-five to fifty,[7,8] whereas Pinterest reaches an equally narrow audience of relatively wealthy women, ages eighteen to forty-nine (Duggan, 2013).[9] Whereas advertising on network television offers a broad reach and cable advertising offers a slightly narrower audience, most Internet advertising reaches an even more specific audience, usually one whose demographics and interests are known by cookies that store viewer characteristics and track online behavior.

Reaching a narrow audience is important for marketers because a company's most loyal customers are almost always its most profitable customers (Jain & Singh, 2002; Reichheld & Teal, 2001). The 80/20 rule says that 20 percent of customers are responsible for 80 percent of sales (Juran, 1995; Pareto, 1896/1965). This rule of thumb has been found to apply to Internet traffic, consumer purchases, wealth distribution, and a host of other phenomena (Faloutsos, Faloutsos, & Faloutsos, 1999). It is common for a small number of people to account for a large percentage of the activity. Using social media to find the most relevant audience, companies can potentially communicate with its most valuable customers more cheaply than ever before. The only trouble is that you first have to find them.

THE PURCHASE FUNNEL
AND THE DECISION JOURNEY

Once a good has been produced, what leads someone to buy it? The purchase funnel is one model for how people learn about marketplace objects. For example, think of the last time you wanted a new pair of jeans. Sure, you might see ads for Levi's on bus stops, television, or Internet banner ads. But there are also a number of things you might have done to gather information about the best jeans. You might have visited a fashion blog or have seen a celebrity wearing them in *US Magazine*. Or you might have asked your friend where she got hers and how she liked them. In sum, marketing communication comes from any number of sources and in a variety of ways, through information we seek out, information that is forced on us, and even through communication we create. The **purchase funnel** applies most often to a primarily rational decision process (as rational as it can be to spend $150 on jeans) where consumers do extensive information search before purchase.

The funnel begins with **awareness,** your knowledge that the product or product category exists.[10] For example, as a person likely living in the United States, you have probably heard of these things called jeans. However, social media messages such as mentions on Twitter can make the product mentally accessible (Berger & Schwartz, 2011; Higgins & King, 1981). Maybe you were not thinking of buying jeans for the new school year until your friends started talking about it and posting photos of their new hauls. As we discussed in Chapter 4, creating awareness is not always easy in a clouded attention economy. Social media marketers may also take advantage of large reach of some events through

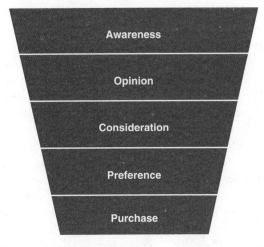

Figure 11.1 The Purchase Funnel.

moment marketing in which the company will improvise to circulate something timely in social media channel like Twitter. For example, Oreo and Audi took advantage of the power outage during the 2013 Superbowl. While Oreos tweeted "you can still dunk in the dark," Audi created a tie-in to a product feature, their LED headlights.

The next stage of the funnel is **opinion**—what you think of the options— which is largely influenced by how familiar you are with them. In this stage, you are likely gathering information and weighing it against what you need, want, or like. What do you think of jeans, either as a category or as a particular brand like Levi's? Here, many factors can affect opinion. Opinion may be shaped by your tastes, those preferences that sometimes reflect your cultural capital and social context. You might not be aware of the latest trends in jean styles. Here, social media content from others such as fashion blogs might play a role in shaping opinion. In this way, electronic word of mouth can play a role, particularly in tastes of particular subcultures.

Next, **consideration** is the stage in which you weigh different options against one another or consider other alternatives like not buying. Here, customer ratings on social shopping sites like Amazon or Zappos can have an impact on your consideration process, particularly for items you feel lukewarm about or where you do not have much information. For example, seeing others who are similar to you on a brand's Facebook page will increase brand evaluation and your purchase intention (Naylor, Lamberton, & West, 2012; see also Babic et al 2015). Seeing people who are not like you, on the other hand, decreases brand evaluations and makes you less likely to purchase. The other alternatives in your consideration set may shift your opinion as well (Hamilton, Hong, & Chernev, 2007; Hamilton, 2003; Huber, Payne, & Puto, 1982; Simonson & Tversky, 1992). For example, if you are shopping online, you might be likely to pick the item that is priced in between the other items, a pattern known as the "compromise effect" (Huber et al., 1982; Wernerfelt, 1995). After considering the options, you will form a **preference** and an intention to buy.

Finally, you **purchase** the good or service. Purchase can be as straightforward as buying a pair of jeans, but it can also stand for any decision that costs time or money. For example, you might decide to spend your weekend volunteering at Habitat for Humanity instead of going to the beach with your friends. You would likely go through the same process of awareness, opinion, consideration, preference, and purchase or choice. Or imagine you are donating to Kiva, a site that provides microlending to people throughout the world. You would still have to become aware of the platform, form an opinion about whether to donate, consider to whom to donate, form a preference, and finally decide to make the loan.

Social media can play a role at each step of the decision funnel. But company–consumer interaction does not end there. Consumers produce feedback from their experience with the product in the form of word-of-mouth communication on Twitter, producing a haul video of their own, or griping on Yelp. Although confirmation bias tends to lead people to like the item more after purchase, consumer regret is also possible, as people reevaluate purchases made on impulse.

Internet shopping comes with risk, and some of these risks can be mitigated through social media channels. On the one hand, a site like Zappos can offer a wide assortment of shoes and easy comparison (Alba et al., 1997). Yet on the other hand, buying online can be risky because you cannot experience the product before buying it, and shipping is potentially costly (Alba et al., 1997; Balasubramanian, Raghunathan, & Mahajan, 2005). However, reviews from other customers—those who actually have experienced the product—can inform you about experiential aspects. On Zappos, for example, other customers will not only provide open-ended feedback, but also rate shoes on fit, support, and style.

Decision Journey

One alternative to the purchase funnel is a model called the **decision journey** (Figure 11.2). In the decision journey model, purchases are not always so rational, and consumers can be triggered to buy something without much thought or planning. For example, say you are in a store to buy those jeans and you see a great sweater to go with them. You may not ask a friend, build awareness, or anything of the type. Maybe, if you are really savvy, you will compare prices with an app like RedLaser, but chances are you will just buy the product that is there. So what role does social media play in this model?

It may not be so different from the role it plays in the funnel. Observe in Figure 11.2 that after the initial trigger, people evaluate the product and may provide feedback. This feedback often ends up on review sites or apps like Yelp!, where it can create a loyal following for a particular restaurant or café, or Zappos or Amazon, where it can inform future purchasers. We will discuss the effects of this kind of word of mouth in the next section.

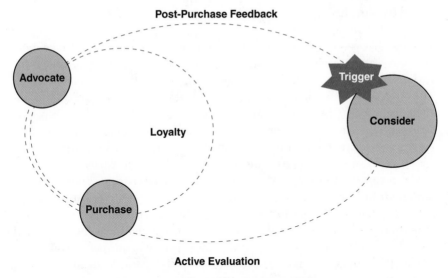

Figure 11.2 The Decision Journey. Adapted from McKinsey & Co.

Social media can also play a role in reminding people to repurchase and to deepen their love for the product, something called the **loyalty loop**. For example, devoted fans of Jessica Alba's Honest Company post glowing word-of-mouth endorsements on mommy blogging sites, and this feedback prompts others to try the products as well. As we can see, the decision journey model suits contexts where purchase is less rationally planned and when people purchase a product multiple times while potentially creating feedback that might influence others. We will now turn to understanding exactly what kinds of influence consumers can have on one another.

ADVERTISING MESSAGES AND CHANNELS

Search Advertising

As consumers go through the purchase funnel or the decision journey, use of social media can vary. Although you might be learning about products and services through your friends, on blogs, and in magazines, when it comes time to purchase online, search plays a key role. Researchers find that the closer you are to purchasing, the more precise your search term will be. For example, if you are close to buying a car, you probably will not search for "four door sedan" but rather "Volkswagen TDI used" (Jerath, Ma, & Park, 2014). This means that advertisers will pay more for placing ads in pages with these concrete words rather than less specific terms. As we discussed in Chapter 4, through search engine optimization, companies and nonprofit organizations pay money to optimize their search results, ensuring that their organization comes up at the top of the list.

Word of Mouth
Impact of Word of Mouth

Imagine that you need a new hairdryer. Whose opinion would you take more seriously—a spokesperson on a television advertisement, your best friend, or the reviews on Amazon.com? If you are like most people, the recommendation of others, either your friend or your friends on Amazon, has an impact on your ultimate purchase (Chevalier & Mayzlin, 2006; Godes & Mayzlin, 2004; Brown & Reingen, 1987; Liu, 2006). **Word-of-mouth** communication is when product or service information is transmitted from one person to another (Arndt, 1967). This type of communication occurs more frequently, is more trusted, and has a larger impact on decision making than traditional advertising (Brown & Reingen, 1987; Money, Gilly, & Graham, 1998). There are many reasons we would trust people in our social network over an institutionalized media source such as a news program, and most of these reasons have to do with the effects of social capital that we discussed in Chapter 9. Because people in our network are more like us, they know our unique preferences, and because we like them, we tend to be more persuaded by them (Cialdini, 1993; Eagly & Chaiken, 1975). Also, if they lead us astray, we certainly know where to find them.

Traditional word of mouth was conceptualized as the transmission of marketplace information face to face (Katz & Lazarsfeld, 1970). For example, housewives in the 1960s were known as key influencers of each others' purchases and were thus targeted by marketers for products from coffee to Jell-O to processed meats. However, unlike fifty years ago, when word of mouth passed quite routinely from person to person, today there is an onslaught of word of mouth in the form of product reviews, Twitter comments, and message board conversations. In this new communication model, word of mouth is not only given and received, but also observed. Roughly two-thirds of all online shoppers consult at least four reviews before they make a purchase (Kee, 2008). Likewise, two-thirds of car shoppers read reviews before they step on the car lot (McGran, 2005). **Social shopping sites** integrate these forms of word of mouth into the purchase infrastructure itself, which attracts more shoppers to the site (Stephen and Toubia, 2010).

And it is not just chatter; word of mouth has a dramatic impact on important company metrics such as sales (Babic, Sotgiu, de Valeck, and Bijmolt, 2015; Chevalier & Mayzlin, 2006; Dellarocas, Zhang, & Awad, 2007; Godes & Mayzlin, 2004, 2009; Godes & Silva, 2012; Li & Hitt, 2008; Van den Bulte & Joshi, 2007), brand equity (Moe & Schweidel, 2012; Schivinski & Dabrowski, 2014), and even stock price (Moe & Schweidel, 2012; Tirunillai & Tellis, 2012). In contrast to traditional advertising, it has longer term effects on sales (Trusov, Bucklin, & Pauwels, 2009) and profits (Villanueva, Yoo, & Hanssens, 2008). Word of mouth has never been more important, and understanding its dynamics in social media provides rewards to the companies who skillfully navigate it versus those who do not. From the consumer point of view, you might be surprised by the effects that it may have on your attitudes and behavior.

Characteristics of word of mouth

Word of mouth can be measured in terms of valence, variance, and volume (Dellarocas, Gao, & Narayan, 2010). **Valence** is the positivity or negativity of the review. People are more influenced by negative reviews than they are by positive reviews, primarily because people tend to be risk averse and trust negative information more than positive information. Just one negative eBay review can decrease sales by 13 percent (Cabral & Hortacsu, 2010), whereas a one-star increase in a Yelp! review increases revenue by only 5 to 9 percent (Luca, 2011). One study found that a one-star review on Amazon and BarnesandNoble.com had a greater negative impact on sales than the positive impact of a five-star review (Chevalier & Mayzlin, 2006). The valence of social media content can also vary across genre. Blogs, for example, tend to be relatively positive, whereas microblogging and message boards will have more negative and neutral comments (Moe & Schweidel, 2012).

When grouped together, online reviews also have **variance**, similarity or dissimilarity to each other. Imagine you go to Amazon to buy a computer, and it has high five-star reviews and low one-star reviews. Would you think twice about buying that computer? Probably so, especially because you have a lot to lose (namely, a couple thousand dollars and all of your data). When reading reviews, people are cognitive misers—they use heuristics that will help them quickly make a decision without combing through a lot of information. For example, the first few hotel reviews have a huge impact on booking intentions, particularly if they are negative and particularly for unfamiliar hotels (Sparks & Browning, 2011; Vermeulen & Seegers, 2009).

Volume is the total number of online reviews. If there are a lot of reviews, you will probably feel more confident about their validity because it seems you have enough information from others to make a decision. Valance and volume have the greatest impact on sales (Babic et al., 2015; Chevalier & Mayzlin, 2006), but variance can also be important for more specialized categories such as craft beer (Clemons, Gao, & Hitt, 2006).

When writing reviews, people consider their audience, and word-of-mouth communication is itself prone to the kinds of social influence as discussed in Chapters 8 and 9 (Moe & Trusov, 2011). For example, reading negative reviews will make you more likely to write a negative review (Schlosser, 2005). If you log on to see a wide variety of reviews, some positive some negative, you will be more likely to write a more balanced review (Schlosser, 2005). In general, reviews trend downward over time because of these effects (Godes & Silva, 2012; Moe & Trusov, 2011), and over the past ten to fifteen years, online reviews in general have become more negative (Godes & Silva, 2012). Think of it this way: people have little incentive to post one more positive review about an item, but will often invest the time to post a negative review if they are unhappy (Godes & Silva, 2012; Wu & Huberman, 2008). Scholars find that, as time goes on, people will tend to post more negative reviews than positive reviews, particularly when volume is high (Moe & Trusov, 2011).

Photo 11.3 Word of Mouth on Yelp!

Lots of companies take consumer comments on social media seriously and keep track of them through **social media monitoring**. Nabisco, for example, removed transfats from its Oreo cookies following an extensive period of social media monitoring (Moe & Schweidel, 2012).

Drivers of Word of Mouth
So where does word of mouth come from? Loyal customers are more likely to spread word of mouth (Lambrecht, Tucker, & Wiertz, 2014), and yet **opinion leaders**, those with a lot of social capital, are more influential, albeit more selective with their opinions (Godes & Mayzlin, 2009). Word of mouth can also say as much about the poster as it does about the product, and self-enhancement can be a motive for writing reviews (Angelis, Bonezzi, Peluso, Rucker, & Costabile, 2012; Bagozzi & Dholakia, 2002) because offering word of mouth can make people feel like an expert or a helpful friend (Hennig-Thurau, Gwinner, Walsh, & Gremler, 2004).

To spur people to talk, a product must be interesting and it must be relevant (Berger & Schwartz, 2011; Higgins & King, 1981; Rosen, 2009). For example, people are much more likely to share opinions about their iPhone than about their socks. However, relevance also plays an important role. People are more

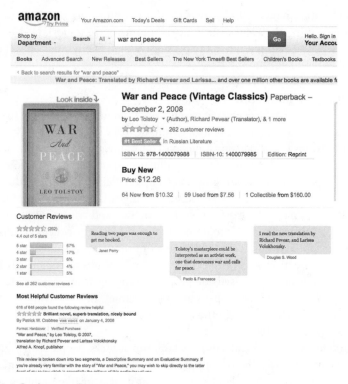

Photo 11.4 Reviews on Amazon.com.

likely to give their opinion on restaurants to others simply because there are so many contexts in which food is relevant. Relevance can be created by just about anything. Even socks can be relevant if, say, you are posting on a message board about running. In the short run, both interest and relevance create a lot of word of mouth, but over time, a product continues to be talked about only if it is relevant (Berger & Schwartz, 2011).

Yet not all word-of-mouth communication is equally effective. Think back to what we learned from the purchase funnel. Word of mouth can play different roles at different times in our path to purchase. Sometimes word of mouth can raise awareness, whereas other times it can affect preference. Coming from weak ties, word of mouth is good at raising awareness (Godes & Mayzlin, 2009). Yet surprisingly, communication from loyal customers with which we have strong ties is not always best, and products with low awareness actually benefit more from word of mouth coming from weak ties than from loyal customers whom we know well (Godes & Mayzlin, 2009). To understand why, think back to what we learned about the strength of weak ties in Chapter 9. Weak ties are valuable because they can provide more new information. We are likely to already know what our strong ties know. If they are loyal to a product, it is likely that either we are loyal as well or we have already considered and dismissed the product. Weak ties, on the other hand, tell us things we did not know previously. Yet, when it comes to affecting preference, strong ties become more important. Nonanonymous reviews, for example, are more persuasive than anonymous ones (Forman, Ghose, & Wiesenfeld, 2008).

Word-of-mouth Marketing

Social media has provided a whole new forum for companies not only to observe and measure word of mouth, but also to pursue word of mouth publicity of their own. Companies know person-to-person communication is influential, and so they attempt to use this type of social influence through **word-of-mouth marketing**, the practice of encouraging the transmission of positive product information, or "buzz." Campaigns aimed at creating this kind of buzz represent a hybrid between naturally existing word of mouth and advertising campaigns. For example, Proctor and Gamble maintains a platform called Vocalpoint, a panel of customers who receive early trials of products with the hope that they will share their experiences with others (Godes & Mayzlin, 2009). This kind of buzz marketing has been used for products ranging from jeans to television shows like *The Biggest Loser* to pens and video games. In some contexts, this increases sales, particularly when the aim is to create awareness of a new product (Godes & Mayzlin, 2009).

Marketers with product trials target opinion leaders, people with high social and/or cultural capital who occupy the roles of a connector, market maven, or bridge as we have discussed. For example, using a measure like Klout, companies offer promotions to a select group of people with an active social media presence and large following. Companies will try to increase word of mouth through **seeding** products with consumers, a technique of giving products to lead users or opinion leaders. By seeding new products with key influencers, companies hope to generate positive word-of-mouth marketing, authentic product reviews, and heightened exposure.

However, when doing this, companies face an inherent tension: they want people to communicate about their products because it seems more authentic, but *prompting* people to communicate about certain products undermines their authenticity (Friestad & Wright, 1994). Seeding products with bloggers and other Internet personalities must itself be carefully managed to avoid appearing inauthentic (Hinz, Skiera, Barrot, & Becker, 2011; Kozinets, De Valck, Wojnicki, & Wilner, 2010). So how do bloggers communicate product endorsements when challenged with these problems of inauthenticity? Seeding works best when it is congruent with the celebrity's persona and interests. Bloggers tend to adopt one of four strategies—evaluation, embracing, explanation, or endorsement—when reviewing products (Kozinets et al., 2010). Depending on the personal narrative of the blogger and the norms and expectations of fans, these would-be spokespeople either explicitly disclose the promotion (explanation or endorsement) and paradoxically win approval of their followers by being upfront or implicitly disclose the promotion (evaluation or embracing), which meets with much less approval unless their followers accept the commercial endorsement.

Crisis Management and Firestorms

Online word of mouth has had some spectacular failures. For example, McDonald's launched a Twitter campaign in which they encouraged people to tweet stories using the hashtag #McDStories.[11] As you might imagine, this unleashed a torrent of negative and spectacularly gross tales about visiting the restaurant chain (Photo 11.5A). By creating the hashtag #askJPM, the investment bank JP Morgan found itself in a similar firestorm following the financial crisis (Photo 11.5B). Scholars call this phenomenon an online **firestorm**, "the sudden discharge of large quantities of messages containing negative WOM [word of mouth] and complaint behavior against a person, company, or group in social media networks" (Pfeffer, Zorbach, & Carley, 2014). Because of the dynamics of networked digital communications, firestorms have become increasingly common, as public figures and companies are lambasted for everything from criminal behavior to homophobic and racist attitudes to customer mistreatment. The reputations of many famous figures have been destroyed by the increased potential for negative publicity brought about by social media (Garrett, 2009; Key & Cummings, 1966). Companies are also subject to criticism on social media. In the case of United Airlines, for example, one upset customer, Pete Carroll, took to YouTube to create a music video and song detailing his experience when United broke his Taylor guitar during baggage handling on a flight from Chicago to Halifax (Carroll, 2012; Deighton & Kornfeld, 2010). The video ultimately garnered more than 14 million views and eventually forced United to respond.

So why do firestorms happen? Both the speed of networked communications and its capacity for volume facilitate firestorms (Pfeffer et al., 2014). In contrast to traditional media, the half-life (or time it takes to reach 50% of the overall traffic (Burton & Kebler, 1960)—for Twitter hashtags, YouTube memes, and Facebook posts is hours or minutes rather than days (Wu & Huberman, 2007). This kind of cycling means that messages spread exponentially more quickly than in traditional media. Twitter is probably the "fastest" genre, but firestorms can equally happen on Facebook or in message boards, crossing over to traditional media outlets overnight (Diakopoulos, De Choudhury, & Naaman, 2012). This crossover then creates a second wave of social media attention, accounting for about 30% of the mentions on social media.

Message characteristics such as length can also contribute to the phenomenon of firestorms. People are more likely to post extreme sentiments on Twitter because of the word constraints relative to more nuanced statements in other genres. Facebook posts inspire binary choices between liking or not liking—showing approval or disapproval rather than expressing more nuanced sentiments about the topic of the firestorm. Such affordances can lead to simplified messages and extreme sentiments.

Further, the structure of networks can impact how firestorms are spread. Because of clustering—the likelihood of your knowing someone that I also know

is high—the story comes at you from multiple directions, creating repeated exposure to a message from different people. This adds to normative pressure some
may feel to weigh in on and circulate outrage about a topic about which they may
have previously been neutral or in which they previously had little interest (Pfeffer et al., 2014).

McDonald's @McDonalds   18 jan
"When u make something w/pride, people can taste it," - McD potato
supplier #McDStories mcd.to/zIIXXu
▶ View video

Chris Woods @chrismwoods   31m
When a hash tag-based campaign goes wrong. McDonald's with
#McDStories: bit.out via   @ paidContent

Stephenie King @stephenie_king   1h
McDonald's tried to deal with out of control #McDStories hashtag
campaign m.theglobeandmail.com/news/technolog...

Kim Stallwood @grumpyvegan   21 Jan
My warm memories of McDonald's is to use them as public toilets.
#McDStories

CTV Vancouver Island @CTVNewsVI   21 Jan
CTV News Video: @ McDonalds gets grilled by Twitter #McDStories.
@ CTVNewsAndrew reports- bit.ly/zMYJiV @yyj

Vegan @vegan   20 Jan
My memories of walking into a McDonalds: the sensory experience of
inhaling deeply from a freshly-opened can of dog food. #McDStories

Mark Zohar @markzohar   20 Jan
McDonald's customets don't eant to tell #McDStories. They just want
their fries, mechanically seperated chicken parts & wallow in shake.

Melissa. ❥ @XoMelissaEmily   18 Jan
#mcdstories it's made of 100% beef, but they use stuff like cow eyes
& cow tongues in thier hamburgers. Learned this today../:

Killuminati @JetsOnJeTsOnJet   18 Jan
i will never set mcdonalds ever again after seeing that rat crawl threw
the pack of buns on worldstarhiphop.com smh lol #McDStories

Jeremy Drummond @ImSoCelebrity   18 Jan
Hoodrats is goin in on that #McDStories trent. "One time I only had
$1.06 and didn't know if i wanted a Sweet Tea or 2 apple Pies."

The Undateable Girl @Undateable_Girl   18 Jan
#McDStories Paid for my food but almost left cause I was high and
convinced that the worker called the cops and were using my food

Photo 11.5A Twitter Campaigns Gone Wrong: McDonald's.

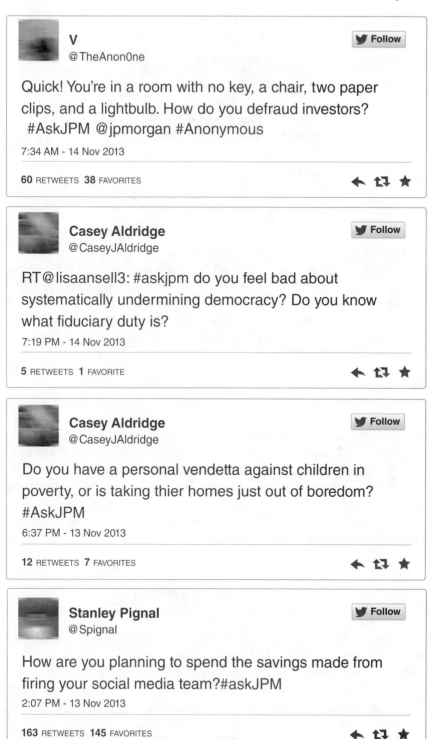

V
@TheAnonOne

Follow

Quick! You're in a room with no key, a chair, two paper clips, and a lightbulb. How do you defraud investors? #AskJPM @jpmorgan #Anonymous

7:34 AM - 14 Nov 2013

60 RETWEETS **38** FAVORITES

Casey Aldridge
@CaseyJAldridge

Follow

RT@lisaansell3: #askjpm do you feel bad about systematically undermining democracy? Do you know what fiduciary duty is?

7:19 PM - 14 Nov 2013

5 RETWEETS **1** FAVORITE

Casey Aldridge
@CaseyJAldridge

Follow

Do you have a personal vendetta against children in poverty, or is taking thier homes just out of boredom? #AskJPM

6:37 PM - 13 Nov 2013

12 RETWEETS **7** FAVORITES

Stanley Pignal
@Spignal

Follow

How are you planning to spend the savings made from firing your social media team?#askJPM

2:07 PM - 13 Nov 2013

163 RETWEETS **145** FAVORITES

Photo 11.5B Twitter Campaigns Gone Wrong: JP Morgan.

Photo 11.6 Image from "United Breaks Guitars" by Pete Carroll.

Social Media Campaigns and Offline Promotions

Social media campaigns can include offline elements as well. For example, the Korean chain Megabox held a series of special movie events for singles. Using Facebook, people could nominate their single friends to receive tickets to a movie with a randomly selected stranger of the opposite sex. Flashmobs and promotional events are just a few ways that social media can be used to coordinate offline efforts through social media.

Sometimes social media can be used to simply do old things in a new way. For example, Starbucks is well known for offering creative promotions on its Facebook page such as sharing a coffee on Valentine's Day or a contest to name a Starbucks' new coffee blend. These kinds of promotions have gained more than 30 million likes on Facebook and more than 99,000 followers on Twitter.[12] Transactional brands like Starbucks work well for short-term promotions, but lifestyle or luxury brands require longer-term brand-building that includes multiple social media platforms and more organic "fan" recruitment. For example, the Burberry brand has a Facebook page that represents its musical tastes, while its Instagram profile provides backstage content of photo shoots and runway shows. These are complemented by the Mulberry blog, which conveys lifestyle information such as travel, events, and recipes (Dubois, 2014).

SOCIAL MEDIA MARKETING AND THE VALUE CHAIN

Despite their interchangeability in popular discourse, advertising and marketing are actually slightly different endeavors. Advertising describes the communication of an organization with its customers, whereas marketing encompasses other activities performed by the organization to meet the needs of its customers. These activities might go well beyond communication to product development, customer service, sales, and customer retention. In the next section, we will go beyond advertising to consider how marketing more generally uses social media.

As we have seen, social media can be a communication channel, but it can also be integral to more fundamental changes in the way that organizations operate (Li, 2010). Organizational tasks ranging from product development to customer service have shifted because of the incorporation of co-creation and co-production like the types we saw in Chapter 5. Recall the value chain: market research, design, production, distribution, sales, and service. Each stage of this process presents the opportunity—not always cost-effective or ideal—for the incorporation of consumer input into company processes, usually facilitated by social media platforms.

Market Research

Companies can use social media "listening" software to conduct market research. Through methods like netnography discussed in Chapter 4, they conduct unobtrusive observation and participant observation into message boards and forums of some of their most loyal customers. Market research can help companies gain insight into the needs and values of their target customers and track how products are doing on the market. For example, to learn about the market potential for launching Cayenne, Porsche conducted research in a forum of Porsche enthusiasts (Deighton, Avery, & Fear, 2011). However, they found that hardcore Porsche fans largely *hated* the idea of debasing their beloved Porsche 911, a symbol of masculine virility, by making it a "mini-van" for "moms." And yet, Porsche went ahead with the launch, and the Cayenne was a huge success among a new demographic. Thus, although social media presents valuable opportunities for conducting market research relatively cheaply, its data must be viewed with some perspective. Further, although Internet use is nearly ubiquitous, and it may seem as if any interest group has a presence, recalling what we learned in Chapters 7 and 8, the digital world can still be a remarkably segmented place.

Design

Companies have incorporated consumers into the design process by communicating with both average Joe customers and "lead users" through social media platforms (Hautz, Hutter, Fuller, Matzler, & Rieger, 2010). For example, in 2008, Starbucks launched MyStarbucksIdea.com to solicit ideas from customers. The campaign enrolled more than 180,000 users and generated 80,000 ideas, which ultimately produced fifty adopted innovations such as the green stick that prevents coffee from spilling out of the top when carried (York, 2010).

Production

Production is probably the step in the chain least likely to incorporate consumer input through social media. After all, the purpose of most companies is to produce something—put together raw resources into a new product that has value (Vargo & Lusch, 2004)—and yet there are a few examples where consumers have actually played a role in production. For example, groups like Soylife sell the components to make shakes and host forums dedicated to assembling them.

Homebrewed beers operate similarly. In general, companies taking advantage of a broader cultural do-it-yourself trend, use the knowledge produced in online forums, and supply the materials so that users can make their own. Interestingly, this is not so different from how computers themselves used to be sold to hobbyists.

Distribution and Sales

Distribution and sales are perhaps the clearest place where social media has been incorporated into the supply chain. As we discussed in the previous section, word-of-mouth communication from other consumers on social media is persuasive and impactful. Companies will often use networks of loyal consumers to distribute new products and develop a sales force. For example, a natural health company called Shaklee distributes its products in large part through "health advocates," many of whom use social media marketing to reach leads through Facebook and other social media platforms.

Service

Perhaps the most surprising place that social media platforms have played a role in commercial life is through technical support and service. Companies like Adobe, for example, host forums that provide extensive support for computer software by and for consumers. Finally, as we have seen in several places throughout the book, online communities provide resources for companies to develop value by studying new target markets, developing new products, or enrolling people in sharing a message (Schau, Muniz, & Arnould, 2009).

SUMMARY AND CONCLUSION

Whether it is convincing a friend to listen to your band, gathering donations for ALS, or simply persuading someone to buy a Coke, organizations both formal and informal, profit and non-profit, are often trying to persuade. In this chapter we have seen the many ways in which social media practices and content have been incorporated into existing advertising practices, but also more fundamentally changed business practices for some organizations. Using existing frameworks such as the purchase funnel and the value chain, we have examined the ways that social media can inform some basic processes in marketing. In studying word of mouth, we have seen what can go right, and in the case of firestorms, what can go wrong. The next chapter on cultural life will give us a broader context for considering how communication and value creation take place.

TOPICS

- Purchase funnel
- Decision journey
- Push versus pull marketing

- Paid, earned, owned media
- Valence, volume, variance of word of mouth
- Firestorms

DISCUSSION QUESTIONS

1. Do you think advertising is information or persuasion?
2. When was the last time you used word-of-mouth communication from social media? Was it effective? Why or why not?

EXERCISES

1. Think of the last time you decided to buy something online. Illustrate the process that led you to that purchase with the purchase funnel or the decision journey. Is there anything that does not fit? If so, how would you conceptualize the process?
2. It is time to design your own social media campaign. Imagine that you have just been tasked with selling a new smartphone. Plan your campaign, including your target audience and intended social media platforms. Consider decisions of where and how to involve consumers in the value chain. Would you include any offline elements? If you are feeling adventurous, include a budget.

NOTES

1. http://www.projectrebrief.com/coke/#page=original
2. The new campaign can be found here: https://www.youtube.com/watch?v=45Z-GevoYB8#t=48/. An interview with Bill Backer, the creator of the campaign can be found here: https://www.youtube.com/watch?v=tSNU1TvF4pc/ Other versions of the commercial include the Christmas version: https://www.youtube.com/watch?v=_zCsFvVg0UY/. The reprised 1990 commercial and https://www.youtube.com/watch?v=Wqd5K5goiIo/ and 2010 versions https://www.youtube.com/watch?v=kWa1tNbHYEg/. The song has also had an afterlife in popular culture, with the band Oasis using much of the melody and lyrics in their song "Shakermaker," https://www.youtube.com/watch?v=JUoVQ-kB7DQ/. The making of the new campaign can be found here: http://vimeo.com/42035286/.
3. http://www.coca-colacompany.com/holidays/the-true-history-of-the-modern-day-santa-claus/
4. http://www.nytimes.com/2014/08/18/business/ice-bucket-challenge-has-raised-millions-for-als-association.html?_r=2/.
5. https://www.youtube.com/watch?v=h_2osOb2SMU/; https://www.youtube.com/watch?v=hKoB0MHVBvM/.
6. http://www.businessweek.com/stories/2007-01-16/the-diet-coke-and-mentos-explosionbusinessweek-business-news-stock-market-and-financial-advice/.
7. http://www.entrepreneur.com/article/231970/.

8. https://www.quantcast.com/linkedin.com/, http://www.pewinternet.org/fact-sheets/social-networking-fact-sheet/.
9. http://watier.org/katherine/list-of-us-social-media-demographics/.
10. Some more sociologically oriented scholars will refer to awareness as cultural-cognitive legitimacy, acknowledging the role that cultural categories play in creating awareness of some products (see, e.g., Humphreys & Latour, 2013).
11. http://www.forbes.com/sites/kashmirhill/2012/01/24/mcdstories-when-a-hashtag-becomes-a-bashtag/.
12. http://www.socialbakers.com/all-social-media-stats/facebook/.

FURTHER READINGS

Arvidsson, A. (2006). *Brands: Meaning and value in media culture.* New York: Psychology Press.
Li, C. (2010). *Open leadership: How social technology can transform the way you lead.* New York: Wiley.
Moe, Wendy W., & Schweidel, D. A. (2014), *Social media intelligence.* Cambridge, UK: Cambridge University Press.

REFERENCES

Alba, J., Lynch, J., Weitz, B., Janiszewski, C., Lutz, R., Sawyer, A., & Wood, S. (1997). Interactive home shopping: Consumer, retailer, and manufacturer incentives to participate in electronic marketplaces. *The Journal of Marketing*, 38–53.
Angelis, M. D., Bonezzi, A., Peluso, A. M., Rucker, D. D., & Costabile, M. (2012). On braggarts and gossips: A self-enhancement account of word-of-mouth generation and transmission. *Journal of Marketing Research, 49*(4), 551–563.
Arndt, J. (1967). Role of product-related conversations in the diffusion of a new product. *Journal of Marketing Research*, 291–295.
Babić, A., Sotgiu, F., de Valck, K., Bijmolt, T.H.A. (2015). The Effect of Electronic Word of Mouth on Sales: A Meta-Analytic Review of Platform, Product, and Metric Factors. *Journal of Marketing Research,* forthcoming.
Bagozzi, R. P., & Dholakia, U. M. (2002). Intentional social action in virtual communities. *Journal of Interactive Marketing, 16*(2), 2–21.
Balasubramanian, S., Raghunathan, R., & Mahajan, V. (2005). Consumers in a multichannel environment: Product utility, process utility, and channel choice. *Journal of Interactive Marketing, 19*(2), 12–30.
Baumgartner, J. C., Mackay, J. B., Morris, J. S., Otenyo, E. E., Powell, L., Smith, M. M., . . . Hendricks, J. A. (2010). *Communicator-in-chief: How Barack Obama used new media technology to win the White House.* Lanham, MD: Lexington Books.
Berger, J., & Schwartz, E. M. (2011). What drives immediate and ongoing word of mouth? *Journal of Marketing Research, 48*(5), 869–880.

Brown, J. J., & Reingen, P. H. (1987). Social ties and word-of-mouth referral behavior. *Journal of Consumer Research*, 350–362.

Burton, R. E., & Kebler, R. (1960). The "half-life" of some scientific and technical literatures. *American Documentation, 11*(1), 18–22.

Cabral, L., & Hortacsu, A. (2010). The dynamics of seller reputation: Evidence from Ebay. *The Journal of Industrial Economics, 58*(1), 54–78.

Carroll, D. (2012). *United breaks guitars*. London: Hay House.

Chevalier, J. A., & Mayzlin, D. (2006). The effect of word of mouth on sales: Online book reviews. *Journal of Marketing Research, 43*(3), 345–354.

Cialdini, R. B. (1993). *Influence: The psychology of persuasion*. New York: HarperCollins.

Clemons, E. K., Gao, G. G., & Hitt, L. M. (2006). When online reviews meet hyperdifferentiation: A study of the craft beer industry. *Journal of Management Information Systems, 23*(2), 149–171.

Cogburn, D. L., & Espinoza-Vasquez, F. K. (2011). From networked nominee to networked nation: Examining the impact of Web 2.0 and social media on political participation and civic engagement in the 2008 Obama campaign. *Journal of Political Marketing, 10*(1–2), 189–213.

Deighton, J., Avery, J., & Fear, J. (2011). Porsche: The Cayenne launch. *Harvard Business School Marketing Unit Case* (511-068).

Deighton, J., & Kornfeld, L. (2010). United breaks guitars. *HBS Case* (510-057).

Deighton, J., & Kornfeld, L. (2011). Coca-Cola on Facebook. *Harvard Business School Marketing Unit Case* (511-110).

Dellarocas, C., Gao, G., & Narayan, R. (2010). Are consumers more likely to contribute online reviews for hit or niche products? *Journal of Management Information Systems, 27*(2), 127–158.

Dellarocas, C., Zhang, X. M., & Awad, N. F. (2007). Exploring the value of online product reviews in forecasting sales: The case of motion pictures. *Journal of Interactive Marketing, 21*(4), 23–45.

Diakopoulos, N., De Choudhury, M., & Naaman, M. (2012). *Finding and assessing social media information sources in the context of journalism*. Paper presented at the Proceedings of the SIGCHI Conference on Human Factors in Computing Systems. Austin, Texas, USA.

Diamond, N., Sherry, J. F. Jr., Muñiz, A. M. Jr., McGrath, M. A., Kozinets, R. V., & Borghini, S. (2009). American Girl and the brand gestalt: Closing the loop on sociocultural branding research. *Journal of Marketing, 73*(3), 118–134.

Duggan, M., & Brenner, J. (2013). *The demographics of social media users—2012*. Retrieved from http://www.pewinternet.org/2013/02/14/the-demographics-of-social-media-users-2012/.

Eagly, A. H., & Chaiken, S. (1975). An attribution analysis of the effect of communicator characteristics on opinion change: The case of communicator attractiveness. *Journal of Personality and Social Psychology, 32*(1), 136.

Faloutsos, M., Faloutsos, P., & Faloutsos, C. (1999). *On power-law relationships of the Internet topology.* Paper presented at the ACM SIGCOMM Computer Communication Review. Cambridge, Massachussetts, USA.

Forman, C., Ghose, A., & Wiesenfeld, B. (2008). Examining the relationship between reviews and sales: The role of reviewer identity disclosure in electronic markets. *Information Systems Research, 19*(3), 291–313.

Friestad, M., & Wright, P. (1994). The persuasion knowledge model: How people cope with persuasion attempts. *Journal of Consumer Research*, 1–31.

Garrett, R. K. (2009). Echo chambers online?: Politically motivated selective exposure among Internet news users1. *Journal of Computer-Mediated Communication, 14*(2), 265–285.

Godes, D., & Mayzlin, D. (2004). Using online conversations to study word-of-mouth communication. *Marketing Science, 23*(4), 545–560.

Godes, D., & Mayzlin, D. (2009). Firm-created word-of-mouth communication: Evidence from a field test. *Marketing Science, 28*(4), 721–739.

Godes, D., & Silva, J. C. (2012). Sequential and temporal dynamics of online opinion. *Marketing Science, 31*(3), 448–473.

Hamilton, R., Hong, J., & Chernev, A. (2007). Perceptual focus effects in choice. *Journal of Consumer Research, 34*(2), 187–199.

Hamilton, R. W. (2003). Why do people suggest what they do not want? Using context effects to influence others' choices. *Journal of Consumer Research, 29*(4), 492–506.

Hautz, J., Hutter, K., Fuller, J., Matzler, K., & Rieger, M. (2010). *How to establish an online innovation community? The role of users and their innovative content.* Paper presented at the 2010 43rd Hawaii International Conference on System Sciences. Manoa, Hawaii, USA.

Hennig-Thurau, T., Gwinner, K. P., Walsh, G., & Gremler, D. D. (2004). Electronic word-of-mouth via consumer-opinion platforms: What motivates consumers to articulate themselves on the internet? *Journal of Interactive Marketing, 18*(1), 38–52.

Higgins, E. T., & King, G. (1981). Accessibility of social constructs: Information processing consequences of individual and contextual variability. *Personality, Cognition, and Social Interaction, 69*, 121.

Hinz, O., Skiera, B., Barrot, C., & Becker, J. U. (2011). Seeding strategies for viral marketing: An empirical comparison. *Journal of Marketing, 75*(6), 55–71.

Huber, J., Payne, J. W., & Puto, C. (1982). Adding asymmetrically dominated alternatives: Violations of regularity and the similarity hypothesis. *Journal of Consumer Research*, 90–98.

Jain, D., & Singh, S. S. (2002). Customer lifetime value research in marketing: A review and future directions. *Journal of Interactive Marketing, 16*(2), 34–46. doi:http://dx.doi.org/10.1002/dir.10032.

Jerath, K., Ma, L., & Park, Y.-H. (2014). Consumer click behavior at a search engine: The role of keyword popularity. *Journal of Marketing Research, 51*(4), 480–486.

Juran, J. M. (1995). *Managerial breakthrough: The classic book on improving management performance*. New York: McGraw–Hill.

Katz, E., & Lazarsfeld, P. F. (1970). *Personal influence, The part played by people in the flow of mass communications*. New Brunswick, NJ: Transaction.

Kee, T. (2008, February 19). Majority of online shoppers check at least four reviews before buying. *Online Media Daily*.

Keller, E., & Libai, B. (2009). A holistic approach to the measurement of WOM. Its impact on consumers. Part 5/the Power of Social Media. WM3-Worldwide Multi Media Measurement 2009. Paper presented at the I nternational Conference, Stockholm.

Key, V. O., & Cummings, M. C. (1966). *The responsible electorate*. Cambridge, MA: Belknap Press of Harvard University Press.

Kotler, P., & Levy, S. J. (1969). Broadening the concept of marketing. *The Journal of Marketing*, 10–15.

Kotler, P., & Zaltman, G. (1971). Social marketing: An approach to planned social change. *The Journal of Marketing*, 3–12.

Kozinets, R. V., De Valck, K., Wojnicki, A. C., & Wilner, S. J. (2010). Networked narratives: Understanding word-of-mouth marketing in online communities. *Journal of Marketing, 74*(2), 71–89.

Lambrecht, A., Tucker, C., & Wiertz, C. (2014, April 1). *Should you target early trend propagators? Evidence from Twitter*.

Li, C. (2010). *Open leadership: How social technology can transform the way you lead*. New York: Wiley.

Li, X., & Hitt, L. M. (2008). Self-selection and information role of online product reviews. *Information Systems Research, 19*(4), 456–474.

Liu, Y. (2006). Word of mouth for movies: Its dynamics and impact on box office revenue. *Journal of Marketing, 70*(3), 74–89.

Luca, M. (2011). *Reviews, reputation, and revenue: The case of Yelp.com*. Watertown, MA: Harvard Business School.

McGran, K. (2005, November 12). Internet hurting dealer profits; savvy shoppers hunt for bargains buyers often know more than sellers. *Toronto Star*, G4.

Moe, W. W., & Schweidel, D. A. (2012). Online product opinions: Incidence, evaluation, and evolution. *Marketing Science, 31*(3), 372–386.

Moe, W. W., & Trusov, M. (2011). The value of social dynamics in online product ratings forums. *Journal of Marketing Research, 48*(3), 444–456.

Money, R. B., Gilly, M. C., & Graham, J. L. (1998). Explorations of national culture and word-of-mouth referral behavior in the purchase of industrial services in the United States and Japan. *The Journal of Marketing*, 76–87.

Naylor, R. W., Lamberton, C. P., & West, P. M. (2012). Beyond the "like" button: The impact of mere virtual presence on brand evaluations and purchase intentions in social media settings. *Journal of Marketing, 76*(6), 105–120.

Pareto, V. (1896/1965). *Oeuvres complètes: Écrits sur la courbe de la répartition de la richesse*. Geneva: Droz.

Pfeffer, J., Zorbach, T., & Carley, K. (2014). Understanding online firestorms: Negative word-of-mouth dynamics in social media networks. *Journal of Marketing Communications, 20*(1–2), 117–128.

Powell, L., Hendricks, J., & Denton, R. Jr. (2010). Obama and Obama girl: YouTube, viral videos, and the 2008 presidential campaign. *Communicator-In-Chief*. Lanham, MD: Lexington Books.

Reichheld, F. F., & Teal, T. (2001). *The loyalty effect: The hidden force behind growth, profits, and lasting value*. Watertown, MA: Harvard Business Press.

Rosen, E. (2009). *The anatomy of buzz revisited: Real-life lessons in word-of-mouth marketing*. New York: Random House.

Schau, H. J., Muniz, A. M. Jr., & Arnould, E. J. (2009). How brand community practices create value. *Journal of Marketing, 73*(5), 30–51.

Schivinski, B., & Dabrowski, D. (2014). The effect of social media communication on consumer perceptions of brands. *Journal of Marketing Communications*. doi:10.1080/13527266.2013.871323.

Schlosser, A. E. (2005). Posting versus lurking: Communicating in a multiple audience context. *Journal of Consumer Research, 32*(2), 260–265.

Schudson, M. (2013). *Advertising, The uneasy persuasion (RLE Advertising): Its dubious impact on American society*. New York: Routledge.

Simonson, I., & Tversky, A. (1992). Choice in context: Tradeoff contrast and extremeness aversion. *Journal of Marketing Research, 29*(3), 281.

Solop, F. I. (2010). RT@ BarackObama We just made history: Twitter and the 2008 presidential election. *Communicator-In-Chief*, 37–49.

Sparks, B. A., & Browning, V. (2011). The impact of online reviews on hotel booking intentions and perception of trust. *Tourism Management, 32*(6), 1310–1323. doi:http://dx.doi.org/10.1016/j.tourman.2010.12.011.

Stephen, A. T., & Galak, J. (2012). The effects of traditional and social earned media on sales: A study of a microlending marketplace. *Journal of Marketing Research, 49*(5), 624–639.

Stephen, A. T., & Toubia, O. (2010). *Deriving value from social commerce networks. Journal of Marketing Research*, 47(2), 215–228.

Tirunillai, S., & Tellis, G. J. (2012). Does chatter really matter? Dynamics of user-generated content and stock performance. *Marketing Science, 31*(2), 198–215.

Trusov, M., Bucklin, R. E., & Pauwels, K. (2009). Effects of word-of-mouth versus traditional marketing: Findings from an Internet social networking site. *Journal of Marketing, 73*(5), 90–102.

Twitchell, J. B. (2004). *Branded nation: The marketing of megachurch, college inc., and museumworld*. New York: Simon & Schuster.

Van den Bulte, C., & Joshi, Y. V. (2007). New product diffusion with influentials and imitators. *Marketing Science, 26*(3), 400–421.

Vargo, S. L., & Lusch, R. F. (2004). Evolving to a new dominant logic for marketing. *Journal of Marketing, 68*(1), 1–17.

Vermeulen, I. E., & Seegers, D. (2009). Tried and tested: The impact of online hotel reviews on consumer consideration. *Tourism Management, 30*(1), 123–127.

Villanueva, J., Yoo, S., & Hanssens, D. M. (2008). The impact of marketing-induced versus word-of-mouth customer acquisition on customer equity growth. *Journal of Marketing Research, 45*(1), 48–59.

Wernerfelt, B. (1995). A rational reconstruction of the compromise effect: Using market data to infer utilities. *Journal of Consumer Research*, 627–633.

Wu, F., & Huberman, B. A. (2007). Novelty and collective attention. *Proceedings of the National Academy of Sciences, 104*(45), 17599–17601.

Wu, F., & Huberman, B. A. (2008). How public opinion forms. In *Internet and Network Economics* (pp. 334–341). New York: Springer.

York, E. B. (2010). Starbucks gets its business brewing again with social media. *Advertising Age, 81*(8), 34.

CHAPTER 12

———

Cultural Representations and Practices

Nick lives in a small town and has never really fit in with guys his age. He does not particularly like football or cars and would rather make music, watch movies, or read books. Online one day, a female friend sends him a link from YouTube that just says "Don't judge, just WATCH THIS." Nick curiously clicks the link and three bright, animated ponies gallop onto the screen. Turns out this is the fourth generation of a show called *My Little Pony*, a franchise of toys started in the 1980s. Sure, it is ripped from cable television, which most people pay for, but Nick is not particularly concerned about copyright. Despite his initial reservations, Nick cannot deny that there is something compelling about the show—the fast animation, the music, the colors, the storylines and characters. Soon he is staying up late to chat with other fans online and making remixes of music from the show, which are a big hit among the community members. He freely shares these at first—after all, he has gotten a lot of great artwork from the community—but then people begin requesting custom compositions. He cheaply sets up a website where people can share their music and starts selling his own mp3s on iTunes. It is tough going at first. He gets a cease-and-desist letter from the copyright holder, but he is relatively undeterred. People love this stuff and deserve to hear it. The bigger problem is that he has to get a critical mass of people to start coming to his site and draw a mix of people who not only want to download, but also upload songs. Eventually, he sets up a YouTube sponsor account, which pays him for each view he gets, and within six months Nick has made $10,000. This is *too* easy, the thinks. Then, one day, he logs on only to find that *his* music is being distributed without with permission. "I guess now you've *really* made it!" his friend quips over gchat.

In this chapter, we will discuss the many cultural styles, artifacts, and practices that permeate online life and evaluate how these interact with and are themselves embedded in offline culture. We will begin with an examination of exactly what culture is and then apply some of this thinking to look at cultural practices online. Recall that in the introduction and throughout the book we have evaluated how social media practices are continuous with things people have been doing for a long time. Cultural practices—the ways people create, share, and interpret meaning—are certainly no exception. Social media practices of discussion, collaboration, or co-creation have facilitated existing cultural practices like fandom and interpretation of cultural artifacts like books, movies, or music. Further, social media practices themselves have reshaped parts of culture, creating remixes, viral videos, and memes.

THEORIES OF CULTURE

But just what is culture? Culture can be a tricky concept to understand because it is so pervasive. If we are fish, culture is the water in which we swim. Cultural norms and values are so ubiquitous and so deeply socialized that it takes practice and a lot of analysis to understand their effects on behavior and social structure. This section will discuss three perspectives on culture from three different disciplines—anthropology, sociology, and the humanities. Each of these disciplines has a slightly different perspective, but all are helpful for understanding the rich intersection of cultural and social media practices.

Coming from anthropology, one widely held view of culture is that it is the broad web of norms, values, practices, and artifacts of a particular group of people (Geertz, 1973). For example, tools like Facebook and YouTube are products that come out of a particular San Francisco Bay culture that prizes individual achievement and prosocial engineering (Marwick, 2013), a mix of entrepreneurial capitalism and hippie-era idealism. These values show up in features of the cultural artifacts produced such as the Facebook "status update," the like button, and more broadly in the technology for broadcasting individual achievements. In this sense, the "culture" of social media startups is a relatively consistent web of meanings and values that become institutionalized in its practices and products.

Another view of culture coming from sociology sees culture as a toolkit—a system of norms, values, practices, and artifacts from which people draw strategically for their own purposes (Swidler, 2013). For example, in the introductory vignette, Nick draws from meanings and values associated with the show *My Little Pony* such as caring and friendship to cope with tensions between his own identity and the culture where he happens to live (well, that, and there is catchy music). Yet, although he may draw from *My Little Pony* to achieve these self-related goals, he may use *Mean Girls* for cognitive models of high school and movies like *Sleepless in Seattle* for scripts of love. According to the toolkit model, these systems of meaning are not themselves necessarily consistent.

In contrast to these two views of culture from social science, perspectives from humanities tend to emphasize cultural artifacts and the people who produce them. In this view, culture is a set of idealized and valorized ideas and artifacts, "the best which has been thought and said" (Arnold, 1883). Coming from the humanities rather than anthropology or sociology, this view of culture sees it as an ideal for which humans should strive, and it often follows that "high culture" should not only be cultivated but also protected and preserved. Drawing on this model, some scholars view high culture as a worthy endeavor and "mass" or "popular" culture as inferior, and worse, as corrupting or enslaving (Adorno & Horkheimer, 2007).

For example, some may argue that Internet cycles of news and trends create a climate of superficial culture that is fleeting rather than one that builds lasting, meaningful ideas and productive debate (Keen, 2007).

Against this model, scholars like John Fiske argue that popular culture, a mix of texts and meanings that represent the ethos of a heterogeneous group of people, is itself worthy of study and preservation. From this perspective, mass culture refers to how culture is produced, whereas popular culture refers to how people use, embrace, and appropriate those products. As Fiske (1989/2010) says, "[P]opular culture is made by the people, not produced by the culture industry" (p. 24). Consider, for example, what one might learn about scripts of romance by studying *The Bachelor* or by sitting with reading groups of an Oprah book group (Daniels, 2002; Striphas, 2003). In this view, products of popular culture are so pervasive, so treasured, so *meaningful* to people that by understanding them, we might better understand ourselves and our world. Work following in this tradition has studied the *uses* people make of popular culture, such as how late-twentieth-century women read and discussed romance novels (Radway, 1991) or how nineteenth-century working-class men read dime novels (Demming, 1998).

Entire books—rather, entire libraries—could be written about how social media has become embedded in—and perhaps in some ways changed—cultural norms, values, and practices. Although this chapter will cover some of this territory, it will concern itself primarily with the cultural practices behind the creation of cultural objects—videos, fan fiction, mashups—that are one of the most fascinating outgrowths of social media. This chapter will provide a framework for understanding the place of these cultural products in society and within the groups of users that produce, consume, and circulate them.

CULTURAL STYLES AND PRACTICES

Participatory Culture

Participatory culture is "a culture with relatively low barriers to artistic expression and civic engagement, strong support for creating and sharing one's creations, and some type of informal mentorship whereby what is known by the most experienced is passed along to novices" (Jenkins, 2013, p.3; Jenkins, Clinton, Purushotma, Robinson, & Weigel, 2006). In participatory cultures, the audience is or can become active in producing, modifying, or curating cultural objects.

First studied in the context of fan communities, participatory culture emphasizes the ability of anyone to engage in cultural production, but usually stresses the degree to which people work and rework elements of cultural products distributed through traditional media. As Jenkins notes, "Modern participatory culture has some relationship to traditional folk culture in terms of the principles of informal learning and social reproduction" (Jenkins, 2013, p. xxvii). Thus, theories for studying participatory culture come most notably from studies of popular culture, but also incorporate an understanding of cultural norms, values, and practices that are the hallmark of an anthropological approach to culture as a web of meaning.

Social media platforms, together with the technology to edit cultural content, have increased participation in producing or modifying cultural objects online (Pew, 2007). Whereas participatory cultures might have formerly produced zines, formed letter rings, or sent tapes through the mail, people now write blogs, create message boards, and post videos. Indeed, participatory cultural practices, which existed prior to social media, are one model on which many social media practices are now based. Social media platforms certainly make it easier to collaborate on cultural objects, but this kind of collaboration existed long before social media. For example, fans of baseball, science fiction, and soap operas have long gathered to produce cultural artifacts. Further, it is not inevitable that participatory culture will naturally be enabled by social media. Rather, some have suggested that initial possibilities for cultural production offered by the Internet have been foreclosed by increasing commercialization and decreasing transparency (Heffernan, 2010; Lanier, 2014).

Participatory cultures form social bonds around the cultural objects that people admire. This process itself produces cultural materials—anything from texts of conversations about interpretation of a particular episode, to fan fiction, to handmade replicas of cultural objects. For example, the fan community for *My Little Pony* discussed in the opening vignette is one example of a participatory culture. Fans of the show hold conventions, produce fan fiction, and make and remake animations from the show. Members of the culture form a community, the type of which we discussed in Chapter 10. Strong social bonds exist between group members, and some have even met their spouses through the community (Malaquais, 2012). Antifans can be equally active in interpreting and reacting to texts or celebrities (Marwick, 2013). The book and movie series *Twilight*, for example, inspired the creation of several antifan groups online (Pinkowitz, 2010).

Online participatory fan cultures can sometimes even influence the television show, movie, or artist of which they are a fan. For example, major changes to the television series *Babylon 5* were made after fan feedback to the pilot (Booth, 2010). The writers for *The X-Files* famously read the fan message boards, incorporated posters' screen names into the show as bit characters, and increased the prominence of certain characters based on fan feedback. In response to a prominent community member dying, the writers even dedicated an episode to that fan (Deery, 2003).

These fan communities also sometimes work as a collective to take an active role in promoting their interests. For example, taking a note from tactics common in social movements, fans of the Backstreet Boys in Thailand organized a petition, submitted to their record company, for the group to visit an Asian country that was not Japan or China (Earl & Schussman, 2008). In fact, entertainment petitions were the largest category of petitions offered by PetitionOnline, a site that hosts petitions, which hosted 14,395 active entertainment-oriented petitions. The next largest category was international government issues, with a mere 3,470 petitions (Earl & Schussman, 2008). The purpose of these fan petitions was primarily advocacy, with fans demanding revivals or continuations of their favorite shows. Twenty-one percent of these petitions were pleas to add or expand existing cultural objects such as a petition to bring the band Pearl Jam to Columbia. Many of these petitions, roughly one-third, called on a particular public or fan community such as those discussed in Chapter 10.

Fan Fiction

Fan communities not only read, interpret, and discuss texts, but also often produce texts themselves. Fan fiction is perhaps the clearest example in which fan communities rework the narrative of their favorite television show or movie, often using the same characters and the same worlds. As opposed to the "canon," the original, usually copyright-protected narrative and characters, fan fiction takes elements of the story and remixes them in a variety of ways for a variety of purposes. For example, Harry Potter fan fiction is a corpus of text unto itself, with the largest site (http://www.fanalley.com/) offering more than 30,000 stories written by fans of all ages (Anelli, 2008; Booth, 2010; Jenkins, 2006). Harry Potter fan fiction runs the gamut in terms of genres from comedy, to news, to gay and straight pornography, horror, and humor (Booth, 2010; Jenkins, 2006), and fans have elaborate systems for marking genres or combinations of genres. For example "AU" stands for alternate universe and signifies that the story takes place with the same characters, but in a different world. "Gen" stands for "general" and means that the narrative is not romantic.

In producing fan fiction, fans may develop feelings of moral authority, the right to play with characters and plot, often feeling they have more ownership over the cultural object than do its creators (Booth, 2010; Jenkins, 2006). As Booth (2010) says, "Fan fiction is, in a way, both an appreciation and a re-appreciation of the object of that fandom. Appreciation involves reading for meaning, but re-appreciation is reading the media object again through the lens of the fan

Photo 12.1 Star Trek fans were early producers of fan fiction.

community" (Booth, 2010, p. 104). As we discussed in Chapter 10, fans can create audience communities that develop their own unique interpretations of focal texts. For example, one *Simpsons* fan group on reddit became convinced that the show was all Homer's dream, against the expressed protests of head creator Matt Groening (Vlastelica, 2015).

In addition to fan fiction, communities will produce many other different types of cultural products from videos, to music, to wikis, collectively created compendiums of characters and elements from the narratives. For example, the fan community for *Game of Thrones* maintains an extensive wiki to organize 2,777 characters and families from both the books and the television series.[1] These wikis reconfigure the narrative from a "chrono logic" of a narrative that unfolds in time to a spatial logic that is connected through hyperlinks (Booth, 2010, p. 82).

Online fan communities may seem unique—and indeed they have long been stigmatized (Jenkins, 1993/2013), but the models of engagement practiced in these

@ABCScandal followers

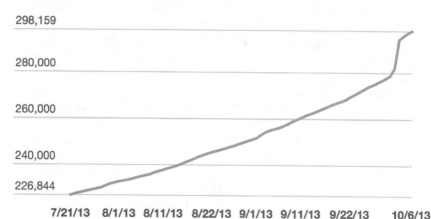

298,159

280,000

260,000

240,000

226,844

7/21/13   8/1/13   8/11/13   8/22/13   9/1/13   9/11/13   9/22/13   10/6/13

Source: Twitter Media Blog, Get the data, Embed this chart

Scandal @ScandalABC · Feb 25
We're with you. sister! Tune in next thursday for an all-new #Scandal. #MellieForPresident #Scandal

↩   ↻ 248   ★ 561   •••

Figure 12.1 and Figure 12.2 Twitter Followers for @ScandalABC Have Increased Rapidly over Time.

communities have actually become a model for attracting and engaging all kinds of audiences. After all, everyone is a fan of something. Take, for example, the ABC show *Scandal*. Early on, producers of the show realized that cultivating loyalists through Twitter and other platforms was a key promotional vehicle.[2] When viewed as cultural narratives, sports, news, and politics and the communities of fans that surround them are not terribly different from science fiction and soap operas, and people form participatory cultures around them in similar ways.

Repetition, Mashups, Remixes, and Parody

Tools for manipulating and creating cultural objects have become less expensive and widely available (Benkler, 2006). Studies show that many people—but certainly not all—create their own cultural products to circulate online. A Pew survey reports that 33% of "online teens report sharing their own artwork, photos, stories, or videos with others" online (Lenhart, 2005) which is comparable to adults' participation rate of approximately 30% (Schradie, 2011). User-produced texts can take a variety of forms, several of which we have discussed in the previous section. Online tools, particularly video and music editing, have made it more common to create and circulate cultural products reassembled from others in the form of tribute, mashup, remix, and parody.

With these tools, people add commentary to cultural products, remaking them as tribute, parody, or play. For example, a video called "The Harlem Shake v1 (TSCS original)" was posted on TheSunnyCoastSkate on February 2, 2013, and touched off a wave of repetition. Seven days later, more than 12,000 videos had been uploaded, at the rate of 4,000 videos every day. By February 14, twelve days later, more than 40,000 videos using the meme had been posted, and the creators included not only people in their living rooms and college dorms, but also the U.S. Olympic Swim team on a plane, the band Matt and Kim, and employees at companies ranging from Buzzfeed to Sea World. Firefighters, soccer teams, senior citizens, kids, the University of Kansas basketball team—all of them and many more had posted Harlem Shake videos.[3] In another vein of repetition, people will post "tribute" videos, clips that remake an original music or viral video, a kind of visual "cover" of the original.

Through these iterations, social media also creates the opportunity for parody. For example, music videos from Lady Gaga, Kanye West, Katy Perry, and Ke$ha routinely unleash a wave of imitation videos. However, the line between tribute and parody is not always clear. For example, in response to the show *Mad Men*, advertising executives made Twitter names for each of the characters on the show, impersonating characters from the show in their tweets. One female advertising professional created a Twitter account for @PeggyOlson, who, through her tweets, would offer a perspective into her internal monologue as events from the show unraveled. These tweets were obviously made in the spirit of admiration, but also poked fun at the characters' personality and the norms of work environments of the 1960s (Jenkins, Ford, & Green, 2013). By inhabiting these roles, fans can play with the characters in a new way.

Videos can also emerge from fan collaboration. For example, on a site called Star Wars Uncut (http://www.starwarsuncut.com/), a fan named Casey Pugh set up platform where other fans could choose and then remake a fifteen-second clip of the first *Star Wars* release, *A New Hope*. Some fans chose to remake scenes with their kids, others used action figures, and some reenacted them in their pajamas. Then, the site creator put the clips together, forming a new, two and a half–hour movie that is a replica of the original (Booth, 2010).

It has never been easier to produce cultural content, but it has also never been easier to decompose it and reconstitute it in another form. A **mashup** is when two or more cultural products are combined into one (Kendall & Schmidt, 2007). For example, DJ Dangermouse combined the Beatle's *White Album* with Jay-Z's the *Black Album* to create the *Grey Album*. The artist Girl Talk combines old and new popular songs into dance hits. A **remix** is when elements of a cultural object are reconfigured into a new cultural object, often also by adding musical or visual elements or changing the pacing. Repetition, mashup, remix, and parody, of course, all challenge boundaries of copyright, as we will discuss in Chapter 14.

Language

All of these new cultural forms provide new aesthetic styles and new vocabulary in popular culture. As we discussed in Chapter 3, social media interaction can breed particular, and unique, linguistic styles. For example, the animated gif can be used on message boards to provide witty or sarcastic commentary. The constraints of texting can produce new language patterns such as abbreviation, the abandonment of sentence structure, and use of symbols. **Phatic communication** is language used for social purposes, not necessarily to communicate information (Miller, 2008). For example, when someone Tweets "OMG I can't believe the new album is out!!" he or she is likely trying to express affiliation and loyalty to a particular artist rather than convey information about an album release. Tweets can be used in this way to create and maintain social bonds, particularly when they share the same linguistic style and expression (Crawford, 2009; Marwick & boyd, 2011). Memes, which we will discuss in the next section, can be more than passing fads, becoming lasting parts of culture. For example, terms like sexting and selfie have generally passed into common usage, at least for now.

CULTURAL TRANSMISSION

Social media platforms provide the infrastructure for collaboration on and with cultural products and create new styles and aesthetics of their own. But how do cultural products, once made, circulate? Metaphors of transmission—circulation, virality, memes, stickiness, spreadability—are all attempts to represent the process through which digital content moves from one person, or a group of people, to another, sometimes changing in the process. Viral video is perhaps the most popular way to refer to cultural transmission online. A **viral** video is one that becomes popular quickly through person-to-person referral on social media platforms. As we discussed in Chapter 11, the short half-life of networked communication as well as network structure can lead to rapid diffusion of cultural material.

And, yes, studies even provisionally confirm the stereotype of viral videos as clips of cats doing crazy things. The most "socially" shared videos are from the pets and animals categories; 42% of highly shared videos were pets and animals, compared to 31.7% for news, 28% for sports, and 12% for music (Broxton, Interian, Vaver, & Wattenhofer, 2013; see also Burgess & Green, 2009). Coming initially from science fiction depictions of how ideas might spread (Jenkins et al., 2013; Stephenson, 2003), the viral metaphor has predominated how many people think of this movement.

A **meme** is "an idea, behavior, or style that spreads from person to person within a culture" (Dawkins, 1976, p. 192). First proposed by the evolutionary biologist Richard Dawkins, a meme is a carrier of cultural content, like a gene, but filled with cultural meaning. Named from the term *mimesis*, which means imitation in Ancient Greek (Plato, 380 BC), this metaphor for transmission emphasizes the reproductive nature of ideas and implies that success is determined through a process of selection from a vast amount of competing memes. Given what we know about the vast amount and availability of cultural material and the limited capacity of one person to attend to the ideas that emerge in public consciousness, ideas do seem to make it through a process of cultural filtering, albeit a somewhat more socially and culturally complex one than what the biological metaphor suggests (Hilgartner & Bosk, 1988).

Shifman distinguishes between viral videos, which generally circulate without modification, and memes, which tend to be modified with each transmission. These modifications come primarily in two forms: parody and remix (Shifman, 2012). One of the most circulated image memes is LOLcats, a style of meme that depicts cats in funny poses with captions in altered or broken English such as

Photo 12.2 Can I Has Cheezburger?

"I can haz cheezburger?" (Photo 12.3) (Gawne & Vaughan, 2011). A study of the most popular memes on YouTube finds that they have distinct characteristics relative to other videos. They tend to contain ordinary people and a number of traits that make them relatively easy to reproduce, such as a simple background and repetitive concept. For instance, the "Leave Britney Alone" video made by Chris Crocker contains a simple setting—the protagonist with a sheet over his head—and contains a repeated phrase, which makes them seem easy to reproduce.

Mimetic videos tend to contain humor and often work from unexpected incongruities, such as a frumpy woman singing a beautiful song or a young boy belting it out with the voice of a large man (Shifman, 2012). For instance, in the video "Chocolate Rain," the singer's boyish appearance contradicts his deep singing voice. They often represent forms of flawed masculinity; twenty-four of the thirty viral videos studied had men as leading characters, but these characters did not fit the dominant norm of stoic, fit men (Shifman, 2012). These properties, taken together, can help us understand what spreads and what does not.

Stickiness is another concept, first introduced by organizational scholars, to further understand what makes ideas particularly successful (Szulanski, 1996). Although many claim to identify properties of stickiness (Heath & Heath, 2007), studies of this kind of cultural transmission tend to suffer from selection bias in that they only study cases of successful diffusion. That is, many cultural ideas and products may have these traits, but understanding their success or failure also requires understanding the social and cultural environment in which they exist.

Attempting to overcome the biological metaphors of these previous models of transmission, some scholars have argued that terms like viral and meme fail to account for the agency that people have in sharing an idea. That is, audience members are active in shaping the flow of media content rather than passive carriers of content (Jenkins et al., 2013, pp. 2, 20). **Spreadability** is "the potential—both technical and cultural—for audiences to share content for their own purposes" (Jenkins et al., 2013, p. 3). In contrast to stickiness, spreadability recognizes that audiences often exist as collectives rather than individuals,

Photo 12.3 "Leave Britney Alone."

that they are diverse rather than homogenous, and that cultural transmission requires not holding attention through stickiness, but rather motivating continued engagement. For example, an idea like the ALS ice bucket challenge becomes circulated because people find it resonant (Schudson, 1989) and want to participate by sharing it with their friends. By sharing it with someone else, you are saying something about yourself to a community of people who interpret that behavior in a particular way, perhaps with some esteem or interest. By following Kim Kierkegaardashian (Photo 12.4), one is signifying knowledge of both high culture—the Danish philosopher Søren Kierkegaard—and low culture—the celebrity Kim Kardashian.

Metaphors of virality, and even stickiness and spreadability, will often omit the role of gatekeepers in the process of cultural diffusion. One often thinks of social media, and the Internet more broadly, as a democratic realm of equals. But this is not the case when we observe the patterns of circulation of online content. Large news organizations, celebrities, bloggers, and the platforms themselves often play an important role in shaping which cultural products get shared and which do not. Gatekeepers, who we read about in Chapter 9, play a critical role in the transmission of media, sometimes practically because of technology, but more often because of social or cultural capital. For example, being featured on the front page of YouTube has a dramatic effect on a video's popularity (Figueiredo, Benevenuto, & Almeida, 2011). In fact, videos have three distinctive growth patterns: those that become popular because they are helped by a key gatekeeper such as the front page of YouTube, those that become popular because of a simple random process, and those that achieve popularity rapidly through online word of mouth (i.e. viral videos) (Figueiredo et al., 2011). For example, if a video is circulated on a popular blog like *Talking Points Memo*, the mention by this gatekeeper dramatically increases the video's circulation. In a context where attention is limited and cultural material is plentiful, gatekeepers with cultural and social capital play a pivotal—and often overlooked—role in promoting some content, whereas other content gets overlooked.

Photo 12.4 Existential Insights from Kim Kierkegaardashian.

Circulation

Circulation describes the movement of an object or sign in and out of different cultural, economic, and social contexts (Appadurai, 1988; Kopytoff, 1988). For example, the K-pop group Super Junior became hugely popular in Indonesia, partly because of an Indonesian parody video of one of their songs (Jung, 2011). Riding on a wave called Hyluu, Korean pop music diffused throughout East and Southeast Asia, overtaking Japan in terms of cultural exports (Jung, 2011). Notably, in this case and others, political and economic structures play a role in structuring circulation (Kopytoff, 1986). For example, Indonesia was culturally and economically closed from 1966 to 1998, and only after the political and cultural opening in 1998 did products from East Asia begin circulating, first with Japanese pop (or J-pop) and then later with K-pop. Social media provides not only a venue for the circulation of official songs and parody videos, but also a platform for consumer co-creation that facilitates circulation. For example, bilingual Indonesian fans translated and subtitled K-pop videos into Indonesian, posting them to a wiki for other fans.

Cross-cultural circulation is obviously an important part of cultural transmission. Yet digital products in circulation are not always cleanly replicated, without regard to material realities. As Larkin has found, the circulation of pirated movies like *Shrek* in Nigeria show signs of material degradation as they are copied from their original forms to cheaper and sometimes more portable media (Larkin, 2004). Posters on YouTube in the United States will often complain of the poor quality of nostalgia videos because of their preservation on modes of media like VHS. We may think of cultural transmission online as a free-flowing process, but material realities such as compression and bandwidth play a role in shaping the form of the product. Circulation calls attention to these realities, particularly as they exist as differences between core and periphery, first and third worlds.

CULTURAL CONTENT

Narrative

So how have our beloved narrative structures—epic, comedy, tragedy, romance—fared in this new system of cultural transmission? Streams of research point in two opposing directions. On the one hand, viral videos can be mind-numbingly simple. For example, keyboard cat (Photo 12.5) depicts a cat being manipulated as a puppet to play a simple, repeated musical riff. Indeed, the simplicity makes it endlessly repeatable, open to parody, and imitation (Shifman, 2012). On the other hand, texts have also gotten increasingly complex (Johnson, 2006). Aware that devoted fan communities surround some media properties, producers of cultural products might embed secret or hidden "clues" or "keys" within the narrative or write complex multiple plots with many richly developed characters. Yet, despite their complexity, these narratives are nonetheless structured according to classic mythic structures such as a hero narrative or a romance. **Cult texts** are

Photo 12.5 "Keyboard Cat."

"vast, elaborate and densely populated fictional world[s] that [are] constructed episode-by-episode, extended and embellished by official secondary-level texts (episode guides, novelizations, comics, magazines) and fan-produced tertiary texts (fan fiction, cultural criticism essays, art, scratch videos)" (Gwenllian-Jones & Pearson, 2004). For example, the television show *Lost* contains allusions to philosophy, literature, and myth, which spurred extensive investigation and discussion among fans in online forums.

Transmedia Storytelling

In a complex media ecology such as the one outlined in Chapter 2, narratives can be written to span multiple media. **Transmedia** is a "story [that] unfolds across multiple media platforms, with each new text making a distinctive and valuable contribution to the whole" (Jenkins, 2006, p. 97). For example, the *Matrix* franchise expanded well beyond movies to tell the story through video games and graphic novels (Jenkins, 2006). Similar properties exist in movies like *Star Wars*, which generated a video game and a series of books, and Indiana Jones, which spawned a TV series (*Young Indiana Jones*). Transmedia storytelling is often dependent on social media, and fans gather on social media platforms to compare notes and make connections between different parts of the narrative. These fans circulate knowledge about the storylines and puzzle out clues in the narrative in a process of **collective reasoning**, a type of collective intelligence and co-creation discussed in Chapter 5. Notably, many media producers have attempted to cultivate and cater to fan engagement, at least partly out of economic interest, because it creates more products for people to buy (Jenkins, 2006). Although ideally transmedia products can be consumed a la carte, execution requires coordination among writers, producers, game developers, and many others. Transmedia products have led to deep fan engagement, yet they can also demand extensive fan time, interest, and commitment (Jenkins, 2006, p. 131). Imagine how much time it would take to see all three *Matrix* movies, play the video games, read the comics, and still have time to go through the boards on *Matrix Online*!

Transparency is another important shift that has been partly facilitated by social media. Fans become intimately familiar with the "backstage" machinations of cultural products because a host of formerly inaccessible figures are now accessible online. Actors now routinely post backstage pictures of the show's production for promotion, and hardcore fans will endlessly puzzle out the motivations of the writers and production teams. Booth argues that a philosophy of playfulness constitutes viewer activities, not only encompassing fan fiction, videos, songs, and conversation, but also structuring how fans "play" with creators of the show (Booth, 2010, p. 2).

Celebrity

Taking a step back, it can be helpful to better understand the people and organizations that shape the context of cultural production. Participatory culture can of course be influential—but it exists within a system of selling cultural products. In fact, we can understand many cultural products as the result of several different, but overlapping microsystems (Van Dijk, 2005).

One system that has had significant incursion into social media is celebrity. **Microcelebrity** is "a state of being famous to a niche group of people, but it is also a behavior: the presentation of oneself as a celebrity regardless of who is paying attention" (Marwick, 2013, p. 114; see also Marwick & boyd, 2011; Senft, 2008). Beauty bloggers on YouTube, creators of certain viral videos, and legendary creators of some online platforms all have the potential to be "Internet famous." Microcelebrities develop carefully crafted personas, produce content strategically crafted for their audience, and attempt to "authentically" relate to their fans (Humphreys & Kozinets, 2009; Marwick, 2013). By exchanging either public @ replies or private DMs, celebrities large and small can create a sense of "digital intimacy" (Thompson, 2008) with their fans and followers (Marwick, 2013). For example, Mariah Carey responds to tweets sent by fans, who then preserve and circulate them as a form of badging, giving them status among other Mariah fans (Marwick & boyd, 2011).

Photo 12.6 The Real Kim Kardashian.

Another way celebrities form this kind of digital intimacy is by offering followers a look into the backstage of their world. For example, celebrities like James Franco, Beyoncé and Questlove tweet pictures of themselves from bed having just woken up, hanging out with other celebrities, or behind the scenes of a "frontstage" cultural product like a play or concert. Reflecting on what we learned about self-presentation in Chapter 6, we see that such glimpses can create a sense of authenticity that may be missing from traditional mediated performances such as a movie or television show. Celebrities must be "special," but also "real" because they both produce work and are worked on by those charged with elevating them to capture attention by creating a personal "brand" (Gamson, 2011).

Celebrities are surprisingly active when it comes to producing unique content. According to one study, 42% of celebrity tweets were @replies, whereas only 5% were retweets, and 6% included hashtags (Marwick & boyd, 2011). This indicates that they are writing original content, not simply passing things along. For example, Kim Kardashian is one such celebrity who regularly contributes personal thoughts and photos via platforms like Instagram and Twitter in addition to tweeting on behalf of corporate sponsors (Photo 12.6). In contrast to previous models of **parasocial relationships** with characters in traditional media, where fans will form a quasi-relationship via media products (Thompson, 1995), these celebrity–fan interactions can cross into relationships that entail direct communication and exchange of affection (Marwick & boyd, 2011).

SUMMARY AND CONCLUSION

This chapter has provided an overview of how cultural practices and representations exist in and are enabled by social media, focusing on three ways of looking at culture. Using the perspective of participatory culture, we have examined some ways that social media practices have reshaped cultural production and transmission and other ways in which cultural products have maintained their structure despite the new economic and technological context. As we have seen in this chapter, culture is deeply embedded in our media practices and consumer lives. In the next two chapters, we will examine two other important domains—politics and economics—that both shape and have been shaped by social media.

TOPICS

- Viral video
- Memes
- Participatory culture
- Transmedia
- Circulation
- Parasocial relationships

DISCUSSION QUESTIONS

1. Are online fan communities important to a cultural product? Why or why not?
2. Which model of culture do you think most accurately describes your observations of culture? Give two examples that support your view and at least one example that may challenge the model.
3. Why do you think cultural products have become more transparent? Is there anything that remains mysterious or illusive about either the product or its creators?

EXERCISES

1. Pick a recent meme and research its cultural transmission. How did it become popular? Through what connections did it become popular and were any gatekeepers involved? Finally, what, if any, properties of its content made it spreadable?
2. Select a microcelebrity online and analyze his or her persona, performance, and authenticity. What kind of work makes them "Internet famous," and how do they curate a persona and digital intimacy? Are they successful at this? Why or why not?

NOTES

1. http://awoiaf.westeros.org/index.php/List_of_Characters/.
2. https://media.Twitter.com/success/abc-scandal-recruits-fans-on-Twitter/.
3. http://youtube-trends.blogspot.com/2013/02/the-harlem-shake-has-exploded.html/.

FURTHER READINGS

Jenkins, H., Ford, S., & Green, J. (2013). *Spreadable media: Creating value and meaning in a networked culture*. New York: New York University Press.

Marwick, A.E. (2013). *Status update: Celebrity, publicity, and branding in the social media age*. New Haven, CT: Yale University Press.

Van Dijck, Jose (2013), *The culture of connectivity: A critical history of social media*. Oxford: Oxford University Press.

REFERENCES

Adorno, T., & Horkheimer, M. (2007). The culture industry: Enlightenment as mass deception. In *Stardom and celebrity: A reader* (pp. 34–43). London and Thousand Oaks, CA: Sage.

Anelli, M. (2008). *Harry, a history-now updated with JK Rowling interview, new chapter & photos: The true story of a boy wizard, his fans, and life inside the Harry Potter phenomenon*. New York: Simon & Schuster.

Appadurai, A. (1988). *The social life of things: Commodities in cultural perspective.* Cambridge, UK: Cambridge University Press.

Arnold, M. (1883). *Culture & anarchy: An essay in political and social critisicm.* New York: Macmillan.

Benkler, Y. (2006). *The wealth of networks: How social production transforms markets and freedom.* New Haven, CT: Yale University Press.

Booth, P. (2010). *Digital fandom: New media studies* (Vol. 68). New York: Lang.

Broxton, T., Interian, Y., Vaver, J., & Wattenhofer, M. (2013). Catching a viral video. *Journal of Intelligent Information Systems, 40*(2), 241–259.

Burgess, J. E., & Green, J. B. (2009). The entrepreneurial vlogger: Participatory culture beyond the professional-amateur divide. *The YouTube Reader,* 89–107.

Crawford, K. (2009). Following you: Disciplines of listening in social media. *Continuum: Journal of Media & Cultural Studies, 23*(4), 525–535.

Daniels, H. (2002). *Literature circles: Voice and choice in book clubs and reading groups.* Portland, ME: Stenhouse.

Dawkins, R. (1976). *The selfish gene* (pp. 1, 976). New York: Oxford University Press.

Deery, J. (2003). TV. com: Participatory viewing on the Web. *The Journal of Popular Culture, 37*(2), 161–183.

Demming, M. (1998). *Mechanic accents: Dime novels and working class culture of America.* New York: Verso.

Earl, J., & Schussman, A. (2008). Contesting cultural control: Youth culture and online petitioning. In *Civic life online: Learning how digital media can engage youth* (pp. 71–95). Cambridge, MA: MIT Press.

Figueiredo, F., Benevenuto, F., & Almeida, J. M. (2011). *The tube over time: Characterizing popularity growth of youtube videos.* Paper presented at the Proceedings of the Fourth ACM International Conference on Web Search and Data Mining –WSDM. Hong Kong, China

Fiske, J. (1989/2010). *Understanding popular culture.* New York: Routledge.

Gamson, J. (2011). The unwatched life is not worth living: The elevation of the ordinary in celebrity culture. *PMLA, 126*(4), 1061–1069.

Gawne, L., & Vaughan, J. (2011). *I can haz language play: The construction of language and identity in LOLspeak.* In M. Ponsonnet, L. Dao & M. Bowler (Eds), Proceedings of the 42nd Australian Linguistic Society Conference—2011. Australian National University, Canberra ACT, 2–4 December 2011 (pp. 97–122).

Geertz, C. (1973). *The interpretation of cultures: Selected essays* (Vol. 5019). New York: Basic Books.

Gwenllian-Jones, S., & Pearson, R. E. (2004). *Cult television.* Minneapolis: University of Minnesota Press.

Heath, C., & Heath, D. (2007). *Made to stick: Why some ideas survive and others die.* New York: Random House.

Heffernan, V. (2010). *The death of the open web. New York Times.* Retrieved from http://www.nytimes.com/2010/05/23/magazine/23FOB-medium-t.html?_r=0/.

Hilgartner, S., & Bosk, C. L. (1988). The rise and fall of social problems: A public arenas model. *American Journal of Sociology, 94*(1), 53–78.

Humphreys, A., & Kozinets, R. V. (2009). The construction of value in attention economies. *Advances in Consumer Research, 36,* 689–690.

Jenkins, H. (1993/2013). *Textual poachers: Television fans and participatory culture.* New York: Routledge.

Jenkins, H. (2006). *Convergence culture: Where old and new media collide.* New York: New York University Press.

Jenkins, H. (2013). *Textual poachers: Television fans and participatory culture.* New York: Routledge.

Jenkins, H., Clinton, K., Purushotma, R., Robinson, A. J., & Weigel, M. (2006). *Confronting the challenges of participatory culture: Media education for the 21st century.* Chicago: The John D. and Catherine T. MacArthur Foundation. Retrieved from http://www.newmedialiteracies.Org/.

Jenkins, H., Ford, S., & Green, J. (2013). *Spreadable media: Creating value and meaning in a networked culture.* New York: New York University Press.

Johnson, S. (2006). *Everything bad is good for you.* New York: Penguin.

Jung, S. (2011). K-pop, Indonesian fandom, and social media. *Transformative Works and Cultures, 8,* 281–305.

Keen, A. (2007). *The cult of the amateur: How blogs, MySpace, YouTube, and the rest of today's user-generated media are destroying our economy, our culture, and our values.* New York: Broadway Business.

Kendall, K. E., & Schmidt, A. (2007). Mashups: The art of creating new applications by combining two or more web sites. *Decision Line, 38*(2).

Kopytoff, I. (1988). The cultural biography of things. In Appadurai, A. (Ed.), *The social life of things: Commodities in cultural perspective.* Cambridge, UK: Cambridge University Press.

Lanier, J. (2014). *Who owns the future?* New York: Simon & Schuster.

Larkin, B. (2004). Degraded images, distorted sounds: Nigerian video and the infrastructure of piracy. *Public Culture, 16*(2), 289–314.

Lenhart, A. M., & Madden, M. (2005). *Teen content creators and consumers.* Retrieved from http://www.pewinternet.org/2005/11/02/teen-content-creators-and-consumers/.

Malaquais, L. (Writer). (2012). Bronies: The extremely unexpected adult fans of *My Little Pony* [Film]. In Silk, D. S., Silk, L., Foxley, S. R., Brown, A., Wackernagel, H., Peterson, M., Faust, L., Chow, T. (Producer). BronyDoc, Inc.

Marwick, A. E. (2013). *Status update: Celebrity, publicity, and branding in the social media age.* New Haven, CT: Yale University Press.

Marwick, A. E., & boyd, d. (2011). I tweet honestly, I tweet passionately: Twitter users, context collapse, and the imagined audience. *New Media & Society, 13*(1), 114–133.

Miller, V. (2008). New media, networking and phatic culture. *Convergence: The International Journal of Research into New Media Technologies, 14*(4), 387–400.

Pew. (2007). *Teens creating content.* Retrieved from http://www.pewinternet .org/2007/12/19/teens-creating-content/.

Pinkowitz, J. M. (2010). "The rabid fans that take [Twilight] much too seriously": The construction and rejection of excess in Twilight antifandom. *Transformative Works and Cultures, 7.* doi:10.3983/twc.2011.0247.

Plato. (380 BC). *The Republic.*

Radway, J. A. (1991). *Reading the romance: Women, patriarchy, and popular literature.* Chapel Hill: University of North Carolina Press.

Schradie, J. (2011). The digital production gap: The digital divide and Web 2.0 collide. *Poetics, 39*(2), 145–168.

Schudson, M. (1989). How culture works. *Theory and Society, 18*(2), 153–180.

Senft, T. M. (2008). *Camgirls: Celebrity and community in the age of social networks* (Vol. 4). New York: Lang.

Shifman, L. (2012). An anatomy of a YouTube meme. *New Media & Society, 14*(2), 187–203.

Stephenson, N. (2003). *Snow crash.* New York: Random House.

Striphas, T. (2003). A dialectic with the everyday: Communication and cultural politics on Oprah Winfrey's book club. *Critical Studies in Media Communication, 20*(3), 295–316.

Swidler, A. (2013). *Talk of love: How culture matters.* Chicago: University of Chicago Press.

Szulanski, G. (1996). Exploring internal stickiness: Impediments to the transfer of best practice within the firm. *Strategic Management Journal, 17*(S2), 27–43.

Thompson, C. (2008). Brave new world of digital intimacy. *The New York Times.*

Van Dijk, J. A. (2005). *The deepening divide: Inequality in the information society.* Thousand Oaks, CA: Sage.

Vlastelica, R. (2015). *New fan theory says most of The Simpsons takes place in Homer's mind.* AV Club. Retrieved from http://www.avclub.com/article/ new-fan-theory-says-most-simpsons-takes-place-home-215301/.

CHAPTER 13

—

Political Life

Catherine cannot wait to go to Istanbul this summer. An avid traveler, she reads constantly about the city's history as a global trading center since the fourth century BCE. On the day she arrives, Catherine gets a Facebook message from her friend Zeynep that the street to her hotel is blocked because of a protest in Taksim Square. She has read about the protests in Egypt, Libya, and Tunisia, but she never thought she would be in the middle of a mass protest herself, let alone on her vacation. On the ride from the airport, she checks Twitter to get the latest on what is going on. The subway has been shut down. One group of protesters plans to meet by Starbucks for another night of blocking police attempts to clear the square. Another group plans to organize a theatrical performance at sundown, and still another group is getting together to march through Gezi Park around lunchtime. To understand exactly why all of these people are out there, Catherine goes to http://www.nytimes.com to read about the shopping mall that President Erdoğan plans to develop in the park. This all started with a few people protecting trees? The comments, largely from people in the United States, are generally supportive of the protestors, but debate issues of U.S. intervention. She reads all that she can until her cab stops at a homemade barricade, made up of road signs, gates, and a burned out car. "You'll have to walk from here," the driver says, and she gets out and hikes to her hotel.

Chapter 13 will examine the role of social media practices in civic and political life. Some basic concepts and theories from sociology, journalism, and political science will be used to assess how social media has changed the nature of political action and more broadly how it has become integrated with civic life. Theories covered will include social movements theory, agenda setting, and empirically grounded research on civic engagement and online activism.

But first, the big questions: Does social media enable political movements or hinder their formation? Is it inherently democratizing or does it potentially serve the interests of dictatorships, intelligence agencies, or state organizations? These are hotly debated topics about which many people have an opinion, but they have only recently been empirically investigated (for perspectives see Fandy, 1999; Morozov, 2009; Sunstein, 2009). Some have argued that social media is a tool for political activism, as when a political organization like Human Rights Watch

Photo 13.1 A Protestor in Taksim Square.

uses Facebook to rally citizens or when protesters in Turkey take to Twitter to organize opposition to government plans. Others have pointed out that terrorists, insurgents, and hackers use the same networks to communicate, whereas social media also furnishes states with powerful tools for monitoring citizens' political activities. As we will see in this chapter, the reality is more complicated than any one-sided generalization about the role of social media in political life. Throughout the examples in this book, we have seen how social media can enable new ways of doings things, but also how it can reinforce preexisting norms, values, and institutions. Nonetheless, new technologies may provide certain affordances that make engagement in political life easier or harder, safer or more dangerous, more powerful or less effective. Ultimately, deciding whether social media is changing politics will be a matter of evaluating different cases and examining the contextual factors that enable or inhibit its potential to change the way people organize politically (boyd, 2008).

POWER

To begin to understand the influence that social media may have on political life, it helps to start with an understanding of power. **Power** is the ability to influence people or things. It is a deceptively simple term for a complex concept. Social theorists have developed different ways of understanding power and the ability of people or organizations to influence social structures such as laws, norms, and values. The sociologist Max Weber (1864–1920) argues that there are three kinds of power: charismatic power, totalitarian power, and bureaucratic power (Weber, 1978). Each of these can be used to understand social media. For instance, the charisma of a politician or a celebrity like Bono may give him or her influence over an extensive group of followers and fans. Totalitarian power is seen more often in **states** or territories where one person has control over what Weber calls the means of violence, the military and the legal system for enforcing punishment. We can see, for example, how totalitarian power might play a role in structuring access to social media. For example, during the Egyptian protests of 2011, representatives of the state cut Internet access to much of the nation (Arthur, 2011). The Chinese government has periodically blocked Google, Facebook, and Twitter, which has nurtured the growth of companies like Baidu, Tencent, and Weibo (Levin, 2014; Woollaston, 2013). Bureaucratic power is the ability to influence people or practices based on rules or procedures in some organized hierarchy. For example, the Recording Industry Association of America lobbied to pass a law in 2007 that strengthened enforcement of copyright in the United States (Bangeman, 2008), potentially affecting digital and social media platforms. In an organization like Wikipedia, administrators exercise bureaucratic power by adjudicating disputes according to agreed-on rules and procedures such as having a neutral point of view (NPOV) (Joyce, Pike, & Butler, 2013).[1]

Power can be obvious, but it can also be more implicit. The French philosopher and social theorist Michel Foucault (1926–1984) argued that power can be much more subtle and pervasive. He shows that **discourse**, or of the systems of ideas and practices concerning individuals throughout history, can have profound influence on personal freedom and autonomy. In his classic study of nineteenth-century prisons, Foucault argues that the panoptic structure of the prison gives the guard in the center a profound power (see Cartoon 13.1). If prisoners feel that they are always being watched, over time they come to internalize the gaze of the guard and willingly conform to the prison rules without any physical compulsion (Foucault, 1977). As a fundamental observation about surveillance, Foucault's work has implications for online behavior, which may be monitored by corporations or government institutions. For example, terms-of-service agreements often grant companies broad rights of surveillance and ownership over personal data, but few people read them (Skandia, 2011). Further, existing power differences between users and companies mean that users have little choice but to agree to terms if they want to participate. If all of your relatives, friends, and co-workers use Facebook, do you truly have a free choice whether to join it?

Foucault's work also discusses the power of surveillance through record keeping. For instance, the ability of a psychologist to keep a record of a patient's medical history gives the psychologist power over the patient. Keeping records of mental illness enables doctors to identify new illnesses, but also creates new categories of stigmatized people. Scholars studying social media have gone on to apply this observation to understanding the power of user histories and profiles. Amazon's "recommended" feature, for example, which is based on your purchase history, shapes what you are exposed to and therefore what you might later purchase. This running record of your purchases, changing tastes, and browsing habits can shape what kind of person you perceive yourself to be (Humphreys, 2006). Your Google search data likely has some private information about you, and many people are not comfortable with existing company uses for this data

Cartoon 13.1   Credit: "Surveillance," charcoal and pencil on paper, © Laurie Lipton.

(Tene, 2007). The data itself can also be sold, enabling companies to assemble detailed profiles of individual consumers' tastes, credit history, and medical history from multiple databases, profiles over which users have little direct control. Although these profiles have primarily commercial applications, they also represent new ways of classifying people, with profound implications for privacy, credit, insurance, and medicine.

Public Sphere

In addition to theories about the power of leaders, states, and bureaucracies, there are also theories about the political power of groups. These theories address the more or less peaceful interaction between the government and the people and attempt to understand how it is possible to discuss, debate, and adjudicate issues rationally and fairly. The philosopher Jürgen Habermas has proposed the term **public sphere** to describe the space where people can come together to debate social issues, including the rules that govern people (Habermas, 1991). This could be your local coffee shop, student lounge, or bar. Opinion in a truly public sphere is based on the validity of one's arguments, not on the wealth or rank of the speaker. The ideal public sphere, Habermas argues, has three traits: disregard of status, common concerns, and inclusiveness. Public spheres coalesce around common concerns, or issues that everyone cares about, and they are open. Ideally, anyone can have an opinion, and ideas are judged on their merit. Initially theorized as based on face-to-face and print communication, the public sphere has required some rethinking in cases of digital communication.

Some argue that mediated debate in newspapers and online can have the traits of a public sphere (Benkler, 2006) and that citizens online form a **networked public**, a group of people who debate civic issues in digital forums such as message boards, comment threads, and chat rooms, rather than or in addition to public spaces like coffee shops and bars (Varnelis, 2008). For example, in the case of debate about online privacy legislation (SOPA-PIPA), networked publics offered considerable and varied debate among both individuals and organizations (Benkler, Roberts, Faris, Solow-Niederman, & Etling, 2013). Sites like CreateDebate and Debate.org offer forums for people to debate topical issues, creating formal arguments and having others vote for a winner. The comments sections of many news articles on *Huffington Post* and *The New York Times* will often lapse into public sphere–like debate, although these forums are, notably, often moderated.

However, as anyone who has interacted with a troll or witnessed a flame war can attest, digital spaces of public discourse can clearly diverge from this ideal (Freelon, 2010). To further understand how publics vary, scholars divide political discussion in online forums into different types (Freelon, 2010). Some platforms have norms of individual liberalism where personal testimony is valued and often trumps discussion. Communitarian platforms emphasize in-group boundaries and contain discussion among people with similar opinion and values. Deliberative groups—those perhaps closest to Habermas's ideal of rational and open public discourse—contain discussion among people with opposing views and involve true questioning of values and opinions.

Publics emphasize collectivities of people, and we certainly see that online publics surround political issues from gay rights to gun control. In contrast, a **networked society** perspective sees individuals as connected, but embedded in larger, overlapping publics and potentially able to switch between publics (Castells, 2004). In this networked perspective, societies are more complex than publics. In this view, groups of people have compatible as well as competing interests. They are "constituted of multiple, overlapping and interacting sociospatial networks of power" (Mann, 1986). Power, then, works through **assemblages**, loosely affiliated groups of actors that come together for a shared interest, but may also be reconfigured when the context changes (DeLanda, 2006). Because assemblages can be reconfigured, power from the networked society point of view consists of controlling networks. People exercise power by enabling or blocking connections between nodes in the network or changing the "program" that structures their communication and structure of influence (Castells, 2004).

Publics further play a foundational role in how people think about themselves and their relation to groups (Warner, 2002). As we saw in Chapter 10, virtual communities of fans and subcultures can constitute powerful constituencies that influence public debate and culture. In some cases, they can grow to be **counterpublics**. Counterpublics are formed in opposition to dominant cultural norms and values. Political action is not a requirement of a counterpublic, but it sometimes follows from membership in one. Counterpublics can push public debate in one direction, even transforming mainstream norms, institutions, and values. For example, counterpublics of individuals with stigmatized sexual orientations have coalesced into political action groups and lobbied for changes to criminal codes as well as to laws regulating marriage. Social media has created entirely new spaces for the formation of publics and counterpublics that may eventually pursue political action. The next section will examine how social media may in turn shape the nature of political action and civic participation.

Citizenship and Civic Participation

So far this chapter has discussed how people relate to each other politically. But how has social media changed perceptions of citizenship and civic action more broadly? Scholars find that models of citizenship have actually shifted in the past thirty years from a model of dutiful citizenship, where citizens feel they should be involved in civic life by voting, to one of actualizing citizenship, where citizens feel that participating in civic life is a way to be their best self (Bennett, 2008). Civic norms may now be based more on self-expression rather than feelings of obligation. Although definitions of citizenship are inevitably normative, many pursue politics to achieve an ideal self, not just out of a sense of obligation. For example, liberal activists organized online to sign a position opposing the impeachment of President Bill Clinton. From this assemblage, MoveOn.org was founded to take concrete action on liberal political issues, and the group, aligned around a particular set of liberal issues absent from traditional nongovernmental organizations (NGOs), grew despite George W. Bush's victory in 2000. As a platform for sharing information and building alliances between like-minded groups, MoveOn.org built resources that made it a powerful NGO (Bennett, 2008).

This self-actualization model of civic activism has produced political messages that integrate art and play (Photo 13.2). For example, during the presidential election of 2008, the street artist Sheppard Fairy produced an illustrated poster of Obama called Hope that became an icon of the campaign (Baumgartner et al., 2010; Powell, Hendricks, & Denton, 2010). Protest leaders like Reverend Billy and the Church of Stop Shopping[2] in New York draw from performance art rather than purely from scripts of sit-ins and marches.

Many point out that models of civic participation show increasing integration with consumer and cultural issues that one would not normally consider political (Earl & Schussman, 2008). Adopting methods formerly used for civic action to protest cultural or lifestyle issues signals a transformation in the way people think about culture and politics (Earl & Kimport, 2009, p. 72). For example, consumers angry about the cancelation of a television show like Heroes may petition the network to reinstate it or even physically protest its cancelation. When Facebook changed its features in 2006, users formed groups on the site as a way to protest the sharing of private information (Bates & Waugh, 2011). Scholars argue that there has been a historical trend toward **movement society**, the tendency for people to use political tactics to solve issues that are not explicitly political but rather cultural, consumerist, or even personal (Earl & Kimport, 2009).

Photo 13.2 Art and Performance during the Protests in Taksim Square, Istanbul, Turkey.

Fan communities that we discussed in Chapter 9 can therefore use some of the same tactics that we discuss as political activism. To better understand how people act to enhance their lives and the lives of others in civil society, it helps to understand the theoretical elements of social movements, both past and present.

SOCIAL MOVEMENT THEORY

Social Issue Formation

Social movement theory is the study of how groups originate, evolve, and become effective in taking political action (McAdam, McCarthy, & Zald, 1996). Such movements tend to be organized around a particular **social issue**, a topic that people collectively agree should be addressed politically, economically, or culturally. But how does an issue come to be a public concern? In the public sphere, there is limited attention, and activists therefore must compete in contests to garner public attention and make their issues a priority (Hilgartner & Bosk, 1988). Social issues are constructed through the actions and language of activists, journalists, and the general public. For example, an occurrence like girls being kidnapped in Nigeria moves from a news story to a situation in which action is demanded by raising awareness, linking it with other issues, and providing scripts for public action (Soergel, 2015). Through mediated publics, issues take shape and become causes for action.

Another, more subtle way that social issues are constructed online is through a "link economy," a system of reciprocal linking between topic pages that signals mutual affiliation (Rogers, 2010; Young & Leonardi, 2012). In designing a webpage, creators decide what links to include as related to a social issue and therefore create a particular cognitive map of what that social issue

Photo 13.3 Equal Rights Amendment Protest, 1982.

entails. Sometimes this is done intuitively, but linking practices can also be governed by norms of a particular institution. For example, NGOs tend to have a broad set of links that span different points of view while government organizations tend to have a narrower set of officially sanctioned links (Rogers & Marres, 2000).

Social Movement Tactics

So, a social issue has been identified among a public online. But what is to be done about it? Cultural and cognitive models of social action, which are called **tactics**, can emerge and change over time (Tilly, 2005). As available scripts for how to take action, things like petitions, marches, and sit-ins form **repertoires of protest**, models of how to collectively organize to change society (Tilly, 2005). These repertoires can be relatively consistent over time, although there may be subtle changes in them depending on the actors involved and the political context (Photo 13.3).

Many repertoires that have defined political protests of the past have found a home online and quickly circulate through social network sites, Twitter, and blogs. These forms of protest, or **etactics**, are hybrid adaptations of traditional repertoires such as petitioning, letter writing, and boycotting to the online world (Earl & Kimport, 2011). For instance, sites such as change.org and MoveOn.org enable users to create and circulate their own petitions and help citizens write letters to their representatives in the U.S. Congress. Sites like theethicalconsumer.org list consumer boycotts occurring nationally and internationally on a variety of topics in a searchable database (Earl & Schussman, 2008).

Mobilization

Social media can enhance political activism in several ways. First, it can lower costs for organizing, publicizing, and participating in protest and therefore make mobilization more efficient in terms of time and money (Earl & Kimport, 2009). **Mobilization** is the ability of political activists to translate existing resources such as money, people, or ideas into meaningful political

Photo 13.4 Protests in Iran.

action (McAdam et al., 1996; see also Sewell, 1992), and eMobilization describes the use of digital technologies, including social media, to mobilize resources, often for the purposes of offline protest activities (Earl & Kimport, 2011). For example, social media was used to spread the word about the antiwar protest in Washington, DC, in 2008, making it easier and more efficient to circulate information about the march, coordinate rides to the march, and arrange lodging for out-of-town guests (Earl & Kimport, 2011). However, there are limits to the political power of digital tools. Social media made organizing and executing the march faster and less costly, but it did not change the overall dynamics of how the protest unfolded. This "supersize" model, scholars argue, suggests that digital technology simply enhances and facilitates existing activist activities and, when leveraged effectively, can change the scope, scale, and pace of social movements (Earl & Kimport, 2011).

During the protests in Egypt in 2011, many people learned about the protests through social media tools like Facebook in addition to phone and face-to-face contact. Further, roughly half of protesters (48%) documented the unfolding events with pictures or video and used social media or phones to distribute the content to others (Tufekci & Wilson, 2012). Few protestors learned about them through mainstream media. In these two examples, we can see how the ability to share information through social media has transformed some aspects of political action.

Coordination

Second, social media can help coordinate efforts within and across different activist groups. For example, early in their widespread adoption, cellphones were used to coordinate protest against the World Bank in 2001 (Ahrens, 2001). Protesters in Syria used tools like Facebook to coordinate rallies and document their efforts, circulating videos of police brutality. These tools, often operated through proxies in the United States, provide the needed size for rallies that would otherwise be repressed by the military (Piscatella, 2013).

Photo 13.5 Protestor in Tehran.

Further, social media can draw together publics and focus attention for an extended period of time. For example, mobilization of Egyptian protestors in Tehrir Square did not happen overnight (Lim, 2012). Rather, previous protests were coordinated through blogs and on Facebook several months prior to the large-scale protest. Critical in the mobilization of Egyptians was a Facebook page called "I am Kalihd Said" that rallied attention around the case of a middle-class Egyptian who had been killed by police.

Some of these coordination examples lead scholars to conclude that in some cases social media can fundamentally change the basic processes and tactics usually seen in social movements. Sometimes social media affects the movement more fundamentally—what kind of people participate, how they participate, and why they participate. Because social movements can be organized more quickly and with fewer organizational resources, the role of traditional activist organizations can sometimes be challenged (Earl & Kimport, 2011). Whereas NGOs like the American Civil Liberties Union or the National Association for the Advancement of Colored People have historically offered financial and organizational resources that gives social issues a continuity over decades, contemporary movements may be short lived and organized by small, independent, and entrepreneurial groups (or sometimes individuals) because of their lowered costs. So-called **flash activism** describes activism that appears and then disappears overnight as attention toward to cause waxes and wanes (Mehta, 2011). For example, Invisible Children mobilized primarily through a video, "Kony 2012," which circulated widely and called for the removal of Ugandan warlord Joseph Kony. Although it generated almost 100 million views on YouTube in six days and raised $20 million for the cause,[3] group organizers were criticized for accomplishing little of practical value with the attention and money their campaign generated.[4]

Older models of collective action that revolve around a structured organization have to some extent been replaced by contemporary models of connective action, which tend to be self-organized (Bennett & Segerberg, 2012). For example, during the Occupy Wall Street movement, the attention of independent groups of protestors was drawn together under the slogan "We are the 99%," which acted as a simple frame around which actions were mobilized (Bennett & Segerberg, 2012; Photo 13.6). Drawing from Castell's idea of networked society, many scholars have examined how "leaderless" movements, nonhierarchical networks of people, organize for civic action. In the case of Occupy Wall Street, a system of hand gestures was used in collective deliberations, and the "code" for hand gestures was circulated through blogs and other forms of social media (Conover, Ferrara, Menczer, & Flammini, 2013).

Yet, as we have discovered many times throughout this book, much depends not on the physical structure of technology but on the *uses* of that technology. Keeping in mind what we learned in Chapter 2 about affordances, we can see that the capabilities of social media platforms can structure what use people make of them for political ends. As Earl and Kimport (2011) note, "Another way of saying

Photo 13.6 A Protestor Documents at Occupy Wall Street.

Photo 13.7 Occupy Wall Street.

this is that it is people's usage of the technology—not the technology itself—that can change social processes" (Earl & Kimport, 2011, p. 14).

In a similar way, social media can coordinate how movements get funded. Digital platforms enable **microcontributions**, which are often made by people who are not normally involved in activism (Earl & Kimport, 2011; Garrett, 2009). These small contributions of money, when aggregated on a large scale, can add up (Garrett, 2009). For example, sites like Kiva and Microcredit allows contributors to make microloans to individuals and organizations throughout the world to grow their small businesses. During natural disasters like Hurricane Sandy, the Red Cross raised millions of dollars in donations through cellphone text donations, a tactic also used by presidential campaigns.

Slacktivism

Despite these shifts in coordination and information sharing, some have critiqued the ability of digital technology to enable changes in offline power structures. So-called slacktivism describes the idea that online activism substitutes for offline action and therefore may lead to little change on existing power structures (Rotman et al., 2011). Support for slacktivism has been mixed. For example, research shows that liking a post on Facebook can make you less likely to donate because it relieves your feelings of obligation to act (Kristofferson, White, & Peloza, 2014). This supports the substitution thesis—the idea that online activity will be a substitute for offline activism. Yet other studies have demonstrated that online activism heightens awareness and engages those who would not otherwise participate (Christensen, 2011). In this way, some argue that these waves of political awareness prompted by social media are, at worst, harmless (Christensen, 2011). Whether you see social media action as efficacious may depend on what kind of movements one studies and what the criteria are for "making a difference" (Earl, 2007).

Hacktivism and Alternative Means of Communication

Last, social media can also help activist groups avoid state surveillance (Garrett & Edwards, 2007). For example, the Zapatista movement in Mexico used digital networks to coordinate efforts without the knowledge of the government, and anti-Apartheid fighters used then still-primitive Internet connections to coordinate action inside and outside of South Africa (Garrett & Edwards, 2007). Social media provides a space for the coordination of actions that can range from legal mischief, to legal gray areas, to outright illegal cyberattacks.

In this way, the Internet has added to the repertoires of tactics for some movements. **Hacktivism** describes using digital technology to disrupt organizations or individuals that the social movement opposes. For example, in 2008, Anonymous, a loosely affiliated collective of hackers, bombarded the Church of Scientology with actions ranging from unsolicited pizza deliveries and taxies to attacks on Church servers, activities coordinated by the group primarily through social media[5] (Coleman, 2011). Represented by the trademark Guy Folkes mask (Photo 13.7), Anonymous originated primarily from the 4chan community and has participated in hacktivism of all sorts ranging from involvement in Occupy Wall Street and the Tunisian uprisings to Julian Assange's Wikileaks initiative (Coleman, 2014). One tool in their arsenal is a distributed denial of service, an attack that floods servers with requests, debilitating a website and its servers. In 2012, for instance, Anonymous hackers, or Anons, executed such attacks on behalf of Wikileaks to banks that refused help to Wikileaks founder Julian Assange. As Gabriella Coleman (2014) found, the members of the group tend to be motivated by *lulz*, "a spirited but often malevolent brand of humor etymologically derived from lol" (p. 4). The pursuit of lulz gives Anonymous actions a particular brand of humor and hijinks that are the trademark of Internet trolls.

Another trademark tool of the group and of hacktivism more generally is doxing, the discovery and circulation of private information such as one's home address, place of employment, or social security number, a form of revenge we last discussed in Chapter 6 (Coleman, 2011, p. 7). Through "ruin life" campaigns and RIP trolling, members of Anonymous can wreak havoc on both those in power and seemingly innocent bystanders alike. However, no one group has the monopoly on hacktivism, as we saw in perhaps its most notable case in 2014 when North Korea hacked Sony Pictures, exposing embarrassing emails and trade secrets to protest the movie *The Interview* (Kang, 2015).

Social Media Use and Amount of Participation

These and many other examples illustrate how social media can increase participation in protest activities, particularly among normally disinterested parties. At the beginning of 2012, almost no one in America had heard of Joseph Kony, and one week later half of young adults in the United States had[6] (Rainie, 2012). However, it is also important to note, as we discussed in Chapter 4, that human attention is scarce. People only have so much time and attention to devote to social issues, and it can be hard to get and sustain attention. This means that although social media *can* enable social activists to distribute their message to a broad audience quickly, it may not always translate into a social movement and in some cases may impede mobilization. Thus, it is also important to consider the issues of resonance and relevance, not just capacity (Schudson, 1989). In Chile, for example, Facebook use was associated with political behavior, but only if Facebook was used for social life and news gathering (Valenzuela, Arriagada, & Scherman, 2012). When Facebook was used only for self-expression, its use did not translate into increased protesting behavior.

Different genres of social media can play different roles in a social movement. For example, consider the different roles played by media in the opening vignette. Catherine was first alerted to the social issue privately through a social networking site. She then went to listen in on the ways in which people were mobilizing online through a feed (Twitter). On the feed, she received not only text, but also pictures of injuries from police brutality and other vivid images. To get broader context and commentary, she went to the website of a mainstream news source, *New York Times*, albeit one that also offers comments from a particular audience of readers. As a public sphere, she observed commenters debating the salient issues, albeit from a distance in the United States. Rather than viewing social media in terms of isolated platforms, we may want to think of it as part of the broader media ecology that shapes political knowledge, motivation, and practice.

FRAMING

So far this chapter has discussed how social media can change the scope and structure of political action. However, the content of communication is also important. Language can have meaningful political effects because it shapes the way we categorize and form attitudes about objects, people, and ideas (Humphreys & Latour, 2013). What effect does social media have on what people say about politics? One important tool for understanding its effects is through the concept of **framing** (Gamson & Modigliani, 1989; Snow & Benford, 1988). Framing is the process of strategically referring to a social issue, practice, or group to heighten some of its attributes and downplay other aspects. For example, workers who were not born in the United States can be labeled either "illegal immigrants" or "undocumented workers," depending on who is talking. We can speak of "global warming" or "climate change," the "estate tax" or the "death tax," "gaming" or "gambling," and each of these choices has implications for the way the political issue is perceived and acted on (Entman, 2004; Lakoff, 2012). Framing decisions have been studied by media scholars for decades (Gamson & Modigliani, 1989), but now frames have new life, as they are circulated quickly and easily through social media.

What role has social media played in changing the landscape of media frames? Linguistically and cognitively, frames work much the same way online as they do in print or conversation. However, the ability of people to produce and circulate media has led to a shift in the dynamics of frames in the media ecology. The fact that many people can broadcast their views on social media means that there are many more available frames (Walgrave & Van Aelst, 2004). Although it may liberate individuals to frame issues themselves, social media can also lead to frame "clouding," or the multiplication of many conflicting frames for viewing an issue, which causes confusion among non- or would be activists and may therefore inhibit coordinated political action (Le Grignou & Patou, 2004). However, sometimes ordinary people will generate new frames that gain wide usage on social media, such as when Occupy Wall Street's concept of the wealthy "1%" and remaining "99%" became a new way of framing income inequality. Practices such as hashtagging are also a way to frame an issue, such as when protestors of misogyny and violence against women created the hashtag #YesAllWomen to emphasize the pervasiveness of sexism or when the hashtag #BlackLivesMatter was used to frame the shooting in Ferguson, Missouri. Yet although social media has given more people the ability to attempt to frame an issue, gatekeepers such as politicians, mainstream media, high-profile activists, and corporations still play a pivotal role by legitimizing some frames over others (Meraz, 2006).

Agenda setting is "the ability [of news media] to influence the salience of topics" in the public sphere (McCombs & Shaw, 1972, p. 181). Whether social media coverage leads to a popular groundswell of activism often depends on who leads the agenda. One study of blogs shows that social effects can be different depending on whether the story breaks in traditional or social media first. When blogs lead the agenda by covering an issue before mainstream media, it often creates a "pressure cooker" situation and mainstream media actors are compelled to cover an issue that might have otherwise been ignored. However, when mainstream media covers an issue first, blogs act as more of a "safety value" where people can talk about the headlines and rehash the mainstream coverage (Hassid, 2012).

NEWS CONSUMPTION AND CIVIC ENGAGEMENT

Gatekeepers such as news organizations are clearly important in linking online and offline knowledge and action. Known as one of the key pillars in liberal democracy (Lippmann, 1946), the mainstream press provides oversight of government action, on-the-ground reporting of important issues throughout the world, and fact checking of what would otherwise be gossip, rumors, or propaganda. What journalists find, report, and publish can dramatically increase public awareness of an issue. This section will discuss some ways that social media has become integrated with traditional journalism and in some cases changed it.

Social versus Mainstream News Media

How does news on social media differ from traditional media? Does social media work with or against traditional methods for conveying news? First, social media has changed elements of the news cycle in some important ways. Because feeds like Twitter offer breaking news at a pace never before conceivable, traditional media have begun to change their practices as well (Papacharissi, 2011). In an examination of tweets sent during the Egyptian protests of 2011, Papacharissi (2011) describes how this kind of newsgathering provides an affective rhythm to the occurrences, meaning that dispatches coming in 140 characters take on a sense of urgency and recency as events unfold. Scholars have found that the addition of Twitter as a tool for news delivery to the media ecology has taken over some tasks formerly allocated to traditional news organizations, but it has also made other functions of mainstream media such as their gatekeeping and fact checking role more valuable (Meraz, 2006).

Second, content may be different on social media. Think of what your Facebook feed contains right now (or even better, go look). Social media can be a mashup of news stories, personal updates, and pop culture ephemera. The news that people access through social media tends to be circulated among people in a particular social network, which means that people are more likely to encounter congruent points of view and less likely to encounter incongruent points of view. This congruency can reinforce and thus strengthen existing attitudes. Confirmation bias means that people look for information that confirms their own beliefs and discount information that is contradictory. Research finds that people do indeed look for news that confirms their beliefs; however, we do not necessarily shy away from news that has alternative points of view (Garrett, 2009). In fact, people who are particularly interested in news and politics, so-called "news-junkies," will often read alternative points of view for knowledge and entertainment. Thus, recent research into people's actual online news consumption practices somewhat complicates the view of narrowcasting, the idea that audiences rarely receive oppositional viewpoints because of social media (Sunstein, 2009).

Citizen Journalism

When hundreds of thousands of people in Egypt took to the street in January 2011 to protest the continuing leadership of President Hosni Mubarak, the first reports came from tweets depicting the protests and, perhaps more important, the military crackdown. When the situation transformed in Taksim Square in Turkey from a nonviolent protest to protect a park into a national movement against a conservative leader, as in the opening vignette, Twitter was used to broadcast developments and coordinate action. In political movements particularly, normal people take to media to chronicle events and let others know what is going on. **Citizen journalism**, a type of co-creation that we discussed in Chapter 5, is the practice of news gathering and production by nonprofessionals (Bruns, 2008). For example, CNN offers iReport, a platform for the production and circulation of citizen journalism on important topics such as the Treyvon Martin shooting. In other ways, mainstream news media have begun to incorporate social media, such as when organizations like MSNBC rely on Twitter for updated reports on events taking place in war zones. The *Nightly News on NBC* has even been known to make corrections on air in response to Twitter responses (Burkey, 2015). Citizen journalism can take several forms: reporting news, investigative blogging, hyperlocal journalism, fact checking, or digital storytelling (Rheingold, 1993), and citizen journalism can occur at various stages in the news production process (Bruns, 2008). Yet when someone is tweeting an eyewitness report of violence in Tehrir Square, is he or she a source or a journalist?

When everyone participates in information gathering and dissemination, credibility can be seriously challenged. Journalists have long been governed by a formal and informal code of ethics (Lippmann, 2012; Tuchman, 1978), and professional journalists operate within particular rules and standards such as two-source verification. Citizen journalists gather and disseminate information, but they may not always follow the same procedures as professional journalists. For example, during the Boston bombing, false reports on 4chan led to death threats and the harassment of two innocent people. In contrast, Twitter also brought us live, up-to-the second coverage of the apprehension of the real suspect in a Watertown, Massachusetts, neighborhood.

Social media has also become an important form of civic communication in many places. As the opening vignette to this book points out, gathering and disseminating eyewitness reports can ease navigation, but during a natural disaster it can save lives. For example, during the earthquake in Japan, Honda, working with Google maps, quickly took action to track and map all cars with a navigational device. This produced a map of roads that were open and highlighted those that were closed because of the disaster, allowing medical and fire rescue to get to victims more quickly. Social media such as Twitter has also been used for more mundane civic communication. For example, a mayor in Spain handles issues like broken streetlights or mail delivery through tweets (Spiro, Acton, & Butts, 2013). In Minneapolis, the city government developed an app for residents to use for the same purpose as 311 calls, addressing issues like potholes, noise violations, and other civic concerns (Watson, 2014).

In more controversial cases, social media can be used to circulate information from whistleblowers. For example, Wikileaks gathered information from anonymous sources within the military community and shared it with the public, facilitated by a system of online servers for disguising location. Edward Snowden similarly made use of his blog to publicize information about U.S. government surveillance of online activities of both citizens and noncitizens. Coming back around to hacktivism, we see that the ability of social media to quickly disseminate information, sometimes anonymously, can have consequences when it comes to fighting existing power structures.

SUMMARY AND CONCLUSION

This chapter has examined the ways in which social media practices have become integrated with political life as well as some ways in which they have simply augmented existing political actions. As we have seen, sometimes they may change a great deal, whereas other times they may not. It depends heavily on the context—including the political structures at play, the technological capabilities, the existing social structure, and user knowledge for using technology. Theories like social movement theory, agenda setting, and framing enlighten us to the ways that politics has been practiced and offer hints as to how social media may shift these practices.

TOPICS

- Three types of power (charismatic, totalitarian, bureaucratic)
- Public sphere
- Network society
- Framing
- Agenda setting
- Citizen journalism

DISCUSSION QUESTIONS

1. This chapter discusses three types of power. Which kind of power do you think is most important in having influence in social media? Does this differ from having power offline?
2. Is the public sphere, originally conceptualized as occurring face to face, the same online? What makes it similar or different and what might those differences mean for power?
3. From a political perspective, consider the impact of citizen journalists on the media ecosystem. How might mainstream journalism be affected and is this a loss or gain to civil society?

EXERCISES

1. Pick one case that you think is an important site of power struggle. Who currently has power and why? How could one or more people mobilize to change the existing power structure? Develop a campaign using social media and consider not only medium but also content using tactics such as framing and agenda setting.
2. Choose three sites online that you think could represent different publics. What kind of public does each represent, and how do you know?
3. Pick a recent social movement. What were its online tactics and repertoires of protest? What did the movement seek to achieve, and how did social media facilitate or hinder these goals?

NOTES

1. http://en.wikipedia.org/wiki/Wikipedia:List_of_policies/.
2. http://www.revbilly.com/.
3. http://www.buzzfeed.com/jtes/two-years-after-kony-2012-has-invisible-children-grown-up#3ymoa1x/.
4. http://www.news.com.au/world/remember-kony-2012-well-its-2013-what-happened/story-fndir2ev-1226550575923/.
5. http://www.newyorker.com/magazine/2014/09/08/masked-avengers/.
6. http://www.pewinternet.org/2012/03/15/the-viral-kony-2012-video/.

FURTHER READINGS

Coleman, G. (2014). *Hacker, hoaxer, whistleblower, spy: The many faces of Anonymous*. New York: Verso Books.

Earl, J., & Kimport, K. (2011). *Digitally enabled social change: Activism in the Internet age*. Cambridge, MA: MIT Press.

Morozov, E. (2009). Iran: Downside to the "Twitter revolution." *Dissent, 56*(4), 10–14.

Piscatella, J. (Writer). (2013). *#chicagoGirl*. B. G. Roberts, David (Producer). Los Angeles, CA: Revolutio.

REFERENCES

Ahrens, F. (2001). For activists today, it's marks, not Marx. *The Washington Post*.

Arthur, C. (2011, January 28, 2011). *Egypt cuts off Internet access*. *The Guardian*. Retrieved from http://www.theguardian.com/technology/2011/jan/28/egypt-cuts-off-internet-access/.

Bangeman, E. (2008, April 21). *RIAA spent $2 million lobbying for tougher IP laws in 2007*. *Ars Technica*. Retrieved from http://arstechnica.com/tech-policy/2008/04/riaa-spent-2-million-lobbying-for-tougher-ip-laws-in-2007/.

Bates & Waugh. (2011, November 22). *Facebook blog is inundated with thousands of protests as users start Facebook group "We Hate the New News Feed."* *The Daily Mail*. Retrieved from http://www.dailymail.co.uk/sciencetech/article-2039726/Facebook-changes-Thousands-protests-We-hate-new-news-feed-group.html/.

Baumgartner, J. C., Mackay, J. B., Morris, J. S., Otenyo, E. E., Powell, L., Smith, M. M., . . . Hendricks, J. A. (2010). *Communicator-in-chief: How Barack Obama used new media technology to win the White House*. Lanham, MD: Lexington Books.

Benkler, Y. (2006). *The wealth of networks: How social production transforms markets and freedom*. New Haven, CT: Yale University Press.

Benkler, Y., Roberts, H., Faris, R., Solow-Niederman, A., & Etling, B. (2013). *Social mobilization and the networked public sphere: Mapping the SOPA-PIPA debate*. Berkman Center Research Publication (2013–16).

Bennett, W. L. (2008). Changing citizenship in the digital age. *Civic life online: Learning how digital media can engage youth, 1*, 1–24.

Bennett, W. L., & Segerberg, A. (2012). The logic of connective action: Digital media and the personalization of contentious politics. *Information, Communication & Society, 15*(5), 739–768.

boyd, d. (2008). Can social network sites enable political action? *International Journal of Media & Cultural Politics, 4*(2), 241–244.

Bruns, A. (2008). *Blogs, Wikipedia, Second Life, and beyond: From production to produsage* (Vol. 45). New York: Lang.

Burkey, P., (Writer) & Burkey, P. (Director). (2015). NBC Nightly News with Brian Williams [Television]. In P. Burkey (Producer), *NBC Nightly News with Brian Williams*: NBC.

Castells, M. (2004). Informationalism, networks, and the network society: A theoretical blueprint. In Castells, M. (ed.), *The network society: A cross-cultural perspective* (pp. 3–45). Cheltenham, UK: Elgar.

Christensen, H. S. (2011). Political activities on the Internet: Slacktivism or political participation by other means? *First Monday, 16*(2).

Coleman, G. (2011). Anonymous: From the Lulz to collective action. *The new everyday: A media commons project, 6*.

Conover, M. D., Ferrara, E., Menczer, F., & Flammini, A. (2013). The digital evolution of Occupy Wall Street. *PloS One, 8*(5), e64679.

DeLanda, M. (2006). *A new philosophy of society: Assemblage theory and social complexity*. London: A&C Black.

Earl, J. (2007). Leading tasks in a leaderless movement: The case of strategic voting. *American Behavioral Scientist, 50*(10), 1327–1349.

Earl, J., & Kimport, K. (2009). Movement societies and digital protest: Fan activism and other nonpolitical protest online. *Sociological Theory, 27*(3), 220–243.

Earl, J., & Kimport, K. (2011). *Digitally enabled social change: Activism in the Internet age.* Cambridge, MA: MIT Press.

Earl, J., & Schussman, A. (2008). Contesting cultural control: Youth culture and online petitioning. In Bennett, W. L. (ed.), *Civic life online: Learning how digital media can engage youth* (pp. 71–95). Cambridge, MA: MIT Press.

Entman, R. M. (2004). *Projections of power: Framing news, public opinion, and US foreign policy.* Chicago: University of Chicago Press.

Fandy, M. (1999). CyberResistance: Saudi opposition between globalization and localization. *Comparative Studies in Society and History, 41*(1), 124–147.

Foucault, M. (1977). *Discipline and punish: The birth of the prison.* New York: Random House.

Freelon, D. G. (2010). Analyzing online political discussion using three models of democratic communication. *New Media & Society, 12*(7), 1172–1190.

Gamson, W. A., & Modigliani, A. (1989). Media discourse and public opinion on nuclear power: A constructionist approach. *American Journal of Sociology, 95*(1), 1–37.

Garrett, R. K. (2009). Echo chambers online?: Politically motivated selective exposure among Internet news users. *Journal of Computer-Mediated Communication, 14*(2), 265–285.

Garrett, R. K., & Edwards, P. N. (2007). Revolutionary secrets: Technology's role in the South African anti-apartheid movement. *Social Science Computer Review, 25*(1), 13–26.

Habermas, J. (1991). *The structural transformation of the public sphere: An inquiry into a category of bourgeois society.* Cambridge, MA: MIT Press.

Hassid, J. (2012). Safety valve or pressure cooker? Blogs in Chinese political life. *Journal of Communication, 62*(2), 212–230.

Hilgartner, S., & Bosk, C. L. (1988). The rise and fall of social problems: A public arenas model. *American Journal of Sociology, 94*(1), 53–78.

Humphreys, A. (2006). The consumer as Foucauldian "object of knowledge." *Social Science Computer Review, 24*(3), 296–309.

Humphreys, A., & Latour, K. A. (2013). Framing the game: Assessing the impact of cultural representations on consumer perceptions of legitimacy. *Journal of Consumer Research, 40*(4), 773–795.

Joyce, E., Pike, J. C., & Butler, B. S. (2013). Rules and roles vs. consensus self-governed deliberative mass collaboration bureaucracies. *American Behavioral Scientist, 57*(5), 576–594.

Kang, C. (2015, February 4). *Sony Pictures hack cost the movie studio at least $15 million. The Washington Post.* Retrieved from http://www.washington post.com/news/business/wp/2015/02/04/sony-pictures-hack-cost-the-movie-studio-at-least-15-million/.

Kristofferson, K., White, K., & Peloza, J. (2014). The nature of slacktivism: How the social observability of an initial act of token support affects subsequent prosocial action. *Journal of Consumer Research, 40*(6), 1149–1166.

Lakoff, G. (2012). Explaining embodied cognition results. *Topics in Cognitive Science, 4*(4), 773–785.

Le Grignou, B., & Patou, C. (2004). ATTAC (k) ing expertise. Does the Internet really democratize knowledge? In van de Donk, W. B. H. J. et al. (eds.) *Cyberprotest: New Media, Citizens, and Social Movements* (pp. 145–158). London: Routledge.

Levin, D. (2014, June 2). *China escalating attack on Google. The New York Times.* Retrieved from http://www.nytimes.com/2014/06/03/business/chinas-battle-against-google-heats-up.html/.

Lim, M. (2012). Clicks, cabs, and coffee houses: Social media and oppositional movements in Egypt, 2004–2011. *Journal of Communication, 62*(2), 231–248.

Lippmann, W. (1946). *Public opinion.* New Brunswick, NJ: Transaction.

Lippmann, W. (2012). *Liberty and the news.* Mineola, NY: Courier Dover.

Mann, M. (1986). *The sources of social power,* Vol. 1.: *A history of power from the beginnings to AD 1760.* Cambridge, UK: Cambridge University Press.

McAdam, D., McCarthy, J. D., & Zald, M. N. (1996). *Comparative perspectives on social movements: Political opportunities, mobilizing structures, and cultural framings.* Cambridge, UK: Cambridge University Press.

McCombs, M. E., & Shaw, D. L. (1972). The agenda-setting function of mass media. *Public Opinion Quarterly, 36*(2), 176–187.

Mehta, R. (2011). Flash activism: How a Bollywood film catalyzed civic justice toward a murder trial. *Transformative Works and Cultures, 10.* doi:10.3983/twc.2012.0345.

Meraz, S. (2006). *Citizen journalism, citizen activism, and technology: Positioning technology as a "second superpower" in times of disaster and terrorism.* Paper presented at the 7th International Symposium on Online Journalism. Austin, TX.

Morozov, E. (2009). Iran: Downside to the "Twitter Revolution." *Dissent, 56*(4), 10–14.

Papacharissi, Z. (2011). *A networked self: Identity, community and culture on social network sites.* New York: Taylor & Francis.

Piscatella, J. (Writer). (2013). *#chicagoGirl.* Joe Piscatella, Mark Rinehart (Producers). Los Angeles, CA: Revolutio.

Powell, L., Hendricks, J., & Denton, R. Jr. (2010). Obama and Obama girl: YouTube, viral videos, and the 2008 presidential campaign. In *Communicator-in-chief.* Lanham, MD: Lexington Books.

Rainie, L., Hitlin, P., Jurkowitz, M., Dimock, M., & Neidorf, S. (2012). *The viral Kony 2012 video.* http://www.pewinternet.org/2012/03/15/the-viral-kony-2012-video/.

Rheingold, H. (1993). *The virtual community: Homesteading on the electronic frontier.* New York: Basic Books.

Rogers, E. M. (2010). *Diffusion of innovations*. New York: Simon & Schuster.

Rogers, R., & Marres, N. (2000). Landscaping climate change: A mapping technique for understanding science and technology debates on the World Wide Web. *Public Understanding of Science, 9*(2), 141–163.

Rotman, D., Vieweg, S., Yardi, S., Chi, E., Preece, J., Shneiderman, B., . . . Glaisyer, T. (2011). *From slacktivism to activism: Participatory culture in the age of social media*. Paper presented at the CHI'11 Extended Abstracts on Human Factors in Computing Systems. Vancouver, BC, Canada.

Sewell, W. H. Jr. (1992). A theory of structure: Duality, agency, and transformation. *American Journal of Sociology, 98*(1), 1–29.

Skandia. (2011). *Skandia takes the terminal out of terms and conditions* [Press release]. Retrieved from http://www2.skandia.co.uk/Media-Centre/2011-press-releases/May-2011/skandia-takes-the-terminal-outof-terms-and-conditions/.

Snow, D. A., & Benford, R. D. (1988). Ideology, frame resonance, and participant mobilization. *International Social Movement Research, 1*(1), 197–217.

Soergel, A. (2015, January 29). *Beyond #BringBackOurGirls: What's being done about Boko Haram. U.S. News & World Report*. Retrieved from http://www.usnews.com/news/articles/2015/01/27/beyond-bringbackourgirls-whats-being-done-about-boko-haram/.

Spiro, E. S., Acton, R. M., & Butts, C. T. (2013). Extended structures of mediation: Re-examining brokerage in dynamic networks. *Social Networks, 35*(1), 130–143.

Sunstein, C. R. (2009). *Republic. com 2.0*. Princeton, NJ: Princeton University Press.

Tene, O. (2007). What Google knows: Privacy and internet search engines. *Utah Law Review, 2008*(4), 1433–1492.

Tilly, C. (2005). *Social movements, 1768–2004*. Boulder, CO: Paradigm.

Tuchman, G. (1978). *Making news* (Vol. 147). New York: Free Press.

Tufekci, Z., & Wilson, C. (2012). Social media and the decision to participate in political protest: Observations from Tahrir Square. *Journal of Communication, 62*(2), 363–379.

Valenzuela, S., Arriagada, A., & Scherman, A. (2012). The social media basis of youth protest behavior: The case of Chile. *Journal of Communication, 62*(2), 299–314.

Varnelis, K. (2008). Conclusion: The meaning of network culture. In *Networked Publics* (pp. 145–160). Cambridge, MA: MIT Press.

Walgrave, S., & Van Aelst, P. (2004). Much ado about (almost) nothing. *Over de electorale effecten van Doe de Stemtest, 12*(2), 61–72.

Warner, M. (2002). Publics and counterpublics. *Public Culture, 14*(1), 49–90.

Watson, B. R. (2014), "Is mobile expanding political participation?: The digital divide and demographic patterns in telephone, web, and mobile-based requests for city services," presented at Association for Education in Journalism & Mass Communication (AEJMC) conference in Montreal, Canada,

Aug. 2014.Weber, M. (1978). *Economy and society: An outline of interpretive sociology.* Berkeley: University of California Press.

Woollaston, V. (2013, September 25). *China lifts ban on Facebook–But only for people living in a 17 square mile area of Shanghai. The Daily Mail.* Retrieved from http://www.dailymail.co.uk/sciencetech/article-2431861/China-lifts-ban-Facebook--people-living-working-small-area-Shanghai.html/.

Young, L. E., & Leonardi, P. M. (2012). Social issue emergence on the web: A dual structurational model. *Journal of Computer-Mediated Communication, 17*(2), 231–246.

CHAPTER 14

———

Economic and Legal Structures

Nancy has always loved what she does. As the owner of a jazz record store, she meets all kinds of interesting people, and visitors even come from out of town to check out her collection of old albums from the 1920s. However, in the past few years, things have been tough. People have started buying music off iTunes, and her sales have dwindled. Doesn't anyone appreciate album art anymore? One day Nancy hears that the bookstore down the street is doing a good business online. "What have I got to lose?" Nancy thinks, as she sets up her eBay account to sell some Miles Davis and Billie Holliday. Soon, things have taken off in a big way. She has doubled her sales and has buyers from all over the world (who knew people in Japan were this into jazz?). Nancy starts chatting with a few of them through the seller comments. They have a lot of the same interests, and the people she is talking to certainly want to know more. Things are going so well that she decides to stop paying eBay a commission and just set up her own shop online, complete with a platform for discussing old records and posting clips of music from them. She needs not only people who have clips to upload, but also people who are looking for clips to download. She gamely sets up this feature, and it is a big hit. She is selling more records, and she even starts making money from advertising. Maybe she won't have to quit the business after all! Things are going great when one day she gets a cease-and-desist letter from one of her favorite record companies. People have been remixing the clips for old silent movies on YouTube. Nancy sighs. Maybe she shouldn't quit her day job.

Chapter 14 provides a broad overview of the ways that social media has become integrated with economic life and legal structures. The costs of producing, distributing, and storing information have decreased dramatically over the past few decades and have prompted a number of shifts in commerce, particularly in knowledge and culture industries such as music and film. Social media platforms play an important role in the formation of fan communities and in how companies track the success of their products. They offer a way for consumers to share and create their own content, often in violation of copyrights laws, as well as a way for companies to capitalize on consumer-created products, many times without paying for them. In this chapter, we will cover several concepts in economic theory such as marginal cost, network effects, and two-sided markets and use these concepts to understand changes in consumer practices, business models, and legal structures for selling and distributing goods, services, and information. As a result of the shifting economic and technological landscape, the boundaries around cultural and knowledge-based properties that used to be tethered to materials like books and albums have also been challenged. In this chapter, we will therefore also cover copyright law and its challenges to legal theory and practice.

Unlike the treatment of co-creation in Chapter 5 and social media marketing found in Chapter 11, this chapter on economic life takes a broader approach, looking at shifts in media production and future directions for economic growth. The Internet and digital technologies have touched off changes in many industries. However, the boundary between changes related to the Internet and digital technology—bandwidth, storage, and processing speed—and those related to social media—collaborative production, sharing, and co-creation—are not always clear. For the sake of brevity, this chapter will first briefly review broad changes related to the Internet before focusing more specifically on the particular economic shifts engendered by social media itself. Throughout the chapter, we will examine some of the consequences of this shift for regulation and policy such as copyright law and net neutrality.

SHIFTS IN ECONOMIC STRUCTURE

To understand social media's impact on economic life, it is first necessary to consider the changes that gave social media economic importance in the first place. For example, it would not be possible to upload a video of your favorite performer taken on your phone without cheap technology for storing large amounts of information, social and legal norms that allow such uploading, and networks of others engaged in similar acts of publication. The development and diffusion of digital technology and the Internet have prompted three major shifts that have transformed traditional economic structures and given social media economic value: decreasing costs of technology, blurred ownership of digital objects, and networked exchange (Benkler, 2006). This section will examine the consequences

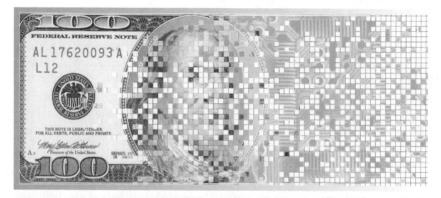

Photo 14.1 Digital Currency.

of these three shifts for economic life before examining their meaning for understanding social media.

Decreasing Costs of Production, Storage, and Dissemination

The first, most sweeping change is that the costs of production, consumption, and distribution of information have radically decreased in the past two decades (Benkler, 2006). The costs of storage space, bandwidth, and processing power have all fallen over time. Intel's president, Gordon E. Moore, was the first to observe that the processing speed of computer chips doubles every two years (1965). This pattern, called **Moore's Law**, has proven true for at least thirty years, although it might not prove true forever. The capacity of storage space and bandwidth have similarly increased, leading to a decrease in their costs (Benkler, 2006).

This decrease in the cost of production, transfer, and storage of information has had several implications for economic life, some of which are still unfolding. The widespread availability of tools such as networked computers that can be used to produce texts, videos, and music has prompted a "radical change in the organization of information production" (Benkler, 2006, p. 1). Whereas the startup costs for a printing press, a television station, or a recording studio were once quite large, one can now obtain the means to produce and circulate texts, videos, or music for a few thousand dollars. The costs of producing the first copy of a book, software, or innovation are called the **fixed costs**, and for entrepreneurs, this means that the costs of entering certain markets can be considerably lower. Fixed costs may now be slightly lower because of these effects, but they are still nowhere close to zero.

The adoption of digital technology can mean that the **marginal cost**, the cost of producing and distributing one more of the item, is considerably lower as well. For example, whereas a physical book costs about $3.25 to print, an eBook costs considerably less per copy.[1] Yet fixed costs are still about the same. Paying the writer, copy-editor, and jacket designers has not significantly changed. One study shows that consumers feel justified in pirating something that has low marginal costs, but perhaps high fixed cost (Nunes, Hsee, & Weber, 2004; Xia, Monroe, & Cox, 2004). It is easier for people to think of the "cost" of a book as what it costs to produce one more rather than to think about the cost of producing the first one.

To understand why the decreasing cost of processing, storage, and bandwidth would affect anything, we will start with the idea of a good. An economic **good** is any object that satisfies a human need or want (Varian, 1992). Goods can be privately held, public, common, or jointly owned. As the price of a good goes down, people can (and usually do) buy more of it. However, if a good is cheap, there is little incentive for a company to produce it. The same applies to services. For example, if someone has the capacity to give a great haircut, she can charge a lot for it. But as more people learn this skill, the price will go down because the service is more readily available. In most markets, value comes from scarcity.

Scarce goods tend to be more valuable because there are fewer of them and more people competing to buy them. For example, diamonds are relatively rare (compared to, say, sugar), and so they cost more per ounce. This basic insight, that price is determined by supply and demand, is generally called the **economic theory of value**.[2]

In many ways, information as a good has become plentiful and therefore cheap. For example, if you want to know who won the 1986 World Series, you do not have to buy a sports almanac or take the time to visit the library, but can simply look up the information on Wikipedia for the cost of your regular Internet access (I will save you the trouble: it is the New York Mets). Information is plentiful, which means that you are not likely to pay someone to answer this question (although as discussed in Chapter 7, it will require you to buy or access a computer or mobile device and have the literacy to find the information at a site like Wikipedia). So information is relatively plentiful and accessible—perhaps more so now than any other time in human history.

But recall what we learned in Chapter 4 about attention. Attention is scarce, which means that the curation and filtering mechanisms for this information become more valuable as information itself becomes more plentiful (see Davenport & Beck, 2013; Simon, 1971). Thus although search engines make it possible to access information, filtering and curating information still has a lot of value, and social media plays a role in such filtering. For example, if you want to know the best place in town to eat, you can find the location, hours, and menus of virtually every place online, but to make a decision, it might make more sense to ask your friends—who are the most like you—or consult online reviews by strangers. This filtering, then, can come to have value because it saves you time and sometimes wasted money.

Blurred Rights of Ownership

The speed at which computers transfer and process information has gotten faster; storage capacity has dramatically increased, and cultural products like music and movies as well as medical, geographic, and scientific knowledge have therefore become dramatically easier to access. But has this actually changed anything about these goods as products themselves? It turns out that the ability of people to access and store information has also challenged some of its more basic boundaries. Although we may think of ownership as one legal right, it is actually a bundle of three rights: the right to use, the right to exclude others from using, and the right to transfer these two rights to someone else (Reeve, 1986). When someone owns a physical object, these rights are easy to bundle. If you own a car, you can decide whether to use it, can exclude others from using it, and can decide when to transfer those rights. **Enclosure** describes the process of putting boundaries around property to ensure these rights (Boyle, 2003). Enclosure is easy enough for a plot of land or your beloved car. However, digital objects are a little different. First, they are **nonrival**, which means that using them does not decrease the value to others. For example, reading an article on *Huffington Post* does not alter the content of the article, and so it is just as valuable to the next reader. Or if you look through your friend's pictures on Facebook, they are still there for someone else to see. Information in this sense does not become depleted when used. In contrast, if you buy a sandwich and consume some of that sandwich, it has considerably less value to the next person!

Second, digital objects can be more easily transferred than previously. This reduction in **transactions costs** (Williamson, 1979), or the cost of exchanging a good, which can include shipping or the physical or mental effort of making a transaction, means that people are more likely to exchange material like songs, news stories, or photographs if bandwidth is large and storage is plentiful. Consider the transaction costs of taking and sharing a photograph twenty years ago. Showing someone a picture required film, a camera, a visit to the film developer, and then being physically co-present with someone or using the postal service. Now, transaction costs for sharing a photo amount to snapping a picture, uploading it to a website, or emailing it to a friend. The transaction costs for music fell precipitously when people were first able to transfer it for free using services like Napster and Limewire (ancient history—but ask your parents). Profits from the music industry fell, and the industry was slow to respond with a new business model (Giesler, 2006, 2008). Although transaction costs for obtaining information goods like a song or movie are now lower, they are still not negligible because one must purchase electronic devices and access to networks, invest time in search and download, and perhaps risk punishment if the transfer is illegal. Yet this shift in transaction costs has fundamentally changed the music industry. Apple, for example, sells songs on iTunes, and Amazon has fought to take a cut of publishing profits from the sale of ebooks.[3]

Another important trait of knowledge and other social media content is that it is often considered a **public good**. A public good is one that anyone can use. When a public good is shared by a group of people, it is called a **commons.** Keeping and cultivating a commons is tricky business and one that has fascinated economists for decades. From an economic point of view, people should have no incentive for contributing to a commons. Why spend time writing a Wikipedia article when someone else will do it? Why waste your time without getting paid? Further, if a resource is available for everyone to use, then people may feel less responsible for maintaining it, primarily because of the social phenomenon called diffusion of responsibility we discussed in Chapter 10. Appropriately enough, this tendency for groups of people to overuse and neglect collectively held property is called the **tragedy of the commons.** That is, it is a tragedy because something that seems so plentiful can be quickly overrun if everyone exploits it (Hardin, 1968). For example, bandwidth is a shared resource, yet if everyone uses it at the same time to download large files, the resource can quickly become scarce, particularly during peak times of the day or night. For this reason, hotels have started charging for "premium" Internet access for those who want to stream movies, and some speculate that broadband providers may follow suit by "metering" Internet use (Alor-Hernandez, Chavez-Trejo, Pelaez-Camarena, & Gomez, 2006).

Historically, Internet access has been neutral in the sense that all data on the Internet are treated equally, no matter its sender, receiver, or content (Wu, 2003). Many see this principle, called **net neutrality**, as vital to maintaining the public interest and preventing monopoly (Lessig & McChesney, 2006; Wu, 2003). Based on the same precedent as telephone service called "common carrier" laws, this net neutrality structure is normative but also protected by agencies like the Federal Communications Commission, who confirmed their position that the Internet should be regulated like a utility by a three-to-two vote in 2015 (Rebecca & Lohr, 2015). The fact that anyone can access the Internet for the same cost (as long as you have the right equipment) has led to unprecedented entrepreneurship and innovation. Many argue that if this were to change it would stifle development and innovation and allow those who own the "pipeline," companies like Comcast and Time Warner, to exert monopoly power in pricing (Lessig, 2004). The interplay between public goods and commercial development is precarious because many companies use public resources for commercial purposes. For example, the inter-state highway system—expanded in 1956 by President Dwight D. Eisenhower—provided efficient trucking routes for companies in the United States. Many argue that the Internet, as a "highway" that everyone uses, is the same kind of public resource that should be protected.

However, consider what we learned in Chapter 10 about community norms. Because of social agreements and informal pressures, the tragedy of the commons might not always occur. There are a number of informal social (rather than legal) ways to resolve the tragedy of the commons (Ostrom, 2008). For example, in peer-to-peer file sharing, users who download but do not upload take up server bandwidth. As a social check on this, peer-to-peer file sharing communities adopt strong norms about "leeching" and punish leechers by expelling and then banning them from the site (Giesler, 2006).

The tragedy of the commons is clearly an issue for physical goods that can be depleted. But what about informational goods? If a digital good cannot be depleted, what is wrong with sharing it? After all, as lawyer and cultural critic Lawrence Lessig says, "Information wants to be free" (Lessig, 2004). However, if information is free, then how do people who produce and circulate it get paid? And who profits from any value produced by its circulation? The question is hotly debated and considering it requires an examination of copyright.

Copyright

Copyright is a system of laws for delineating and enforcing the rights of intellectual property. Protecting intellectual property involves a tradeoff between public and private interests (Collins, 2010). On the one hand, knowledge can enhance human life and spur developments in science and culture, which is in the collective public interest. For instance, the information offered on WebMD about how to treat a venomous spider bite can increase human welfare, particularly if the information is not widely known. However, on the other hand, if all information is free, some argue, people will not spend much time or energy trying to produce it because it has no value. And yet people have many other, nonmarket motivations for producing information such as pursuing scientific knowledge, valuing artistic production, helping others, or gaining social esteem and fame (Hyde 1983). In the face of decreasing costs to certain kinds of information, these factors, rather than economic interest, appear to motivate production. We will return to some of the implications of these motivations for business models later in the chapter.

Protecting intellectual property is a balance between collective and individual interests, but it also presents a tradeoff between short- and long-term social gains. Inhibiting knowledge dissemination in the short term may be socially inefficient because information often costs little to reproduce and may be sorely needed by others for their own innovations. However, many have argued that it is important to protect intellectual property in the long term to offer an incentive for people to produce it (Hunt, 1999). This later point that there is long-term benefit to copyright protections has come under scrutiny lately as industries have attempted to lengthen the period of copyright. One analysis of intellectual property policy in sixty countries, for example, finds that stronger copyright protection actually decreased the number of innovations in a country (Lerner, 2009).

So how are these tradeoffs resolved? Not easily, as it turns out. A number of legal and practical provisions provide an unsteady stalemate. For instance, the policy of **fair use** says that small portions of copyrighted material can be used for educational or commentary purposes. Fair use was created to try to resolve the basic tension between the good of the public and the good of the individual creator. Intellectual property can be appropriated for the sake of commentary, education, news reporting, or a variety of other actions in the public interest. Yet there are still bounds on how much can be used and for exactly what purpose.

Another provision is the so-called Mickey Mouse rule, a piece of legislation first introduced to protect the intellectual property of Disney. The Copyright Act of 1976 says that intellectual property is protected from the moment of its creation through fifty years after its author's death or for seventy-five years if it has a corporate author (Public Law 94-553), and this term was extended in 1998 (Public

Photo 14.2 Copyright.

Law 105-298). This law was meant to protect the economic interests of the creator and yet ensure the eventual passing of knowledge into the public domain. As such, it is an attempt to resolve the tradeoff between short-term individual rights and long-term public good (Benkler, 2006).

Blurred rights of ownership apply not only to companies, but also to consumers. Several scholars have pointed out that companies like Google and Amazon collect, store, and use large amounts of consumer-produced data to provide services like search. What rights do users have to the data they produce? As it stands, none. Solutions to this issue range from schemes to allow you to enclose and then sell your private information (Lanier, 2013, 2014) to proposals to enforce the use of rights-management technologies and facilities on behalf of private users (Linn, 2005). In Chapter 4 we discussed the kind of value that large amounts of data can have for companies like Google and Facebook when it comes to measuring and selling an audience to advertisers. Chapter 5 examined its explicit and implicit creation of value for both companies and users. Clearly, this thorny issue concerns economics, politics, and technology and is still in flux (Morozov, 2013).

Networked Consumers

As we have seen, the costs of goods have changed, and the boundaries around digital goods have themselves shifted. But what about consumers? The fact that people can easily communicate, work collaboratively, and share digital objects has changed many aspects of economic life. For example, groups of people can collaborate either on things they create themselves or by modifying existing cultural objects. For instance, research shows that group work using Google docs to collaborate is best done when participants give feedback that is specifically about the work, not about the creator (Birnholtz, Steinhardt, & Pavese, 2013). Fan communities and cultures produce cultural texts, talk about modifications to their favorite shows, and gripe about new characters and plotlines. This audience feedback has in some ways changed how the mainstream media operates. For example, shows like *Pretty Little Liars* explicitly depend on consumer input because they incorporate fan suggestions into plots and characters (Keveney, 2013). Chapters 5 and 10 have covered many of these value-producing activities by networked consumers.

One particularly financial form of this kind of consumer coordination is crowdfunding. **Crowdfunding** is when a business idea or project is supported by a large and disaggregated group of people, usually through relatively small donations. For example, Kickstarter is cited as the platform responsible for coordinating fans of the show *Veronica Mars* to fund a movie many years after the show went off the air ("Veronica Mars," 2013). Zach Braff also raised money for his movie *Wish I Was Here* using Kickstarter and was met with a furious backlash (Child, 2013; O'Hehir, 2014). As we discussed in the previous chapter, fan communities will often use political tactics to back their favorite cultural products, and in many cases they will put their money where their mouth is (Earl & Kimport, 2009).

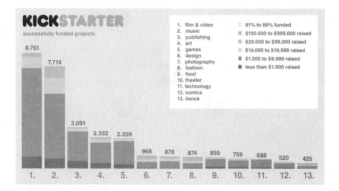

Photo 14.3 Kickstarter Projects, sorted by Quantity.

More broadly, the production of cultural or informational content can be funded by small amounts of money, called **micropayments**, that can be collected from a large number of people and distributed to the content creators. For example, the crowdfunding platform GoFundMe, which processed more than $470 million in micropayments in 2014, enables individuals or groups to fundraise all over the world in support of their health, communities, education, or charitable goals, among other causes (Hurst, 2015).

However, micropayments can have paradoxical effects on economic behavior. Although they may work when consumers have a passionate interest, micropayments have been less successful for everyday products about which people feel lukewarm (Anderson, 2009). Being free is fundamentally psychologically different from costing one cent (Shampanier, Mazar, & Ariely, 2007), and this is because of transaction costs, the mental effort one might have to expend to complete the payment. For example, imagine that every time you wanted to hear your favorite song, you had to get out a credit card and make an online payment. Or every time you wanted to read a news article you had to enter your credit card information. The transaction costs, in this case the psychological costs of getting out your wallet, ensuring the website is trustworthy, and processing a payment are likely to deter you from buying a simple newspaper article or watching a clip of last night's *Daily Show*. Even if the transaction were relatively frictionless, the mental task of even thinking of spending one cent would make one less likely to watch the show.

Platforms and the Chicken and Egg Problem

To set up a thriving social network site, you need people. But to get people, you need other people. Recall that when Nancy wanted to set up a music-sharing site, she had to attract both downloaders and uploaders (or at least enough people who do both). How does this type of platform ever get off the ground? Economists call this the Chicken and Egg problem, and it is an issue for all kinds of platforms (Evans & Schmalensee, 2010). Economists use the term network effects to describe the positive or negative value that additional users have to other users of

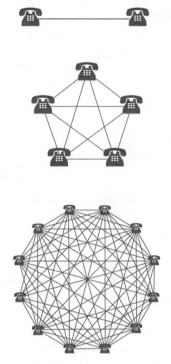

Figure 14.1 Network Effects: Public Domain.

the platform (Figure 14.1). The Chicken and Egg problem exists because of network effects, and understanding network effects is crucial if you want to attempt to solve it.

Direct network effects mean that current users get value out of additional users joining. For example, if you are on the old social networking site Friendster, it is not valuable if none of your friends is on the platform. However, as more people are added, there are more pictures to look at, more comments to read, and more messages to send. In this way, more users make the platform more valuable. Direct network effects can also be negative. For example, more users being added to Friendster may cause the service to be congested or may clutter the service with repetitive content, decreasing the overall value (boyd & Ellison, 2007).

But platforms are not always so simple. Sometimes there are distinct segments of users that can have network effects on each other. Recall the concept of a two-sided market, which we discussed in Chapter 3. A two-sided market provides value by linking two or more groups of people together for economic exchange. The traditional way of thinking about a two-sided market is when a company supports itself through both advertising and subscriptions. For example, on Deadspin, there are advertisers who pay the site and users who visit the site. In this market, there are two groups—a group of advertisers and a group of users. Advertisers fund the production of content, and users provide the "eyeballs" that may generate a sale for the advertiser. There are many other variants to this basic platform structure, and they are ubiquitous in social media. For example, eBay provides a platform on which buyers and sellers meet, and then eBay charges a fee for uniting the two parties. Task rabbit provides a platform for uniting service seekers and service providers. Uber unites riders with drivers. Even match.com provides a platform for the dating "market," uniting date-seekers (Piskorski, 2014).[4] Figure 14.2 shows a typical platform with two user groups.

Indirect or **cross-side network effects** describe the effects of additional users of one segment on another segment. For example, if Facebook adds 2 million users, this has a positive cross-side network effect for advertisers on Facebook because there are now more eyeballs on the site. However, if Facebook added 2 million new advertisers, there certainly would be cross-network effects, but they definitely would not be positive for users, whose experience of the site would be cluttered with even more advertising.

The trick to managing a successful platform is balancing the tension among the many "sides" of the platform—uploaders and downloaders, advertisers and readers, voyeurs and exhibitionists. Although network effects are not new—they have been studied in the context of telephone networks, credit cards, and newspapers for a long time—they have become much more common; after all, the Internet is a "platform of platforms" (Eisenmann, Parker, & Van Alstyne, 2006). Social media markets—services like Uber, AirBnB, and Etsy—have created many new business models based on the simple idea of a platform. The ubiquity of platforms for sharing cultural content—uniting people who want to listen to songs or watch videos with those who post them—has presented challenges to those wishing to prosecute copyright infringement. If a company wants to punish someone for circulating clips of a television show, but the uploader has disappeared, can they punish the platform? Turns out, no. As long as the platform provider responds to requests to remove the content, it cannot be sued for distributing illegal content. This seemingly trivial distinction protects platforms like YouTube under a "safe harbor" provision in the Digital Millennium Copyright Act (DMCA, Title II: Online Copyright Infringement Liability Limitation Act 1998).

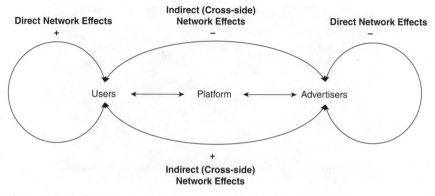

Figure 14.2 Platform Structure with Direct and Indirect Network Effects.

Monopolies, Switching Costs, and Multihoming

As we saw in the previous section, much of a platform's value comes from its size. The bigger the network, the greater potential value it has to users. But is it right for Google to control 67.6% of the market for search in the United States[5] (comScore Explicit, 2014)? What about Facebook? And will the users of Facebook evaporate from the platform just as they did for Myspace? Economists have been puzzling this out and argue that the answer depends on a couple of factors.

A **monopoly**, when one organization controls most of the market, is usually thought to be a bad thing because the organization has the power to increase prices and reduce quality (if you need an example, reflect for a moment on your cable provider). However, consider what we just discussed about network effects. More customers can be a good thing for everyone. Thus some platforms will tend toward monopoly status, and this might benefit users as well.

One factor that can make a difference on whether a platform has a monopoly is the switching cost for users. **Switching costs** are a specific type of transaction costs, the costs to the user of changing a product or platforms (Evans & Schmalensee, 2010; Schmalensee, 1972). People find switching inherently risky or needlessly time consuming. For example, consider the costs of switching from an iPhone to an Android-based Samsung. You would have to spend time transferring contacts and data and learn how to use the product, and after that, you may not like it. Switching costs can be different for different platforms, however. For example, switching from Bing to Google is not costly, but switching from Mac to PC is considerably harder. Switching costs can also exist on the other side of the market. Consider, for example, seller reputations on eBay. When a seller builds a particular history of favorable ratings from buyers, she can charge higher prices and sell more goods (Haucap & Heimeshoff, 2014). But this reputation score is only available to users on eBay and only exists on the eBay platform. This fact would make any seller think twice before switching to another auction site. Switching costs for some platforms, like your operating system, might be high, but they may be much lower for other platforms, like your social networking or search

Photo 14.4 Switching Costs.

site. The ability to use more than one platform, called **multihoming**, also clearly affects the ability of the platform to have monopoly power (Rochet & Tirole, 2003).

SHIFTS IN ECONOMIC PRACTICE AND PRODUCTION

The major shifts covered in the previous section—decrease in costs, blurred property rights, and networked consumers—have had concrete implications for real products and real markets. This section will cover a few of these implications for innovation and consumer sharing.

User Innovation

Product development and innovation is one aspect of economic life that has changed because of some of the effects of social media described in this book. Co-creation, the decreased costs of sharing information, and increased availability of materials to produce things have all led to shifts in innovation. In industries ranging from software development to hiking gear to surgical devices, **user innovation** has altered the creation of new products. User-centric (as opposed to manufacturer-centric) design occurs when users—any firm or individual whose primary interest is in using rather than selling the product—develop a new product or modify an existing product, usually to suit their own needs (Von Hippel, 2005). For example, a community of windsurfers in the mid-1970s created boards that could be used for jumping and spinning (Von Hippel, 2005). Mini-motorcross bikes began with a user community that modified bikes originally built for kids (Martin & Schouten, 2014). Studies suggest that user innovation is common; between 10 and 40 percent of users participate in some kind of innovation, depending on the product. For example, about 40 percent of users who participate in extreme sports like hiking modify their gear at some point (Franke & Shah, 2003). About 22 percent of surgeons in Germany report modifying their instruments for more effective use (Lüthje, 2003).

However, not everyone who uses a product innovates with it. **Lead users**, experts who know the product well, are some of the best innovators. These users have a lot to gain by developing better tools, and they also have the extensive knowledge to contribute helpful innovations. Studies show that objects developed by lead users rather than nonexpert users end up being more commercially attractive innovations (Franke & von Hippel, 2003). Innovation or knowledge communities like those discussed in Chapter 9 will often collaborate to produce innovations and freely share the fruits of their labor, both because it can be mutually beneficial to group members and because it is perceived as altruistic. In some cases this community process is called **open innovation**, innovation where anyone can contribute and the resulting ideas and products are freely shared. Many communities like software development groups institutionalize open innovation into the rules for enclosing property. For example, the Linux platform contains explicit previsions that legally prevent another party from taking ownership of the collectively developed product.

Although "freely revealing" information has existed for hundreds of years (Nuvolar, 2004; Lim, 2000; Morrison, Roberts, & Von Hippel, 2000; Allen, Hyman, & Pinckney, 1983), transaction costs for diffusing information are now lower because of networked, digital communication—message boards, online forums, and blogs that comprise the platforms that coordinate community members. A combination of online and offline social events and connections bring these types of group together for information sharing and collaboration (Martin & Schouten, 2014).

However, although innovation communities can improve knowledge products such as software or music, most products still profoundly benefit from the economies of scale of professional manufacturers. For example, although car aficionados may modify their vehicles as a form of expression, their ability to do so is constrained by the product lines of car-parts manufacturers, who possess economies of scale that no amount of social-media networking could ever hope to replicate. Still, exceptions to this constraint can be found in arts and crafts that do not require economies of scale to produce. Sites like Etsy, where users sell homemade wares, demonstrate that entrepreneurs can make and distribute products themselves when facilitated by online platforms.

Sharing

Sharing goods and services is another shift that has emerged partly as a result of the increased ability to coordinate people through social media tools. **Sharing** is "nonreciprocal pro-social behavior" (Benkler, 2004) in which one or more people pool resources for distribution to others and conversely access resources from this pool for their own use without direct reciprocation. It can encompass a range of practices along a spectrum—from commercial sharing in the case of services like ZipCar to gift-oriented economies such as food sharing, book sharing, and file sharing (Botsman and Rogers 2010). Social media often provides a platform to facilitate sharing. For example, couchsurfing.com coordinates people looking for free lodging with people happy to offer it.

Sharing practices are related to, but distinct from, both commercial exchange and gift giving (Belk, 2010; Dubois, Schor, & Carfagna, 2014). Commercial exchange is when two parties exchange a good or service for money. Although payment can be deferred, it is contractually obligated and enforceable according to a system of legal sanctions. Commercial exchange has long been a part of human cultures, but gift giving is also a fundamental social practice that has structured societies for tens of thousands of years (Mauss, 1954; Polanyi, 2001; Sahlins, 1972). In a traditional **gift economy**, the giver prepares an object for an intended receiver, presents the object in a socially appropriate way, and has no ostensible motive for the gift, although the norms of reciprocity usually indebt the receiver to the giver over a period of time until the gift is reciprocated (Derrida, 1992; Mauss, 1954; Sherry, 1983). This kind of gift giving is called dyadic because it involves two people.

Sharing is like commercial exchange in that it is a relatively mundane exchange practice where people exchange common material or cultural resources.

Photo 14.5 Book Exchanges as a form of Offline Sharing.

However, unlike economic exchange, payment is not always required. Sharing is like gift exchange in that goods, services, or information can be exchanged without payment. However, unlike gift giving, sharing tends to involve more than two people, and the norm of reciprocity can be somewhat looser, although perhaps not completely absent. As one scholar studying fan communities points out, "the digital gift . . . is a gift without obligation to reciprocate. Instead of reciprocity, what the gift in the digital age requires for 'membership' into the fan community, is merely an obligation to reply" (Booth, 2010, p. 134). Instead of being dyadic as in gift exchange, it is **rhizomatic**, meaning social connections are not just one to one, but rather fan out in an exponential pattern similar to what we saw in our discussion of social networks (Giesler, 2006). These systems, also called peer-to-peer network exchange, facilitate sharing of information or cultural products. Studies of file sharing show that those who download from a resource are usually expected to share their own files. Taking without giving violates a norm well known to sharing communities, as we saw in Chapter 9. However, unlike gift giving, reciprocity in sharing communities need not necessarily be one to one. The norm of reciprocity in sharing can be satisfied by contributing one item to an extensive pool of resources (Giesler, 2006). In one experiment, researchers found that the majority of movie downloaders (75%) shared their files, although there was no monetary incentive to do so and sharing even involved heightened risk of legal penalties under copyright law (Schade, Nitschke, & Sattler, 2005).

Certain kinds of objects lend themselves to sharing. Goods that have excess capacity and those that are commonly and privately owned are likely candidates for communal arrangements (Benkler, 2002). For example, if you own a computer, it likely sits on your desk or couch for most of the day without being used, when in fact this excess processing capacity could be donated to a project like SETI@home, a program that uses networks of home computers to look for extraterrestrial life (Benkler, 2004). More commonly, your car has excess capacity that could be used by others if you were to share access to it. Lawn equipment, books, yards, apartments, and toys are all physical goods that find themselves amenable to sharing, and many of these sharing arrangements are coordinated by social media platforms (see, e.g., Ozanne & Ozanne, 2010).

Yet, sharing can also be a threat to intellectual property and challenge other legal structures such as zoning and permitting laws. Despite much debate (*The Economist*, 2002), some research has shown that file sharing can cut into movie theater revenue (Hennig-Thurau, Henning, & Sattler, 2007; Liebowitz, 2006; Michel, 2006; Montoro-Pons & Cuadrado-García, 2006; Peitz & Waelbroeck, 2004; Zentner, 2006). For instance, in a survey of German movie goers, about 19% of those surveyed had downloaded a movie, and about two-thirds of those watched their download. By looking at movie-going intentions prior to downloading, researchers found that file downloading decreased the probability that the consumer would see the movie in the theater (Hennig-Thurau, Henning, & Sattler, 2007). However, there is a silver lining for those selling DVDs. People who had downloaded a copy of the movie but had not watched it were more likely to buy the DVD. These researchers estimate that in Germany, file sharing accounts for a 12.6% decline in revenues, but that does not fully account for the observed 16% decrease, thus supporting claims that the movie business has bigger problems than mere piracy.

However, in many cases, offering something for free critically supports promotion of a product and can expand one's audience enough to offset any losses. As we will see in the next section, freemium business models and online file sharing can also provide a lift to experience goods such as music or video games by providing a free sample and thus decreasing risk of trial (Gopal, Bhattacharjee, & Sanders, 2006). Sharing can clearly enhance network effects, helping some products to get off the ground and thus solve the Chicken and Egg problem. So how is one to know when to encourage or discourage sharing? This question has inspired new business models that attempt to profit from the widespread sharing of information.

Business Models for Social Media

In response to these clear and obvious transformations in economic life, new ways of making money from information goods and social media practices have come to the fore. In this section, we will examine just a few of the models that have been adopted by companies in a number of domains.

As companies and other organizations tackle the economic transitions discussed in this chapter, at least five ways to make money from noncopyrighted material have been proposed and tested (Benkler, 2006). First, some organizations seek government or extramarket support through foundations, patrons, or nonprofit organizations. For example, podcast networks like Radiotopia benefit from grants from organizations like the Knight Foundation. The National Endowment for the Arts provides funding for interactive digital projects like funding Poets.org, the website for the leading poetry journal, *American Poetry*, to incorporate user-generated content, and the National Science Foundation sponsors radio and podcast programing like Radiolab.

The second business model, the so-called **freemium** model, involves offering a free version of the product to encourage trial, with the hopes that some percentage of users convert to a paid version or to buying related services and goods like concerts or appearances rather than the content itself. For example, Dropbox developed a successful freemium model based on a referral program. Users could use the platform for free with some *de facto* amount of storage and received extra storage space as an incentive for referring other users. In 2010, about 70% of users referred others, which led to a huge growth in the number of users. By 2013, about 1.6 to 4% of users converted to paid membership, yielding a lot of revenue (Teixeira & Watkins, 2013). Spotify, with a conversion rate of 20%, is also considered a successful example of the freemium model. The basic principle of freemium pricing is related to the attention economy discussed in Chapter 4. Offering a free product expands the audience dramatically, such that a platform can make money even if only 1% of those trials become paying members (Teixeira & Watkins, 2013). Seventy-seven percent of apps in the Apple store in 2013 used the freemium model. In many cases, content producers can earn money through the same platforms used by pirates. The band Radiohead, for example, let fans pay what they wanted for an album, earning significant profits despite the many free downloads (Warner Chappell Records, 2008). Monty Python set up a free YouTube channel to rival fans who were disseminating copies of their videos online, and within weeks, Monty Python's DVDs rose to #2 bestseller on Amazon (Anderson, 2009).

The third, and most common, business model is a commercial sponsorship model that funds activities through advertising. Although this is how platforms like newspapers have operated for decades, the idea is also now used by social media celebrities like Michelle Pham, who gained sponsorship from Lancôme and Dr. Pepper and blogs like *TechCrunch*, *Grantland*, and *Mashable*. Although commercial sponsorship is one of the easiest and most intuitive business models in social media, it does come with some pitfalls like loss of authenticity, as discussed in Chapter 11.

A fourth, increasingly important business model has arisen from companies with access and control of user data. Twitter, for example, charges for access to its

Photo 14.6 Free!

"fire hose" of user Tweets, and companies buy these data for market research. Facebook, with its control over interactional and personal data, sells to advertisers, who use it for segmentation (Maurer & Wiegmann, 2011). As the "big data" approaches discussed in Chapter 4 gain traction among managers, companies that collect and store user data are increasingly looking for ways to monetize the resource. Here, the ethical issues of co-creative activities discussed in Chapter 5 take on new and important meaning.

A fifth business model exists based on an understanding of what social media platforms actually *do*. Mikołaj Jan Piskorski argues that companies should base their social media activities around social failures, those missed opportunities for connection such as structural holes that we discussed in Chapter 9. By understanding why these social failures happen—because of social norms, distance, or personal reticence—companies can better facilitate them by creating social solutions (Piskorski, 2014). For example, Piskorski (2014) describes how LinkedIn provided a solution to job seekers who did not want to violate the norm of looking for a job while employed and to recruiters, who could facilitate a match. Tinder, OkCupid, and match.com overcome similar social failures on the dating market, often for a fee. By operating a platform, these companies coordinate connections that wouldn't otherwise occur. Further, for companies not interested in operating a social platform, understanding that people want to connect with others (and not be spammed with advertising) can focus managerial thinking on the uses and benefits that people are seeking rather than trying to get attention from people who do not want to give it.

SUMMARY AND CONCLUSION

This chapter has covered some of the fundamental shifts in economic life spurred by producer and consumer uses of networked digital technology, and social media in particular. It is important to remember that economic shifts do not just happen—they are enacted by people using technology. Although they may be bound by the affordances of particular tools, people adapt these technologies and economic structures to new and sometimes surprising ends. The economic shifts engendered by changes in costs and availability of technology, together with new social practices, have posed challenges for many areas of law and economic practice—from data collection and privacy to copyright and competition in the marketplace. Importantly, these shifts are not just economic, but also political and cultural.

TOPICS

- Copyright
- Good
- Fixed and marginal cost
- Network effects

- Tragedy of the commons
- Sharing
- Switching costs
- Transaction costs
- Net neutrality

DISCUSSION QUESTIONS

1. Is it ever OK for a platform to have a monopoly? Why or why not? Compare a platform like Google Search with a social networking site like Facebook. What are the differences and do these matter when it comes to monopoly power?
2. The sharing examples discussed in this chapter seem to involve contexts where people are relatively homogeneous. What are some potential challenges that might emerge when the people sharing are different from each other? Provide an example where this works and one where it fails.

EXERCISE

Imagine that you have been tasked with setting up a successful platform for sharing recipes. What would you do first? How would you create positive network effects? How would you mitigate negative network effects? Create a business plan for your platform that covers three stages of growth.

NOTES

1. http://www.nytimes.com/2010/03/01/business/media/01ebooks.html?page wanted=all&_r=0/.
2. There are other important and interesting theories of value that will not be discussed at length in this chapter. The labor theory of value, for example, says that value comes from the amount of labor that is put into the object (which is then sold, thereby alienating the worker from his product) (Marx, 1867). Another theory of value is the cost theory of value, which says that a good's value is the cost it took to make that objects, including the land, labor, and capital (Smith, 1887).
3. http://www.nytimes.com/2014/05/29/technology/amazon-hachette-book-publisher-dispute.html/.
4. http://www.nytimes.com/2014/08/08/business/media/plot-thickens-as-900-writers-battle-amazon.html/.
5. Interestingly, however, there are platforms that foster repeat transactions such as Uber and others where successful pairing closes the market, as with match.com. Thanks to John Deighton for this insight.
6. https://www.comscore.com/Insights/Market-Rankings/comScore-Releases-June-2014-US-Search-Engine-Rankings/.

FURTHER READINGS

Benkler, Y. (2006). *The wealth of networks: How social production transforms markets and freedom.* New Haven, CT: Yale University Press.

Piskorski, M. J. (2014). *A social strategy: How we profit from social media.* Princeton, NJ: Princeton University Press.

REFERENCES

Allen, T. J., Hyman, D. B., & Pinckney, D. L. (1983). Transferring technology to the small manufacturing firm: a study of technology transfer in three countries. *Research Policy, 12*(4), 199–211.

Alor-Hernandez, G., Chavez-Trejo, A. M., Pelaez-Camarena, G., & Gomez, J. M. (2006). *A framework for Web Services Procurement.* Paper presented at the 2006 3rd International Conference on Electrical and Electronics Engineering. Veracruz, Mexico, September 6–8, 2006.

Anderson, C. (2009). *Free: The future of a radical price.* New York: Random House.

Belk, R. (2010). Sharing. *Journal of Consumer Research, 36*(5), 715–734.

Benkler, Y. (2002). Coase's Penguin, or, Linux and "The Nature of the Firm." *Yale Law Journal, 112*(3), 369–446.

Benkler, Y. (2004). Sharing nicely: On shareable goods and the emergence of sharing as a modality of economic production. *Yale Law Journal, 114,* 273–358.

Benkler, Y. (2006). *The wealth of networks: How social production transforms markets and freedom.* New Haven, CT: Yale University Press.

Birnholtz, J., Steinhardt, S., & Pavese, A. (2013). *Write here, write now!: An experimental study of group maintenance in collaborative writing.* Paper presented at the Proceedings of the SIGCHI Conference on Human Factors in Computing Systems. Paris, France—April 27–May 02, 2013.

Booth, P. (2010). *Digital fandom: New media studies* (Vol. 68). New York: Lang.

Botsman, R., & Rogers, R. (2010). What's mine is yours. *The Rise of Collaborative Consumption.* New York: HarperBusiness.

boyd, d., & Ellison, N. B. (2007). Social network sites: Definition, history, and scholarship. *Journal of Computer-Mediated Communication, 13*(1), 210–230.

Boyle, J. (2003). The second enclosure movement and the construction of the public domain. *Law and Contemporary Problems, 66,* 33–74.

Child, B. (2013, May 16). Zach Braff Kickstarter controversy deepens after financier bolsters budget. *The Guardian.* Retrieved from http://www.theguardian.com/film/2013/may/16/zach-braff-kickstarter-controversy-deepens/.

Collins, S. (2010). Digital fair prosumption and the fair use defence. *Journal of Consumer Culture, 10*(1), 37–55.

Davenport, T. H., & Beck, J. C. (2013). *The attention economy: Understanding the new currency of business.* Watertown, MA: Harvard Business Press.

Derrida, J. (1992). *Given time: I. Counterfeit money* (Vol. 1). Chicago: University of Chicago Press.

Dubois, E. A., Schor, J. B., & Carfagna, L. B. (2014). New cultures of connection in a Boston time bank. In *Sustainable lifestyles and the quest for plenitude: case studies of the new economy* (p. 95). New Haven, CT: Yale University Press.

Earl, J., & Kimport, K. (2009). Movement societies and digital protest: Fan activism and other nonpolitical protest online. *Sociological Theory, 27*(3), 220–243.

The Economist (2002, March 25). The Oscars get Napsterised. March 25, 2002. http://www.economist.com/node/1049624?zid=292&ah=165a5788fdb0726c01b1374d8e1ea285.

Eisenmann, T., Parker, G., & Van Alstyne, M. W. (2006). Strategies for two-sided markets. *Harvard Business Review, 84*(10), 92.

Evans, D. S., & Schmalensee, R. (2010). Failure to launch: Critical mass in platform businesses. *Review of Network Economics, 9*(4), 1–26.

Franke, N., & Shah, S. (2003). How communities support innovative activities: An exploration of assistance and sharing among end-users. *Research Policy, 32*(1), 157–178.

Franke, N., & Von Hippel, E. (2003). Satisfying heterogeneous user needs via innovation toolkits: The case of Apache security software. *Research policy, 32*(7), 1199–1215.

Giesler, M. (2006). Consumer gift systems. *Journal of Consumer Research, 33*(2), 283–290.

Giesler, M. (2008). Conflict and compromise: Drama in marketplace evolution. *Journal of Consumer Research, 34*(6), 739–753.

Gopal, R. D., Bhattacharjee, S., & Sanders, G. L. (2006). Do Artists benefit from online music sharing? *The Journal of Business, 79*(3), 1503–1533.

Hardin, G. (1968). The tragedy of the commons. *Science, 162*, 1243–1248.

Haucap, J., & Heimeshoff, U. (2014). Google, Facebook, Amazon, eBay: Is the Internet driving competition or market monopolization? *International Economics and Economic Policy, 11*(1–2), 49–61.

Hennig-Thurau, T., Henning, V., & Sattler, H. (2007). Consumer file sharing of motion pictures. *Journal of Marketing, 71*(4), 1–18.

Hunt, R. M. (1999). *Nonobviousness and the incentive to innovate: An economic analysis of intellectual property reform*. Philadelphia: Economic Research Division, Federal Reserve Bank of Philadelphia.

Hurst, S. (2015, January 13). GoFundMe reportedly brings in $470M in 2014; claims to top Kickstarter. *Crowdfund Insider*.

Hyde, L. (1983). *The gift: Imagination and the erotic life of property*. New York: Vintage.

Keveney, B. (2013, June 10). The true sign of "Liars" success is in social media. *USA Today*. Retrieved from http://www.usatoday.com/story/life/tv/2013/06/10/pretty-little-liarsabc-family-social-media/2399921/.

Lanier, J. (2013). How should we think about privacy? *Scientific American, 309*(5), 64–71.

Lanier, J. (2014). *Who owns the future?* New York: Simon & Schuster.

Lerner, J. (2009). The empirical impact of intellectual property rights on innovation: Puzzles and clues. *The American Economic Review, 99,* 343–348.

Lessig, L. (2004). *Free culture: How big media uses technology and the law to lock down culture and control creativity.* New York: Penguin.

Lessig, L., & McChesney, R. W. (2006, June 8). No tolls on the Internet. *Washington Post, 8,* A23.

Liebowitz, S. J. (2006). File Sharing: Creative Destruction or Just Plain Destruction?*. *Journal of Law and Economics, 49*(1), 1–28.

Linn, J. (2005). Technology and Web user data privacy. *IEEE Security & Privacy, 3*(1), 52–58.

Lüthje, C., & Herstatt, C. (2004). The Lead User method: An outline of empirical findings and issues for future research. *R&D Management, 34*(5), 553–568.

Martin, D. M., & Schouten, J. W. (2014). Consumption-driven market emergence. *Journal of Consumer Research, 40*(5), 855–870.

Marx, K. (1867). *Capital, A critical analysis of capitalist production, Volume I.* Moscow: Progress.

Maurer, C., & Wiegmann, R. (2011). *Effectiveness of advertising on social network sites: A case study on Facebook.* New York: Springer.

Mauss, M. (1954). *The gift: The form and reason for exchange in archaic societies.* New York and London: Norton, 1990 [1950], 11.

Michel, N. J. (2006). The impact of digital file sharing on the music industry: An empirical analysis. *Topics in Economic Analysis & Policy, 6*(1).

Montoro-Pons, J. D., & Cuadrado-García, M. (2006, May). Digital goods and the effects of copying: an empirical study of the music market. In *14th International Conference on Cultural Economics, Vienna.*

Moore, G. (1965). Moore's law. *Electronics Magazine, 38*(8).

Morrison, P. D., Roberts, J. H., & Von Hippel, E. (2000). Determinants of user innovation and innovation sharing in a local market. *Management science, 46*(12), 1513–1527.

Morozov, E. (2013, October 22). *The real privacy problem. Technology Review.* Retrieved from http://www.technologyreview.com/featuredstory/520426/the-real-privacyproblem/.

Nunes, J. C., Hsee, C. K., & Weber, E. U. (2004). Why are people so prone to steal software? The effect of cost structure on consumer purchase and payment intentions. *Journal of Public Policy and Marketing, 23*(1), 43–53.

O'Hehir, A. (2014, July 17). "Wish I was here": Zach Braff's controversial Kickstarter comeback. *Salon.*

Ostrom, E. (2008). *Tragedy of the commons.* New York: Palgrave Macmillan.

Ozanne, L. K., & Ballantine, P. W. (2010). Sharing as a form of anti-consumption? An examination of toy library users. *Journal of Consumer Behaviour, 9*(6), 485–498.

Peitz, M., & Waelbroeck, P. (2004). File-sharing, sampling, and music distribution. *International University in Germany Working Paper*, (26).

Piskorski, M. J. (2014). *A social strategy: How we profit from social media*. Princeton, NJ: Princeton University Press.

Polanyi, K. (2001). *The great transformation: The political and economic origins of our time*. Boston: Beacon Press.

Rebecca, R., & Lohr, S. (2015). *F.C.C. approves net neutrality rules, classifying broadband Internet service as a utility*. New York Times, Retrieved from http://www.nytimes.com/2015/02/27/technology/net-neutrality-fcc-vote-internet-utility.html/.

Reeve, A. (1986). *Property*. Atlantic Highlands, NJ: Humanities Press.

Rochet, J. C., & Tirole, J. (2003). Platform competition in two-sided markets. *Journal of the European Economic Association, 1*(4), 990–1029.

Sahlins, M. D. (1972). *Stone age economics*. New Brunswick, NJ: Transaction.

Schade, C., Nitschke, T., & Sattler, H. (2005). Reciprocity with video file sharing: Experimental evidence. *Advances in consumer research, 32*, 58.

Schmalensee, R. (1972). Product differentiation advantages of pioneering brands. *American Economic Review, 72*(3), 349–366.

Shampanier, K., Mazar, N., & Ariely, D. (2007). Zero as a special price: The true value of free products. *Marketing Science, 26*(6), 742–757.

Sherry, J. F. Jr. (1983). Gift giving in anthropological perspective. *Journal of Consumer Research, 10*, 157–168.

Simon, H. A. (1971). Designing organizations for an information-rich world. *Computers, Communications, and the Public Interest, 72*, 37–72.

Smith, A. (1887). *An inquiry into the nature and causes of the Wealth of Nations*. Edinburgh: Nelson.

Teixeira, T. S., & Watkins, E. A. (2013). *Freemium pricing at Dropbox. Harvard Business Review*. Retrieved from https://hbr.org/product/freemium-pricing-at-dropbox/514053-PDF-ENG/.

Varian, H. R. (1992). *Microeconomic analysis* (Vol. 2). New York: Norton.

Von Hippel, E. (2005). *Democratizing innovation*. Cambridge, MA: MIT Press.

Williamson, O. E. (1979). Transaction-cost economics: The governance of contractual relations. *Journal of Law and Economics, 22*(2), 233–261.

Warner Chappell Records (2008), "Radiohead Record Sales," Presented at the You are in Control Conference, Reykjavik, Iceland, October 2008. http://musically.com/2008/10/15/exclusive-warner-chappell-reveals-radioheads-in-rainbows-pot-of-gold/

Wu, T. (2003). Network neutrality, broadband discrimination. *Journal of Telecommunications and High Technology Law, 2*, 141–178.

Xia, L., Monroe, K. B., & Cox, J. L. (2004). The price is unfair! A conceptual framework of price fairness perceptions. *Journal of Marketing, 68*(4), 1–15.

Zentner, A. (2006). Measuring the effect of file sharing on music purchases*. *Journal of Law and Economics, 49*(1), 63–90.

Glossary

Advertising Forms of communication aimed at persuading or informing an audience, usually pertaining to a commercial goal.

Affordances Capabilities of an object or technology resulting from the fit between an object or technology's material properties and human needs or goals.

Age cohort A group of people who are about the same age.

Agenda setting The ability of news media to influence the salience of topics in the public sphere.

Algorithm Executable formulae or programs used to take particular inputs of data and provide an output that is a prediction or simplified result.

Anonymity A trait describing when someone's speech, writing, or actions do not contain personally identifiable information and thus cannot be linked to personal identity.

Archetypes Common categories of people formed by past experience, or common cultural narrative or myth.

Assemblages Loosely affiliated groups of actors that come together for a shared interest, but may also be reconfigured when the context changes.

Asynchronous communication Communication occurring while participants are not in the same digital space at the same time.

Attention economy A system in which people's attention comes to have economic value.

Attention The ability to focus on a given task or piece of information.

Audience community A social group that forms around a particular media product such as a movie, television show, or book.

Awareness The first stage in the purchase funnel consisting of the consumer's existing knowledge of a product or product category.

Balance theory The idea that people seek a balance in their attitudes and opinions about others.

Bonding social capital The value a relationship might have to provide lasting and meaningful social support.

Bridging social capital The value that friendship has in uniting two different groups of people.

Centrality A measure of how important a node is in a particular network.

Centralized network A network in which there are only one or two people with a lot of connections, which gives them power in the network.

Circulation The movement of an object or sign in and out of different cultural, economic, and social contexts.

Citizen journalism The practice of nonprofessional journalists producing and disseminating journalistic knowledge.

Click-through rate A measurement of whether a user clicked on a link.

Clustering A phenomenon occurring in networks in which nodes tend to be closely related by one-degree connections.

Co-creation The practice of an audience or consumers producing goods or content, often collaboratively with other consumers or with a company.

Cognitive dissonance A theory arguing that people experience a sense of psychological discomfort when they encounter disconfirming information to their own beliefs or are blocked from pursuing a goal and seek to reduce the discomfort as much as possible.

Collaborative production A type of co-creation that happens when fans or community members collaborate on a product.

Collective reasoning A type of collective intelligence and co-creation.

Commons The term for when a public good is shared by a group of people.

Communitas The feeling of being in a social group or part of a collective of like-minded individuals.

Community of practice A group that is informally bound together by shared expertise and passion for a joint enterprise.

Conformation bias The tendency for people to seek out or attend to information that confirms their existing belief or beliefs.

Connectors Those individuals in a network with a large number of acquaintances, who might otherwise be unrelated.

Consideration The third stage of the purchase funnel in which the consumer weighs different options against one another or considers other alternatives.

Content analysis A method of systematically collecting, analyzing, and interpreting textual or visual data online, usually with the intent of quantifying patterns for comparison or to draw inferences across time.

Context collapse Situations in which two or more social worlds collide, particularly online.

Contextual integrity Acknowledging and ensuring "adequate protection for privacy to norms of specific contexts, demanding that information gathering and dissemination be appropriate to that context and obey the governing norms of distribution within it" (Nissenbaum, 2004, p. 101).

Convergence The process through which certain institutional, functional, and user practices have merged into one platform and/or sphere.

Conversational analysis The method used by linguists to study dyadic, interpersonal communication.

Conversion attribution The process of linking exposure to conversion.

Conversion When the user takes some action that the sender of a message desires.

Cool media Media requiring more active audience engagement.

Copyright A system of laws for delineating and enforcing the rights of intellectual property.

Counterpublics Publics formed in opposition to dominant cultural norms and values.

Creative Commons license An agreement that allows work to be used and reappropriated freely for creative purposes with both commercial and noncommercial options.

Cross-side network effects The effects of additional users of one user segment on another user segment.

Crowdfunding The practice of financially supporting a business idea or project through small donations from a large and disaggregated group of people.

Crowdsourcing Using collectively produced knowledge, often from external sources, to solve a problem.

Cult texts Vast, elaborate, and densely populated fictional worlds that are constructed episode by episode, extended, and embellished by official and secondary-level texts and fan-produced tertiary texts.

Cultural capital The articulation of tastes, embodied practices, or institutionalized formal education that constitutes a resource in the reproduction or advancement of social class.

Cyberbullying The practice of socially or physically intimidating someone online, which can include spreading rumors, circulating illicitly taken pictures, or taunting.

Decentralized network A network in which most people are connected to most of the other people.

Decision journey A model of consumer decision making in which purchases are not always rational, and a purchase may be triggered without much thought or planning.

Degree centrality A measure of how many connections a node has.

Degree The measure of how far removed one person or node is from another person or node.

Deindividuation A concept describing the sense of a mass of people acting as one entity.

Demotic turn A term used to understand the historical turn toward participatory culture, namely the widespread ability for ordinary people to produce, distribute, and play with cultural objects.

Diffusion of responsibility A phenomenon in which individuals participating in a group activity feel less responsible for the outcome as a result of being part of a group.

Digital anthropology Studies the cultural and social structures that frame human interaction that occurs through digital technology (Horst & Miller, 2013). This perspective often includes the analysis of interactions between the digital and non-digital worlds and incorporates an understanding of the material elements of the digital.

Digital Inequality The differential access people have to the social, cultural and material resources necessary to use understand, and interpret digital information and technologies.

Digital literacy The ability to perform alphanumeric literacy, information literacy, computer literacy, computer-mediated communication literacy, and multimedia literacy in concert to understand digitally-provided information

Direct network effects The value of additional users joining a network to existing users.

Directionality A property of edges illustrating the flow of relationships from one node to another.

Discourse analysis A method for studying text that focuses on interpreting the material with reference to broader patterns and structures in society usually by taking into account the social role, position, and power of the speaker.

Discourse The systems of ideas and practices concerning individual subjectivity throughout history that construct the limits of personal freedom and autonomy.

Disinhibition The feeling describing unrestrained or impulsive behavior without regard for social norms or consequences.

Dramaturgical theory of self A theory of self that argues we are always performing different roles or selves on a "stage" with "props" for an intended audience.

Dyadic communication Communication that is primarily based on the interpersonal dynamics of two people.

Dyadic relationship A relationship between two people.

Earned media Media coverage of a company created by someone else for which that company did not pay.

Economic theory of value The theory that price is determined by supply and demand.

Edge The link representing the relationship between two people or objects in a network.

Emergence "Any order, structure, or pattern appearing in complex random events that cannot be attributed to some specific prepensive, purposeful activity or decision by some identifiable official or unofficial component or entity." (McKelvey 1997)

Enclosure The process of putting boundaries around property to ensure rights of the owner.

Engagement Category referring to measures of audience involvement with or responsiveness to a particular message.

Etactics Adaptations of traditional repertoires of protest such as petitioning, letter writing, and boycotting to the online world.

Exchange value The value produced whenever a person or company exchanges a good or service for another good, service, or money.

Extended self The notion that we can extend ourselves in objects beyond physical and temporal limitations.

Fair use A policy stating that small portions of copyrighted material can be used for educational or commentary purposes.

Filter bubble The notion that users receive personalized search results or recommendations online that determine the content to which they are exposed with potential political and cultural consequences.

Firestorm The sudden discharge of large quantities of messages containing negative word of mouth or complaint behavior against a person, company, or group in social media networks.

Fixed costs Startup costs required to obtain the means to produce and circulate content.

Flaming The use of hostile language online including swearing, insults, and otherwise offensive language.

Flash activism Activism that appears and then disappears overnight as attention toward a cause waxes and wanes.

Flow Total absorption in a task that creates the feeling of escape and losing track of time.

Form The type of media that results from a particular technology.

Framing The process of strategically referring to a social issue, practice, or group to heighten some of its attributes and downplay other aspects.

Freemium model A business model involving offering a free version of a product to encourage trial with the hope that some percentage of users will convert to a paid version later on.

Frequency Metric used to describe the number of times a user has seen online content.

Gatekeeper A role in an online community or network in which a person regulates the flow of information or curates content.

General public license An agreement that work can be shared freely, used by anyone, and modified.

Generalized reciprocity A social norm dictating that people may contribute to the group without any particular expectation of immediate payback, but expect to use the group's resources in the future.

Genre A particular set of conventions within a form.

Gift economy An economy in which the giver prepares an object for an intended receiver, presents the object in a socially appropriate way, and has no motive for the gift although there are often implied norms of reciprocity.

Goal A desired end state.

Good Any object that satisfies a human need or want.

Graph theory An area of research in mathematics that studies the properties of nodes, their connections, and their relationships.

Habitus The cultural and social context into which one is socialized.

Hacktivism The use of digital technology to disrupt organizations or individuals that a social movement opposes.

Hardcore members Members in an online community who contribute substantially and have subcultural capital that gives them status in the community.

Hate speech Speech that attacks, threatens or insults a person or group based on race, religion, national origin, gender, sexual orientation, disability, or other traits.

Heteronormativity The normative assumption that individuals are heterosexual and occupy traditional gender roles.

Homophily The tendency for people to affiliate with others who are like them.

Hot media Media that requires less audience involvement.

Hubs Individuals in a network with a large and diverse number of acquaintances, aiding in information flow throughout a network.

Hyperpersonal model of communication The idea that in the absence of other cues, people will exaggerate features of their communication partners when communicating and develop strong interpersonal attachment quickly.

Ideal self The self we hope to project by emphasizing some usually positive or culturally meaningful aspects of self and deemphasizing others.

Imagined community The way in which media such as newspapers create a sense of belonging to one nation or one community.

Information gatherers People who bring specialized knowledge to a group.

Information overload The idea that the ubiquity of technologies causes us to "overdose" on information, leading to decreases in attention, concentration, and analytical thinking.

Information regime Collective agreements codified in payment schemes, contracts, standards, processes, and expectations used to develop standards of measuring attention.

Interpellation The process by which the dominant meanings of a social role come to constitute subjective identity.

Interpersonal communication An approach to studying communication that is primarily based on the face-to-face dynamics of two people.

Lead users Experts who know a product well and are most likely to innovate.

Looking-glass self A perspective of self that suggests people express and modify a collection of relatively stable attributes and feelings about these attributes as a result of interaction and feedback from the social and physical world.

Loyalty loop The process by which consumers repurchase and deepen their love for a product.

Lurkers Online community members who are passive participants and rarely contribute content to the community.

Machine learning A process through which predictive information is produced using observed patterns in a large database.

Marginal cost The cost of producing and distributing an additional item.

Market mavens Actors who gather and disseminate marketplace information about prices, products, and consumption practices.

Mashup The resulting product when two or more cultural products are combined.

Mass communication An approach to studying communication that provides explanations of what people, either users or providers of media, do in the aggregate.

Means of production Factories, equipment, or money that can be used to reproduce wealth.

Media ecology The perspective that the mode of communication shapes human activity in both interactional and historical domains.

Media replicability The degree to which information is easy to reproduce.

Media richness A factor describing the amount of sensory information transferred between a sender and receiver.

Meme An idea, behavior, or style that spreads from person to person within a culture.

Mere exposure effect The finding that the more frequently people are exposed to a stimulus the more they like that stimulus.

Methodological individualism The idea that if we can understand how one person responds, we can build that into an understanding of how a group of people will respond.

Microcelebrity A state of being famous to a niche group of people and the presentation of oneself as a celebrity regardless of who is paying attention.

Microcontributions Small monetary contributions to social movements often made by people who are not normally involved in activism on digital platforms.

Micropayments Small amounts of money targeted toward the production of cultural or informative content.

Mobile The degree to which a medium is "heavy" (durable, but difficult to transport) versus "light" (portable).

Mobilization The ability of political activists to translate existing resources such as money, people, or ideas into meaningful political action.

Monopoly Economic structure in which one firm controls most of the market for a good or service.

Moore's Law The observation that the processing speed of computer chips doubles every two years.

Movement society The tendency for people to use political tactics to solve issues that are not political but rather cultural, consumer-oriented, or personal.

Multihoming The ability to use more than one platform.

Net neutrality The notion that all activity on the Internet is treated equally, no matter its sender, receiver, or content.

Netnography The practice of conducting field research online.

Network analysis A method of mapping and analyzing patterns of connection or information flow between people online.

Network effects The resulting gains in a system when more and more people use the network.

Networked individualism The argument that individuals act as nodes in many different networks where they operate as individuals but draw from latent network connections in seeking help or sharing information.

Networked public A real or imaged group of people constituted by discussion of civic and social issues in digital forums such as message boards, comment threads, and chat rooms.

Networked society A perspective that views individuals as connected, but embedded in larger, overlapping publics with the ability to switch between publics.

Newbies New members to the community who are sometimes ignored or flamed and have the lowest status in a community.

Nonrival A type of good that can be consumed without decreasing its value to others.

Norms informal rules of collective agreement that govern behavior.

Online disinhibition effect The tendency to experience disinhibition because of the effects of computer-mediated communication. Anonymity online is one factor widely assumed to be associated with disinhibition.

Online vigilantes Social media users who investigate and harass people suspected of harassment or assault.

Open innovation Innovation where anyone can contribute and resulting ideas and products are freely shared.

Open-access/freemium models Those services that offer content for free, hoping to build an audience that will support the production of content through advertising. These services often have premium content available for a fee.

Opinion leaders People with high social and/or cultural capital who occupy the roles of a connector, market maven, or bridge.

Opinion The second stage in the purchase funnel in which a consumer forms an opinion of the product options available through information gathering.

Owned media A company's use of time or space on a marketing channel that it owns.

Paid media A company's purchase of time or space on an existing channel.

Parasocial relationships Relationships in which fans form a quasi-relationship with characters in traditional media via media products.

Participatory culture A culture with relatively low barriers to artistic expression and civic engagement, strong support for creating and sharing one's creations, and some type of informal mentorship whereby what is known by the most experienced is passed along to novices.

Participatory/citizen journalism The practice of nonprofessional journalists producing and disseminating journalistic knowledge.

Pay-per-click A measurement of whether a user purchased a product as a result of an online advertisement.

Pay-per-use platforms Those services that expect users to pay for each piece of content discretely.

Phatic communication Language used for social purposes and not necessarily to communicate information.

Platform A system that coordinates the exchange or interaction between two or more groups of people.

Play Human activity that has no end goal, is pleasurable, and is often spontaneous.

Post-human Theories that see technology and human bodies as increasingly intertwined, thus challenging the boundary between human and machine and potentially also essentialist concepts of gender.

Power The ability to influence people or things.

Preference The fourth stage in the purchase funnel in which consumers either form an intention to buy or abandon the purchase.

Privacy An interpersonal boundary process by which a person or group regulates interaction with others.

Propinquity Physical nearness.

Prosumption The practice of consumers modifying goods or services to fulfill their own needs.

Pseudonymity The trait describing when a person's actions may be linked to a particular name, but not traced to an offline person.

Public good A good that anyone can use and is nonexcludable.

Public sphere The space where people can come together to debate social issues, including the rules that govern them.

Public "A discursive space in which individuals and groups congregate to discuss matters of mutual interest and, where possible, to reach a common judgment." (Hauser 1998)

Pull marketing The practice of consumers seeking out information about a company.

Purchase funnel The sequence of states a consumer goes through during a rational decision process of making a purchase.

Purchase The final stage in the purchase funnel in which a consumer decides to purchase the good or service.

Push marketing The practice of conveying a message to the consumer through company channels or advertising.

Reach Metric used to describe the total number of people who have seen an advertisement or other content online.

Reciprocity A social norm dictating that a person is obligated to give back to an individual or group in some way if he or she has taken something from the individual or group.

Relational norms Informal rules that govern communicative behavior between people.

Remediation The idea that stylistic elements from previous genres are carried forward into new styles and genres of communication.

Remix The resulting product when elements of a cultural object are reconfigured into a new cultural object, often by adding musical or visual elements or changing the pacing.

Repertoires of protest Models of how to collectively organize to change society.

Rhizomatic A pattern where social exchange is not just one to one or linear, but rather occurs in an exponential pattern similar to that of social networks.

Ritual An action or series of actions, usually performed collectively, that has meaning for the actor or the group.

Role theory A theory arguing that people inhabit different roles which consist of social and cultural norms for how to behave.

Sample A smaller subset of available data.

Search engine optimization A process through which companies design webpages and other online infrastructure to be as search friendly as possible and to reach the highest position in the results of search algorithms.

Seeding A technique in which companies give products to lead users or opinion leaders with the hope that this will increase word-of-mouth communication.

Self A collection of relatively stable attributes and feelings about these attributes.

Self-disclosure The norm that one is expected to, at least gradually, disclose information about oneself to others.

Selfie A picture one takes of oneself, usually close up and facing the camera.

Self-presentation A theory arguing that we are always presenting ourselves for a perceived audience.

Self-regulation The process through which one controls short-term impulses.

Sharing A nonreciprocal prosocial behavior in which one or more people pool resources for distribution to others and conversely access resources from this pool for their own use without direct reciprocation.

Signaling theory A theory arguing that we are always "giving" and "giving off" social signals, either purposefully or unintentionally.

Situated communication Communication used according to personal needs and goals as well as practical and social conventions.

Social capital Connections with other people that serve as a resource.

Social class The combination of education, income, and prestige of occupation that places one in a hierarchy relative to others.

Social comparison theory A theory arguing that we form evaluations of ourselves through comparison with others.

Social construction The idea that reality is shaped by collective understandings.

Social exchange theory A theory arguing that the exchange of goods or services over time will lead to the development of social ties.

Social identity The intersection of who we see ourselves to be and how others see us.

Social identity deindividuation (SIDE) model A model of interpersonal communication that argues that we use social categories rather than interpersonal cues when we communicate online to interpret and understand identity, behavior, and intentions.

Social Information Processing (SIP) A model of interpersonal communication that argues that we use interpersonal cues from others when we communicate online in order to form conceptions of their identity and intentions.

Social issue A topic that people collectively agree should be addressed politically, economically, or culturally.

Social marketing Communication aimed at persuading or informing an audience about a social issue, goal, or organization, usually one that is non-commercial in nature.

Social media monitoring The practice of tracking consumer comments on social media.

Social network sites Web-based services that allow individuals to construct a public or semipublic profile within a bounded system, articulate a list of other users with whom they share a connection, and view and traverse their list of connections and those made by others within the system.

Social norms Informal rules of collective agreement.

Social presence The degree to which a medium permits users to experience others as being psychologically present.

Social role A systemic pattern of behavior in interaction with others.

Social shopping sites Sites that integrate word-of-mouth communications like reviews into the purchase infrastructure itself.

Sock puppets Alias identities in an online community or message board.

Spreadability The potential—both technical and cultural—for audiences to share content because it resonates with the norms, values, or identity of a particular social group or individual.

States Territories where one person has control over the means of violence, the military, and the legal system for enforcing punishment.

Status A person's relative place within a social grouping.

Structural hole A phenomenon occurring when two different clusters in a network have complementary information or resources, but no way to share them.

Structuration The idea that the larger normative patterns are created and structured by the interactions of individuals, and that these are in turn structured by larger normative patterns.

Subcultural capital The knowledge, tastes, and practices that are valued within a particular subculture or group.

Subculture A smaller grouping within a culture that shares particular norms, values, and practices that may run counter to the dominant culture.

Subscription services Those services that offer membership for a fee, usually on a monthly or annual basis.

Surveillance studies A branch of sociology that examines the appropriate boundaries and techniques of surveillance in society.

Switching costs A type of transaction cost expressed as the cost to the user of changing to a different product or platform from the one he or she is currently using.

Synchronous communication Communication occurring while participants are co-present in the same digital space.

Tactics Cultural and cognitive models of social action.

Technological determinism The perspective that technology determines the nature of human communication and that technology is a force autonomous from human thought or action.

Technology A material configuration that allows for the production or reception of media.

Tie strength The closeness between nodes.

Tragedy of the commons The tendency for groups of people to overuse and/or neglect collectively held property.

Transactions costs The costs of exchanging a good or service.

Transmedia A story that unfolds across multiple media platforms, with each new text making a distinctive and valuable contribution to the whole.

Triadic relationship A relationship in which three people are interconnected.

Trolls Users who attempt to disrupt online communication in some way.

Two-sided market An economic platform where a company provides value to two or more different groups.

Use value The value that one gets from using an object.

User-generated content The textual, visual, or structural material produced by users and user groups.

User innovation The process whereby a group or individual whose primary interest is in using rather than selling the product develops a new product or modifies an existing product, usually to suit their own needs.

Uses and gratification theory The notion that people consume media for some purpose and to receive some reward.

Valence The degree positivity or negativity associated with a review.

Value chain Michael Porter's theory describing the process that leads to the creation of a consumable good.

Variance The degree of similarity or dissimilarity between online reviews.

Viral video A video that becomes popular quickly through person-to-person referral on social media platforms.

Virtual self The self-presented in representations, particularly in representations online.

Volume The total number of online reviews.

Web 2.0 A term used to indicate the historical turn toward creating communication and commercial platforms that are sustained by collective participation.

Word-of-mouth marketing The leveraging of word-of-mouth communications to encourage the transmission of positive product information or "buzz."

Word-of-mouth Communication occurring when product or service information is transmitted from one person to another.

Credits

Page 9, *Cartoon 2.1*: Peter Steiner / The New Yorker Collections / The Cartoon Bank.

Page 15, *Photo 2.2*: CBC Still Photo Collection.

Page 30, *Cartoon 3.1*: Mike Keefe, InToon.com.

Page 32, *Photo 3.1 (Top)*: Luca Bruno/Associated Press; *Photo 3.1 (Bottom)*, Michael Sohn/Associated Press.

Page 33, *Photo 3.2*: Courtesy mytemplatez.com.

Page 34, *Figure 3.2*: From 'Social Network Sites: Definition, History, and Scholarship' by danah m. boyd, and Nicole B. Ellison in Journal of Computer-Mediated Communication 13 (2008) pp. 210 to 230. Copyright 2008 International Communication Association and published by John Wiley and Sons. http://onlinelibrary.wiley.com/doi/10.1111/j.1083-6101.2007.00395.x/full

Page 46, *Photo 4.1*: Photo: Rachel Topham, Vancouver Art Gallery.

Page 48, *Photo 4.3*: Oli Scarff/Staff/Getty Images.

Page 63, *Photo 5.1*: Courtesy Threadless Designs.

Page 85, *Photo 6.1*: Courtesy Street Art News.

Page 87, *Photo 6.2*: Vintage print from the private collection of Jeffrey Goldstein.

Page 89, *Photo 6.4*: PM Images / Getty Images.

Page 95, *Figure 6.1*: "Anonymity, Privacy, and Security Online" Pew Research Center, Washington, DC (September 5, 2013). http://www.pewinternet .org/2013/09/05/part-1-the-quest-for-anonymity-online/.

Page 97, *Cartoon 6.1*: Courtesy Sarah Lazarovic.

Page 99, *Photo 6.5*: Art by 2wenty. Reproduced with permission.

Page 100, *Photo 6.6*: Erin Baiano/ The New York Times/ Redux.

Page 110, *Photo 7.1*: Lily Dale / Contributor.

Page 117, *Photo 7.2*: Ed Clark/The LIFE Picture Collection/Getty Images.

Page 120, *Photo 7.4*: Jamie Kingham/Getty Images.

Page 122, *Photo 7.5*: Jamie Kingham/Getty Images.

Page 138, *Photo 8.2*: David Goldman/Associated Press.

Page 157, *Photo 9.3*: Courtesy Challenger Network.

Index